The Private Civil War

THE
PRIVATE
CIVIL WAR

POPULAR THOUGHT DURING
THE SECTIONAL CONFLICT

Randall C. Jimerson

Louisiana State University Press
Baton Rouge and London

Copyright © 1988 by Louisiana State University Press
All rights reserved
Manufactured in the United States of America
96 95 94 93 92 91 90 89 88   5 4 3 2 1

Designer: Sylvia Malik Loftin
Typeface: Palatino
Typesetter: Composing Room of Michigan
Printer: Thomson-Shore, Inc.
Binder: John H. Dekker & Sons, Inc.

Library of Congress Cataloging-in-Publication Data

Jimerson, Randall C.
    The private Civil War: popular thought during the sectional
conflict / Randall C. Jimerson.
        p.   cm.
    Bibliography: p.
    Includes index.
    ISBN 0-8071-1454-5 (alk. paper)
    1. United States—History—Civil War, 1861–1865—Public opinion.
    2. United States—History—Civil War, 1861–1865—Social aspects.
    I. Title.
    E468.9.J55 1988   88-11765
    973.7—dc19   CIP

The paper in this book meets the guidelines for permanence and durability
of the Committee on Production Guidelines for Book Longevity of the
Council on Library Resources. ∞

For Joyce

The deeper meaning of the American Civil War, for the people who lived through it and for us today, goes beyond the historian's grasp. Here was an event so complex, so deeply based in human emotions, so far-reaching in its final effects, that understanding it is likely to be a matter primarily for the emotions rather than for the cold analysis of facts. It was an experience that was probably felt more deeply than anything else that ever happened to us. We cannot hope to understand it unless we share in that feeling, simply because the depth and intensity of the feeling are among the war's principal legacies.

—Bruce Catton
Prefaces to History

CONTENTS

ILLUSTRATIONS

following page 123

ACKNOWLEDGMENTS

A project that takes more than ten years to complete cannot be accomplished without the generous advice and support of many teachers, colleagues, and friends. At an early stage in my research, I was fortunate to receive advice from the two leading historians of Civil War participants. Bell I. Wiley kindly answered my inquiry about research strategies, guiding me to the richest archival collections. Bruce Catton spent an hour talking with me about our mutual fascination with the response of ordinary people to the Civil War. I regret that with the passing of these two great historians, who inspired much of my approach to understanding the Civil War, my own musings on the war could not benefit from their critical review.

During my first drafting of this study of Civil War sectionalism, Gerald F. Linderman provided valuable direction and painstaking editorial assistance, smoothing my prose and offering a model of scholarly achievement. Shaw Livermore, Jr., sharpened my critical acumen during many free-flowing discussions covering a wide range of topics but always ending in a clearer understanding of nineteenth-century Americans. Cecil D. Eby, Jr., Leslie H. Owens, and John W. Shy freely offered advice on research sources and critical comments on my early efforts to make sense of them.

During my rewriting of the manuscript, Joel Williamson has given freely of his advice and encouragement. He coined the term *popular thought* to describe my approach to intellectual history from the bottom up, and his comments have helped clarify my interpretation and analysis. As a teacher, counselor, and critic, William W. Freehling has provided an outstanding example and continuing inspiration. At a critical juncture, Leon F. Litwack made valuable suggestions for revision and encouraged me to persevere. Clarence L. Mohr and Paul D. Escott offered valuable critiques of the manuscript, which saved me from errors of omission and commission. Beverly Jarrett of Louisiana State University Press has provided encouragement and support during a long period of revising the manuscript, and John Easterly and Catherine Barton have supervised the final editing and publication. Trudie Calvert has been a superb and understanding editor, working magic charms with a blue pencil. For their many contributions I would also like to thank Russell L. Blake, Janice Bittner, Frank Crowley, Daria D'Arienzo, Carole Drescher, Howard Drescher, David Garnes, Jan Lewis, Tony Mingrone, and Norman Stevens. The University of Connecticut Research Foundation provided some needed financial assistance.

For permission to publish brief quotations from the Ella Gertrude (Clanton) Thomas Diary, I wish to thank Mrs. Donald H. Burr and Mrs. Frank B. Despeaux. Cecil D. Eby, Jr., May Davis Hill, and John Sickler generously permitted me to use and cite manuscripts in their possession. For permission to reproduce photographs I gratefully acknowledge the Southern Historical Collection, the University of North Carolina Press, the University of Wisconsin Press, and Indiana University Press.

Without dedicated archivists, working with inadequate resources but exceptional commitment to researchers, historical studies such as this could never be undertaken. The many archivists at the repositories I visited in my research forays have been particularly helpful. I especially thank the staff members of the Southern Historical Collection, the Manuscript Department at Duke, the Bentley Historical Library, the State Historical Society of Wisconsin, Louisiana State University Library, the Manuscripts and Archives Department at Yale, the Connecticut Historical Society, and the Burton Historical Collection. Special thanks for assistance above all reasonable expectations I gratefully offer to Francis X. Blouin, Jr., John Dann, Ellen Garrison, Ellen Gartrell, Mary Jo Pugh, Mattie Russell, Richard Schrader, and Carolyn Wallace. The example set by these and other dedicated archivists lured me from teaching and research to the archival profession. I hope they will accept that as the high praise for which it is intended.

My greatest thanks are reserved for my family, who had little direct involvement with my research and writing. From my parents, Norman and Melva Jimerson, I have learned a profound respect for all people, a commitment to reducing prejudice and injustice, and a dedication to securing a peaceful world. Ann, Paul, Sue, and Mark have made their brother's experiences broader, richer, and happier. Laura and Beth have given their father more joy and love than they yet imagine. Finally, this book is dedicated to Joyce Sorrows Jimerson, who has given me love, laughter, hope, and compassion. I am proud to be her husband.

ABBREVIATIONS

BHC	Burton Historical Collection, Detroit Public Library
CHS	Connecticut Historical Society, Hartford
DU	Duke University Library, Manuscript Department, Durham, North Carolina
LC	Library of Congress, Washington, D.C.
LSU	Louisiana State University Libraries, Louisiana and Lower Mississippi Valley Collections, Baton Rouge
MHC	Michigan Historical Collections, Bentley Historical Library, University of Michigan, Ann Arbor
OR	*The War of the Rebellion: A Compilation of the Official Records of the Union and Confederate Armies.* 130 vols. Washington, D.C., 1880–1901.
SHC	Southern Historical Collection, Library of the University of North Carolina, Chapel Hill
WSHS	State Historical Society of Wisconsin, Archives Division, Madison
UV	University of Virginia Library, Manuscripts Department, Charlottesville
WLC	William L. Clements Library, University of Michigan, Ann Arbor
Yale	Yale University Library, Manuscripts and Archives Department, New Haven, Connecticut

The Private Civil War

PREFACE

I wish the Union could be preserved," declared Henry Watson, Jr., a Greensboro, Alabama, lawyer and plantation owner, in January, 1861. Two weeks earlier, Alabama had become the fourth Deep South state to secede from the Union. A native of East Windsor, Connecticut, Watson had lived in Alabama since 1834. He initially opposed secession and argued that the sectional conflict resulted from a mere misunderstanding between northerners and southerners. "It is desirable that brothers & sisters in a family should live in peace & harmony & do kindnesses for each other," Watson concluded, "but if strife commences and all efforts at reconciliation fail, rather than that they should continue under one roof to be *always* wrangling & quarreling it is better that one party go off & set up for themselves. As with a family so with our Union."[1]

Americans repeatedly viewed the sectional conflict as a family quarrel. The great compromiser, Senator Henry Clay of Kentucky, in 1850 called the Union "a marriage that no human authority can dissolve or divorce the parties from." Yet that is precisely what eleven southern states did in 1860 and 1861. "We separated because of incompatibility of temper," proclaimed Mary Chesnut, wife of a prominent South Carolina planter-politician, in March, 1861. "We are divorced, North from South, because we hated each other so."[2] The fierce war that followed deepened this sense of estrangement, perpetuating the conviction that northerners and southerners were two different peoples. More than a century after reunion and reconciliation, this sectional consciousness remains a troubling legacy.

In tracing the contours of Americans' sectional consciousness, this study examines the meaning of the Civil War to those individuals who fought its battles and endured its hardships, rather than the opinions of politicians, generals, and editors, who sought to articulate the views

1. Henry Watson, Jr., letter fragment, January 27, 1861, in Henry Watson, Jr., Papers, DU.
2. Paul C. Nagel, *One Nation Indivisible: The Union in American Thought, 1776–1861* (New York, 1964), 267; C. Vann Woodward (ed.), *Mary Chesnut's Civil War* (New Haven, 1981), 25.

of broad constituencies. Historians have extensively studied the leaders, but the opinions of common soldiers and civilians have received inadequate attention. This study of popular thought during the Civil War explores the ways in which the "plain people" responded to the conflict between North and South. Their opinions reveal a great deal about sectional identity and American character.

Sectional consciousness is nearly as old as the Union. As early as 1785, Thomas Jefferson prepared a detailed list of contrasting personal characteristics that distinguished northerners from southerners. Sectional interests collided during the Constitutional Convention and again during political contests between Federalists and Jeffersonians. Yet as late as 1819, citizens of the southern states exhibited little sense of sectional identity. The Missouri controversy forced sectional differences to center stage. For the next forty years, almost every national political issue related in some way to the competing interests of the free-soil North and the slave South. Black revolts and abolitionist attacks soon led southerners to assess national issues, such as the tariff, according to their potential impact on slavery. Contrasts between North and South turned to conflict when each side became convinced that its survival required westward expansion. Beginning with the Missouri Compromise in 1820, careful political maneuverings maintained the sectional balance of power for over a generation. By the 1850s, however, ideological conflict became irrevocably polarized. Radicals on both sides refused to compromise.[3]

The dichotomy between the slave South and the free-labor North created political and economic divisions, but armed conflict would not have resulted if northerners and southerners had not regarded each other as members of antagonistic cultures vying for ideological supremacy. Belief in sectional differences overpowered the reality of cultural homogeneity. Ironically, northerners and southerners could hardly be distinguished in their commitment to liberty, democracy, individualism, and equality. Yet slavery and the black presence created an intense ideological and social clash that ultimately resisted all efforts

3. John R. Alden, *The First South* (Baton Rouge, 1961), 3–73; Charles S. Sydnor, *The Development of Southern Sectionalism, 1819–1848* (Baton Rouge, 1948); Jesse T. Carpenter, *The South as a Conscious Minority, 1789–1861: A Study in Political Thought* (New York, 1930); David M. Potter, *The Impending Crisis, 1848–1861* (New York, 1976); Eric Foner, *Free Soil, Free Labor, Free Men: The Ideology of the Republican Party Before the Civil War* (New York, 1970), esp. 310–13.

at compromise. With Abraham Lincoln's election as candidate of an exclusively northern party, the sectional conflict reached a point of no return. The psychological division of the American people encouraged political and military disruptions. As William R. Taylor concludes, the lasting distinction between North and South was "a psychological, not a physical division, which often cut like a cleaver through the mentality of individual men and women everywhere in the country." In seeking to define national character according to their own values, southerners and northerners engaged in an ideological rivalry that would have tragic consequences. The Civil War reveals, above all, an American people divided by their perceptions of conflicting sectional identities.[4]

To understand the depth of this sectional consciousness, it is necessary to look beyond the clamor of public debates and examine the Civil War's private side. The principal sources for this study of popular thought are the countless letters and diaries written by Civil War participants. Many excellent diaries and collections have been published, but the richest sources remain in archives, libraries, and historical societies throughout the country. These exceptional sources have been preserved for over a century by dedicated family members, archivists, and librarians. The diversity of people who left records of their thoughts and experiences makes this an exceptionally rich period for studying common people's opinions on social and political issues.

War thrusts ideology to the forefront. The sectional conflict focused attention on issues that divided southerners and northerners, thereby creating a unique opportunity for discovering the contours of sectional consciousness. According to Bell I. Wiley, the foremost historian of common people during the Civil War, "The obscurity imposed on the rank and file [in most historical writings] is especially unfortunate because it is only during war that the plain people become articulate in a degree comparable to the more privileged classes." Separated from home and family, virtually every soldier wrote frequent and informative letters or recorded daily observations in private diaries. The war affected the whole population, which was highly literate. As Henry Steele Commager observes, "Surely no other chapter of modern history has been so faithfully or so elaborately recorded by ordinary men

4. William R. Taylor, *Cavalier and Yankee: The Old South and American National Character* (New York, 1961), 333; Nagel, *One Nation*, 175–76; David H. Donald, *Liberty and Union* (Boston, 1978), esp. 80–81.

and women; in the American Civil War Everyman was, indeed, his own historian."[5]

Participating in momentous events, many people kept private journals of their experiences so that in later years they could recall the details of this important period of their lives. The time for reflection would come later; now was the time for action. Colonel Charles Wainwright of New York noted in his diary the arrival of some books he had ordered: "By books, I do not mean to read, but books to write in. We are making history, not studying it." Wainwright's diary served as a record of his own deeds and observations. At the end of the first of several volumes, he wrote: "I think I have accomplished my object in the journal, which is to so fix the events of my soldiering in time and place, that I may easily recall them in years to come, should my life be spared. I do not expect that anyone else will see it." Similarly, Louisiana quartermaster Robert Patrick explained, "I have determined to jot down a few memoranda of my doings and thoughts during the war, not that I expect it to interest anyone else, for I do not intend that any other person besides myself shall ever read it, but I write it, *first*, for amusement, *secondly*, because in after years it may afford me some pleasure to peruse it." For many, the major benefits of diary writing were to relieve boredom and vent frustration. Corporal Edmund Patterson of Alabama wrote that his diary had become "a sort of task of duty" without which the daily routine would seem incomplete. "I feel better satisfied with writing than at any other time, whether writing a letter to a friend or penning my thoughts here for my own perusal," he commented. Sarah Morgan of Baton Rouge, Louisiana, filled "many inexpressibly dreary days" by writing in her journal: "How many disagreeable affairs it has caused me to pass over without another thought, how many times it has proved a relief to me where my tongue was forced to remain quiet!"[6]

Many diarists recognized that their writings might prove interesting

5. Bell Irvin Wiley (ed.), *Confederate Letters of John W. Hagan* (Athens, Ga., 1954), 1; Henry Steele Commager (ed.), *The Blue and the Gray: The Story of the Civil War as Told by Participants* (2 vols.; Indianapolis, 1950), I, xxi.

6. Allan Nevins (ed.), *A Diary of Battle: The Personal Journals of Colonel Charles S. Wainwright, 1861–1865* (New York, 1962), 432, 152–53; F. Jay Taylor (ed.), *Reluctant Rebel: The Secret Diary of Robert Patrick, 1861–1865* (Baton Rouge, 1959), 18–19; John G. Barrett (ed.), *Yankee Rebel: The Civil War Journal of Edmund Dewitt Patterson* (Chapel Hill, 1966), 133; Sarah Morgan Dawson, *A Confederate Girl's Diary*, ed. James I. Robertson, Jr. (Bloomington, 1960), 76.

to others. On the flyleaf of "Vol. xxvi" of his journal, Edward O. Guerrant of the 4th Kentucky Cavalry wrote: "To whoever it may concern:
Inclosed will be found short records of my life as a soldier, some reflections on the persons & things I have seen, & I hope modest notices of
my own unworthy actions—in this great war for Independence." Many
who had kept diaries before the war to record their spiritual or intellectual progress continued writing during the war, but with a new focus.
Ella Thomas of Georgia, like many of her contemporaries, hoped that a
record of her experiences would later provide lessons and examples for
her children. "In writing now I have an eye always to the future when I
shall read portions to my children or submit the book to their perusal,"
she explained.[7]

For soldiers letter writing broke the monotony of camp life and afforded moments of solace and communication with the folks back
home. Their correspondence describes the universal incidents of army
life and their personal responses to novel experiences. "I mention all
these little details . . . to keep you posted as to the events which now
make up the sum of our life," Lieutenant William W. Gordon of Georgia
wrote to his wife. "It seems childish to talk so much about eating and
sleeping and yet one needs to be a true Philosopher to avoid doing so
when deprived of or stinted in them." With extensive newspaper reporting of campaigns, battle tactics, and war rumors, many soldiers
found they could offer the home folks only accounts of their own
personal experiences and opinions. "News with us is scarce as hens
teeth," complained Georgia private Irby Scott. "We hardly know anything that does not come under our own observation." In explaining
his reasons for writing home, Private Constant C. Hanks of New York
concluded, "It is not that I think that I can write any news, for you get
that in the papers long before I could write it, but I expect that you want
to know what I am about, how I get along." In explaining how they "got
along," Union and Confederate soldiers offered their own interpretations of the war's meaning and their reflections on the political and
social issues raised by these years of national crisis.[8]

Despite the broad spectrum of individuals who wrote letters and

7. Edward Owings Guerrant Diary, [February, 1865], in Edward Owings Guerrant
Papers, SHC; Ella Gertrude (Clanton) Thomas Diary, July 31, 1863, DU.
8. William W. Gordon to his wife, December 19, 1861, in Gordon Family Papers, SHC;
Irby G. Scott to his family, July 20, 1862, in Irby H. Scott Papers, DU; Constant C. Hanks
to his mother, May 23, 1863, in Constant C. Hanks Papers, DU.

diaries, certain biases appear in the sources available for use. Such sources always disproportionately represent well-educated individuals from higher socioeconomic classes. This gap, however, is narrower during the Civil War than for any other time in American history. Officers are better represented than enlisted men; likewise, soldiers' letters are more common than those of civilians. Certain states, such as North Carolina, are more fully documented than others. Although the manuscript collections consulted represent only a small portion of available resources, I have made painstaking efforts to counter these biases. I have consulted a broad cross section of letters and diaries, covering all states, social classes, and military ranks. If this approach sacrifices some of the depth afforded by focusing on a narrow spectrum, it compensates by providing a comprehensive overview. In this way, true sectional comparisons can be made.

Such a study is by necessity subjective. Until statisticians invent a system for quantifying idealism, courage, hope, fear, love, or anything else that makes us human, I see no way to avoid this. In fact, this study began with the objective of exploring the opinions and values of Civil War participants much as Studs Terkel and Robert Coles have studied contemporary Americans.[9] Unable to interview my subjects or study them directly, I have relied on the best available evidence, their personal letters and diaries. I have examined these sources with a historian's critical eye, but I have used them with respect for the individuals who wrote openly (in most cases) of their deepest personal feelings. Whether they always revealed their subconscious motivations—whether, even, they were always unflinchingly candid about their conscious motivations—their words hauntingly depict their own perceptions of reality. The sum of these individual, private viewpoints constitutes the popular thought of the Civil War era.

This study reveals a remarkable diversity of opinion among individuals of all social groups. Civil War participants expressed every nuance of interpretation that subsequent historians have presented and debated on the war's social and political issues. Their comments, written amid the maelstrom of war, are frequently more eloquent than the rhetoric of contemporary public statements and more perceptive than the hindsight of historical analysis. In examining these personal narra-

9. See, in particular, Studs Terkel, *Hard Times: An Oral History of the Great Depression* (New York, 1970); Terkel, *The Good War* (New York, 1984); and Robert Coles, *Children of Crisis: A Study of Courage and Fear* (New York, 1967).

tives, however, some of this diversity must be sacrificed to identify common themes. Neither northerners nor southerners always thought alike as one unit. Use of the terms *northern* and *southern* is simply the historian's shorthand for the most common ideas in regions of sometimes remarkable diversity. Because of its focus on sectional consciousness, this study pays only passing attention to black Americans. Their actions and opinions exerted major influences on the war's outcome, as shown in Chapters 3 and 4. Yet a full examination of the black experience would require a separate book.

Because the words through which ideas are expressed convey important nuances of meaning, I present individual viewpoints, whenever possible, by direct quotation from letters and diaries. In most cases, I include full sentences rather than brief phrases or summaries. Errors of spelling and punctuation are corrected only when absolutely necessary to avoid confusion.

The individuals represented in these pages spoke only for themselves, in the intimate, personal language of family letters and private diaries. Their writings reflect their intimate emotional involvement in events of tremendous national significance. They reveal a people who faced incalculable danger with courage, suffering with endurance, and tragedy with fortitude. There were also many who denounced the folly and tragedy of war, recognizing that bloodshed can seldom heal, that destruction does not resolve differences. Whatever their viewpoints, participants presented their ideas clearly and passionately. Above all else, the Civil War was an intensely felt personal experience. This is a major reason for the war's enduring fascination.

1 / ALL THAT WE HOLD DEAR

When Abraham Lincoln was elected president in November, 1860, Elizabeth Grimball was visiting her aunt in Philadelphia, far away from the excitement that prevailed at her home in Charleston, South Carolina. Her father, John Berkley Grimball, feared Lincoln's victory as a dangerous omen. A prominent rice planter and member of Charleston's select society, Grimball soon became an ardent advocate of secession, which he justified as a defense of southern rights. "The prospect before us in regard to our Slave property, if we continue in the Union, is nothing less than utter ruin," he wrote in his private diary. "The people have therefore with unexampled unanimity resolved to secede and to dare any consequence that may follow the act."[1] Elizabeth could not understand such alarms. She had observed virtually no hostility toward the South during her stay in Philadelphia and could see no justification for the secession fever that raged in South Carolina.

Acting as family spokesmen, Elizabeth's brothers wrote several letters trying to convince her that southern rights were indeed threatened and that secession was the only remedy. "You, at the North cannot comprehend the irritation and hatred which animate without exception every man here," William Grimball wrote on November 13. "There have been two tremendous meetings here, which were addressed by Barnwell Rhett, Magrath, James Conner and others, all declaring that our safety, our honor demanded from us as freemen no longer to submit to their insults and sneers, no longer to own as country-man men whose highest wish is to invade the sacred rights of our homes with poison in one hand and the incendiary's torch in the other." He concluded that "we are fighting for existence." One week later William declared that South Carolina property holders had united "in the belief that now a stand must be made for African slavery or it is forever lost." He told Elizabeth that her father and brothers carried loaded pistols to protect the family from "dishonor and death." He then enumerated the wrongs suffered by the South: "Is it nothing to *yell* about that we are

---

1. John Berkley Grimball Diary, December 17, 1860, SHC. In calling for secession, the Charleston *Mercury* on November 3 had similarly proclaimed, "The issue before the country is the extinction of slavery" (Dwight L. Dumond [ed.], *Southern Editorials on Secession* [New York, 1931], 204–207).

prevented from carrying our property into the common territory of the United States. Is it nothing to yell for that the government is to be in the hands of men pledged to carry on the 'irrepressible conflict' against us. Is it nothing that they send incendiaries to stir up the slaves to poison & murder us? Is it nothing that our brothers at the North robb us of our property and beat us when we reclaim it?" Surely such abuses justified secession. William Grimball insisted that secession was not a revolution but the legitimate action of a sovereign state. The South could not keep for itself the "golden egg" of taxation. "Opening our ports to free trade, we will break down the manufacturing monopolies at the north," he proclaimed. Thus freed from the North, the South would enjoy peace and prosperity.[2]

Elizabeth was not persuaded by her brother's arguments. She replied that the Republicans would have little power to carry out their hostile purposes because the Democratic majority in both houses of Congress could easily thwart the president's actions. Her brother Lewis responded on November 27, arguing that "every one at the North, who does not own slaves, is opposed to the Institution. They are all enemies of Slavery and hope for its extinction." Even conservative Democrats had supported Stephen A. Douglas' "squatter sovereignty" doctrine, which Lewis Grimball characterized as a treacherous compromise, "*disastrous* to the *South*." The North was now ruled by "Frantic Fanaticism," he warned. "I tell you Fanaticism has murdered Justice, and reigning there supreme publishes to the world the Irrepressible conflict its first mandate." The time for compromise had passed, he insisted: "We will have no more Compromises, and we *will have our rights*. If there be a man in South Carolina, who proposes delay in action, and a further continuance in this Union, he is a *vile traitor* and should be *hung* to the first *limb* that he can be *dragged* to. *Aye hang him higher than Haman*. South Carolina must go now, if she goes alone. There is no step backward, but to disgrace—vile submission and slavish chains." There could be no alternative but secession, Lewis told his sister. South Carolina would stand firmly in defense of "the glorious cause of Liberty," against all northern assaults on her rights.[3]

From Philadelphia, Elizabeth had written that South Carolina

2. William H. Grimball to Elizabeth Grimball, November 13, 20, 1860, in John Berkley Grimball Papers, DU. "The Irrepressible Conflict" was the title of a speech given by Senator William H. Seward of New York on October 25, 1858; see George E. Baker (ed.), *The Works of William Seward* (5 vols.; Boston, 1884), IV, 289–302.

3. Lewis M. Grimball to Elizabeth Grimball, November 27, 1860, in Grimball Family Papers, SHC.

seemed ungrateful in demanding separation from the Union that had nourished and protected her rights for eighty years. Such action would gain the state no friends, she warned. "My God Lizzie! what are you writing?" Lewis exploded. "You speak as if we are the aggressors, and would dissolve the union in Blood shed, upon a *mere abstract principle*, when the fact is we are *oppressed* and are contending for all that we hold dear—our Property—our Institutions—our Honor—aye and our very lives!" Finally, in another letter Elizabeth's brother Berkley Grimball also hailed South Carolina's secession. "I hope it will end in establishing a Southern Confederacy who will have among themselves slavery a bond of union stronger than any which holds the north together," he wrote. The southern cause, as outlined by the Grimball men, demanded total commitment from every southern patriot. Defense of slavery and their rights would bring unity.[4]

The arguments advanced by the Grimballs in justification of secession encompassed the southern interpretation of the war's meaning. Few southerners attributed the conflict to a single cause. They fought not for one clearly defined purpose but for a combination of interrelated motives, which formed a logical chain of reasoning. From specific incidents of injury they foresaw potential consequences fatal to their way of life, and they built their ideological defense on fundamental American principles. The southern interpretation of the war derived from one basic premise: that a hostile northern majority opposed slavery. Southerners anticipated an attack on slavery that would eventually result in destruction of their property rights, emancipation, and disruption of race relations. With an antagonistic northern majority wielding such power, all of southerners' cherished constitutional rights would be endangered. Liberty itself would be overthrown, as the majority forced the helpless minority to submit to its will. The result would be to jeopardize all that southerners most dearly treasured—honor, family, home, religion, and their entire social order. As the cornerstone of their civilization, slavery must be protected at all costs.[5]

    4. *Ibid.*; Berkley Grimball to Elizabeth Grimball, December 8, 1860, in Grimball Family Papers. For similar statements, see the Charleston *Mercury*, October 11, 1860, in Dumond (ed.), *Southern Editorials*, 178–81.
    5. Stephen A. Channing, *Crisis of Fear: Secession in South Carolina* (New York, 1970), 261–73, 286–93; Eugene D. Genovese, *The Political Economy of Slavery: Studies in the Economy and Society of the Slave South* (New York, 1965), 260–70; Eric Foner, *Free Soil, Free Labor, Free Men: The Ideology of the Republican Party Before the Civil War* (New York, 1970), 308–17.

Except among a small group of planters, slavery was not frequently discussed as a reason for fighting. Yet it was the danger to slavery that first prompted appeals to constitutional rights and liberty. Whether deliberately or inadvertently, secessionists quickly advanced from the narrow defense of property interests to appeals to principle. They assumed a defensive posture by portraying the danger to existing institutions as a threat to law, social order, family, and true religion. It was on this ground that most southerners could unite in protecting their identity and pride. Abstractions, moreover, have an emotional force greater than that called forth by specific cases of injury. The Civil War became a total war involving the entire population precisely because both sides fought for ideological principles. Compromise and surrender were unthinkable when so much was at stake.[6]

Overt northern actions could not justify the emotional intensity displayed by secessionists such as Lewis Grimball at the end of 1860. Only a small number of radical abolitionists advocated emancipation, and President-elect Lincoln had publicly disavowed any intention of interfering with slavery. Specific incidents of injury were few; only John Brown's raid and scattered violations of the fugitive slave law indicated any northern intent to meddle with southern institutions. Nevertheless, once a Republican majority gained power in the North the sectional balance was disrupted. White southerners feared that they would become a perpetual minority within the Union. From this perspective, it seemed probable that the South would soon stand helpless before an overwhelming northern majority. The Republican party did want to restrict the expansion of slavery, thereby limiting the spread of southern influence, disrupting the sectional balance in politics, and striking at southern pride in the beneficial effects of slavery. The South would be powerless to stop such developments. From this premise, southerners deduced a succession of anticipated dangers, finally reaching the conclusion that their entire way of life was threatened. Although relatively few recognized the logic behind this ideological

6. James L. Roark, *Masters Without Slaves: Southern Planters in the Civil War and Reconstruction* (New York, 1977), 1–37; David B. Davis, *The Slave Power Conspiracy and the Paranoid Style* (Baton Rouge, 1969), 51; David H. Donald, *Liberty and Union* (Boston, 1978), 14–17; Foner, *Free Soil, Free Labor, Free Men*, 1–10; John McCardell, *The Idea of a Southern Nation: Southern Nationalists and Southern Nationalism, 1830–1860* (New York, 1979), 3–4; Genovese, *Political Economy of Slavery*, 7; William L. Barney, *Flawed Victory: A New Perspective on the Civil War* (New York, 1975), 26–42.

defense of the Confederate cause, most southerners felt the compelling emotional force of these arguments.[7]

Lincoln's election confirmed southerners' fears that a malignant sectional majority dominated public opinion in the North. Shortly after the election, Frank Steel of Kentucky charged that "the *whole* responsibility for the present state of affairs lies with the Republican party." If the Republicans refused to enforce the fugitive slave law and continued to violate "the clearest constitutional rights of the South," he predicted, "this Union will be dissolved—and that very soon." Even new laws and constitutional amendments would not be sufficient guarantees, argued Henry Watson, Jr., an Alabama lawyer and planter, who had long deplored secession. "The only remedy is a *change* of *public* opinion north," he wrote to a friend in Connecticut in December, 1860. "Such a change *cannot* be *hoped for*." The Republicans could not be trusted. Richard L. Dixon, a wealthy Mississippi planter and lawyer, insisted that the South should demand "a full recognition of territorial rights, and execution of the fugitive act by constitutional amendment." Yet he believed it already too late for any such compromise to stop the movement toward secession, because "many think that even positive constitutional provisions and guarantees, if conceded to us now, will soon be overridden by a 'higher law' doctrine, and the same insecurity and depreciation of our property" would result.[8]

Southern radicals depicted all northerners as fanatical "Black Republicans" determined to subjugate the South. During three decades of sectional controversy, southerners had portrayed themselves as victims of northern fanaticism: the Yankees threatened their institutions

7. For the impact of John Brown's raid, see C. Vann Woodward, *The Burden of Southern History* (rev. ed.; Baton Rouge, 1968), 41–68; David M. Potter, *The Impending Crisis, 1848–1861* (New York, 1976), 356–84; and Channing, *Crisis of Fear*, 18–23, 28–34, 286. On the issue of slavery expansion, see Charles W. Ramsdell, "The Natural Limits of Slavery Expansion," *Mississippi Valley Historical Review*, XVI (1929), 151–71; Genovese, *Political Economy of Slavery*, 243–70; and the Charleston *Mercury* editorial of February 28, 1860, in Dumond (ed.), *Southern Editorials*, 40–48. Concerning the South's minority position, see Jesse T. Carpenter, *The South as a Conscious Minority, 1789–1861* (New York, 1930); Avery Craven, *An Historian and the Civil War* (Chicago, 1964), 151; and Potter, *Impending Crisis*, 475–78.

8. Frank Steel to his sister, December 8, 1860, in Frank F. Steel Letters, SHC; Henry Watson, Jr., to Henry Barnard, December 23, 1860, in Henry Watson, Jr., Papers, DU; Richard L. Dixon to Harry St. John Dixon, November 27, December 8, 1860, in Harry St. John Dixon Papers, SHC. The "higher law" was invoked by William H. Seward in his March 11, 1850, speech in the Senate; see *Congressional Globe*, 31st Cong., 2nd Sess., 262–76. For northern responses to the fugitive slave law see Potter, *Impending Crisis*, 130–40, 294–95. Northern opinion on slavery is analyzed in Foner, *Free Soil, Free Labor, Free Men*, 40–72.

and constitutional rights, fostered sectional animosity, and endangered the country's peace and harmony. If southerners occasionally spoke or acted as radicals, it was only in justifiable defense of their treasured rights and institutions. Harry St. John Dixon, a student at the University of Virginia and the son of a Mississippi planter, predicted that the impending conflict would be the bloodiest and most horrible ever waged by men. "Blind religious fanaticism on one side, and outraged liberties on the other, will incite both parties to dire extremities," he warned. The fanatics, the aggressors, were all to be found on the northern side. According to Dixon, southerners would resort to extreme measures only when forced to defend their liberties. During the weeks of preparation for war following the attack on Fort Sumter, Alabama lawyer and planter James D. Webb anticipated the "ruthless assault of a relentless foe who threatens to invade us to subjugate our people." War had resulted from "the fanaticism of our opponents," he told his wife. "They have tendered us the issue."[9] It was a challenge that proud southerners would meet forcefully.

Lincoln's election had destroyed slaveowners' confidence that their interests would be protected by the federal government and that the Republicans represented only a small radical faction in the North. "I always knew that all the North lacked to work our ruin was *Power*," David Schenck warned. Now that the Republicans controlled the government, southerners feared that northern fanaticism would lead to tyranny. A delegate to North Carolina's secession convention, Schenck rejoiced when his state seceded, hailing the event as a liberation from "the bondage and unjust oppression of our degenerate brethren in the North." Similarly, Edmund Patterson, an Ohio native who moved to Alabama in 1859 and enlisted in the 9th Alabama Regiment in May, 1861, wrote at the end of that year that the war had commenced because "the Southern people [were] unable longer to bear the tyranny of the North, or rather of Northern fanaticism," just as their ancestors had revolted against British tyranny.[10]

9. Harry St. John Dixon to his father, March 24, 1861, in Dixon Papers; James D. Webb to his wife, May 18, 1861, in Walton Family Papers, SHC. Lewis Cass of Michigan predicted in 1850 that a civil war would be the worst war man ever saw. (Paul C. Nagel, *One Nation Indivisible: The Union in American Thought, 1776–1861* [New York, 1964], 268–69).

10. David Schenck Diary, May 20, 1861, SHC; John G. Barrett (ed.), *Yankee Rebel: The Civil War Journal of Edmund DeWitt Patterson* (Chapel Hill, 1966), 11. For additional comments on northern tyranny, see Dumond (ed.), *Southern Editorials*, 5–11, 140; Clement Eaton, *A History of the Southern Confederacy* (New York, 1954), 61; Nagel, *One Nation Indivisible*, 248–49.

Slaveowners perceived a clear threat to their slave property. For many this was the central issue, from which all other fears derived. "We of the South see nothing now in Union but danger to our sacred rights," declared Susan Cornwall Shewmake, a graduate of Wesleyan College and wife of a Georgia slaveowner, in January, 1861. "The Black Republicans rejoice that they are to be the instruments of final emancipation for that is undoubtedly their aim in spite of their declarations that they will not interfere with slavery in the states where it now exists." Henry Watson of Alabama predicted that the coming war would soon become "a raid against slavery." Likewise, William W. Gordon, son of a wealthy Savannah railroad president and slaveowner, feared that "the violent Red-black-republicans," with a majority in Congress, would pursue their policy of "freeing and arming all the slaves in the South." In depicting all Republicans as abolitionists, southerners gave more prominence to the small radical faction than its numbers or influence warranted. Their fear, based on potential dangers rather than the current situation, was nevertheless reasonable. Even Abraham Lincoln based his apparently moderate determination to resist the expansion of slavery on a belief that such containment would guarantee its ultimate extinction.[11]

As the cornerstone of southern society, slavery seemed essential for the survival of southern civilization. Not only was slave labor necessary for the economy, but the institution was essential to maintain control of the large black population and to preserve the structure of the social order. Mississippi lawyer William L. Nugent, who owned no slaves himself, declared that without slave labor the country would be "a barren waste and desolate plain" not worth fighting for. "We can only live and exist by this species of labor," he wrote, "and hence I am willing to continue the fight to the last." David Schenck, a North Carolina lawyer who owned nine slaves, asserted that the "fundamental principle" of the Republican party was "war on our property" and that its object was the "Equality of the negro and white man." He therefore gave the "cause of Revolution" his hearty approval: "Free negro equality or resistance is the issue."[12] Few white southerners would hesitate in choosing between such alternatives.

11. Susan Cornwall Diary, January 31, 1861, SHC; Henry Watson, Jr., to Dr. John Parrish, July 15, 1861, in Watson Papers; William W. Gordon to his wife, February 22, 1862, in Gordon Family Papers, SHC. On the containment and ultimate extinction of slavery, see Potter, *Impending Crisis*, 445–46; and Foner, *Free Soil, Free Labor, Free Men*, 313–17.
12. William M. Cash and Lucy Somerville Howarth (eds.), *My Dear Nellie: Letters of*

Threats to slavery and southern race control would jeopardize all other constitutional rights. For most white southerners, protecting their rights transcended loyalty to the Union that had established and nourished those principles. The decision often caused anguish and pain, even for ardent defenders of southern rights. Kentucky schoolteacher Edward Guerrant joined the Confederate cavalry in January, 1862, after "having resolved to make an effort to preserve those inalienable rights descended as a glorious legacy from immortal, patriotic sires . . . and purchased by the best blood of our fathers—and perceiving most plainly that it could not be done in the *once* free and chivalric land of my birth." Guerrant fought to protect his constitutional rights, which were threatened by the North. On the anniversary of his enlistment he explained his motives to a friend. "A year ago I resolved to expatriate myself from the land I loved as a mother, to preserve my dearest and almost only birthright—my liberties—which I forsaw were to be wrested from me there."[13]

The right of self-government was foremost among the constitutional rights for which southerners contended. In justification of their cause they invoked America's revolutionary heritage and the ghosts of the founding fathers, those "immortal, patriotic sires" who had declared their independence from British tyranny. Ella Clanton Thomas, a graduate of Wesleyan College and wife of a wealthy Georgia planter, stated the issue clearly: "We are only asking for self government and freedom to decide our own destinys. We claim nothing of the North but—*to be let alone*—and *they*, a people like ourselves whose republican independence was won by a rebellion, whose liberty was achieved by a secession—to think that they should attempt to coerce us—the idea is preposterous." She charged that the North wanted "to force us to a state of vassalage," and she vowed resistance until "all the rivers should be filled with blood and every mountain top covered with the bleached bone of our countryman." If this right of self-government were taken away, southerners warned, they would be reduced to being slaves to the North. North Carolina judge Asa Biggs, a former United States senator, believed that the suffering and horrors of war were but the

---

William L. Nugent to Eleanor Smith Nugent (Jackson, Miss., 1977), 132, 117; Schenck Diary, November 6, 1860, March 18, 1861. See Steven Hahn, *The Roots of Southern Populism: Yeoman Farmers and the Transformation of the Georgia Upcountry, 1850–1890* (New York, 1983), 108–13.

13. Edward O. Guerrant Diary, January 30, 31, 1863 (copy of letter to Tom Pickett), in Edward Owings Guerrant Papers, SHC.

"price of Liberty" that must be borne as preferable to the loss of freedom. "We only claim the right of self-government," he wrote to his son in the army, "& we cannot & will not surrender this vital principle to become the most abject people upon the face of the earth."[14]

A New Orleans woman likewise invoked the principle of self-government in an effort to convince her sister, a western Virginia Unionist, that the southern states had just cause for secession. "As for seceding peacably 'tis what the South has tried to do. All she has *ever wanted*, was to have her *own government* & be let alone," she argued. Surely to be let alone was a modest request, southerners insisted. "All we asked was freedom from molestation. All we have done is to withdraw from the Union when it fails to guarantee our safety," wrote Sue Sparks Keitt, wife of a prominent South Carolina secessionist, to a friend in Philadelphia. The same claim was made by a Virginia private, who described his fellow Confederates as a "noble & gallant people fighting for nothing under High Heaven but 'to be let alone' to manage their own affairs."[15]

If the North denied their right of self-government, southerners feared the loss of their American liberties. Susan Cornwall Shewmake distrusted Republican intentions. "They fight for dominion," she wrote. "We fight for our liberty and our constitutional rights." Echoing Patrick Henry, a North Carolina woman declared in June, 1861, that the South was engaged in "busy preparation for *liberty* or death." The sins of the North were legion and must be resisted: "Infatuation, total blindness has spread over the whole North—the Bible and the Constitution trampled under foot—God forgotten—the 'Father of his Country' forgotten—the memory of patriot fathers insulted—the 'star[s] and stripes' glorious emblems of the free, forever *forever* disgraced." The Confederacy, she believed, would now become the great bastion of liberty for the world. "May our Southern Constellation take [the] high place from which America has fallen, and shine the brighter, to the oppressed of all nations, to guide them on to liberty," she proclaimed.[16]

14. Ella Gertrude (Clanton) Thomas Diary, July 15, 1861, DU; Asa Biggs to William Biggs, June 22, 1864, in Asa Biggs Papers, DU. Jefferson Davis voiced similar opinions; see Thomas J. Pressly, *Americans Interpret Their Civil War* (2nd ed.; Princeton, 1962), 83, 89–92.

15. Mrs. Bettie Thornhill to Mrs. J. S. Tavenner, May 26, 1861, in Cabell Tavenner and Alexander Scott Withers Papers, DU; Sue Sparks Keitt to Mrs. Frederick Brown, March 4, 1861, in Laurence Massillon Keitt Papers, DU; Richard W. Waldrop to his father, September 24, 1864, in Richard W. Waldrop Papers, SHC.

16. Cornwall Diary, April 27, 1861; Clara Hoyt to Mrs. Fannie Hamilton, June 1, 1861, in Ruffin, Roulhac, and Hamilton Family Papers, SHC.

Liberty was central to the war's meaning for many Southern patriots. To a people whose social order faced assault by an external foe, liberty meant being free to direct their own affairs without interference. Shortly before the first battle of Manassas, Ella Thomas of Georgia warned of northern efforts to curtail the South's liberty. "Our country is invaded—our homes are in danger," she exclaimed. "We are deprived or they are attempting to deprive us of that glorious liberty for which our Fathers fought and bled and shall we tamely submit to this? Never!" Confederate soldiers were soon fighting and dying in the cause of liberty. "How we should prize our liberties if ever gained—when they are bought at such a price!" Kentucky soldier Edward Guerrant wrote early in 1862. "Every day witnesses the sacrifice of tens and hundreds of bloody victims laid upon the bloody altar of Freedom's Cause." Invasion proved that the North intended "to crush out freedom in the South, and compel our return to the 'Union,'" Susan Cornwall Shewmake charged. "'The Union,' once our pride and our glory now symbolical of everything detestable to a freeman, is utterly destroyed." The war was draining "the life blood of our fairest and best," yet she believed that the cause of liberty was worth even this fearful cost. "Liberty, Liberty, how many thousands have been sacrificed at thine altar," she lamented. "May God approve the sacrifice and perpetuate the liberties for which we are contending."[17] This fundamental American principle represented for southerners both a personal and a social right to freedom—freedom from outside interference, freedom to be different, freedom to pursue their own special destiny. "Liberty!" became their rallying cry.

Southerners fought for liberty because the only alternative they knew was slavery. White southerners saw every day the effects of slavery and hence gained special appreciation for the benefits of liberty. Using language common to revolutionary movements, but particularly meaningful for a slave society, they repeatedly vowed that defeat would mean slavery, which they would undertake any sacrifice to avoid. On the day that Lincoln issued his first call for volunteers to defend the Union, University of Virginia student Harry St. John Dixon wrote to his father in Mississippi: "Ere this letter . . . reaches you, the news of Lincoln's determination to invade our beloved country will have reached you. Beyond the shadow of a doubt no alternative is left but war or

17. Thomas Diary, July 15, 1861; Guerrant Diary, February 22, 1862; Cornwall Diary, February 17, 1863.

slavery."[18] Through their experience with Negro slavery, white southerners had come to believe that there was no middle ground between total freedom and absolute slavery. Liberty and equality for white men, they thought, depended on permitting no freedom for blacks. Since the South recognized virtually no gradations between freedom and slavery, infringement of even one of a man's rights would lead quickly to enslavement.

Such was their expectation of treatment at the hands of the North. In May, 1861, a Virginia volunteer warned that southerners must defend their liberty or accept servitude to the Yankees. "Now, in the condition in which our country is now plunged, it is the *duty* of every man, woman & child who can understand the difference between Liberty and Vassalism, to do all in their power no matter what that may be . . . and assist in driving back the foe," he urged his cousin. William L. Nugent of Mississippi likewise portrayed the alternative to victory as "vassalage and slavery all our lives." Shortly before the war's first major battle, a South Carolina private wrote from Manassas Junction that defeat for either side would mean utter ruin. "Should we be the unfortunate we can but expect tyrany to supersede our laws," he predicted. Therefore, "in this Cause our people value life as little as any in the world, for liberty is their watchword."[19]

Warning that northern actions endangered southern liberty, Susan Cornwall Shewmake denounced the Republicans as "a horde of ambitious tyrants and their tools," determined to force the South into submission. The attempt to coerce the southern states to remain in the Union presented an intolerable threat to southerners' liberty. "Do they think that we are as degenerate as our slaves, to be whipped into obedience at the command of our self styled masters?" she demanded. "Has freedom made them the slaves of their own passions?" Her choice of imagery is significant. White southerners had intimate daily experience with slavery and coercion. Now they feared that they were to become victims rather than masters, to lose the rights and liberties they had cherished as the exclusive prerogatives of free white Americans.

18. Harry St. John Dixon to his father, April 15, 1861, in Dixon Papers.
19. A. H. Robins to his cousin, May 8, 1861, in Sarah A. Rootes Papers, DU; Cash and Howarth (eds.), *My Dear Nellie*, 196; W. R. McCormick to Irene Cohen, July 4, 1861, in Alonzo B. Cohen Papers, DU. The editor of the Yorksville *Enquirer* wrote: "The reproach of weak and spiritless vassalage should be fully ours should we return to the vomit of Union" (quoted in Bell I. Wiley, *Southern Negroes, 1861–1865* [rev. ed.; New Haven, 1965], 165).

Yet in another sense they accused their would-be masters of being slaves—to their own passions. "Folly and fanaticism blind the eyes of those who are at the head of affairs," Shewmake charged. "A domineering spirit influences them to desire to have their way or break asunder every tie that has hitherto bound us together. We *will not be ruled* by them."[20]

The prospect of subjugation sustained Confederate soldiers in their dedication to the southern cause. At the beginning of the 1863 spring campaign, a Tennessee soldier wrote from Virginia that he anticipated hard fighting and hoped that this would be the war's last campaign. Yet even if the war did not end soon, he told his father, "I have one glorious consolation: that as long as a yankee can stand the war for my subjugation, I can stand it for my honor and liberty." One year later, Samuel Lockhart, a North Carolina farmer and private who later died in battle, mourned the growing lists of "noble officers" and "gallant" privates who had met their deaths. Nevertheless, he justified such sacrifices as "part of the heavy price we must pay for deliverance from servile subjugation and ruin." Georgia lieutenant William R. Redding stated in 1864 that he was willing to endure still more hardships and sacrifices to protect his liberty from northern despotism. "I do not regret the hardships if I can gain my Independance," he told his wife. "I consider it a duty that I owe to my children to battle for their liberty as well as my own, for where is the Nation who has ever submitted to the yoke of despotism that have ever regained their liberty."[21]

This belief that the loss of liberty was irrevocable made white southerners adamant in defending their freedom. They had good cause, in their knowledge of their own system of Negro slavery, to perceive clear, rigid distinctions between freedom and slavery. A slave had little chance to become free. Unlike the slave systems in Latin America, in the South slavery meant not only a total lack of freedom but also, in most cases, its permanent loss. Just as their own slaves had little hope of gaining freedom, so southerners feared that they could never regain their cherished liberties once they bowed to northern rule. Absolute and permanent slavery was an unbearable prospect for people dedi-

---

20. Cornwall Diary, January 31, February 4, 1861.
21. Felix Buchanan to his father, April 27, 1863, in Buchanan and McClellan Family Papers, SHC; Samuel P. Lockhart to Ellen Lockhart, June 26, 1864, in Hugh Conway Browning Papers, DU; W. R. Redding to his wife, April 8, 1864, in W. R. Redding Papers, SHC.

cated to liberty, and white southerners reacted violently when their freedom seemed jeopardized.[22]

The irony of slaveholders claiming to be the champions of liberty was not apparent to most white southerners. So completely had they excluded blacks from consideration as members of society that they scarcely entertained the possibility that civil rights or liberty could apply to this subservient race. There were, of course, exceptions. Religious humanitarianism led to occasional efforts to ameliorate slavery's harshness, including a wartime campaign for legal reform. Some slaveowners, chiefly women, expressed a measure of guilt. Yet virtually none questioned the necessity of white domination. The vast majority of white southerners entertained no feelings of guilt over slaveholding. Nor did they perceive any conflict between the ideal of liberty and the reality of slavery. Slavery was the foundation of southern society, and the planters proclaimed that the superiority and beauty of the gracious edifice sprang from the divinely ordained institution that supported it.[23]

Far from expressing guilt over slavery, most Confederate patriots boasted that God would lead them to victory over the corrupt and aggressively hostile North. Religious arguments had long been advanced to justify slavery and the social order it supported, and slaveholders easily transferred this belief in divine favor to the Confederate cause. Confident of the justice of their struggle for independence, they predicted victory. "I believe God is on our side," wrote Captain William L. Nugent of Mississippi. "Our cause is right and God will give us the victory," proclaimed Kate Stone of Louisiana on the Fourth of July, 1861. Many Christians warned that victory would come only if the South trusted in God. As Susan Cornwall Shewmake of Georgia predicted, "Yes if we only are a faithful God serving people, we shall surely

22. Eugene D. Genovese, *Roll, Jordan, Roll: The World the Slaves Made* (New York, 1974), 50–53, 179, 689 n. 8; Stanley M. Elkins, *Slavery: A Problem in American Institutional and Intellectual Life* (New York, 1976), 62, 72; Frank Tannenbaum, *Slave and Citizen: The Negro in the Americas* (New York, 1947), 50–58.

23. Channing, *Crisis of Fear*, 56–57; Roark, *Masters Without Slaves*, 97–98; Potter, *Impending Crisis*, 458–61; Leon F. Litwack, " 'Blues Falling Down Like Hail': The Ordeal of Black Freedom," in Robert H. Abzug and Stephen E. Maizlish (eds.), *New Perspectives on Race and Slavery in America* (Lexington, Ky., 1986), 113. Concerning religious reform efforts, see Clarence L. Mohr, *On the Threshold of Freedom: Masters and Slaves in Civil War Georgia* (Athens, Ga., 1986), 235–71; and Donald G. Mathews, *Religion in the Old South* (Chicago, 1977), 136–84. For an opposing view of southern guilt over slavery see Charles Grier Sellers, Jr., *The Southerner as American* (Chapel Hill, 1960), 40–71; and Richard E. Beringer, Herman Hattaway, Archer Jones, and William N. Still, Jr., *Why the South Lost the Civil War* (Athens, Ga., 1986), 352–67.

triumph."[24] God would not desert a devout people fighting in a righteous cause.

Belief in a just God who punished sinners but redeemed the faithful led many southerners to attribute defeats to their people's moral failings. They implored their countrymen to turn to God for salvation. "Our people is so wicked that the good being is determined to punish them for it," wrote Virginia lieutenant Ben Andrews during the gloomy days of December, 1864. "When ever we become humble and feel our dependence on him then I believe our cause will brighten and the sunny bright days of peace will return."[25] When such hopes were finally crushed at Appomattox, some of the Confederate faithful found their religious convictions severely tested. Most, however, refused to doubt either God or the justice of their cause.

Faith in the righteousness of their crusade found strength in contrast to the wickedness of the Yankee war of conquest. The North's determination to coerce the Rebel states into submission converted many southern Unionists to the Confederate cause. Lincoln's call for seventy-five thousand volunteers following the attack on Fort Sumter was the decisive act prompting the secession of the Upper South states—Virginia, Tennessee, and North Carolina. "I see nothing left us but to secede lawful or not," concluded the Reverend Richard Wills of North Carolina. "I do not wish to fight . . . but if fight we must let it not be in favor of the North against the South."[26]

Faced with a choice between loyalty to the Union or to the South, most southerners joined the Confederate cause. John Houston Bills, a Tennessee slaveowner and Unionist, predicted that not a single man from the slave states would respond to Lincoln's call for volunteers. "*Now* the south will be a unit," he predicted, "however wrong the leaders may have acted, no one will see the south Coerced into submission to such a Motley Abolition Crew as is headed by Lincoln." Bills

24. Cash and Howarth (eds.), *My Dear Nellie*, 180; John Q. Anderson (ed.), *Brokenburn: The Journal of Kate Stone, 1861–1868* (Baton Rouge, 1955), 36; Cornwall Diary, February 17, 1863. See also Beringer *et al.*, *Why the South Lost*, 82–102.

25. William B. G. Andrews to his father, December 26, 1864, in William B. G. Andrews Papers, DU. See Mohr, *On the Threshold of Freedom*, 262–68, and Beringer *et al.*, *Why the South Lost*, 268–93.

26. Richard H. Wills to George Wills, April 18, 1861, in William Henry Wills Papers, SHC. For information on Lincoln's call for troops and the secession of Upper South states, see Allan Nevins, *The War for the Union* (4 vols.; New York, 1959–71), I, 92–107; James C. McGregor, *The Disruption of Virginia* (New York, 1922), 179; and several editorials from border states in Dumond (ed.), *Southern Editorials*, 494–511.

blamed "bad politicians north & south" for dividing the Union but charged that the North's refusal to compromise had brought on the war. "I go with my section come what will," he vowed, "but give up the government as I would an old friend; in sorrow."[27] For those who had treasured their identity as citizens of the United States, secession was often a painful action taken with deep regret.

More than any other group of southerners, Virginians felt the pangs of divided loyalties. Their own state was split by the creation of West Virginia as a Unionist state after Virginia seceded. Caroline L. Bedinger, widow of a former Democratic congressman, deplored the coming of the war. Born in New York, she now lived along the Potomac River in Shepherdstown, which would soon be part of West Virginia. In January, 1861, she wrote to her son at the University of Virginia that she thought a plan would be arranged to ensure the rights of the South in the Union. If that failed, she thought the South would be allowed peaceably to form a separate Confederacy. After Lincoln's call for troops, she wrote to her mother in New York that "infatuation seems to possess the people North and South Eager for a War that can only ruin them." Virginia would send no troops, she predicted, and there could be "no neutrality in such a war." Virginia immediately seceded. "The strongest Union men now feel that it was impossible to hold out longer," Bedinger told her mother, "even Mr. Lee who has been the most bitter enemy of secession acknowledges that Virginia was forced to take the step she has." "There is a stern purpose to resist aggression," she announced, "every man will die at his post before they will make the slightest concession." This threat of subjugation united the South as no list of grievances or appeals to principle could do. The prospect of invasion made compromise unthinkable.[28]

Few white southerners could remain loyal to the Union after their "sacred soil" was invaded. One of the most prominent Unionist spokesmen in Shepherdstown was the Reverend Charles Wesley Andrews, rector of the Protestant Episcopal church. A former advocate of freeing the slaves and colonizing them in Africa, Andrews in May, 1861,

27. John Houston Bills Diary, April 16, June 8, and January 8, 1861, in John Houston Bills Papers, SHC.
28. Caroline L. Bedinger to George Bedinger, January 8, 1861, and to her mother, April 16, 22, May 3, 1861, in Bedinger-Dandridge Family Papers, DU. On the separation of West Virginia, see Richard O. Curry, *A House Divided: A Study of Statehood Politics and the Copperhead Movement in West Virginia* (Pittsburgh, 1964); Nevins, *War for the Union*, I, 139–47; and McGregor, *Disruption of Virginia*.

voted against secession, which he called "a monstrous delusion & a monstrous wrong." Secession was not only "wrong in principle," but it would be "ruinous" to the South and result in widespread destruction and death. Yet his son Matthew, a young lawyer in Moorefield, canvassed for votes in favor of secession and sought his parents' consent to enlist. "I cannot reconcile Union with my obligations to Virginia," he told his mother after the state had seceded. He stated that he had been "a Union man up to the last and opposed to secession," but that rather than submit to the North he would "sacrifice life property and Everything else that was dear to me in the world."[29]

By early June, the Reverend Mr. Andrews saw neutrality as the only course to follow. "Secession is doctrinally & practically wrong, wrong, wrong," he still insisted, but he saw also the "greater wickedness of a coercive cruel & vindictive war" in which the North sought to subjugate eleven states even if it meant the "destruction of all their brethren." By the beginning of August, however, he had reluctantly become reconciled to secession. He wrote to a friend in Cincinnati that the southern people had been separated from the North "by an impassable gulph" and that they were even more earnest than Patrick Henry in proclaiming, "Give me liberty or give me death."[30] Here, as elsewhere, southerners appropriated the revolutionary heritage to justify resistance to oppression. When threatened by invasion, all but the staunchest Unionists abandoned their hopes for reconciling southern interests with maintenance of the Union.

Even nonslaveowners, who had little vested interest in slavery and no concern for legalistic arguments over the fugitive slave law, felt the importance of protecting home and family from an invading army. Here was a danger so immediate, so palpable, that few could doubt its magnitude. North Carolina private Jonathan F. Coghill explained to his mother and sister the importance he attached to the war: "I love you all for I know that you love me and I love my country too it has called me fourth to proteck you and I will do my best for you and my country and I pray that god may proteck me and defend me wherever I go." Listing his reasons for fighting, a barely literate Georgia private covered the

29. Charles W. Andrews to his wife, May 17, 1861, and to Matthew P. Andrews, May 21, 1861, Matthew P. Andrews to his mother, May 19, 1861, and to his wife, August 23, 1861, in Charles Wesley Andrews Papers, DU.

30. Charles W. Andrews to his wife, June 12, 1861, and to Charles P. McIlvaine, August 1, 1861, in *ibid*.

major points of the southern rationale for the war: "i am fiten for a go[o]d cos I fite for my rits and for my fredom and for my poor brother and sisters and espe[cial]ly for my seethart."[31] Every Confederate soldier believed that in some way he fought to protect his own home and family. Even when suffering seemed to engulf the South, this belief remained the strongest support for soldiers' morale.

Confederate soldiers were willing to sacrifice their lives in defending their homes. This masculine duty to protect the family has always been one of the most powerful motivations for warriors, and it has been evoked repeatedly by political and military leaders seeking to arouse the fighting spirit of their people. Even when invasion is not a distinct threat, the enemy is often depicted as vicious and eager to despoil homes and murder women and children. Embattled southerners saw an immediate, tangible danger. "I shall fight like I was standing at the threshold of my door fighting against robbers and savages for the defense of my wife & family," Texas lieutenant Theophilus Perry vowed at the beginning of the 1864 campaign in Louisiana. "This is a time for brave hearts, and I feel like I can fight by the side of the foremost men." Two weeks later, Perry was mortally wounded in battle, one of many thousands who made the ultimate sacrifice. Perry's brother-in-law Jesse Person had left college to enlist in the 1st North Carolina Cavalry. During the summer campaign of 1862, he explained to his sister the conviction that sustained him through the trials of military service: "We will soon have to conquer or die, but I am willing to give up my life in defence of my Home and Kindred. I had rather be dead than to see the Yanks rule this country." Less than a year later, Jesse Person was mortally wounded at Gettysburg. Just as Perry and Person willingly died for a cause in which they believed, so other Confederate patriots justified the ever-increasing sacrifices by the necessity to avoid subjugation. There could be no nobler cause than defense of home and family.[32]

Invasion posed for southerners an all-inclusive danger. Not only might their property be stolen, their rights trampled, and their liberty

31. Jonathan F. Coghill to his mother and sister, March 15, 1863, in James O. Coghill Papers, DU; Walden Wise to Mrs. G. W. Freeman, December 22, 1861, in John Cumming Papers, DU.

32. Theophilus Perry to his wife, March 23, 1864, and Jesse Person to his sister, February 23, August 21, 1862, in Presley Carter Person Papers, DU. Concerning depictions of the enemy as ruthless despoiler, see J. Glenn Gray, *The Warriors: Reflections on Men in Battle* (New York, 1959), 135–59.

extinguished, but even their homes and their very lives were now directly threatened. Defeat would be total. Following the battle of Manassas in July, 1861, Charles C. Jones, Jr., scion of a prominent Georgia plantation family, summed up the Confederate cause: "A freeman's heart can beat in no nobler behalf, and no more sacred obligations can rest upon any people than those now devolved upon us to protect our homes, our loves, our lives, our property, our religion, and our liberties, from the inhuman and infidel hordes who threaten us with invasion, dishonor, and subjugation." Jones's patriotic rhetoric found echoes in numerous letters and diaries of other Confederate soldiers, who repeatedly proclaimed that everything valuable in life was at stake. William O. Fleming, a Georgia planter turned army officer, declared, "We fight not only for our country—her liberty & independence, but we fight for our homes our firesides, our religion—every thing that makes life dear." So intertwined were the elements of southern civilization that disruption of one part would weaken all. The northern attack on slavery, even though it was mainly indirect in seeking to block the institution's westward expansion, threatened to destroy the social order it supported. The slaveowners fought to protect the essence of their way of life.[33]

Faced with the destruction of their unique civilization, southerners risked all in its defense. Even nonslaveowners recognized the need to protect their homes and their identity as white southerners. "Conquer or die" became the Confederate slogan. As early as January, 1862, Charles C. Jones, Jr., predicted that "we must in meeting the invasions suffer much, and many a brave man surrender his life in the defense of all we hold pure in honor, true in principle, honest in religion, dear in life, and sacred in death." The prospect of defeat made compromise or submission unthinkable. Jones pledged absolute loyalty to the cause, whatever sacrifice was required. "There can be no retreat," he proclaimed. "The ultimatum with every true lover of his country who is able to bare his breast in support of the principles for which we are contending must be *victory or death*."[34] Defeat would mean absolute and permanent subjugation. Just as there was no middle ground be-

33. Charles C. Jones, Jr., to Rev. and Mrs. C. C. Jones, July 29, 1861, in Robert M. Myers (ed.), *The Children of Pride: A True Story of Georgia and the Civil War* (New Haven, 1972), 725; William O. Fleming to his wife, July 18, 1862, in William O. Fleming Papers, SHC; Genovese, *Political Economy of Slavery*, 270.

34. Charles C. Jones, Jr., to Rev. C. C. Jones, January 20, 1862, in Myers (ed.), *Children of Pride*, 834.

tween liberty and slavery, so southerners saw no intermediate condition between victory and desolation. There could be no room for negotiation or compromise. One ideological system or the other must triumph.

As the war entered its fourth year, William Calder, a young junior officer serving in the North Carolina coastal defenses, measured his comrades' morale by the mounting sacrifices they were called on to bear. "During the past week our spirits have been uniformly raised and depressed as the thermometer of war news was more or less favorable to our cause," he explained. The war's progress gave little encouragement, as diminishing resources and military reversals portended defeat. Yet there was one conviction that sustained what patriotism his weary comrades could muster. "Victory now is life to us," he proclaimed. "Defeat is worse than death."[35] Reinforced by this foreboding belief, many Confederate soldiers continued to fight desperately for their cause until the last guns were silenced and all hope destroyed.

35. William Calder to his mother, May 22, 1864, in William Calder Papers, SHC.

2 / FREEDOM, JUSTICE, AND OUR COUNTRY

The northern people entered the war with a divided purpose. Most rallied to the Union cause to protect the nation and its government from the sinister threat of rebellion. They cared only for restoring the Union, without interfering with slavery. An increasingly numerous minority of abolitionists and antislavery Republicans, however, insisted that slavery was the natural parent of secession and war. Republican ideology derived its great appeal from the concept of free labor, which represented a model of the North's superior social order, based on individual liberty and the dignity of labor. As the foundation of a competing social system, slavery posed a threat to the dynamic, expanding capitalist system. Republicans eventually demanded slavery's destruction as the only sure basis of peace. Efforts to define war objectives could not satisfy the conflicting interests of both Unionists and emancipationists unless it could be proven that they were not mutually exclusive.[1]

There was little disagreement about the necessity of preserving the Union. The southern rebellion posed a clear, immediate threat to the Union, which was the strongest bulwark of liberty and independence. Danger to the Union, moreover, jeopardized the entire system of republican government, which Unionists viewed not as a mere abstract principle but as the foundation of American freedom. The war for the Union thus became a war for liberty. When such fundamental principles were involved, compromise would be unthinkable.[2]

Although many northerners had been willing to allow the southern states to secede peaceably, the attack on Fort Sumter on April 12, 1861,

1. Eric Foner, *Free Soil, Free Labor, Free Men: The Ideology of the Republican Party Before the Civil War* (New York, 1970), 11–39, 308–11; David H. Donald, *Liberty and Union* (Boston, 1978), 14–17; Thomas J. Pressly, *Americans Interpret Their Civil War* (2nd ed.; Princeton, 1962), 46–50; Eric Foner, *Politics and Ideology in the Age of the Civil War* (New York, 1980), 34–53.

2. Paul C. Nagel, *One Nation Indivisible: The Union in American Thought, 1776–1861* (New York, 1964), 104–44; Foner, *Free Soil, Free Labor, Free Men,* 1–10, 225; David M. Potter, *The South and the Sectional Conflict* (Baton Rouge, 1968), 34–83; Pressly, *Americans Interpret Their Civil War,* 51–52. For examples of northern editorials on preserving the Union and perpetuating republican government, see Howard C. Perkins (ed.), *Northern Editorials on Secession* (2 vols.; New York, 1942), 121–22, 844–47, 943–45.

united the North in defense of the Union. "Party is forgotten. All feel
that our very nationality is at stake," wrote Maria L. Daly, the staunchly
Democratic wife of a New York judge, "and to save the country from
anarchy . . . every man must do his best to sustain the government,
whoever or whatever the President may be." The Reverend James May
of Philadelphia tried to explain this change in northern attitude to his
fellow clergyman Charles Wesley Andrews of Virginia. "They say the
news of the bombardment of Fort Sumter & of a threat to take Washington was like an electric shock through all the north & roused the
whole body not for invasion nor subjugation, nor revenge, but simply
for defence," he wrote. The South "seized national property by force,
drove off national forces, defied the government, threatened its utter
overthrow, [and] made open war." The question, according to May,
was "whether the U.S. government were to be allowed to exist. . . . The
north only wishes the South to stand on the Constitution just as it did &
all is right," he told his southern friend. "There is no purpose nor wish
to interfere with Slavery." Moderate Unionists such as James May and
Maria Daly represented the North's most conciliatory faction. Apart
from a small number of radical abolitionists and "Peace Democrats," at
opposite ends of the political spectrum, most northerners demanded
restoration of the Union as a minimum condition for peace.[3]

For many Unionists, defense of the Union was the only objective of
the war. Slavery seemed irrelevant. David Hunter Strother, a Virginian, who during the 1850s had contributed sketches and essays to
Harper's New Monthly Magazine, enlisted in the Union army shortly
after war commenced. "There is but one great and paramount question
to be considered," he proclaimed, "'United we stand, Divided we

3. Maria L. Daly, *Diary of a Union Lady, 1861–1865*, ed. Harold Earl Hammond (New
York, 1962), 12; James May to Charles Wesley Andrews, June 26, 5, 1861, in Charles Wesley
Andrews Papers, DU. On the patriotic response to Fort Sumter and the emergence of
conservative Unionism, see Pressly, *Americans Interpret Their Civil War*, 27–43, 129–34;
Christopher Dell, *Lincoln and the War Democrats: The Grand Erosion of Conservative Tradition*
(Rutherford, N.J., 1975), 51–66; William L. Barney, *Flawed Victory: A New Perspective on the
Civil War* (New York, 1975), 44–50; and George M. Fredrickson, *The Inner Civil War:
Northern Intellectuals and the Crisis of the Union* (New York, 1965), 65–78. For the response
of some abolitionists who advocated letting the southern states secede, see James M.
McPherson, *The Struggle for Equality: Abolitionists and the Negro in the Civil War and Recon-
struction* (Princeton, 1964), 34–39, 58–60. The opposition of Peace Democrats to the war is
described in Wood Gray, *The Hidden Civil War: The Story of the Copperheads* (New York,
1942), 41–48, 56–58. For editorials advocating peaceable secession, see Perkins (ed.),
Northern Editorials, 331–34, 337–43, 348–50, 352–59.

fall.'" There were only two alternatives: "The nationality, with independence, power and dignity. Division with anarchy, foreign protection and eternal war." Faced with such a choice, Strother asked, "What then are the minor questions of Negro freedom or slavery, party dogmas and prejudices of race, sectional hatred, compared to the great question?" Writing to a southern friend, Charles P. McIlvaine of Cincinnati insisted that the North could not "submit to any effort of treason, any spoliations, any schemes of disorganization." Volunteers for the Union cause vowed to protect the country from "this monstrous, hellish rebellion," which threatened to dismember the cherished Union.[4]

This northern effort to put down the rebellion assumed the aura of a holy crusade, imbued with the combination of patriotism and religion exemplified by "The Battle Hymn of the Republic." Describing the buildup of troops and weapons before the 1862 spring campaign, Lieutenant Colonel Robert McAllister of New Jersey explained that these preparations had been undertaken "to put down this wicked rebellion and teach the Southerners with force what they would not learn in time of peace—that governments are not so easily broken up, and that God requires obedience to law and order." The conviction that secession constituted unlawful rebellion against the Union reassured many northerners that their cause was righteous and must prevail. "God grant . . . that our cause shall continue to prosper until the unhallowed rebellion is crushed forever," wrote Lieutenant John B. Stickney of Massachusetts, "and the U.S. government shines out with resplendid grandeur richer in resources, material, strength and power." Rebellion was wicked precisely because it threatened the power of the government, and Unionists rallied to defend their country against this assault. A Maine volunteer explained that he had enlisted to serve the Union, "for in defending our country we are but preserving the blessings of the best government the earth affords, for the protection of the dear friends at home." Unlike southerners, he did not fear a direct assault on family and home. The Union served as protector of individual rights, providing the means to safeguard liberty, property, and opportunity. By threatening to destroy this shield, however, rebellion indirectly

4. David H. Strother Diary, August 9, 1863, in David Hunter Strother Collection, West Virginia University Library; Charles P. McIlvaine to Charles Wesley Andrews, August 28, 1861, in Andrews Papers; Nathan Webb Diary, May 24, 1864, WLC.

attacked northern homes. Thus did Unionists invoke defense of family and home for their cause.[5]

The Union not only protected individual citizens but also stood as the world's great citadel of freedom. Those who fought to defend the Union saw themselves as champions of free institutions, endeavoring to perpetuate the great American experiment in republican government. "I think the leaders of the rebelion the meanest men on Gods earth," exclaimed Indiana farmer Brantley Swaim. "They commenced this destructive and bloody war soully for the purpose of putting down free government and planting the infernal institution of Slavery on a firmer rock." Whether or not they viewed slavery as a moral issue, most northerners opposed its extension. Free institutions should not succumb to the encroachments of any competing political and social system. "The cause of free institutions and the *undivided* existence of this Glorious Republic the roused spirit of the North has been sworn to maintain," vowed Sergeant Felix Brannigan of New York, "tho' we had to *exterminate* our brethren of the South in accomplishing it!" The Union was fighting for existence, warned New Hampshire private Oren Farr, a Republican farmer and son of a Baptist minister, "for the question now is country or no country, liberty or slavery." Serving the Union cause thus guaranteed the perpetuation of free institutions.[6]

Union soldiers accepted tremendous sacrifices to preserve the Union's blessings for posterity. During the war's first months, Robert McAllister wrote that he was glad to take part in "the grate struggle for the Union, Constitution, and law." He complained about privations and miserable conditions in the army camps but added: "I do it because I love my country and its institutions, and am willing to sacrifice much—even life itself—to sustain our glorious country and the best Government in the world." Although nearly fifty years old, McAllister had left his work as a railroad contractor to fight for the Union. He insisted that all active young men should join the army, "to help us put down this wicked and unjustifiable rebellion. Our Country and prop-

5. James I. Robertson, Jr. (ed.), *The Civil War Letters of General Robert McAllister* (New Brunswick, N.J., 1965), 159–60; John B. Stickney to his parents, July 6, 1863, in Clinton H. Haskell Collection, WLC; Charles P. Lord to his sister, July 3, 1861, in Charles Phineas Lord Papers, DU. For northern interpretations of the war as a "rebellion," see Pressly, *Americans Interpret Their Civil War*, 25–77.

6. Brantley Swaim to Christopher Hackett, March 25, 1865, in John C. Hackett Papers, DU; Felix Brannigan to his sister, May 30, 1862, in Felix Brannigan Papers, LC; Oren E. Farr to his wife, March 27, 1863, in Oren E. Farr Papers, DU.

erty is worth nothing if we don't, nor will life be secure." Beyond such practical considerations lay a moral obligation. "We will be held responsible before God if we don't do our part in helping to transmit this boon of civil & religious liberty down to succeeding generations," he told a nephew who was reluctant to enlist. "Our glorious institutions are likely to be destroyed; will we not help to save them?" Thus for McAllister, maintaining personal liberty depended on preserving the national government. Liberty and Union stood inseparable.[7]

McAllister's concern for succeeding generations echoed in many northern hearts. A Missouri cavalry officer declared that he enlisted because "it is a duty I owe to my country and to my children to do what I can to preserve this government as I shudder to think what is ahead for them if this government should be overthrown." Connecticut sergeant Henry C. Hall expressed a similar motivation for enlisting. "I thought I saw the free Institutions of our country in danger of being overthrown," he told his brother, "and being desirous of having them perpetuated to all future generations of my children and yours and all others I resolved to be one of the vast numbers that have gone forth to meet in battle those who would do us this great wrong." The same concern for posterity supported the patriotic resolve of an Iowa soldier, who told his wife that he was "willing to make the present sacrifice that our children may enjoy the free institutions that we do."[8]

The Union's importance for future generations led many to believe in its divine sanction. In January, 1861, Juliette A. Kenzie, a socially prominent writer in Chicago, wrote to her daughter, whose husband would soon enlist in a Georgia regiment, charging that "the *crime* of attempting to break up the Union and rend our Nation in pieces is second only to that of an attempt to overthrow the Christian religion." Many northerners viewed the interests of God and the Union as identical. Captain John D. Wilkins of Pennsylvania, a regular army veteran of the Mexican War, told his wife, "If I should fall on the field know that I did so fighting for my country, and, I believe, for my 'God.'" Trusting in the righteousness of their cause, many Unionists expressed faith that God would secure their victory. "Remember it is a good cause you are en-

---

7. Robertson (ed.), *Civil War Letters of McAllister*, 38, 72, 107.
8. Vivian K. McLarty (ed.), "The Civil War Letters of Colonel Bazel F. Lazear," *Missouri Historical Review*, XLIV (1949–50), 265; Henry C. Hall to Alex Hall, November 24, 1861, in Henry C. Hall Papers, DU; Isaac Marsh to his niece, November 21, 1862, in Isaac Marsh Papers, DU.

gaged in," Ruth Whittemore of Oswego, New York, reassured her brother, who was serving in the Virginia campaign, "and have faith in Heaven and the final triumph of right over wrong, of Justice over Injustice and Rebellion, and be not discouraged."[9]

Supporters of both the Union and the Confederacy thus claimed that God was on their side and would ensure the success of their cause. There were theological differences between North and South, and southerners more often expressed religious sentiments, but both sides believed that God influenced political and military events. Most northerners believed that the Union's perpetuation was divinely ordained as part of God's plan for human progress.

Preservation of the Union superseded all other concerns, according to most Unionists, primarily because it provided the strongest bulwark of American liberty. They continually invoked liberty as a rallying cry for defense of the Union. "Rather than see the south conquer," an Ohio soldier solemnly vowed, "let me die, fighting for the great principle of human Liberty." Secession threatened to dismember the United States government, which, according to Virginia Unionist David H. Strother, had "afforded to four or five generations the most entire freedom in any human society." Juliette Kenzie denounced the secessionists as madmen, who "would sacriligiously destroy the fairest temple of Liberty ever constructed on the face of the earth!" Such use of religious metaphors, which abound in Unionists' paeans to liberty, signifies both their belief in its divine sanction and their sense of mission in defending it. "Let the page of history in the future tell how nobly fought the sons of freedom to support the sacred temple of liberty," proclaimed Sergeant Arthur Carpenter of Indiana in typically grandiose style. "Liberty!! May that be the watchword of every American citizen throughout all future ages." Northern Unionists thus claimed to be the true champions of America's greatest ideals, preserving liberty and free government for posterity.[10]

9. Juliette A. Kenzie to Nelly Gordon, January 18, 1861, in Gordon Family Papers, SHC; John D. Wilkins to his wife, May 26, 1862, in John Darragh Wilkins Papers, WLC; Walter Rundell, Jr. (ed.), "'Despotism of Traitors': The Rebellious South Through New York Eyes," *New York History*, XLV (October, 1964), 335. On the Union's divine mission, see Nagel, *One Nation Indivisible*, 20–22, 147–76.

10. W. P. Deland to Mr. and Mrs. E. Crossman, November, 1863, Civil War Correspondence, BHC; Cecil D. Eby, Jr. (ed.), *A Virginia Yankee in the Civil War: The Diaries of David Hunter Strother* (Chapel Hill, 1961), 123; Juliette A. Kenzie to Nelly Gordon, April 26, 1861, in Gordon Family Papers; Arthur Carpenter to his grandmother, November 10, 1861, in Civil War Manuscripts Collection, Yale.

The concept of liberty dominated both northern and southern explanations of the war's meaning. Each side justified its cause by appeals to cherished American principles and claimed the title of true descendant of the founding fathers. Unionists and Confederates alike proclaimed that they fought for liberty. With rare insight, Sergeant Onley Andrus recognized this irony. A twenty-seven-year-old farmer from northern Illinois, he had enlisted in August, 1862, to claim the one-hundred-dollar bounty being offered and to prove to his neighbors that he was a reliable citizen. Shortly after arriving in Tennessee with his regiment, Andrus reported that "the rebs fight like Devils." The reason for their tenacity seemed obvious: "Supposing you were fighting to keep an enemy out of your own neighborhood & protect your property—your own hard earnings. How would you fight? Not that I consider their cause just but, right or wrong, if we thot or believed we was right it would be the same to us as though God (or any other man) should say it. I tell *you* you would fight & to the bitter end too & die in your tracks before you would give up." Although conceding that southerners fought to defend their property and homes, he denied the justice of their cause. He recognized, nevertheless, that they espoused the same principles as his fellow Unionists. "They are fighting for the same thing that we are," he told his wife, "*Liberty*."[11]

The similarities between northern and southern declarations about preserving liberty are striking, yet there are also subtle but significant differences of meaning. The rhetoric, derived from the same sources of American ideology, often sounded identical; each justified sacrifice and suffering as "the price of liberty" and warned that defeat would entail the loss of "cherished liberties." The meaning of liberty, however, differed for northerners and southerners. The same Union which Confederates feared would deprive them of their liberty seemed to Unionists the only safeguard of freedom. A majority of northerners viewed the Union as absolute, an end in itself. For most southerners, it was an experiment to be discarded if it failed to protect their interests. This fundamental distinction between two opposing views of the relationship between Union and liberty had been apparent at least since the founding of the republic. Southerners, for the most part, expressed the Jeffersonian belief that government should exercise minimal power

11. Fred A. Shannon (ed.), *The Civil War Letters of Sergeant Onley Andrus* (Urbana, Ill., 1947), 25–26.

over individuals. Liberty meant being left alone to pursue personal goals, without suffering interference in one's private affairs from either government or fellow citizens. The Federalist position, eventually adopted by most northerners, assumed that liberty required the Union's protection. As Daniel Webster had proclaimed, only the Union could perpetuate political and social freedom and guarantee personal liberties. Whereas Confederates feared the power of the government to interfere, Unionists welcomed its power to protect.[12]

The northern and southern interpretations of liberty thus represented two divergent ideological positions, both deeply rooted in American thought. The desired result, personal freedom of choice and action, was the same, but the means necessary to secure that condition differed dramatically. This difference was an important factor in shaping individual responses to secession and invasion. For northerners, secession threatened liberty by undermining the institutions that guaranteed individual rights. Invasion, by contrast, underscored southern fear of institutional infringements on personal liberty. It was a direct attack on home and family. When Unionists and Confederates went to war, they did so principally because they saw in the events of 1860 and 1861 the culmination of their worst fears about the potential loss of American liberty.

The concept of liberty played another role in northern interpretations of the war. Eager to establish their claim as the true champions of liberty, many Unionists such as Private Constant C. Hanks portrayed the Union cause as the defense of freedom against the onslaught of rebellion and slavery. According to Hanks, the war was an ideological conflict between two civilizations. Each regarded the other as the antithesis of its own virtues and a threat to its continued existence. As the basis of southern society, slavery seemed to Hanks both a moral reproach to American ideals and, more important, a hindrance to national progress. The war precipitated by secession would determine

---

12. The classic statement of the close interrelationship of liberty and Union is Daniel Webster's exhortation during a Senate speech in January, 1830: "Liberty *and* Union, now and forever, one and unseparable!" (quoted in Donald, *Liberty and Union*, 33). On the meaning of liberty and union, see Fred Somkin, *Unquiet Eagle: Memory and Desire in the Idea of American Freedom, 1815–1860* (Ithaca, N.Y., 1967); Nagel, *One Nation Indivisible*, 13–31, 235–80; and Foner, *Free Soil, Free Labor, Free Men*, 139–40, 225. On the origins of divergent views of liberty, see Gordon S. Wood, *The Creation of the American Republic, 1776–1787* (Chapel Hill, 1969), esp. 543–53; and John C. Miller, *The Federalist Era, 1789–1801* (New York, 1960), 20–32.

which social system would shape the future of America. "Freedom justice and our country will tryumph in this mighty struggle with Slavery injustice & Treason, " Hanks reassured his father.[13]

Although most northerners entered the war concerned only with defending the Union, Constant Hanks typified the beliefs of many Republicans, who, though not advocating abolition, perceived the war as a contest between free labor and slavery. A resident of Greene County, New York, Hanks enlisted in September, 1861, as a private in Company K of the 20th New York State Militia. His record of war service is typical. Serving entirely in the Virginia campaigns, he fought at Antietam, was wounded twice (at Second Bull Run and Fort Damnation), spent three months in a Washington hospital with diarrhea, and yet reenlisted in October, 1864. His young son Cyrus, who had enlisted against his parents' wishes, was killed one day before Hanks reenlisted in order to be near him.[14]

Throughout four years of war, Constant Hanks frequently repeated his determination to fight freedom's battles. At the beginning of the 1862 spring campaign, Hanks wrote to his sister Mary Rose that the people of the North must be prepared to "mourn the loss of sons, brothers, fathers, husbands." The sacrifice would not be in vain, however, for "sure as the right will in the end triumph over wrong, so sure will the principles of Freedom, free thought, free speech, free press, free schools, and free labor, free *government* for which we fight, & ask *God's* help, tryumph in the end over Slavery, ignorance, and tyranny and *brutishness*." This array of free institutions, Hanks believed, would overcome slavery and its concomitant evils through sheer force of moral superiority. The South, debased by slavery and devoid of an energetic, prosperous class of white laborers, could be redeemed only by "Yankee skill energy Enterprise, with the *leaven* of free labor, free schools." The concept of free labor was the heart of Hanks's Republican model of the perfect society. His opposition to slavery was not so much an antisouthern position as an active advocacy of northern institutions threatened by disunion.[15]

13. Constant Hanks to his father, October 8, 1862, in Constant C. Hanks Papers, DU.
14. Hanks Papers; Theodore B. Gates, *The "Ulster Guard" and the War of the Rebellion* (New York, 1879), 577.
15. Constant Hanks to Mary Rose, May 1, 1862, in Hanks Papers. For similar statements on the need to make the South conform to the northern free-labor model, see Foner, *Free Soil, Free Labor, Free Men*, 48–54; and Fredrickson, *Inner Civil War*, 117–18.

As the world's strongest bulwark of human freedom and republican government, the Union must be preserved for future generations. At the outset of the spring campaign of 1863, Hanks hopefully declared that the northern people now realized that "they are fighting for their very existence as a free people, and for *Principles* that must tryumph or they will leave only a legacy of shame to their children." President Lincoln's Emancipation Proclamation, which committed the Union to a war against slavery, encouraged him. "Thank God the day of compromises in favor of Slavery with our government is past," Hanks proclaimed, "the contest is now between Slavery & Freedom, & every honest man knows what he is fighting for." He repeatedly predicted that freedom would eventually triumph and that when the war ended, "the foul stain and villainous blot of Slavery with all its unclean family will be forever washed off . . . & our nation will be acknowledged to the ends of the earth as the true champion of human rights, and self-government will no longer remain an unsolved problem, but be established as an *axion* so plain that he who runs may read & understand." Once that "glorious result" was accomplished, Hanks declared, "our country then shall truly be home of the 'brave and the land of the free.'" The Republican goal was to spread northern free institutions throughout the South, molding the entire nation to conform to the free-labor model of the good society. Northern freedom could be guaranteed only if its influence could expand and direct national policy.[16]

In the contest between freedom and slavery, the latter must perish for the Union to be preserved. Recognizing this necessity, many northern soldiers argued that slavery must be destroyed. Abolitionist rhetoric resounds in some of their philippics, such as that of Nathan Webb, a sergeant from Maine:

> O the curse the system has been to the land. All the past wickedness and present horrible cruelties, all the torture, concubinage, the whipping, starving, blaspheming, acts of this people is directly due to Slavery. It is a most cursed institution an originator and promoter of all that's evil, the "sum of all villainies." I hope before this war is closed every vestige of it will be purged from the nation. That no more the bondsman shall cry for mercy, that no more families shall be separated, that no more torture shall

16. Constant Hanks to his mother, April 20, 1863, and to Mary Rose, February 6, 1864, in Hanks Papers. On the conflict between freedom and slavery, see Allan Nevins, *The Emergence of Lincoln* (2 vols.; New York, 1950), II, 359–63, 409–11; Barney, *Flawed Victory*, 56–71; and Foner, *Free Soil, Free Labor, Free Men*, 69–72, 225.

be inflicted upon innocent men and women, that all the cruelties and horrors arising may be swept away by the destruction of the cause.[17]

A few opponents of slavery emphasized cruelties inflicted on slaves themselves, rather than social and moral consequences for the country. Constant Hanks insisted that the North shared responsibility for allowing masters to separate slave families by tearing a child from its mother's arms. "Can we wonder that God punishes our country for the wrong done the poor slave," he demanded. Wisconsin private Jenkin Lloyd Jones announced his willingness to fight so as to redress injustices suffered by slaves. A Unitarian, Jones had moved to Wisconsin from his native Wales at an early age. "How sickening and disgusting is the detail of this sin of slavery, and I thank God that a better day is dawning for the poor wronged African," he wrote in December, 1864. "I can cheerfully bear all the discomforts of a soldier's life for the overthrow of the monster evil."[18]

Nevertheless, what troubled northerners most about slavery was its impact on white society, both South and North of the Potomac. Slavery had transformed the South into a "land of human bondage & oppression." If slavery were eradicated, the South could once more become "the home of freemen and the land of liberty"—in other words, more like the North. The "curse of slavery" was not confined to the South but infected the entire country. It threatened to undermine free institutions, which northerners vowed to defend at all cost. Slavery was a moral reproach to American doctrines of freedom and equality, a "foul blot upon our nations virgin garments," as Ohio chaplain Lucius Chapman described it. Southerners had long insisted that their "peculiar institution" was strictly a domestic concern over which the South should retain sole authority. "Slavery a *private* affair indeed!" objected Nathan Webb. "It affects the whole nation for woe." Webb applauded Lincoln's proposed emancipation edict in September, 1862. "Many at the North are crying this war down as a 'nigger war,' but I tell you that before this is over with this negro question will be settled," Webb predicted. "Now we've got the power and chance, I say take the opportunity to eradicate this evil from the nation."[19] This was exactly what

17. Nathan Webb Diary, July 19, 1863, WLC.
18. Constant Hanks to his mother, October 18, 1862, in Hanks Papers; Jenkin L. Jones, *An Artilleryman's Diary* ([Madison], 1914), 289–90.
19. John B. Foote to his sister, February 8, 1865, in John B. Foote Papers, DU; Lucius W. Chapman Diary, April 7, 1864, WLC; Webb Diary, September 30, 1862.

southerners had feared would happen once the North gained political dominance.

A small number of radical abolitionists believed that the principle of liberty, for which most Unionists claimed to be fighting, should apply to black slaves as well as to white freemen. Their commitment to free institutions made slavery abhorrent. Their dedication to human liberty allowed no exceptions. "I am fighting for Liberty, for the slave & the white man alike," Connecticut private Uriah Parmelee declared early in 1862. Convinced that constitutional guarantees to slavery had been "one & all forfeited by the rebel slave owners & slave drivers of the South," Parmelee left Yale College in his junior year to volunteer as a private in the 6th New York Cavalry. To his brother, Parmelee confided: "I am more of an abolitionist than ever—right up to the handle—if I had money enough to raise a few hundred contrabands & arm them I'd get up an insurrection among the slaves—told Capt. I'd desert to do it." John Brown's martyrdom still inspired Parmelee. His statements would have confirmed southerners' worst fears about northern intentions. Here was abolitionism at its most extreme.[20]

Uriah Parmelee denounced the government's initial war policy, which was limited to restoring the Union on the prewar basis. "The present contest will indeed, settle the question for some years at least, as to whether Union or Secession, the Constitution or Rebellion shall triumph," the young radical warned, "but the great heart wound, Slavery, will not be reached." The administration still did not support emancipation, he complained, in September, 1862. "I thought that the progress of events must surely bring about universal Emancipation," he wrote to his mother, "this either as an indirect result of our subduing the rebels, or a direct result of the light which would dawn on men's minds." Neither had yet occurred, he lamented. Indeed, if the army's principles did not soon change, he thought that his conscience would require him to summon "the moral courage to desert it."[21] Two weeks later, Lincoln officially announced his Emancipation Proclamation.

Parmelee was skeptical at first, doubting whether this emancipation

20. Uriah Parmelee to his mother, April 18, January 10, 1862, and to Sam Parmelee, April 23, 1862, in Samuel Spencer Parmelee and Uriah N. Parmelee Papers, DU.

21. Uriah Parmelee to his mother, November 11, 1861, and September 8, 1862, in *ibid*. A Rhode Island sergeant wrote: "I have talked prayed & voted against [slavery] and now I am here to fight against it" (Henry E. Simmons to his wife, November 23, 1862, Henry E. Simmons Letters, SHC). Concerning abolitionists' efforts to turn the war for the Union into an antislavery struggle, see McPherson, *Struggle for Equality*, 52–74.

proposal would ever be carried out or, if implemented, whether it would help the slaves. By March, 1863, he concluded that emancipation would indeed be achieved, and his attitude toward army life visibly brightened. At the start of the spring campaign, he not only had abandoned thoughts of deserting but even refused to apply for a furlough. He explained this change to his father: "I do not intend to shirk now there is really something to fight for—I mean *Freedom*. Since the First of January it has become more & more evident to my mind that the war is henceforth to be conducted upon a different basis. Those who profess to love the Union are not so anxious to preserve Slavery, while those who are opposed to the war acknowledge in all their actions that its continuance will put an end to that accursed system. So then I am willing to remain & endure whatever may fall to my share." Parmelee went on to complete a distinguished military record. He was promoted to lieutenant of the 1st Connecticut Cavalry for bravery at Chancellorsville, promoted to captain for his actions at the battle of Ashland, and captured and escaped from confinement during the Valley campaign. General John C. Caldwell praised Parmelee, stating that "he had never seen a braver soldier." On April 1, 1865, eight days before General Robert E. Lee surrendered at Appomattox, Uriah Parmelee was killed in battle at Five Forks, Virginia. To the end, he fought for liberty and the Union.[22]

Avowed abolitionists such as Uriah Parmelee were not well liked by most Union soldiers, who blamed extremists on each side for causing the war. Their bitterness toward abolitionists grew stronger because they believed that few of the radicals had enlisted to fight for their convictions. "I am down on the abolitionists," grumbled Private Joseph Osborn, an outspoken New Jersey Democrat. "I believe it is their fault from beginning to end that the country is ruined." Osborn's army experience had taught him at least one important lesson: "to keep out of political wars and let those that have and would cause the trouble fight it out."[23]

Northern Democrats branded all Republicans as abolitionists and railed against their power in the government. Following Democratic

22. Uriah Parmelee to his mother, September 25, 1862, and to his father, March 29, 1863, in Parmelee Papers; Ellsworth Eliot, Jr., *Yale in the Civil War* (New Haven, 1932), 47, 50, 176.
23. Joseph B. Osborn to his father, March 7, 1863, in Joseph Bloomfield Osborn Papers, LC.

victories in the 1862 elections, Major E. B. Grubb of New Jersey said he was glad to see this small sign "that the North is not ruled by a set of infernal fanatics and nigger worshippers." Those responsible for arousing sectional hatred and inciting war should be forced to fight and suffer, Lieutenant William M. Ferry of Michigan declared. "This fighting the 'battles of Freedom' is where I want to see the Abolition priesthood of the Northern states," he insisted.[24]

Even those who disliked slavery and secession sometimes considered abolitionism worse. Lieutenant Charles Wills of Illinois reported that his commanding officer "said that he considered 'slavery a vile blot on the face of the earth,' and that unadulterated abolitionism alone was its equal." To this Wills gave hearty assent, adding only that it was such an obvious truth that recognizing it required little genius. In August, 1862, Indiana private Arthur Carpenter stated that since entering the army he had become convinced that "abolitionism is worse if anything than secession." As early as May, 1861, Juliette Kenzie of Chicago wrote to her daughter in Georgia, "I consider *abolitionism* as great a breach of loyalty and patriotism, as great an engine for destroying the Constitution and the laws, as *secession*." This hostility toward abolitionists reflected both the extent of political conflict within the North and the depth of the division over war objectives.[25]

From the war's beginning, abolitionists had argued that emancipation was both a moral and a military necessity. The Boston Emancipation League, formed in September, 1861, after President Lincoln revoked General John C. Frémont's order freeing the slaves of rebels in Missouri, led a propaganda campaign for emancipation to which most abolitionists contributed. By the spring of 1862, military reverses gradually pushed northern political leaders, slowly and reluctantly, to oppose slavery. In March, the Senate passed an article of war stopping the return of fugitive slaves. In the following months, Congress approved compensated emancipation in the nation's capital, banned slavery from

24. E. B. Grubb to Henry Moffett, November 19, 1862, in Clinton H. Haskell Collection, WLC; William M. Ferry to his wife, May 1, 1862, in Ferry Family Papers, MHC. Christopher Dell disputes the traditional view that Democratic gains in the 1862 elections represented an antiemancipation protest against Lincoln's policies (*Lincoln and the War Democrats*, 181, 231).

25. Charles W. Wills, *Army Life of an Illinois Soldier: Letters and Diary of the Late Charles W. Wills* (Washington, D.C., 1906), 99; Arthur Carpenter to his family, August 19, 1862, in Civil War Manuscripts Collection, Yale; Juliette A. Kenzie to Nelly Gordon, May 21, 1861, in Gordon Family Papers.

the western territories, and passed the Second Confiscation Act, which freed rebels' slaves when they entered Union lines. This law prepared the way for Lincoln's preliminary emancipation announcement in September, 1862. He declared that the slaves of all persons in rebellion against the government on January 1, 1863, would be emancipated. The Emancipation Proclamation actually freed only a portion of the slave population. It excluded slaves in areas under Union occupation—the only places where the government actually could exert its authority— but it did establish emancipation as a northern war objective.[26]

Emancipation unleashed a furious outcry in the North, particularly among Union soldiers. Only about one in ten had enlisted with the aim of freeing the slaves. Those who opposed emancipation either vehemently denied that it was in any way a northern objective or announced that they would rather desert or resign than participate in such an enterprise. "If *anyone* thinks that this army is fighting to free the Negro, or that that is any part of its aim, they are *terribly mistaken*," vowed Sergeant William Pippey of Boston. "I don't believe there is *one abolitionist* in *one thousand*, in the army." Another Massachusetts soldier instructed his sister, "If anyone tells you [the] government is fighting for the nigros tell them they are either ignorant or a traitor." Soldiers who had enlisted in a war to defend the Union felt betrayed by the government's change in policy. They insisted that they had not volunteered to fight against slavery. From Virginia, Private Adam H. Pickel assured his father, a Pennsylvania Peace Democrat, that "if the issue had been the freeing of the Slaves instead of saving the Union as I sometimes think it has come to, I would not have mingled with the dirty job." An Indiana private fighting with the 4th Kentucky (U.S.) Cavalry contemplated desertion. "You say I have done enough fighting for to free the Niggers," Charles H. Sowle told his parents in January, 1863. "I think so too and if old Abe arms them niggers I will quit and go South."[27]

26. McPherson, *Struggle for Equality*, 75–117; John Hope Franklin, *The Emancipation Proclamation* (Garden City, N.Y., 1963); Barney, *Flawed Victory*, 51–68; Allan Nevins, *The War for the Union* (4 vols.; New York, 1959–71), II, 145–50, 231–41; Hans L. Trefousse, *The Radical Republicans: Lincoln's Vanguard for Racial Justice* (New York, 1969), 203–38.

27. Bell Irvin Wiley, *The Life of Billy Yank: The Common Soldier of the Union* (Indianapolis, 1952), 40–43; William T. Pippey to A. Heath and B. Y. Pippey, July 31, 1862, in William T. Pippey Papers, DU; Silas E. Fales to his sister, May 1, 1863, in Silas Everett Fales Papers, SHC; Adam H. Pickel to his father and mother, February 22, 1863, in Adam H. Pickel Papers, DU; Charles H. Sowle to his parents, January 26, 1863, in Charles H. Sowle Papers, DU.

One of the major arguments against emancipation, apart from antipathy toward blacks, was that it might undermine efforts to restore the
Union. Many Unionists feared that attacks on slavery would strengthen
southern resistance and thereby further widen the breach between the
two sections, making reconciliation impossible. At the beginning of
1862, Colonel Charles Wainwright, a member of the Hudson Valley
gentry and a fervent Democrat, worried that radicals in Congress
would succeed in forcing the president to take extreme measures. He
asserted that the sole purpose of the war was "the preservation of the
Union, the putting down of armed rebellion," and charged that if Lincoln "gives way to these 'black Republicans,' and makes it an abolition
war, there will be an end to the Union party at the South, and I for one
shall be sorry that I ever lent a hand to it." When Lincoln issued the
Emancipation Proclamation, Wainwright warned that it would turn all
southern Unionists into rebels and divide the people of the northern
states. He began to despair of victory and even contemplated resigning
from the army, but he concluded that such actions would merely further weaken the defense of the Union. Wainwright remained in service
throughout the war, complaining to the end about Lincoln's policies.[28]

The Emancipation Proclamation disturbed many other Union soldiers, who denounced the administration's partisan action in placing
its own "pet project" above the country's interests. The government's
war goals had suddenly been replaced by radical policies that lacked
clear popular support, these critics contended. Opposition quickly
formed against Lincoln's apparent capitulation to extremists. Lieutenant William M. Ferry, a staunch Democrat, deplored this reversal of
policy, charging that it was caused by bigotry, ambition, and med-
dlesomeness. "To wipe out slavery is more thought of and acted upon
than a restoration of Federal Authority & the Re Union of States," he
lamented. A Vermont private complained that "this war has got to be a
war for the nigger and not for the union." He warned that many more
lives would have to be sacrificed before the war could end.[29]

Although many Unionists objected to emancipation for constitutional and political reasons, the driving force behind their opposition
was racial prejudice. The anticipated influx of free blacks worried many

28. Allan Nevins (ed.), *A Diary of Battle: The Personal Journals of Colonel Charles S.
Wainwright, 1861–1865* (New York, 1962), 9, 109, 156, 472.
29. William M. Ferry to his wife, December 9, 1862, in Ferry Papers; Josephus Jackson
to his wife, February 15, 1863, in Jackson Papers, DU.

northerners, particularly residents of the Middle West. In December, 1860, Juliette Kenzie of Chicago stated that most northerners had no desire "to have a horde of free negroes let loose among us." Private Edward Pippey of Boston vowed that he would "fight for the dear old *land*, the land of the brave and the home of the free providing thay are *white*." A young Hoosier farmer, John McClure, had enlisted for two reasons: to defend the Union and to experience the adventure of war and travel. "I use to think that we were fighting for the union and constitution but we are not," he reported with disgust on January 2, 1863. "We are fighting to free those colored gentlemen." He objected to the prospect of having "all the niggars on an equality with you" and stated, "If I had my way about things I would shoot ever[y] niggar I came across." Racial hatred thus combined with fears for the Union's perpetuation to arouse intense opposition to emancipation.[30]

The prevailing hostility toward blacks prompted a significant minority of northerners to defend slavery as the Negro's proper condition. Blacks must always submit to the dominant white race. Emancipation would create havoc by upsetting the natural relationship between the races, they argued, and must therefore be opposed. "I can not now go in with President Lincoln in fighting for to free niggers who I believe are better off in slavery than anywhere else," Joseph Osborn asserted in February, 1863. When Lincoln announced that only slaves of masters still in rebellion after January 1, 1863, would be freed, Sergeant Onley Andrus declared: "I certainly hope that they may lay down their arms before the first of Jan. in order to keep the Niggers where they belong. Which is in Slavery." He added that "free white citizens" should not be sacrificed in battle to liberate "the Black Devils." As he explained to his wife, "I consider my life & the Happiness of my family of more value than any Nigger." William Ferry proclaimed that slavery was necessary because "the inferior race must be controlled by the superior for the greatest good to the greatest number." Yet the North seemed to be "crazy with the Negro on the brain," and the consequence of this

30. Juliette A. Kenzie to Nelly Gordon, December 1, 1860, in Gordon Family Papers; Edward Pippey to his brother, December 10, 1862, in Pippey Papers; Nancy N. Baxter (ed.), *Hoosier Farm Boy in Lincoln's Army: The Civil War Letters of Pvt. John R. McClure* (N.p., 1971), 44. On northern racism, see V. Jacque Voegeli, *Free But Not Equal: The Midwest and the Negro During the Civil War* (Chicago, 1967), 3–9, 55–65, 88–89; Forrest G. Wood, *Black Scare: The Racist Response to Emancipation and Reconstruction* (Berkeley, 1968), 20–29; C. Vann Woodward, *American Counterpoint: Slavery and Racism in the North-South Dialogue* (Boston, 1971), 140–62.

obsession would be "to enslave the white man & free the nigger." That efforts to free the slaves might undermine the liberties of free white northerners was a compelling fear. Few Union soldiers would risk such a prospect.[31]

Major Henry Withers denounced the Emancipation Proclamation. He predicted that the northern people would not support Lincoln's policy. A Unionist and former participant in the West Virginia statehood movement, he insisted that the border states would have seceded with the other slave states if Lincoln had not made "sacred promises" not to interfere with slavery. Shortly before the Emancipation Proclamation was to take effect, Withers reported that the colonel of his regiment had said "that he would never agree to any Union until slavery was wiped off the territory of the United States." Withers contended that Union should remain paramount to such sectional concerns. Union was an absolute good, not to be overridden or cast aside. He now feared that radicals would attempt "to turn the war into an abolition war, which I would not like to see altho I do not admire the institution [of slavery]." Withers nevertheless remained in the army out of devotion to the Union, convinced that public opinion would not tolerate this change of policy. He denounced those who argued that "the War can't cease until the last Negro is free." In September, 1864, he wrote to his sister, "Nothing will keep me any longer in the army should that policy be adopted by the people of the U.S. in the re-election of Lincoln." True to his word, he resigned his commission three weeks after the November election. Henry Withers had reluctantly concluded that a majority of the northern people were willing to accept emancipation as a war measure, whether or not they personally favored it, in order to preserve the Union.[32]

Public acceptance of emancipation resulted from military necessity. Slavery increasingly appeared to be both a barrier to national unity and progress and a vital source of strength to the Confederacy. Although slavery provided a valuable labor supply for the Confederacy, northerners believed that its long-term effects had been negative. Union

31. Joseph B. Osborn to Louise Landau, February 16, 1863, in Osborn Papers; Shannon (ed.), *Civil War Letters of Andrus*, 28–29; William M. Ferry to his wife, December 9, 1862, in Ferry Papers.

32. Henry Withers to his father, December 13, 1862, to his sister, September 15, 1864, and to his father, January 6, 1865, Cabell Tavenner and Alexander Scott Withers Papers, DU.

soldiers repeatedly attributed the South's poverty to the influence of slavery. "They are behind the times a 1000 years," reported Private John B. Foote, a New York farmer, after seeing the farms in southeastern Virginia: "I thought to myself that it was no wonder there was war as long as slavery was in the land. It is not only a 'Relic of barbarism' but is barbarism its self. I almost pitied the very soil. I[t] seemed as if it were crying out for deliverance." The harmful effects of slavery on white society—not its impact on blacks—made its destruction necessary to further national progress. Although arguing that the administration should conduct the war "as a war for the union and not an abolition war," Private Oren Farr, a New Hampshire Republican, added, "But slavery is a curse to a nation and to humanity not so much to the slave as to the holders." Through this concern for white interests most northerners reached a conservative antislavery position. Emancipation became acceptable—even if not enthusiastically advocated by most Unionists—in large part because it would remove an obstacle to the triumph of free labor. National progress could then proceed unhindered.[33]

Advocates of emancipation found an even stronger argument in denouncing slavery as the source of rebellion and the foundation of Confederate society. Northerners denounced the "slave power" more because it threatened republican government than because of slavery's immorality. Nevertheless, they recognized that slavery united the South and endangered the Union. James T. Ayers, a Methodist minister in Illinois when he enlisted as an army recruiter at age fifty-seven, depicted the war as a slaveowners' conspiracy to destroy free government. Borrowing heavily from abolitionist rhetoric, he linked preservation of the Union to destruction of slavery:

> And my friends when you Reflect that this is A war for slavvery waged by those ungodly Southern Slave drivers and Slave breeders, to spread there unholy and monstrous sistom of making merchandise of Human soals all over this best of all governments and thereby blot out our fair name as A free people and Destroy our free institutions and make us Alike, all not only stink in the Nostrils of men but of God himself and A proverb and A Hissing to the world who will then be astonished at our zeal in this Defensive war, for Defensive it is.

33. John B. Foote to his father, May 22, 1863, in Foote Papers; Oren E. Farr to his wife, January 12, 1863, in Farr Papers. On the "barbarism" of the South see editorial in the Milwaukee *Sentinel*, April 15, 1861, quoted in Kenneth M. Stampp (ed.), *The Causes of the Civil War* (Englewood Cliffs, N.J., 1965), 184.

If slaveowners had launched the rebellion to protect their property, simple logic dictated that emancipation would be a powerful weapon against the Confederacy. Destroy its cornerstone and the edifice of southern society would crash to the ground.[34]

Most Unionists greeted Lincoln's Emancipation Proclamation with skepticism, if not outright hostility. Yet many northerners, weary of a costly war that yielded few signs of victory, expressed their willingness to try any new policy that might promise success. Private Samuel Nichols of Massachusetts, who had enlisted during his sophomore year at Amherst College, observed that opposition had formed because "the North was unprepared" for Lincoln's proclamation. Nevertheless, he recognized "the necessity and patriotism from which this state paper emanated." Private Abraham Stipp, a West Virginia Unionist serving with the 3rd Maryland Volunteers, reported that "the emancipation proclamation has imbittered a great many persons against our Government." Yet he declared that the Union should adopt "any honorable means to put down this wicked rebellion and restore peace to our land." This willingness to accept emancipation as a military necessity was the only basis on which northern opinion would acquiesce in undermining southern institutions. All war measures would be judged on their effectiveness in contributing to the Union's defense.[35]

Many Unionists who had initially opposed emancipation gradually became convinced that it was a valuable weapon for combating the rebellion. Without fully endorsing the policy, they conceded that it assisted the struggle for victory. The fortunes of war took a propitious turn several months after Lincoln signed the Emancipation Proclamation. At the beginning of 1863, northern morale was at its lowest point, particularly among soldiers who had witnessed the futile sacrifice of lives at the battle of Fredericksburg in December, 1862. In the aftermath

34. John Hope Franklin (ed.), *The Diary of James T. Ayers, Civil War Recruiter* (Springfield, Ill., 1947), 26. Ayers' rhetoric borrowed heavily from antebellum warnings of dangers to northern interests posed by a southern "slave power." See David B. Davis, *The Slave Power Conspiracy and the Paranoid Style* (Baton Rouge, 1969); William E. Gienapp, "The Republican Party and the Slave Power," in Robert H. Abzug and Stephen E. Maizlish (eds.), *New Perspectives on Race and Slavery in America* (Lexington, Ky., 1986), 51–78; Michael F. Holt, *The Political Crisis of the 1850s* (New York, 1978), 202–11; and Foner, *Free Soil, Free Labor, Free Men*, 73–102.

35. Charles Sterling Underhill (ed.) *"Your Soldier Boy Samuel": Civil War Letters of Lieut. Samuel Edmund Nichols* (Buffalo, 1929), 35; Abraham Stipp to Helen Shell, June 12, 1863, in Helen L. and Mary Virginia Shell Papers, DU. On emancipation as a military necessity, see McPherson, *Struggle for Equality*, 90–98, 132–33; Voegeli, *Free But Not Equal*, 119–24; Dell, *Lincoln and the War Democrats*, 271; Louis S. Gerteis, *From Contraband to Freedman: Federal Policy Toward Southern Blacks, 1861–1865* (Westport, Conn., 1973), 185.

of Fredericksburg, they greeted Lincoln's proposal with scorn. "I dont think old Abe and all the rest of his niggar lovers can free the slaves because the south has a little to say about that," Indiana private John McClure scoffed. "Old Abe has got to whip the south first and that is a thing that he will not do very soon." After a further reverse at Chancellorsville in May, 1863, however, came the glorious news in July of simultaneous victories at Gettysburg and Vicksburg. Lee's invasion of Pennsylvania failed, and Grant seized control of the Mississippi. "The dawn has broken, and the collapsed confederacy has no place where it can hide its head," Lieutenant William Thompson Lusk of New York exulted. "Slavery has fallen, and I believe Heaven as well as earth rejoices." Lusk overestimated the secular celebration of emancipation, but the North celebrated the improving prospects for victory.[36]

This new military success convinced many early opponents of emancipation that blows against slavery would cripple the Confederacy. Harvey Reid had greeted Lincoln's emancipation policy skeptically. A nineteen-year-old Wisconsin schoolteacher when the war erupted, Reid enlisted in the 22nd Wisconsin Infantry on August 12, 1862. Serving in Kentucky and Tennessee, he found the slaves who sought refuge with Union regiments to be "lazy, saucy, and lousy." He argued that the army should not interfere with slavery. Captured in March, 1863, Reid spent three months in Rebel prisons before being paroled. Soon after his release the victories at Gettysburg and Vicksburg raised new hope for the Union cause. The summer of 1863 also brought proof that black soldiers, enlisted under provisions contained in the Emancipation Proclamation and subsequent legislation, could fight gallantly for their own freedom. Their bravery at Fort Wagner, Port Hudson, and Milliken's Bend prompted Harvey Reid to concede that blacks could be good soldiers. Emancipation would directly contribute to winning the war. "I thought at the time that measure was first introduced that it was unwise," Reid confessed in September, 1863, "but time and experience has, in my opinion, proved it most wise and one of the most powerful weapons yet employed against the rebellion." It was the strength emancipation gave the Union cause, not a moral or political opposition to slavery, that won support from Harvey Reid and his fellow Unionists.[37]

Even conservative Virginia Unionist David H. Strother eventually

36. Baxter (ed.), *Hoosier Farm Boy*, 44; William C. Lusk (ed.), *War Letters of William Thompson Lusk* (New York, 1911), 284–85.
37. Frank L. Byrne (ed.), *The View from Headquarters: Civil War Letters of Harvey Reid* (Madison, 1965), 14–16, 92; see also 9–14, 23, 89–90.

reconciled himself to emancipation. Strother enlisted in the federal army with a fervent devotion to the Union and little concern for such "minor questions" as slavery, party dogmas, and sectional hatred. Although he disliked slavery, he maintained that blacks required firm discipline. He objected to abolition on both practical and constitutional grounds. "For my own part I would be glad to see the whole system wiped out," he wrote in March, 1862, "but the government cannot do it without sacrificing both principle and promises and without involving itself in endless and insupportable troubles." When Lincoln first announced his emancipation policy in September, 1862, Strother reported, "The nigger proclamation seems to have produced very general disgust at home & abroad." One month after the proclamation went into effect, Strother remained skeptical, arguing that it had "no more effect than the blast of a horn." Its limitations would be self-defeating. "All the negroes which it left in slavery were practically free and all it had emancipated were still slaves," he told two friends. "Where the Federal army is not present, the condition of the Negro is totally unchanged." Only military force could secure freedom for blacks.[38]

Following northern victories on all fronts during the summer campaigns of 1863, however, Strother conceded the effectiveness of the administration's new war policy. "As long as the government combatted the Rebellion with conservatism the War for the Union was a failure," he admitted in October, 1863. "When the Emancipation Proclamation came the war took a turn & the Rebellion has been going under from that day." Having insisted throughout the war that the only important issue was preservation of the Union, David Strother now recognized that destruction of slavery was an essential weapon against the rebellion.[39]

These were not enthusiastic endorsements of emancipation. A majority of northerners probably continued, at least until the end of 1864, to oppose abolition except as a matter of absolute military necessity. Yet most Unionists, however reluctantly, gradually came to accept emancipation once that policy had proven its effectiveness as a war measure. The tension between defenders of the Union and opponents of slavery gradually evaporated, dissipated by the winds of victory. Eventually even those who at first vowed simply to defend the Union could join in shouting the battle cry of freedom—for slaves as well as for white men

38. Eby (ed.), *Virginia Yankee*, 10; Strother Diary, October 23, 1862, February 10, 1863.
39. Strother Diary, October 10, 1863.

trying to preserve republican liberty. The two objectives, once believed irreconcilable, in the end were joined in the struggle for the Union and liberty. It was Lincoln's special genius that combined war for the Union with war against slavery at the one point at which antagonisms would be minimized. Emancipation would never win approval on moral or ideological grounds, but northerners accepted it as a pragmatic war policy justified by its contribution to winning the war for the Union.

There was no inherent conflict between emancipation and defense of the Union. Indeed, emancipation could be viewed as a natural extension of northern commitment to liberty. Racial prejudice, however, blocked the inclusion of blacks under guarantees of American liberty and created intense opposition to emancipation. Only by proposing emancipation as a war policy necessary to weaken Confederate strength could it be made palatable to conservative Unionists. The war finally gave liberty to blacks, but northern prejudice would prevent significant progress toward equality.

3 / THE TEST OF SLAVES' LOYALTY

Black slaves played a critical role in the Civil War drama. Without slavery and the black presence, sectional differences would not have erupted into armed conflict. This is not to say that slavery and race were the sole causes of the war. Historians and polemicists have debated the causes of the Civil War for over a century without agreeing on a single explanation. The social forces and human motivations involved are too complex and ambiguous to be reduced to a simple equation. Yet it was clear to most Americans in 1861 that the sectional conflict could not be fully understood without reference to Negro slavery.

The war forced white Americans to reexamine their assumptions about the role of blacks in American society. By threatening and then destroying the system of race relations created by slavery, the war raised possibilities for modifying racial attitudes. Black actions would either challenge or confirm white prejudice. For southerners, the test of their paternalistic system would be whether their slaves would remain faithful through the crisis or rebel against their benevolent masters. The faithful servant would prove that the South's plantation society had nurtured mutual affection between master and slave, controlling and protecting the black bondsman for his own good. For northerners, the crucial issue would be whether blacks could act independently and responsibly as soldiers, both in drill and in combat. Beliefs about black inferiority, laziness, and docility would be challenged if they proved their ability and willingness to fight for freedom. For there to be any possibility of altering white racial attitudes, prevailing assumptions on these two issues would have to change.

The weight of two centuries of experience with black slavery made the intense racial prejudice that pervaded both North and South in 1861 difficult to overturn. Few whites doubted the social, intellectual, and moral inferiority of blacks. Even among antislavery leaders, only a tiny minority advocated any significant steps toward racial equality.[1] Be-

1. Winthrop D. Jordan, *White Over Black: American Attitudes Toward the Negro, 1550–1812* (Chapel Hill, 1968); V. Jacque Voegeli, *Free But Not Equal: The Midwest and the Negro During the Civil War* (Chicago, 1967); Leon F. Litwack, *North of Slavery: The Negro in the Free States, 1790–1860* (Chicago, 1961); Eugene H. Berwanger, *The Frontier Against Slavery:*

cause blacks were involved in the war's central issues, however, their responses and actions would be closely observed. Blacks thus played an active role in shaping their own destiny. Their acts of loyalty, rebellion, military heroism, and cowardice influenced white attitudes toward race and society. Although the examination of racial prejudice in this chapter focuses on white opinions, those opinions were the direct result of black actions. The Civil War reveals an American people divided both by geography and by race. The combination of these divisions has shaped much of our national history.

THE IDEA OF A FAITHFUL SERVANT

Southern planters entered the war professing confidence in their slaves' loyalty and contentment. The paternalistic ideal stressed the mutual dependence and affection of master and slave. According to the southern dogma, kind masters and faithful servants lived in harmony. "Most people here feel an attachment for the servants, similar, in some respects to that we feel for our children," Henry Watson, Jr., of Alabama wrote to his cousin in Connecticut. "We feed them, clothe them, nurse them when sick and in all things provide for them. How can we do this and not love them?" A native of Connecticut, Watson had moved to Alabama in 1834 and established himself as a successful lawyer and planter in the heart of the Black Belt. His cousin Sarah Carrington had suggested that southerners must live in perpetual dread of their black servants. "There could not be possibly a greater mistake," Watson replied in January, 1861. "As well might you suppose that we lived in terror of our children." Blacks fully reciprocated their masters' affection, he claimed: "They too feel an affection for their master, his wife and children and they are proud of his and their success. There seems to be a charm in the name of 'Master.'—they look upon and to their master with the same feeling that a child looks to his father. It is a lovely trait in them. This being the case how can we fear them?"[2] The psychological comfort derived from this paternalistic

Western Anti-Negro Prejudice and the Slavery Extension Controversy (Urbana, Ill., 1967); George M. Fredrickson, The Black Image in the White Mind: The Debate on Afro-American Character and Destiny, 1817–1914 (New York, 1971); David Brion Davis, The Problem of Slavery in Western Culture (Ithaca, 1966); Davis, The Problem of Slavery in the Age of Revolution, 1770–1823 (Ithaca, 1975).

2. Henry Watson, Jr., to Sarah Carrington, January 28, 1861, in Henry Watson, Jr., Papers, DU.

ethos soothed many slaveowners' fears and calmed their doubts about black loyalty. The planters' revolution to protect slavery and the way of life it supported, however, would jeopardize the master-slave relationship. By opening the door to freedom, the Yankee invasion would provide a test of blacks' faithfulness.

The slaves' response to the war and its prospects for freedom would either challenge or confirm southern beliefs about black character. If slaves remained faithful and rejected the illusory promise of freedom, southern convictions of slavery's mutual benefits would be vindicated. Insurrection or disloyalty, however, would lend support to northern charges that slavery was cruel and inhumane. Thus both sides felt a compelling interest in the slaves' response to the Yankees' arrival. Would the slave prove to be a Nat Turner or a Sambo? The black response carried the potential for shattering southern views of slavery and the relationship between the races.[3]

Southerners were convinced that they alone understood the true nature of these mysterious beings. Relations between the two races were complicated and contradictory, but southern whites subconsciously selected black characteristics and actions that met their psychological needs in fashioning a simplified explanation of black character. Long before 1860, a set of racial assumptions had become widespread throughout the South, frequently forming part of southern defenses of slavery. Southerners proclaimed that slavery offered numerous benefits not only to white masters but to black slaves, whose childlike natures rendered them incapable of enjoying the blessings of liberty and who could achieve the rudiments of civilized behavior only under constant discipline and guidance from their white superiors. In return for this protection, blacks expressed their gratitude by remaining loyal to their masters.[4]

At the beginning of the war, Susan Cornwall Shewmake, wife of a Burke County, Georgia, planter, defended slavery with arguments based on prevailing assumptions about black character. Her opinions represent a concise summation of southern racial views. Only the beneficial influences of slavery, she insisted, could raise black savages to

3. Leon F. Litwack, *Been in the Storm So Long: The Aftermath of Slavery* (New York, 1979), 135.

4. On slavery and southern racial views, see Kenneth M. Stampp, *The Peculiar Institution: Slavery in the Ante-Bellum South* (New York, 1956); Eugene D. Genovese, *Roll, Jordan, Roll: The World the Slaves Made* (New York, 1974); and Stanley M. Elkins, *Slavery: A Problem in American Institutional and Intellectual Life* (3rd ed.; Chicago, 1976).

even the rudest graces of civilization or discipline their emotional excesses. "While every feature, every muscle of the negro indicates a low order of intellect mingled with a capacity for endurance, these facts would seem to point out for him a peculiar sphere," she wrote. "With muscular energy sufficient for any purpose he has not mind enough to direct his labors." Deficient in intelligence, calm reasoning, and moral principle, blacks required firm control. Only under discipline such as that afforded by slavery could they coexist in civilized white society. "No evidence can be discovered among them of any state of feeling higher than emotional," Shewmake asserted. "They rejoice over a new dress or a gay kerchief more than in a well ordered home." Their emotional natures made blacks difficult to discipline, she added. "They have no law for the governance of their passions higher than the dread of punishment for an offence, or glimpses of a tangible reward for a correct course of conduct." Slavery afforded the necessary means of punishment, which kind masters tempered with rewards for loyalty and obedience. Only in such an environment could blacks be properly controlled.[5]

Although southerners deeply cherished their personal liberty and went to war to protect it, they contended that blacks, being incapable of responsible action, could never enjoy the blessings of freedom. Susan Cornwall Shewmake insisted that "no encouragement can be found in the past or present of the African races for the hopes of those who pretend to look forward to a career of glory or even usefulness for them in a state of liberty." Slavery alone could protect and control blacks. "Freedom which is to the white man the 'Open Sesame' to a career of honor and everything else desirable or conducive to happiness is with the African merely a synonym for idleness," she contended. "Not a single pulse among them throbs at the thought of freedom as offering them a wider sphere for the exercise of God-given faculties." Even after prolonged contact with southern culture, blacks had failed to absorb the rudiments of civilization and refinement. "And if this is the condition of the negro after so long a residence among a cultivated people enjoying, as most of them do, opportunities of learning what is right, what prospect is there of improvement if left to themselves," Shewmake asked.[6] This proslavery argument denied blacks' capacity for independent action and leadership.

5. Susan Cornwall Diary, January 31, 1861, SHC.
6. *Ibid*.

Slavery thus afforded protection for blacks, who would otherwise be forced to struggle for survival in a world for which neither nature nor experience had prepared them. Beyond any material or psychological rewards which southern masters gained from their peculiar institution, they claimed that slavery benefited an inferior race incapable of self-reliance. "God in *his wisdom & mercy* decreed that the african race *should be slaves* for their good as a people," declared Captain James D. Webb, a Greensboro, Alabama, planter and lawyer. Judged from this perspective, each white master was "the christianizer, the civilizer, the teacher, the protector, of this poor down trodden ignorant people."[7] Southern slaveowners shared Webb's belief that they performed a sacred mission in saving the minds and souls of this race of savages.

By providing protection and guidance, slavery would eventually equip blacks for the trials of freedom, Susan Shewmake believed. Until that slow process had been completed, however, liberty would bring only disaster to these ignorant and childish creatures. "If the Abolitionists desire the good of the negro they will let him alone where he can be kindly treated [and] have the gospel preached to him in a way that he can appreciate and understand," she recommended, "and when his mind is capable of emerging from its present twilight the morning of Truth will illumine its dark corners and gradually usher in the perfect day." Although black slaves remained far behind the better classes of whites, slavery had already made them "more refined and better cultivated than their class at the North," Shewmake contended. "It is certain there is not so much want among them. They are the happiest laboring people on the globe." Under the genial plantation system, blacks had become content with their relatively comfortable existence and were unshakably loyal to their masters. This, at least, was what many white southerners wanted to believe.[8]

Ideally, then, slavery benefited both masters and slaves. Living together in intimate daily contact, both black and white plantation residents sometimes came to feel part of a single extended family. Planters often spoke of their "whole family, black and white," and took great

---

7. James D. Webb to his wife, April 17, 1863, in Walton Family Papers, SHC.
8. Cornwall Diary, January 31, February 12, 1861. Comparisons of slaves to northern or European laborers had been evidence for many antebellum defenders of slavery that the southern system was more beneficial. See George Fitzhugh, "Sociology for the South," in Harvey Wish (ed.), *Ante-bellum: Writings of George Fitzhugh and Hinton Rowan Helper on Slavery* (New York, 1960); and Eric McKitrick (ed.), *Slavery Defended* (Englewood Cliffs, N.J., 1963).

pride in the benevolences they offered their black "children." For many southerners, affection between blacks and whites provided the strongest argument in defense of slavery. Arguments about efficiency, profitability, historical precedent, and even biblical justification for slavery were less compelling for most slaveowners than their emotional attachments to faithful servants. Writing home from an army camp in northern Virginia, Private Charles W. Hutson, son of a wealthy South Carolina Sea Islands planter, thanked the family servants for their efforts to add to his comfort. "They are kind & faithful friends," he told his mother. "What a beneficial system it is! The question of interest may be debated by argument & statistics; but as to *feeling*, we are satisfied on that point from personal observation & experience." Hutson and other slaveowners believed that these feelings were mutual. In response to kind treatment and protection from whites, blacks reciprocated by expressing their gratitude and loyalty.[9]

The most important symbol of this mutually satisfying paternalism was the black mammy. Nothing brought out feelings of affection so fervently as the death of a faithful personal servant. Private Isaac Dunbar Affleck, son of a prominent Louisiana cotton planter and agricultural reformer, wrote that he was very sorry to hear of the death of "old Aunty Annie," an elderly slave woman, "who loved me as if I was some thing more to her than a master." It was important to believe that a servant's affection was genuine and not based on compulsion or deceit. Masters likewise professed their own sincerity. Two Virginia brothers received news of their black mammy's death while they were serving in the army. "How sad and gloomy I feel, after hearing the sad news of the death of poor Rachel," Thomas Andrews wrote, "it looks like it will break my heart, for if ever there was a servant in the world that I was devoted to it was her." His brother William's response was similar: "Poor Rachel was my favorite servant, and I sincerely hope the good Lord has rewarded her goodness on earth with a home in his Kingdom on high."[10]

9. Bell Irvin Wiley (ed.), *Letters of Warren Akin, Confederate Congressman* (Athens, Ga., 1959), 22; Charles W. Hutson to his mother, September 27, 1861, in Charles Woodward Hutson Papers, SHC.

10. Robert W. Williams, Jr., and Ralph A. Wooster (eds.), "Camp Life in Civil War Louisiana: The Letters of Private Isaac Dunbar Affleck" *Louisiana History*, V (Spring, 1964), 199; Thomas F. Andrews to his father, September 11, 1864, William B. Andrews to his father, September 13, 1864, in William B. G. Andrews Papers, DU. On responses to the death of a favorite servant, see Genovese, *Roll, Jordan, Roll*, 347–51.

Loyalty was the quality southerners most admired in their servants. Elizabeth M. Stiles, wife of a prominent Savannah planter and political figure, wrote that the entire household was mourning a servant's death: "He was indeed a faithful servant & kind friend to all the family, one rarely meets with a negro who was so affectionate & took such deep interest in all that concerned the family." This black man's solicitude for the white family's interests clearly reassured her that he found the relationship beneficial, and his faithfulness reinforced that belief. Yet she indicated another, quite different, reason for grief at his death: "Poor Kate looks deeply troubled, he saved her so much care." However important such practical concerns might have been, most southerners claimed that they were outweighed by affection and genuine grief at the loss of a trusted friend. Following a long, poignant description of her servant Hannah's death, Mary Robarts of Georgia concluded: "When we lose our servants, the loss of their services is the last thing we think of; it is the shadow on our household when an attached faithful one is removed."[11]

Trusted blacks sometimes accompanied their masters into the army as body servants. During the war's first year, slaveholders who enlisted often brought servants to cook, wash, and perform routine camp chores. "There is one thing I want and must have, a servant. It is absolutely necessary to have one to cook and wash especially the latter," wrote eighteen-year-old William Calder of North Carolina. An Alabama private told his father, "I hope you received my letter about sending a boy in time to send one by some one of our recruits. You have no idea how I miss Caesar. It's a great pity the rascals don't know how highly they are prised!!" Servants were valued not only for their labor but also for their companionship. Their presence enabled soldiers to retain a semblance of familiar patterns of life at home. Because of his rank, Virginia private Richard W. Waldrop was not permitted to keep a servant. In complaining of this inconvenience, he expressed the dual function of the servant. "Tell Jim I hope he don't feel any worse for not having my boots to clean," Waldrop wrote home, "& I would like to have him here to scold a little for every body here is in such a good humor that we cant get up a quarrel." The jesting tone of this remark

11. Elizabeth Stiles to William H. Stiles, Sr., April 5, 1864, in Mackay and Stiles Family Papers, SHC; Mary E. Robarts to Mary Jones, May 31, 1861, in Myers (ed.), *Children of Pride*, 688.

conceals neither the true affection felt for a favorite servant nor the unequal nature of the relationship.[12]

The potential for slave resistance and insurrection created by the war's disruptions made loyalty even more valuable than before the war. Servants who behaved well thus sometimes received special rewards for their conduct. "John still remains, a model camp servant," Virginia lieutenant Ham Chamberlayne wrote in October, 1862. "I find that he can both cook & wash well enough. He is absolutely content." Several months later, Chamberlayne arranged for John to take a holiday, explaining that "he has been always obedient, faithful & efficient and deserves such an indulgence." Private Frank Richardson, son of a sugar planter from Bayou Teche, Louisiana, sent his body servant Allen home to work in the sugar house. "Allen has done his duty faithfully towards me while with me," Richardson reported with satisfaction. Despite temptations, Allen had behaved well, "though in fact he dont do as much work as a common negro, he being smart enough to make all work as light as possible." Richardson's final admission indicates the indulgence with which many masters favored their faithful servants. Personal affection and a sense of mutual rights and obligations prompted such tolerance, which would quickly disappear if this trust were violated.[13]

The faithful servant proved the moral and social necessity of slavery. On this foundation rested the plantation system and the entire structure of southern society. Masters wanted more than mere obedience from their bondsmen. They expected blacks to internalize obedience and to show duty, respect, and love for their benevolent guardians. Anything less would have opened slaveowners to the charge of being exploitive brutes. They could dismiss abolitionist charges of slavery's evils so long as their self-image as paternalistic masters remained intact. Their self-assurances about the faithful slave led them to ignore or

12. William Calder to his mother, October 29, 1862, in William Calder Papers, SHC; James L. Boardman to his father, August 15, 1861, in James Locke Boardman Papers, DU; Richard W. Waldrop to John Waldrop, May 29, 1861, in Richard W. Waldrop Papers, SHC. For a discussion of Confederate soldiers' use of body servants, see Bell Irvin Wiley, *Southern Negroes, 1861–1865* (rev. ed.; New Haven, 1965), 134–45; Benjamin Quarles, *The Negro in the Civil War* (2nd ed.; Boston, 1969), 262–67; and Genovese, *Roll, Jordan, Roll*, 352–53.

13. C. G. Chamberlayne (ed.), *Ham Chamberlayne—Virginian: Letters and Papers of an Artillery Officer, in the War for Southern Independence, 1861–1865* (Richmond, 1932), 131, 155; Frank Richardson to his father, November 6, 1861, in Frank L. Richardson Papers, SHC.

deny contradictory evidence in slave behavior. Yet slaveowners also worried that they might be wrong.[14]

Doubts about blacks' loyalty had always lurked just below the surface of southern consciousness. John Brown's attack on Harpers Ferry in 1859 unleashed a torrent of rumors of plots, poisonings, and murders, which added to the dangers of civil war the even darker prospect of servile insurrection. Amid this excitement, calmer voices sought to dispel the fear such rumors raised in anxious minds. Hearing in August, 1860, a report that blacks had attempted to poison the local water supply, Matthew Andrews, a young Virginia lawyer, observed that "if any thing goes wrong in the Neighborhood it is immediately laid to the negroes." He pointed out that such an act would be nearly impossible because apothecaries were forbidden to sell poison to blacks. "I hope things will quiet down and people will find out the mistake. Everything that tends to keep up the excitement we had last fall [after John Brown's raid] is just so much worse for the negroes," he added, "and after a while they may really attempt some of these crimes that are now so freely laid to their doors."[15]

Despite such warnings, rumors and fears were not easily suppressed, particularly when the excitement of war increased the potential for insurrection. In May, 1861, Mrs. E. A. Fleming of Liberty County, Georgia, wrote, "No company [of soldiers] has left Liberty yet and I hope none will for I hear that the Negroes in Tatnall have got beside themselves and were planning what they would do when the gentlemen went to fight and said they would take possession of plantations and would not kill the young ladies but take them for wives." She vowed to leave the country if more men were called away. "I am afraid of the lawless Yankee soldiers," a Virginia woman confessed as Union troops approached, "but that is nothing to my fear of the negroes if they should rise against us." In Louisiana there were fears that slaves planned a "great upheaval" for the Fourth of July, 1861. "We live on a mine that the Negroes are suspected of an intention to spring on the fourth of next

14. Genovese, *Roll, Jordan, Roll*, 97; Litwack, *Been in the Storm So Long*, 26–27.
15. Matthew P. Andrews to Anna Robinson, August 26, 1860, in Charles Wesley Andrews Papers, DU. For an account by a frightened Texan, see Enoch T. Withers to his father, August 6, 1860, in Cabell Tavenner and Alexander Scott Withers Papers, DU. See C. Vann Woodward, *The Burden of Southern History* (rev. ed.; Baton Rouge, 1968), 41–68. Fears of insurrection following Harpers Ferry resulted more from imagination than from reality. See Clarence L. Mohr, *On the Threshold of Freedom: Masters and Slaves in Civil War Georgia* (Athens, Ga., 1986), 3–67.

month," wrote young Kate Stone, daughter of a northeastern Louisiana cotton planter who owned 150 slaves. "The information may be true or false, but they are being well watched in every section where there are any suspects." The holiday passed without any trouble from blacks, however. "In some way they have gotten a confused idea of Lincoln's Congress meeting and of the war; they think it is all to help them, and they expected for 'something to turn up,'" she explained. "I hope the house servants will settle to their work now." Left alone in charge of farms and plantations, women felt particularly vulnerable. "We would be practically helpless should the Negroes rise, since there are so few men left at home," Kate Stone wrote later in the war. "It is only because the Negroes do not want to kill us that we are still alive." No matter how much they trusted their bondsmen, white southerners could not help but feel apprehensive in such circumstances. The specter of insurrection, always present since Nat Turner's bloody uprising in 1831, now seemed imminent. If they had miscalculated black faithfulness the future could be disastrous.[16]

Many southerners accused Yankees of attempting to incite slave insurrections. The example of John Brown seemed to confirm fears of external agitation, which had periodically convulsed the South for thirty years. Final proof of northern intentions came with President Lincoln's Emancipation Proclamation. John H. Bills, a Tennessee planter who owned eighty-seven slaves in 1860, charged that this edict was an effort to inaugurate "servile War." In December, 1862, he wrote in his journal that he feared "a great loss of property and perhaps of life" once emancipation became reality. Blacks would be unleashed to seek revenge. "The Paternal Government at Washington has done all in its power to incite a general insurrection throughout the South in hopes of thus getting rid of the women and children in one grand holocaust," Kate Stone charged. Lieutenant Charles C. Jones, Jr., of Georgia called the Emancipation Proclamation "the crowning act of the series of black and diabolical transactions" carried out by the Lincoln administration. "I look upon it as a direct bid for insurrection, as a most infamous attempt to incite flight, murder, and rapine on the part of our slave population," Jones told his father, a prominent Georgia planter and clergyman. He

---

16. Mrs. E. A. Fleming to William O. Fleming, May 27, 1861, in William O. Fleming Papers, SHC; Betty Herndon Maury quoted in Katharine M. Jones, *Heroines of Dixie: Confederate Women Tell Their Story of the War* (Indianapolis, 1955), 118; Anderson (ed.), *Brokenburn*, 28, 37, 298.

predicted that it would "subvert our entire social system, desolate our homes and convert the quiet, ignorant, dependent black son of toil into a savage incendiary and brutal murderer." Such an argument offered several attractions for southern slaveowners. It stressed the natural docility of blacks. It placed blame for insurrection scares on meddlesome Yankees. Above all, it averted suspicion that blacks might not fully accept the paternalistic ethos. Only external influence could make their faithful servants become rebellious.[17]

Blacks responded cautiously to the disruptions of war. If there were few Nat Turners, neither were there many Sambos. Invasion disrupted daily routines. Yet it was not clear what the final outcome would be. Confederate defeat would likely signal the end of slavery, but victory would further tighten their bonds. Black expectations that the war would make a difference in their condition at first led not to insurrection but to restlessness and confusion. "The house servants have been giving a lot of trouble lately—lazy and disobedient," Kate Stone reported in June, 1861. "I suppose the excitement in the air has infected them." According to one Union soldier, a Virginia planter in May, 1862, acknowledged "that he had no authority over his colored servants— that since the war they assumed an indifference to duty that amounted to a refusal to work any more for their master." The situation became particularly difficult when Union troops approached. Early in 1863, Kate Stone wrote that a neighbor had not been able to control his slaves since northern troops entered the area: "He says his Negroes will not even pretend to work and are very impudent, and he thinks they will all go off in a body the next time the Yankees come on his place." The arrival of Union forces marked the end of plantation discipline. Whenever they heard that the Yankees were approaching, blacks became restless in anticipation. "The arrival of the advance of the Yankees alone turned the negroes crazy," reported John H. Ramsdell of Louisiana. "They became utterly demoralized at once and everything like subordination and restraint [came] to an end." Throughout the South, the result was the same. As soon as the Yankees arrived, blacks became impudent, insubordinate, and insolent. "All is anarchy and confusion

17. John H. Bills Diary, December 13, 1862, in John Houston Bills Papers, SHC; Anderson (ed.), *Brokenburn*, 297–98; Charles C. Jones, Jr., to Rev. C. C. Jones, September 27, 1862, in Myers (ed.), *Children of Pride*, 967–68. See James L. Roark, *Masters Without Slaves: Southern Planters in the Civil War and Reconstruction* (New York, 1977), 75–76; and Litwack, *Been in the Storm So Long*, 30.

here," Louisiana overseer Wilmer Shields reported to his employer, "everything going to destruction—and the negroes on the plantation insubordinate." Mary Chesnut, wife of a prominent South Carolina planter-politician, first noticed the subtle signs of change in her servant Dick. "He won't look at me now," she observed. "He looks over my head—he scents freedom in the air."[18]

The deterioration of slave discipline after the arrival of federal troops is vividly depicted in the diary of Tennessee planter John H. Bills. A supporter of Stephen Douglas in the 1860 election, Bills remained a Unionist until Lincoln's call for troops in April, 1861. Throughout the conflict he denounced it as "this War of sections, this *Fratricidal War*." During 1862 and 1863, his diary became an almost daily account of his loss of control over his slaves. Shortly after federal troops arrived in his neighborhood in July, 1862, Bills reported: "Much trouble with our servants. No government. No work doing." A few days later, he wrote that the "Negroes are demoralized." Looking for freedom, large crowds of blacks sought sanctuary with the federal troops, who returned women and children to their owners but put men to work building fortifications. Three of his slaves ran to the Yankees, but Bills caught them and brought them back. "I direct them to be switched which I hope may have a good effect, but doubt it," he wrote, "the negroes having got impudent and desiring an Excuse to run away & join the Northern Army, which many of them are doing." During the fall of 1862, Bills reported several times that his slaves were not working well and that some had run to the Yankees. Yet many of those who sought federal protection became disillusioned and returned, and when Bills visited Hickory Valley plantation in December, he found all his servants on hand. "They profess loyalty to me & declare Constant obedience until universal freedom is the law," he reported skeptically. "We shall see how they will perform."[19]

Bills became increasingly distraught. On the day after Christmas, 1862, Union soldiers took over the houses of his son and daughter for use as barracks, and he feared for his own house. "Great God when

18. Anderson (ed.), *Brokenburn*, 33, 175; Calvin Mehaffey to his mother, May 20, 1862, Calvin Mehaffey Papers, WLC; John H. Ramsdell to Gov. Thomas O. Moore, May 24, 1863, in Harvey Wish, "Slave Disloyalty Under the Confederacy," *Journal of Negro History*, XXIII (1938), 441–42; Wilmer Shields quoted in Litwack, *Been in the Storm So Long*, 135; C. Vann Woodward and Elisabeth Muhlenfeld (eds.), *The Private Mary Chesnut: The Unpublished Civil War Diaries* (New York, 1984), 464.

19. Bills Diary, June 24, 1861, July 28, 31, August 7, 28, December 9, 1862.

will this Cruel war end," Bills lamented. "The Crops of the Country &
stock [are] all gone, slaves demoralized & yet we see no end apparent."
Nevertheless, his slaves were working as usual on New Year's Day,
1863. "They do not perceive that they are free by Lincolns proclamation," he observed. "We have anticipated trouble & I think will yet have
it with regard to holding them." Nine days later he reported, "Negroes
doing no good. they seem to be restless not knowing what to do. [At]
times I pity them at others I blame them much." Throughout the year
his slaves frequently refused to work, and in October Bills wrote: "*They
have* made no crop hardly & will not save what they have, they are not
earning their salt & the sooner I get clear of most of my men the better
for me." He added a revealing comment: "Slavery under the influence
of our Yankey invaders is of no value." Several days later, he wrote that
affairs at the plantation were "in a wretched condition, Negroes not in
mutiny, but a wretched state of idleness & we have not the power to
control them." By July, 1864, Bills had almost given up hope of salvag-
ing his plantation. "Negro slavery is about played out under 'Yankee'
influence," he concluded, "we being deprived of that Control needful
to make them happy and prosperous."[20]

Every southern community touched by the approach of Union forces
felt the same loss of control. When blacks sensed that freedom loomed
within their grasp, daily routines disintegrated. By threatening to destroy planters' control, the war disrupted master-slave relations. As
John H. Bills reported, federal occupation led to a total breakdown of
slavery. Yet even interior regions untouched by invasion experienced
unsettling changes. The departure of large numbers of white males for
military service often led to a decline in control and discipline. By 1863,
even slaves in remote areas assumed that Union victory would end
slavery. They seemed to understand, as one Union officer reported,
"that it was a war for their liberation; that the cause of the war was their
being in slavery, and that the aim and result would be their freedom.
Further than that they did not seem to have any idea of it."[21]

Black responses to the war ranged from passivity to armed resistance. Where white control remained strong or opportunities for direct
action were rare, many blacks simply waited to see what would hap-

20. *Ibid.*, December 26, 1862, January 1, 10, October 8, 17, 1863, July 9, 1864.
21. Quoted in Litwack, *Been in the Storm So Long*, 70. See also Wiley, *Southern Negroes*,
66; and Wish, "Slave Disloyalty," 440–45.

pen. They knew the dangers of rebellion too well to risk it unless the chances for success seemed strong. Minor acts of resistance, however, showed that blacks wanted to participate in their own liberation. Such resistance had always been one means for blacks to demonstrate their opposition to enslavement and maintain a psychological buffer against its dehumanizing forces. Despite the dangers many blacks engaged in active resistance. The absence of major insurrections, which southern whites feared, does not prove that slaves were loyal or content but only shows that they believed such violence would not be necessary. Simply refusing to follow traditional roles would dissolve the paternalistic master-slave relationship. Blacks thus contributed to their own emancipation by refusing to work, striking for wages, refusing to submit to punishment, giving information to the Yankees, and hundreds of minor acts of independence.[22]

Armed insurrection remained a constant danger. Throughout the South, slaveowners faced black resistance similar to that reported by John H. Bills. After Union forces captured New Orleans, slaves on the Mississippi River plantations became unmanageable. "We have a Terrible state of affairs Here," Effingham Lawrence wrote in October, 1862, "negroes refusing to work and women all in their Houses." On Magnolia Plantation his slaves erected a gallows in the slave quarters, explaining that a Union officer told them they must drive their master and his overseer off the plantation, "Hang thier master &c and that then they will be Free." Lawrence concluded, "No one now can tell what a Day may bring Forth—we are all in a State of Great uneasiness." No hangings took place, but the threat of violence could never be forgotten. In rare cases, slave resistance did lead to murder. Isolated acts of slaves poisoning or killing their masters had occurred periodically throughout the history of slavery. John Brown's raid and Yankee invasion gave such acts heightened drama, indicating the tragic possibilities of slave insurrection.[23]

22. W. E. B. Du Bois, *Black Reconstruction in America* (1935; rpr. New York, 1969), 57–67; Wiley, *Southern Negroes*, 73–83; Wish, "Slave Disloyalty," 449–50; Litwack, *Been in the Storm So Long*, 50. On blacks' resistance to slavery throughout the antebellum period, see Eugene D. Genovese, "Rebelliousness and Docility in the Negro Slave: A Critique of the Elkins Thesis," *Civil War History*, XIII (1967), 293–314; Stampp, *Peculiar Institution*; and Genovese, *Roll, Jordan, Roll*. Two of the best studies of black slave culture are John W. Blassingame, *The Slave Community: Plantation Life in the Antebellum South* (New York, 1972); and Leslie Howard Owens, *This Species of Property: Slave Life and Culture in the Old South* (New York, 1976).

Although extremely rare, such incidents sent violent shock waves through the foundations of a slave society. Mary Chesnut, the insightful observer of Confederate social customs, described in detail the murder of her cousin Betsey Witherspoon in September, 1861. "She was smothered—arms & legs bruised & face scratched," Chesnut reported. "William, a man of hers, & several others suspected of her own negroes, people she has pampered & spoiled & done every thing for." Threatened with punishment for using their mistress's china, silver, and house linen at a slave party, the servants killed her while she slept. William reportedly had told the other slaves, "Do as I bid you & there will be no whipping here tomorrow." They smothered Mrs. Witherspoon with her counterpane, and when she revived, begging for her life, "they commenced their hellish work again." The blacks covered up their deed, making it look like a natural death. For several days no one suspected foul play, until the truth gradually emerged. "I always felt that I had never injured any one black especially & therefore feared nothing from them—but *now*. She was so good—so kind—the ground is knocked up from under me," Mary Chesnut confided to her diary. "I sleep & wake with the horrid vision before my eyes of those vile black hands—smothering her." In elaborating on this story twenty years later, she added: "We ought to be grateful that any one of us is alive. But nobody is afraid of their own negroes. These are horrid brutes—savages, monsters—but I find everyone like myself, ready to trust their own yard." This trust in their servants reassured white southerners that theirs was a superior civilization, founded on mutual affection between master and slave. Isolated exceptions could be dismissed. As evidence of black disaffection mounted, however, their ingrained beliefs about black character would be shaken.[24]

The vast majority of slaves never resorted to violence against their masters. The threat of violence, however, made all instances of resistance troubling. Mary Jones, wife of Reverend Charles Colcock Jones, a

23. Effingham Lawrence, Magnolia Plantation Record Book, October 21, 1862, in Henry Clay Warmouth Papers, SHC. For a fuller account of the disruption of slavery at Magnolia Plantation, see William K. Scarborough, *The Overseer: Plantation Management in the Old South* (Baton Rouge, 1966), 153–56.

24. Woodward and Muhlenfeld (eds.), *Private Mary Chesnut*, 162, 174–75, 164; Woodward (ed.), *Mary Chesnut's Civil War*, 211–12. Chesnut also related the story of William Keitt, who was murdered by his slaves in 1860; see *Private Mary Chesnut*, 181–82. For an account by the murdered man's brother see Laurence M. Keitt to his wife, February 29, 1860, Laurence Massillon Keitt Papers, DU.

wealthy Georgia planter, recorded the loss of control following General William T. Sherman's infamous march to the sea. In 1860 Jones owned 129 slaves and three plantations, covering over 3,600 acres. The disruption of slavery thus threatened serious consequences for the Joneses. "The people are all idle on the plantation, most of them seeking their own pleasure," Mary Jones wrote in January, 1865, from Montevideo, their 941-acre rice and sea-island cotton plantation in coastal Georgia. "Many servants have proven faithful, others false and rebellious against all authority or restraint." Two weeks later, the situation had worsened. "Their condition is one of perfect anarchy and rebellion," she wrote. "They have placed themselves in perfect antagonism to their owners and to all government and control. We dare not predict the end of all this, if the Lord in mercy does not restrain the hearts and wills of this deluded people." Three days later she reported that their minister had told her, "Nearly all the house servants have left their homes, and from most of the plantations they have gone in a body, either directly to the enemy or to congregate upon the large plantations in Bryan County, which have been vacated and upon which a plenty of rice remains." In Louisiana, Yankee raiders removed slaves from plantations near Union lines. Many of those who remained declared that they were free and would leave when ready. "The outrages of the Yankees and Negroes are enough to frighten one to death," declared Kate Stone. "The sword of Damocles in a hundred forms is suspended over us, and there is no escape." This sense of impending doom made many slaveowners feel like prisoners on their own plantations. They became masters without mastery.[25]

Blacks most often resisted slavery by running to the Yankees. Slaveowners realized that this action showed that their servants had rejected paternalism. Their kindness and protection had not gained them loyalty or gratitude. Slaves' desertion revealed that they did not fully accept the inequality of the master-slave relationship. The exact number of slaves who actually deserted during the war cannot be determined. Evidence is scattered and contradictory. Some who ran away later returned to their masters, and many left again when circumstances changed. It is clear, however, that the arrival of Union forces in

25. Myers (ed.), *Children of Pride*, 1241, 1247, 1248; Anderson (ed.), *Brokenburn*, 183–84. William W. Freehling coined the phrase "masters without mastery."

any part of the South led to a rapid exodus from the slave quarters, often without the slightest warning. The physical opportunity to obtain freedom determined the escape rate in each area. Most slaves, understandably, hesitated to make a futile flight for freedom, but given a reasonable chance for success, they left in overwhelming numbers. An estimated nineteen thousand slaves, for example, sought freedom behind Sherman's lines during his Georgia campaign in 1864. Once it became clear that the Union army would not return fugitive slaves, blacks poured into federal camps. In some areas, most of the male slave population fled. Those who remained with their masters either lived too far from Union lines, had compelling ties with the local black community or their own families, were too young or too feeble to leave, or feared the dangers of flight and the probable consequences of recapture. Even those who remained, however, frequently refused to work when the Yankees arrived. Blacks thus played an active role in deciding their own destiny.[26]

The reasons why blacks deserted their masters are as elusive and varied as the individuals who made that choice. For some the lure of freedom, which had always been a ray of hope amid the darkness of bondage, impelled them to follow the Yankees. Others fled not so much to freedom as away from slavery. What is significant is that they identified freedom with Union forces and chose the risk of leaving familiar, secure surroundings to seek protection from strangers. Stephen Jordon, a Louisiana slave, had assured his master, "I shall never leave you. Those Yankees are too bad, I hear." But when Mr. Valsin announced plans to remove his slaves to safety in Texas, Jordon joined "all the slaves on our place" in fleeing to meet the Yankees. "Of course I liked Mr. Valsin well enough, but I rather be free than be with him, or be the slave of any body else," Jordon explained. Blacks who entered Union lines offered several reasons for deserting. The oppressiveness of slavery led many to seek the first opportunity to obtain freedom. Others explained that it was difficult to carry out plantation duties and continue traditional routines when freedom was close at hand. For

26. Clarence L. Mohr, "Before Sherman: Georgia Blacks and the Union War Effort, 1861–1864," *Journal of Southern History*, XLV (August, 1979), 331–52; Mohr, *Threshold of Freedom*, 72–86; Litwack, *Been in the Storm So Long*, 137–39; C. Peter Ripley, *Slaves and Freedmen in Civil War Louisiana* (Baton Rouge, 1976), 14–19; Quarles, *Negro in the Civil War*, 63–75; Du Bois, *Black Reconstruction*, 55–83; Wiley, *Southern Negroes*, 3–14, 43, 63–75; Genovese, *Roll, Jordan, Roll*, 97–112, 149–51; Paul D. Escott, "The Context of Freedom: Georgia's Slaves During the Civil War," *Georgia Historical Quarterly*, LVIII (1974), 79–104.

many slaves, however, desertion represented a determination to liberate themselves rather than wait for the Yankees.[27]

In many areas of the Confederacy slave desertions brought agricultural operations to a standstill and left society in chaos. The progress of Union military advances could be measured by the number of runaways slaveowners reported. By June, 1863, Union forces controlled all of the Mississippi River except the besieged city of Vicksburg. "Dan Foley . . . says all the Negroes on Mr. Moore's Woodlawn place and about twenty of those on the Fairview place had gone off with the Yankees," reported William Henry Elder, bishop of Natchez. "The Yankees have abandoned Grand Gulf carrying off about 4,000 Negroes young & old. Many plantations have not a single servant neither for field nor house." Louisiana overseer Wilmer Shields informed his employer that the slaves "will not work for love or money" when Yankee troops reached the area in December, 1863. "Let me again repeat that but very few are faithful," he reported one month later. "Some of those who remain are worse than those who have gone—And I think that all *who are able* will leave as soon as the warm weather sets in." So obsessed was Shields with blacks' conduct that at war's end he compiled a list of how each slave had responded to the test of loyalty. His statistics cannot be verified or applied elsewhere, but they do represent the extent of disloyalty in at least one area. Of 146 adult slaves on the four plantations he supervised, 16 had been "perfectly faithful," 30 had "done well *comparatively*," and the other 100 had "behaved *badly*; many of them Outrageously." Nearly every slave had left the plantation at some time and then returned, "some of them half a dozen times." There could be no doubt that the faithful slave was a myth in this instance. Catherine Edmondston, whose husband owned 85 slaves on his eastern North Carolina plantation, reported a similar situation when Union troops entered the region early in 1865. "Our neighbor's Negroes have either taken a panic or become demoralized and are going off by tens and twenties to the Yankees," she observed. "We see no effect of the panic on our people. Probably the extreme isolation in which we keep them has prevented their being affected by it." This explanation applies throughout the South. Blacks who remained isolated from the Yankee invaders—either through geographical separa-

27. Stephen Jordon quoted in Litwack, *Been in the Storm So Long*, 32; Wiley, *Southern Negroes*, 15–23; Joel Williamson, *After Slavery: The Negro in South Carolina During Reconstruction, 1861–1877* (Chapel Hill, 1965), 3–7.

tion, physical barriers, or lack of information—had little opportunity for escape. Those who did have an opportunity usually took advantage of it.[28]

Samuel A. Agnew, a Tippah County, Mississippi, slaveowner and Reformed Presbyterian minister, recorded the desertion of his slaves during the latter half of 1862. A native of Abbeville, South Carolina, Agnew was now twenty-nine years old. Obsessed with war news and events, he also commented frequently on his servants' behavior, particularly their response to the Yankees. As Union troops arrived, the familiar pattern repeated itself. "There has been a general stampede above here," Reverend Agnew reported in August, 1862. "Jessee Magee has lost 15 of his most valuable slaves. All of Siddalls but 2 have gone [to the Yankees]." Conditions on his own plantation portended more of the same. "Our negroes seem to be restless and hard to please," he observed. "Perhaps they are but seeking a pretext for leaving." Two months later, Agnew returned from a brief absence. "On my arrival was surprised to hear that our negroes stampeded to the Yankees last might, or rather a portion of them," he wrote. Eleven slaves, including men, women, and children, had left. "The children who have been taken away by their misguided parents are to be pitied," he conceded. "I don't commiserate the men and women if they do suffer." A clue to his reasons for judging harshly these unfaithful servants lies in his reaction when another of his slaves deserted. "Wash has gone to the enemy. He is a great rascal, acting in this manner," Agnew declared. "He is an ungrateful and hypocritical wretch."[29]

The ingratitude exhibited by slave runaways particularly galled slaveowners, who prided themselves on the benefits slavery offered blacks. Running away amounted to a rejection of slavery and, by implication, a denial that blacks had anything to be grateful for under the system. To reconcile such behavior with their own conceptions of southern society, slaveowners attributed black actions to the false lure of freedom, which to blacks meant idleness; to the insidious influence of their northern enemies; and to blacks' gullibility, ingratitude, and excitability. If blacks had been mistreated, such behavior would be

28. R. O. Gerow (ed.), *Civil War Diary (1862–1865) of Bishop William Henry Elder* (Natchez, n.d.), 38; Wilmer Shields quoted in Litwack, *Been in the Storm So Long*, 135–36; Margaret Mackay Jones (ed.), *The Journal of Catherine Devereux Edmondston, 1860–1866* (N.p., n.d.), 97. See also Scarborough, *Overseer*, 150.

29. Samuel A. Agnew Diary, August 18, October 29, July 28, 1862, SHC.

understandable. Yet even the most pampered servants often deserted. "As to the idea of a *faithful servant, it is all a fiction*," Catherine Edmondston of North Carolina complained. "I have seen the favorite & most petted negroes the first to leave in every instance." This lamentation arose in all parts of the Confederacy. "The war has taught us the perfect impossibility of placing the least confidence in the negro," Louis Manigault, a patriarchal planter of the South Carolina and Georgia low country, concluded in June, 1862. "In too numerous instances those we esteemed the most have been the first to desert us." An Alabama legislator denounced the infidelity of his body servant, "who had grown up with him from boyhood, who had gone with him to the army and had shared with him, share and share alike, every article of food and clothing," and yet "had seized the first opportunity which presented of deserting him, and joining the Yankees." Such betrayal of trust seemed inexplicable. Kindness should be rewarded with faithfulness. Affection should be reciprocated. "Those we loved best, and who loved us best—as we thought—were the first to leave us," one Virginian lamented. Examples such as these reveal the complexity and ambivalence of master-slave relations. Slaves, particularly house servants, tottered on a precarious balance between the habit of obedience and their strong desire for freedom. Although many remained faithful, that some did not caused consternation among slaveowners.[30]

The desertion of field hands meant financial loss, but the defection of trusted house servants or drivers injured slaveowners' self-esteem. Their recriminations against unfaithful servants reveal that such conduct seemed the ultimate expression of ingratitude, disloyalty, and treason. Had the bonds between master and slave been ephemeral and one-sided? Did blacks merely pretend to be devoted and contented? Was slavery truly cruel and onerous? The extent of disaffection shattered slaveowners' self-image as benevolent patriarchs by showing that the slave's love for his master existed primarily in the planter's own imagination. In their desperate need for the reassurance of their servants' gratitude, the masters had failed to recognize that gratitude and affection can exist only among equals. Blacks had acknowledged

---

30. Catherine D. Edmondston quoted in Roark, *Masters Without Slaves*, 82 (a slightly different version of this quotation, dated one year later and attributed to someone else, is found in Jones [ed.], *Journal of Catherine Devereux Edmondston*, 72); Louis Manigault quoted in Genovese, *Roll, Jordan, Roll*, 101; other quotations in Litwack, *Been in the Storm So Long*, 41–42, 154.

their masters' power over them. In exchange for the limited protection of slavery they returned an equivalent degree of service and respect. Once they received a better offer, from the Yankee liberators, they seized it gladly. Southern whites denounced this black treachery: "Oh! deliver me from the 'citizens of African descent.' I am disgusted forever with the whole race. I have not faith in one single dark individual. They are all alike ungrateful and treacherous—every servant is a spy upon us, & everything we do or say is reported to the Yankees." Such tirades reveal the profound emotional upheaval caused by black desertion.[31]

Confronted by disloyalty, masters frequently disclaimed further obligations to protect their "people." Reverend Charles Colcock Jones of Georgia typifies the transformation from benevolence to hostility. For many years Jones had been a leading proponent of religious instruction for blacks. He prided himself on being a kind Christian master. In July, 1862, large numbers of blacks along the Georgia coast began escaping to federal lines. "Some Negroes (not many) have run away and gone to the enemy, or on the deserted sea islands," Jones wrote to his aunt on July 5. "How extensive the matter may become remains to be seen." Five days later, he reported to his son, a Confederate lieutenant, that fifty-one blacks had left from the county, including five belonging to his brother-in-law and three from his sister's plantation. One of the latter was "Joefinny," a trusted personal servant. Her unfaithfulness bewildered the entire family. "The temptation of *cheap goods, freedom, and paid labor* cannot be withstood. None may be absolutely depended on," Jones explained. Jones himself was fortunate that none of his slaves had left. "Our people *as yet* are all at home," he rejoiced, "and *hope* they may continue faithful." Yet he feared danger from hostile blacks. "They declare themselves enemies and at war with owners by going over to the enemy who is seeking both our lives and property," he charged. "They are traitors of the worst kind, and spies also, who may pilot the enemy into your bedchamber." Those caught returning to their plantations, Jones argued, should be "treated summarily as spies." Charles C. Jones, Jr., agreed with his father. "No mercy should be shown where the party has once absconded and afterwards returns to induce others to accompany him in his act of desertion to the enemy," he responded. "If allowed to desert, our entire social system will be upset if the su-

---

31. Litwack, *Been in the Storm So Long*, 144; Willie Lee Rose, *Slavery and Freedom* (New York, 1982), 84–89.

premacy of the law of servitude and the ownership of such property be not vigorously asserted in cases where recaptures occur." The treachery of runaway slaves thus struck at the heart of southern society. It is no wonder that they received little mercy.[32]

By rejecting the protection of their masters, runaways had forever broken the ties of mutual affection, loyalty, and responsibility. The reaction of slaveholders such as Reverend Charles Colcock Jones came swiftly, full of the fury of rejected friendship and violated trust. Trying to manage the family plantation in Texas, Mrs. W. H. Neblett informed her husband of the steady deterioration of discipline. "The negroes care no more for me than if I was an old free darkey," she complained in the spring of 1864, "and I get so mad sometimes that I think I don't care sometimes if Myers beats the last one of them to death. I cant stay with them another year alone." Blacks' disloyalty led masters to a callous disregard of their suffering. Louisiana cavalry sergeant Edwin Fay, a Harvard graduate, who before the war had been headmaster of a boys' school and partner in a firm that manufactured cotton gins and corn mills, responded angrily when his body servant disappeared from camp. "I wish I had Rich with me, he would be of great assistance," Fay wrote to his wife. "If he went to the Yankees I hope they have killed him ere this."[33]

In moments of exasperation, a few planters might wish death for an unfaithful servant, but many more took quiet satisfaction in believing that blacks would receive harsh treatment from their northern liberators. "The Yankees have taken the Negroes off all the places below Omega, the Negroes generally going most willingly, being promised their freedom by the vandals," Kate Stone observed, with deep skepticism, in June, 1862. "The Negroes are eager to go, leaving wife and children and all for freedom promised them," she reported several days later, "but we hear they are being worked to death on the canal with no shelter at night and not much to eat." Some masters sought to deter slaves from running away by depicting Yankees as devils, savage beasts, or cruel tyrants. As soon as the federal fleet captured the forts guarding the mouth of the Mississippi River in April, 1862, slaves from Effingham Lawrence's nearby Magnolia Plantation began escaping to the enemy. Many of these runaways later returned to Magno-

32. Myers (ed.), *Children of Pride*, 925, 929, 935, 940.
33. Mrs. W. H. Neblett quoted in Wiley, *Southern Negroes*, 52n.; Bell Irvin Wiley (ed.), *"This Infernal War": The Confederate Letters of Sgt. Edwin H. Fay* (Austin, Tex., 1958), 397.

lia, disapappointed in the treatment they received from the Yankees. Nevertheless, to prevent other slaves from leaving before the crops were harvested, Lawrence felt compelled to promise them "a Handsome Present Provided they Resisted the Pressure that is now Felt every where by the Slaves to Run away and Leave there Homes for the Forts and Federal Camps." He warned his slaves that they would find "nothing but *Degredation Missery & Death*" under federal authority and that "it was for there Interest to Remain and be taken Care off Rather than to Leave there Good Homes and Suffer as they was Sure to Do to an immense extent."[34]

Although there were many exceptions, the conduct of Union troops toward blacks frequently confirmed such dire predictions. As Sherman's troops burned their way across Georgia, they abused and stole from black slaves and their white masters indiscriminately. When several of her slaves became restless after the arrival of northern troops, Mary Jones told them to go with the Yankees if they thought they would receive better treatment. "They had seen what their conduct was to the black people—stealing from them, searching their houses, cursing and abusing and insulting their wives and daughters," she wrote, "and if they chose such for their masters to obey and follow, then the sooner they went with them the better; and I had quite a mind to send in a request that they be carried off." She was astonished by the hatred northern soldiers exhibited toward blacks. "In all my life I never heard such expressions of hatred and contempt as the Yankees heap upon our poor servants," she declared. "One of them told me he did not know what God Almighty made Negroes for; all he wished was the power to blow their brains out." Georgia planter William King, a Unionist sympathetic in most respects to the northerners, heard Union soldiers say that "they hated the Negro race, and they would as quickly shoot a negro as a dog." One drunken soldier "cursed the 'damned Nigger' and said he would like to kill the whole race." The future looked bleak for blacks if northerners gained authority over them. "What is to become of this poor race after this War God only knows," King lamented. Mary Jones foresaw a tragic end for blacks. Unprepared for freedom, they would be unable to survive the disintegration

34. Anderson (ed.), *Brokenburn*, 126–28; Effingham Lawrence, Magnolia Plantation Record Book, May 30, September 6, 1862, in Warmouth Papers.

of southern society in the aftermath of war. "The scourge falls with peculiar weight upon them: with their emancipation must come their extermination," she predicted.[35]

Many northerners freely displayed their contempt for blacks. Their conduct varied from condescension to outright brutality. "They carry out their principles by robbing impartially, without regard to 'race, color, or previous condition,'" Eliza F. Andrews of Georgia wrote. "George Palmer's old Maum Betsy says that she has 'knowed white folks all her life, an' some mighty mean ones, but Yankees is de fust ever she seed mean enough to steal fum niggers.'" Further confirmation that northern troops often mistreated blacks comes from the letters of Union soldiers, such as Lieutenant William M. Ferry, a Michigan Democrat, who vociferously opposed emancipation and black equality. Yet he denounced the outrages committed against black contrabands. "The Negro women were debauched by our soldiers—a 'contraband camp' became by the allowance & practice of *officers* & men a scene of prostitution," he charged in February, 1864. "Their sufferings are awful, and many like Old Jack go back to 'Old Massa' not because they love slavery but because they are not subject to the mock philanthropy of money making officials & the lust of unbridled passions." Such behavior was not universal, but it was widespread enough to confirm the southern belief that slavery provided the only protection for blacks. Blacks who congregated in cities and contraband camps under federal control frequently suffered tragic fates. Exposed to disease and suffering from poor diet, lack of medicine, homesickness, filth, and lack of exercise, they had no one to care for them or provide necessary comforts. "The negroes are dying in the streets of Vicksburg," reported the bishop of Natchez, William Elder: "I have asked several Federal Officers what are the intentions or what is the policy of the govt. in regard to the negroes. Everyone whom I have asked has lamented that he thinks there is no policy in their regard, except to deprive the masters of their services & their belief is that as far as the Fed. Govt. & Army prevail, the race will die out like that of the Indians." Despite such intense suffering, blacks continued to seek freedom under the Union banner. Southerners, however, interpreted black suf-

35. Myers (ed.), *Children of Pride*, 1243–44; William King Diary, July 24, 27, 1864, in William King Papers, SHC; Genovese, *Roll, Jordan, Roll*, 152–53.

fering as confirmation of their belief that blacks could not survive without the protection of benevolent white masters.[36]

Southern arguments about black character thus returned to the original premise that blacks could not cope with freedom's responsibilities and would succumb to the dangers of a hostile world. Only slavery could protect them from extermination. Southerners believed that blacks did not even understand what freedom meant and therefore could never enjoy the blessings of liberty and self-government so cherished by free white Americans. According to Sarah Wadley of Louisiana, her family's slaves simply could not recognize that staying on the plantation would be far better for them than fleeing to the Yankees. Amid the war's excitement, blacks had become "dazzled by the false idea of freedom," she explained. Blacks confused freedom with leisure, planters contended, and did not recognize the obligations it entailed. "They are a lazy indolent race. not one in a dozen will make a living without the lash or a certainty of it if they do not work," Tennessee planter John H. Bills declared in 1864. "They all Want freedom *only to Loaf* and do nothing. their idea of freedom is Exemption from Labor." Such an assumption was natural because slavery meant unremitting toil under compulsion. Once this compulsion to work ended, many blacks wanted to take a long overdue vacation. Yet this desire only confirmed southerners' belief in black inferiority and their expectation that without the discipline of slavery, blacks could not survive.[37]

Examples of slaves who resisted the temptation of flight presented the greatest evidence of the soundness of southerners' judgments about black character. It is impossible to know exactly how many slaves ran away and how many remained loyal, but southern assertions that the majority proved faithful appear accurate, largely because many blacks lacked sufficient opportunity to escape successfully. Mary Chesnut, the South Carolina plantation mistress and astute observer of life in the Confederacy, rejoiced at her servants' loyalty. Her neighbors were "horror stricken by the evident exultation they perceive in their servants at the approach of the Yankees," she wrote in November, 1861,

36. Eliza Frances Andrews, *The War-Time Journal of a Georgia Girl, 1864–1865*, ed. Spencer Bidwell King, Jr. (1908; rpr. Macon, Ga., 1960), 283; William M. Ferry to Aunt Hannah, February 29, 1864, Ferry Family Papers, MHC; Gerow (ed.), *Civil War Diary of Elder*, 56–57.

37. Sarah L. Wadley Diary, April 11, 1864, SHC; Bills Diary, August 30, 1864. For a discussion of white complaints about blacks' laziness, see Genovese, *Roll, Jordan, Roll*, 295–309.

when federal forces captured the Sea Islands near Beaufort. "When I hear every body complaining of their Negroes I feel we are blessed. Ours are so well behaved & affectionate—a little lazy but that is no crime & we do no[t] require more of them." Despite enticements from nearby Union troops, most of Effingham Lawrence's Louisiana slaves remained obedient, prodeeding as usual to plant new crops. "There conduct certainly has been when I think of the Terrible ordeal they have Passed thro and the attempts made to Demorralise and Disturb their former Relations most extraordinary," Lawrence boasted. "But they see now the great advantage to them of Remaining under my Protection as they are," he concluded. Many southerners insisted that, in the absence of disruptive external influences, blacks would prefer to continue living under their masters' care. "Father gave all the negroes choice yesterday evening, told them they might go with Willie to a place of safety or they might bundle up their things and go to the Yankees, to take a *free* choice," Sarah Wadley, daughter of a prominent Louisiana railroad contractor and slaveholder, reported. "They might have done so in reality, Father would not have hindered them, but they every one chose to go with Willie."[38]

The most severe test of black loyalty occurred when Union troops raided plantations and attempted to entice slaves to leave. Some of Sherman's "bummers" killed the hogs and ducks belonging to a Milledgeville, Georgia, woman and forced her to cook their dinner. "Mrs. Brooks's servant told many a party her master was a good man, a poor man, and they must not trouble him," one of the woman's friends reported. "They said they could not feed the Negro; they had no love for the Negro. And yet they tried to persuade her to go off with them— which she refused to do. Faithful old soul!" After several bands of ruffians had ransacked her plantation and stolen most of her supplies, a Virginia woman's dread of another such visitation was relieved only by satisfaction with her slaves' conduct. "I never saw people so faithful as all of our servants were," she told her father. "They obeyed every word I said promptly & staid by me as close as they could get, men & all." The loyalty of blacks was crucial because otherwise women left alone to manage plantations would be defenseless against insurrection. Kate Stone admitted that she would be helpless if the blacks

38. Woodward and Muhlenfeld (eds.), *Private Mary Chesnut*, 199–200; Effingham Lawrence, Magnolia Plantation Record Book, January 25, 1863, in Warmouth Papers; Wadley Diary, August 29, 1863.

resisted her authority. "The Negroes have behaved well, far better than anyone anticipated," she wrote in September, 1864. "They have not shown themselves revengeful, have been most biddable, and in many cases have been the only mainstay of their owners."[39]

Even though many slaves left their masters and sought freedom with the federal army southern convictions about black character and the value of slavery remained firm. Southerners denounced rebellious individuals as treacherous, ungrateful wretches, but these seemed a small minority among the loyal masses. The character traits that prompted slaves to run away—ignorance, gullibility, and laziness— were precisely the qualities that rendered slavery necessary for blacks. Furthermore, northern hostility to and harsh treatment of blacks seemed to confirm the humanity and benevolence of southern slavery at its best. Trust and affection between blacks and their former masters had been strained by numerous instances of infidelity and animosity on both sides, but most of these incidents could be attributed to the disruptions caused by war, the hostile intrusions of alien Yankees, natural weaknesses in black character, or the temptations raised by false hopes for freedom, idleness, and luxury. Southerners remained convinced that blacks required the protection and control of white masters.

THEY LONGED TO BE FREE

Northern soldiers who encountered slaves fleeing from their masters took a different view of the situation. The enthusiastic welcome which many slaves gave their assumed liberators impressed the depth of the blacks' desire for freedom even on those who opposed emancipation. Most of those who looked favorably on runaways, however, already held antislavery or abolitionist sentiments. The eagerness of the runaways was seized upon to prove that blacks were an oppressed people yearning to be free and to aid the Union cause. Northerners with less favorable opinions of black character objected that the war's purposes were being diverted from saving the Union to setting loose an inferior race incapable of exercising the responsibilities of freedom.

Most northerners had seldom seen a black face before the war brought them into contact with southern plantation slaves. The blacks

39. Laura Buttolph to Mary Jones, December 10, 1864, in Myers (ed.), *Children of Pride*, 1218–19; Eva M. DeJarnette to her father, June 29, 1864, in John Bowie Magruder Papers, DU; Anderson (ed.), *Brokenburn*, 298.

who sought freedom and protection within Union lines became a great curiosity. Lieutenant William T. Lusk of New York wrote from Virginia in September, 1861, "Our greatest source of entertainment is the article called 'nigger,' a thing I never saw until I came to 'Ole Virginny.'" These black refugees had no means of support other than that provided by soldiers, who gave them small amounts of money or rations in payment for washing, cooking, and other chores. "We own an African of the Pongo species," Lusk told his cousin, "a sort of half-idiotic monkey man, partially possessing the gift of speech, and totally possessing the gift of doing nothing." Enlisted men occasionally pooled their resources to hire a servant, both to ease the drudgery of routine chores and to enjoy the novelty of living like men of wealth and leisure. Union officers frequently hired their own personal servants and thus lived as comfortably as southern gentlemen. "I have a little nigger to wait on me & am growing quite respectably corpulent in my old age," wrote twenty-three-year-old Lieutenant Uriah Parmelee of Guilford, Connecticut, "how much easier it is to have a little nig to take your extra steps for you than it is to do it all yourself when you have arrived at years of maturity & occupy an honorable *posish* more or less." If Parmelee felt any inconsistency between his abolitionist sentiments and his new life of ease, he did not reveal such qualms. The convenience of having a servant appealed greatly to many northerners, who enjoyed the cheaply bought leisure, the power of command, and the novelty of black faces.[40]

Judgments about black character differed according to the predisposition of each individual. Predictably, northerners holding antislavery sentiments expressed very positive opinions of blacks' character and abilities. "There seems to be a good degree of intelligence among the blacks that I have seen, & *they long to be free too*," proclaimed a Connecticut soldier. Massachusetts sergeant William T. Pippey reported that a large group of slaves had escaped and entered Union lines: "They are very intelligent and smart looking chaps, and gave us quite a lot of information." Private Constant Hanks of New York expressed great admiration for the blacks he met. "They are faithful and honest in their work and they improve their leisure in learning to read," the young abolitionist told his mother. "They as a class exhibit

40. William T. Lusk to Cousin Lou, September 21, 1861, in Civil War Manuscripts Collection, Yale; Uriah Parmelee to Sam Parmelee, May 19, 1864, in Samuel Spencer Parmelee and Uriah N. Parmelee Papers, DU.

more native sense than the majority of the white citizens," he boldly concluded.[41]

Soldiers of an invading army like to think of themselves as liberators, welcomed by sympathetic groups in the conquered land. Occasional bands of jubilant slaves provided the only such welcome most Union soldiers found in the South, and this distinction earned for blacks a measure of gratitude. When the 15th Connecticut Regiment returned from a raid in Virginia, large numbers of blacks—men, women, and children—followed it to camp. "It was good to hear & see how joyful they were at our coming," wrote Sergeant Henry G. Marshall. "One gate we passed when we went up & they stood there throwing up their hands & looking as tickled as could be." In North Carolina, runaway slaves "manifest the greatest joy on getting within our lines, calling us their deliverers," New York private John B. Foote boasted. "Ah! Dear sister what a comfort it is to know that liberty goes, where go the stars & stripes." Blacks in Kentucky responded similarly to the arrival of Union troops. "I have often thought how happy they were when we came into Lexington. Som[e] cried for joy others laughed and danced with all manners of demonstration," Michigan private Francis Everett Hall reported. Marching through Virginia, Colonel Robert McAllister of New Jersey met many blacks fleeing from their owners. "You ought to have seen the poor slaves—old and young, men and women— running out to meet us and hobbling along to the 'land of liberty,'" he told his wife. "When asked where they were going, they would an- swer: 'Going with the Union Army!' They know that our flag is the flag of liberty and not oppression." Slave runaways thus implicitly con- firmed the virtue of the Union cause and offered proof that the North, not the South, truly represented freedom.[42]

To substantiate runaways' testimony that the Union symbolized freedom, northerners had to show that blacks understood what free- dom meant and cherished it deeply. Avowed abolitionist Uriah Par- melee depicted slaves as potential fugitives looking northward toward "the dawn of freedom." "I tell you the slave in Virginia is fitted for

41. Jay Nettleton to Seth Hollister, November 13, 1861, in Seth Hollister Papers, DU; William T. Pippey to Mr. H. & B. Y. P., January 26, 1862, in William T. Pippey Papers, DU; Constant Hanks to his mother, September 13, 1863, in Constant C. Hanks Papers, DU.

42. Henry G. Marshall to "dear ones at home," July 4, 1863, in Henry Grimes Marshall Papers, WLC; John B. Foote to his sister, March 9, 1865, in John B. Foote Papers, DU; Francis E. Hall to his mother, November 28, 1862, in Francis Everett Hall Papers, MHC; Robertson (ed.), *Civil War Letters of McAllister*, 553.

Freedom," Parmelee wrote home. "He needs no kind master to enlighten him further as to its advantages or how they are to be turned to the best account." Ohio colonel John Beatty, a Republican banker, claimed the same for Alabama blacks. "All the colored people of Alabama are anxious to go 'wid yer and wait on you folks,'" he observed in May, 1862. "There are not fifty negroes in the South who would not risk their lives for freedom." Working with blacks in a Tidewater Virginia contraband camp in February, 1863, Lucy Chase became fascinated with the tales of these refugees from bondage. The daughter of a highly respected Worcester, Massachusetts, businessman and Quaker, she had volunteered to teach Virginia's freed blacks. "One of them told me that she was very willing to take her share of suffering and all who were in the room with us, said they would suffer still more, rather than again become slaves," this sympathetic observer reported. "The woman said she should die very happy, feeling that her children can spend 'The balance of their days in freedom, though she had been in bonds.'" This statement confirmed Lucy Chase's views that slavery was a cruel and inhumane system and that blacks longed for freedom.[43]

Despite entreaties from abolitionists, government policy until mid-1862 officially prohibited harboring runaway slaves, and many northern soldiers denounced efforts to encourage blacks to leave their masters. Racial prejudice formed a significant barrier against such efforts. Ordered to help catch runaway slaves and return them to their master, Francis E. Hall of Michigan commented: "I often pity the poor fellows so anxious for freedom yet so much feeling against them. There are some boys even in our Squad who would not give a Negroe a bit of Clothing if they saw him dying." During the war's first year, Union officers received orders not to allow runaways to remain in army camps. Although some officers winked at violations of this regulation, many gladly enforced it strictly. Marching through the Kentucky mountains, officers in a Michigan regiment had to decide whether to let a slave running away from his master go with them. Lieutenant James W. Sligh wrote that "the Col & Capt's all refused to have anything to do with him and told him to go back to his master. that we were not here to induce negros to run away, or steel them but to assist to maintain the laws, and put down Rebellion." Union troops stationed at New Or-

---

43. Uriah Parmelee to his mother, July 6, 1862, Parmelee Papers; Harvey S. Ford (ed.), *Memoirs of a Volunteer, 1861–1863* (New York, 1946), 109–10; Henry I. Swint (ed.), *Dear Ones at Home: Letters from Contraband Camps* (Nashville, 1966), 41.

leans likewise refused all requests for sanctuary. "The Niggers here think we have come after them and are flocking in to us every day to go off with Massa Lincon but of course we do not permit them to harbor around at all," Michigan soldier Harrison Soule stated.[44]

By the time official policy changed in 1862, most Union soldiers had become reluctant to return escaped blacks to slavery. Either through antislavery arguments or acquaintance with runaway slaves, many northerners had developed a strong distaste for slavery. Added to this emotional response was a growing conviction that slavery formed a mainstay of the rebellion. Both ideologically and militarily, a blow against slavery might dislodge the Confederacy's "cornerstone." Returning slaves to enemies of the Union became increasingly unpopular. "I do not think there is a man here who pants to be a rescuer [of runaway slaves], & I know there are only a few who can be willingly made slave hunters for secessionists & traitors," Captain Charles V. DeLand of Jackson, Michigan, asserted in March, 1862. Even northerners who did not oppose slavery sometimes found it unpleasant to force blacks back into servitude. "I don't care a damn for the darkies, and know that they are better off with their masters 50 times over than with us," Lieutenant Charles Wills of Illinois admitted, "but of course you know I couldn't help to send a runaway nigger back. I'm blamed if I could."[45]

This reluctance to return runaway slaves resulted from their professed loyalty to the Union and their assistance to northern troops as informants and guides. Northerners wanted to win the contest for blacks' loyalty and affection. Just as southerners seized on instances of faithful service to confirm their belief that blacks recognized the benefits of slavery, northerners emphasized the numbers of runaway slaves to buttress their conviction that blacks cherished freedom and knew that it could be secured only under the Union banner. "The satisfaction of these people in regard to their Negroes is surprising. They seem to believe firmly that their Negroes are so much attached to them that they will not leave them on any terms," David Strother, a Virginian, who served as a Union officer, observed in Virginia. "The Negroes take

44. Francis E. Hall to his mother, November 28, 1862, in Hall Papers; James W. Sligh to his wife, January 4, 1862, in Sligh Family Papers, MHC; Harrison Soule to his wife, May 8, 1862, in Harrison Soule Papers, MHC.

45. Charles V. DeLand to his parents, March 28, 1862, in DeLand Family Papers, MHC; Wills, *Army Life*, 83.

the first opportunity they find of running into our lines and giving information as to where their masters are hidden and conduct our foragers to their retreats," he boasted. In Louisiana, New Hampshire private Oren Farr reported, "As fast as we advance the slaves all leave their masters to come to our lines and then they will go with our boys and act as pilots to show them where their masters have got cotton or sugar hid away and help get it." As friends and allies, blacks gained respect from northern soldiers. "I have increased my confidence so much in the 'old nig' that I credit very nearly every thing I hear from them," Lieutenant Calvin Mehaffey of Lancaster County, Pennsylvania, stated. "They have done us [such] good service in reporting the movements of the enemy that we cannot be altogether unmindful of their services. They are 'Union' and 'fer de North.'" Such faithful service, many northerners argued, should be rewarded with freedom. Blacks had earned their liberty by proving their loyalty to the Union. In fact, they constituted the only large group of southern people who did not renounce the United States government and espouse a treasonable secession.[46]

Nevertheless, serious doubts remained about blacks' capacity for independent action and about their readiness for freedom. Recently freed slaves often had trouble comprehending the change in their status. As Lucy Chase reported, "We asked a colored woman we met in Norfolk, to whom she belonged. She said, 'I don't know, I reckon I'm Massa Lincoln's slave now.'" Having always lived under the protection of white masters, some blacks viewed emancipation as simply an opportunity to find a better guardian. "Such ignorance no where reigns as among contrabands," Cornelia Hancock, a New Jersey nurse, despaired. "They will hang on to a white person as their only hope."[47]

From such evidence of black subservience, many northerners derived conclusions about black character similar to those expressed by southerners. Although many Union soldiers recognized the self-reliance exhibited by bondsmen who risked the dangers of seeking freedom among strangers, others were less generous. Once inside Union lines, many blacks appeared lazy or undisciplined. Plantation hands

46. Eby (ed.), *Virginia Yankee*, 254; Oren E. Farr to his wife, May 6, 1863, in Oren E. Farr Papers, DU; Calvin Mehaffey to his mother, May 11, 1862, in Mehaffey Papers.
47. Swint (ed.), *Dear Ones at Home*, 61; Henrietta Stratton Jaquette (ed.), *South After Gettysburg: Letters of Cornelia Hancock, 1863–1868* (New York, 1956), 37. See Genovese, *Roll, Jordan, Roll*, 139–44.

who sought shelter with federal troops at Hilton Head, South Carolina, had nothing to occupy their time. "Negroes crowd in swarms to our lines," observed Lieutenant William T. Lusk shortly after Union forces occupied the area, "happy in the thought of Freedom, dancing, singing, void of care, & vainly dreaming that all toil is in future to be spared, and that henceforth they are to lead that life of lazy idleness which forms the Nigger Paradise." The outlook for these newly freed people seemed bleak. "I fear that before long they [will] have passed only from the hands of one taskmaster into the hands of another," Lusk concluded ominously. Their apparent indolence led many northerners to conclude that blacks could succeed only if properly disciplined by white supervisors. "I believe [the Negro] capable of improvement by giving him responsibility under a firm and proper discipline," Virginia Yankee David Strother asserted. "The discipline of slavery is his salvation. Continue this discipline and make him at the same time a free man so far as responsibility goes and he will improve within certain limits," Strother concluded. Other than the distinction between a need for discipline under slavery or under nominal freedom, there was little difference between Strother's perception of black character and that of proslavery southerners.[48]

LABORING UNDER A DELUSION

In a letter to the New York *Tribune* in 1865, Augustin L. Taveau of Charleston, South Carolina, evaluated the wartime experience of black conduct. Taveau represented the elite of plantation society. A member of one of South Carolina's most prominent Huguenot families, he had studied law under James L. Petigru, married a French heiress, and established himself as a successful rice planter—all before his thirtieth birthday. Louis Manigault, a leading South Carolina planter, described Taveau as "a gentleman known to our family & a planter." During the war he served as a military staff aide and ordnance official. He signed the loyalty oath in March, 1865, shortly before Lee's surrender at Appomattox. At war's end, Taveau concluded that "the conduct of the Negro in the late crisis of our affairs has convinced me that we were all

48. William T. Lusk to his mother, November 13, 1861, in Civil War Manuscripts Collection, Yale; Eby (ed.), *Virginia Yankee*, 140. Abraham Lincoln's racial views were caught in a similar contradiction by his somewhat arbitrary distinction between slavery and white supremacy, according to Richard Hofstadter, *The American Political Tradition and the Men Who Made It* (New York, 1948), 116–17.

laboring under a delusion." He had come to doubt all of the South's assumptions about black character and the beneficence of the peculiar institution. "Born and raised amid the institution, like a great many others, I believed it was necessary, to our welfare, if not to our very existence," Taveau wrote. "I believed that these people were content, happy, and attached to their master. But events and reflection have caused me to change these opinions." He pronounced slavery unprofitable and charged it with retarding economic well-being. Yet his strongest feelings derived from the black response to freedom. "If they were content, happy and attached to their masters, why did they desert him in the moment of his need and flock to an enemy, whom they did not know; and thus left their, perhaps really good masters whom they did know from infancy?" There was, he thought, no answer except that the mutual affection of master and slave had been a "delusion." His South Carolina plantations ruined, his black property set free, Taveau traveled to Boston to seek aid from his wife's family. The thirty-seven-year-old aristocrat tried to start over on a farm in Maryland. He soon encountered financial difficulties and moved to Baltimore, where he devoted much of his remaining years to literary pursuits. Augustin L. Taveau's painful reassessment of the paternalistic ethos encompasses the South's transition from slavery to freedom.[49]

By rejecting bondage and seeking their own emancipation, blacks had sealed the fate of slavery. After tasting the sweet delights of freedom, they would not return to the bitter diet of servitude. "This war is the certain destruction of slavery," Michigan lieutenant Charles Haydon predicted in January, 1862. "If they are not liberated they will behave so bad that they will have to kill them all." A Union war correspondent traveling in Missouri reached the same conclusion. "These Missouri niggers know a great deal more than the white folks give them credit for," he reported, and the slaves "have learned a lesson too much to ever be useful as slaves." Habits of subservience had been shattered. The evidence of black disaffection remains overwhelming. The vast majority of slaves neither rebelled against their masters nor voluntarily served the Confederate cause. Yet the passive "loyalty" of many could not compensate for the betrayal exhibited by those who deserted to federal lines, refused to work, passed information to the Yankees, or simply became insolent or insubordinate. In only a few

49. Taveau and Manigault quoted in Genovese, *Roll, Jordan, Roll*, 112; biographical information from Augustin Louis Taveau Papers, DU.

exceptional cases were there positive acts of loyalty, and these acts reveal the complexity and personal nature of master-slave relations. Although some slaves remained faithful, personal loyalty to an individual master clearly exceeded loyalty to the institution and acceptance of bondage. The extent of desertion alone discredits the cherished myth of the faithful servant.[50]

The proslavery ideology, however, remained largely intact. Confronted with challenges to their assumptions about black character, white southerners adopted several strategies to explain away this new evidence. They clung to their belief that only slavery could properly control and protect black savages. To prove their own benevolence, they cited examples of northern mistreatment of slave refugees. To prove that blacks could not manage the responsibilities of liberty, they cited examples of indolent, helpless, or impoverished freedmen. Above all, to prove that Yankee agitators had lured "poor deluded wretches" away from the security and contentment of servitude, they cited—over and over again—examples of faithful servants hiding the family silver, concealing their masters from Yankee search parties, and sharing with their impoverished mistresses what little food and provisions they managed to hide from the ruthless invaders. The stories had some basis in fact, but in the telling and retelling they achieved mythic proportions. The myth of the faithful servant, false in its broad claim of black loyalty, nevertheless provided desperately needed reassurance. It offered proof that the Confederate cause had been both just and noble.[51]

The white South thus emerged from the war more than ever convinced that blacks required discipline and control and that some substitute for slavery must be found. Slave behavior had included both docility and rebelliousness, both Sambo and Nat Turner. Masters had feared Nat Turner, but they always discounted the extent of rebellion and resistance among their slaves. According to southern lore, Sambo was the typical plantation slave—docile, irresponsible, lazy, and humble. Above all, Sambo exhibited a childlike attachment and dependence on his master, a faithfulness that was unchanging. Despite ex-

50. Charles Haydon Diary, January 15, 1862, MHC; Cincinnati *Daily Commercial* quoted in Litwack, *Been in the Storm So Long,* 20; Williamson, *After Slavery,* 34–44; Wiley, *Southern Negroes,* 69–73, 83–84; Genovese, *Roll, Jordan, Roll,* 149–50.

51. Roark, *Masters Without Slaves,* 83–85, 100–101; Litwack, *Been in the Storm So Long,* 154; Wiley, *Southern Negroes,* 63–64.

tensive examples of rebellion and resistance during the war, southern whites tenaciously held to their belief in Sambo. When the darker side of black actions became irrefutably visible, white southerners distinguished between loyal "good darkies" and rebellious "uppity niggers." They maintained ties of affection and trust with the former group but would show no forgiveness to unfaithful blacks. If anything had changed in southern racial attitudes, it was a hardening of heart toward blacks who did not "know their place." Disdain and hostility became increasingly significant elements in race relations. There would be no amelioration of southern belief in black inferiority.[52]

The response of northerners to runaway slaves remained at best ambivalent. They welcomed the information given them by blacks and cited black desertions as evidence that the Union represented freedom to all men, but they remained skeptical of blacks' ability to act independently without white control. That blacks undertook the dangers of flight from the security of slavery to the unknown prospects of liberty did not convince northerners that they should be accorded the rights of full citizenship. For the North, a more important test of black character lay ahead: whether they could accept and fulfill the duties of military service.

52. For a provocative but controversial discussion of the Sambo image, see Elkins, *Slavery*, 81–83. Some of the best critiques of Elkins' thesis were collected in Ann J. Lane (ed.), *The Debate Over Slavery* (Urbana, Ill., 1971). On postwar southern whites' responses to freed blacks, see Peter Kolchin, *First Freedom: The Response of Alabama's Blacks to Emancipation and Reconstruction* (Westport, Conn., 1972), 188–90; Lawrence J. Friedman, *The White Savage: Racial Fantasies in the Postbellum South* (Englewood Cliffs, N.J., 1970). The classic history of the origins of segregation is C. Vann Woodward, *The Strange Career of Jim Crow* (1955; 3rd rev. ed., New York, 1974). For a provocative and more extensive treatment of the subject, see Joel Williamson, *The Crucible of Race: Black-White Relations in the American South Since Emancipation* (New York, 1984).

4 / BLACK SOLDIERS

In May, 1862, Major General David Hunter forced into public debate the issue that most directly challenged northern views of black character. A career army officer and graduate of West Point, class of 1822, David Hunter assumed command of the Department of the South in March, 1862. Despite its grand title, the Department of the South consisted only of a small Union-occupied area in the Sea Islands near Port Royal, South Carolina. Hunter soon began putting his abolitionist convictions into action. On May 9, 1862, he issued a brief proclamation declaring all slaves in South Carolina, Georgia, and Florida free, using the dubious logic that these states were under martial law and that "slavery and martial law in a free country are altogether incompatible." On the same day he "requested" his district commanders "to send immediately to these headquarters, under a guard, all the able-bodied negroes capable of bearing arms." Acting without official authorization, General Hunter had undertaken a bold effort to link the issues of emancipation and black enlistment. This had been a major war goal of northern radicals such as black abolitionist Frederick Douglass since the outbreak of war. Yet it was still far from gaining popular approval.[1]

Hunter's efforts to organize the 1st Regiment of South Carolina Volunteers among the Sea Island slaves unleashed a furious protest in the North. Except for the Radical Republicans, most newspaper editors and politicians railed against the idea. On June 9 Representative Charles Wickliffe of Kentucky secured passage of a House resolution asking Secretary of War Edwin Stanton whether General Hunter had organized a regiment of fugitive slaves, whether he had done so with War Department authority, and whether the War Department had furnished uniforms, arms, and equipment for these recruits. Stanton replied on June 14 that Hunter was not authorized to raise troops and then asked Hunter himself to respond to the charges. "To the First Question therefore I reply that no regiment of 'Fugitive Slaves' has

1. Dudley Taylor Cornish, *The Sable Arm: Negro Troops in the Union Army, 1861–1865* (New York, 1956), 36–40; Willie Lee Rose, *Rehearsal for Reconstruction: The Port Royal Experiment* (New York, 1967), 146; *OR*, Ser. I, Vol. XIV, 34; T. Harry Williams, *Lincoln and the Radicals* ([Madison], 1941), 136–38.

been, or is being organized in this Department," Hunter wrote on June 23. "There is, however, a fine regiment of persons whose late masters are 'Fugitive Rebels.'" Hunter's smug retort was read in the House "amid roars of laughter," but by then President Lincoln had already revoked Hunter's order for black enlistments. Lincoln coupled his dismissal of Hunter's proclamation with a declaration that only the president could issue such a far-reaching policy statement and with an appeal to the border states to accept a policy of "gradual abolishment of slavery." As late as August 6, 1862, Lincoln stated that he opposed enlisting blacks as soldiers because "to arm the negroes would turn 50,000 bayonets from the loyal Border States against that were now for us." Without official sanction or public support, General Hunter could not continue his efforts to enlist blacks. On August 10 he disbanded the 1st Regiment of South Carolina Volunteers.[2]

Despite Hunter's failure to organize a permanent black regiment, he succeeded in his larger goal of making black enlistment a major war issue. His attempted conscription of Sea Island slaves stirred distrust, resentment, and opposition both in the North and among blacks themselves. From mid-May to the end of 1862, however, newspaper editors and politicians hotly debated the question of arming blacks. Radicals would not permit the issue to drop, for it was closely tied to the yet unresolved question of emancipation. They wanted to make black enlistment a test of northern commitment to black rights. In July Congress passed the Second Confiscation Act and the Militia Act, which authorized employment of black soldiers and the emancipation of their families.[3]

On August 25, 1862, barely two weeks after General Hunter had disbanded the 1st South Carolina, Secretary of War Stanton authorized General Rufus Saxton "to arm, uniform, equip, and receive into the service of the United States such number of volunteers of African descent as you may deem expedient, not exceeding 5,000." Less rash and abrasive than Hunter, Saxton seemed ideally suited to the task. This first official War Department authorization for enlisting black troops marked a major turning point in President Lincoln's war policy.

2. Cornish, *Sable Arm*, 43–53; Ira Berlin, Joseph P. Reidy, and Leslie S. Rowland (eds.), *The Black Military Experience* (New York, 1982), 51; *OR*, Ser. III, Vol. II, 42–43; Bell Irvin Wiley, *Southern Negroes, 1861–1865* (Rev. ed.; New Haven, 1965), 296–99.

3. Cornish, *Sable Arm*, 40–47; Williams, *Lincoln and the Radicals*, 156–70; James M. McPherson, *The Struggle for Equality: Abolitionists and the Negro in the Civil War and Reconstruction* (Princeton, 1964), 107–12.

Lincoln himself never publicly endorsed the use of blacks as soldiers until adding a clause to that effect to his Emancipation Proclamation of January 1, 1863. It seemed almost an afterthought, yet it would have momentous consequences.[4]

The decision to arm former slaves brought to the forefront critical questions about the role of blacks in American society. As opponents of black enlistment realized, by recognizing that blacks could perform military duties, the government would discredit arguments that they were incapable of fulfilling the responsibilities of free citizens. The door to full equality seemed to be opening. Debate about the policy of black enlistment involved judgments about the capabilities of blacks, their civil and social rights, and the conditions under which they should be permitted to participate in white society. "We had touched the pivot of the war," Colonel Thomas Wentworth Higginson wrote of his efforts in organizing the first officially sanctioned black regiment in November, 1862. "Whether this vast and dusky mass should prove the weakness of the nation or its strength, must depend in great measure, we knew, upon our efforts." The success or failure of this experiment would determine whether blacks could overcome racial prejudice and secure both a greater measure of respect and recognition of their civil rights.[5]

SAMBO'S RIGHT TO BE KILT

The antebellum North, like the South, was a white man's society. Racial prejudice and subjugation did not end at the Mason-Dixon line. Every northern state imposed some legal disabilities on blacks, including prohibiting them from voting, serving in the militia, obtaining an education, testifying against whites in court, and marrying whites. Indiana, Illinois, and Iowa enacted exclusion laws carrying severe penalties for blacks who attempted to settle in those states. Racial segregation and Negrophobia reinforced the doctrine of white supremacy and the social and economic repression of blacks. Almost all northerners held blacks in contempt as members of an inferior race and believed that any

4. Cornish, *Sable Arm*, 53–55, 80–87; Benjamin Quarles, *Lincoln and the Negro* (New York, 1962), 153–55.

5. Thomas Wentworth Higginson, *Army Life in a Black Regiment* (1869; rpr. Boston, 1962), 267; Berlin, Reidy, and Rowland (eds.), *Black Military Experience*, 5; Leon F. Litwack, *Been in the Storm So Long: The Aftermath of Slavery* (New York, 1979), 68.

association with them degraded the white race. It was in this atmosphere that the experiment of black enlistment began.[6]

The odds against eliminating racial prejudice seemed overwhelming. Hatred and fear of blacks, developed during more than two centuries of American slavery, led most northern whites to hold caricatures of them as unknown and loathsome creatures. The Negro's very blackness symbolized baseness, evil, and danger. He represented heathenism, savagery, sexual abandon, and the antithesis of American independence, intelligence, and progress. Blacks seemed more closely related to African apes than to white Americans. In July, 1861, Maria L. Daly, a New York aristocrat and wife of a Democratic judge, overheard "two Negroes, as black as crows with white cravats," discussing the current political situation. "That Black certainly understood himself, though he looked like a dressed-up baboon and little else to me," she commented. "I have an antipathy to Negroes physically and don't like them near me."[7]

According to many northerners, all blacks were ignorant and lazy. Colonel Charles Wainwright, like Maria Daly a New York aristocrat and Democrat, declared that he would employ only white servants because "I cannot possibly stand these wretched 'niggers.'" Blacks were congenitally ignorant, he believed. "To this ignorance must be added the natural laziness, lying, and dirt of the negro which surpasses anything an ordinary white man is capable of," he asserted. "A negro in their present state has no ambition to get money, and no foresight in providing for the future. Enough to eat and drink, with a few dollars to gamble, is all he wants; idleness is his heaven, which no mere bribe can tempt him out of." For Wainwright, blacks represented the antithesis of all admirable human qualities. Education might mitigate these evils but

6. V. Jacque Voegeli, *Free But Not Equal: The Midwest and the Negro During the Civil War* (Chicago, 1967), 1–6; Leon F. Litwack, *North of Slavery: The Negro in the Free States, 1790–1860* (Chicago, 1961), vii–viii; Eugene H. Berwanger, *The Frontier Against Slavery: Western Anti-Negro Prejudice and the Slavery Extension Controversy* (Urbana, Ill., 1967), 33; George Winston Smith and Charles Judah (eds.), *Life in the North During the Civil War: A Source History* (Albuquerque, 1966), xv–xvi, 129–62; Eric Foner, *Free Soil, Free Labor, Free Men: The Ideology of the Republican Party Before the Civil War* (New York, 1970), 261–300.

7. Daly, *Diary of a Union Lady*, 43. See also C. Vann Woodward, *American Counterpoint: Slavery and Racism in the North-South Dialogue* (Boston, 1971), 168. For an excellent discussion of the development of prejudice as a reaction to the color and physical appearance of blacks, see Winthrop D. Jordan, *White Over Black: American Attitudes Toward the Negro, 1550–1812* (Chapel Hill, 1968), 3–98.

only after several generations had passed. "The present generation cannot get rid of [these defects]," he concluded, "and left to themselves will die like sheep with the rot, simply because they are too lazy to live."[8]

Initial impressions of southern blacks frequently strengthened northerners' prejudice against them. "There is no one who has seen the nigger in all its glory on the southern plantations that will vote for emancipation," concluded Indiana soldier Arthur Carpenter after his first close observations of black men. "They will lie & steal and will not work unless they are made to." Such weaknesses were sometimes attributed to blacks' excessively emotional character, which turned even the solemn rites of religious celebration into wild, irreverent outbursts of enthusiasm. One of many Union soldiers who visited black church meetings, Private Jenkin L. Jones, a Wisconsin artilleryman, recorded a typical response: "Their exercise was composed mostly of chanting scraps of every hymn they ever heard, in a gay, dancing tune style, with all jerks and hops for variation." Jones, a Welsh-born Unitarian, referred to them as "poor ignorant souls. They greedily grasp at the most mysterious dogmas, as their judgment and reasoning faculties have never been developed or cultivated."[9]

Aversion to these ignorant, half-civilized black slaves prompted most northerners to insist that they be kept out of the North. Except for the abolitionist minority, Union soldiers deplored the probable consequences of emancipation, particularly the likelihood that hordes of blacks would flood the northern states. Many declared their willingness to let them remain in slavery. Private Charles B. Sartell, a young farmer from Shirley, Massachusetts, complained about his state's reputation for abolitionism among soldiers from other states. "They hate the Massachusetts men because they think that they are fighting to free the negroes they say all that we came here for was to fight for and free them," he reported. "I never came out here for to free the black devils for I think it would be better for to let them stay where they are for they a[re the] ignorant lazy dirtyist class of human beings that I ever see." A Confederate officer, captured in battle, expressed his surprise upon discovering that not all Union soldiers were abolitionists. "We told him that if they would only keep their slaves where they were and not

---

8. Nevins (ed.), *Diary of Battle*, 274.
9. Arthur Carpenter to his parents and brothers, August 19, 1862, December 5, 1861, in Civil War Manuscripts Collection, Yale; Jones, *Artilleryman's Diary*, 207.

trouble us with them, we would be glad to let them alone," reported a Michigan officer, "as we had enough of free ones to satisfy all our yearnings for Sambos company."[10]

This antipathy to associating with blacks had been one motive behind the movement to colonize emancipated slaves in Africa or the Caribbean. Colonization appealed both to antislavery sentiment and to racial intolerance. During the war, President Lincoln and others argued that colonization would render emancipation palatable to those who feared that freed blacks would stream northward. The plan proved impractical and never attracted widespread support, but many northerners liked the idea of resolving the nation's vexing racial problems by removing all blacks from the country. When General David Hunter issued his order freeing slaves in the Department of the South in 1862, many of his subordinates threatened to resign, until Lincoln revoked the controversial edict. One of those officers, Lieutenant Joseph Findley of Pennsylvania, applauded Lincoln's determination "to maintain his strict conservatism" and decided not to resign. "The niggers . . . would be a curse to the people of the whole country if they were set free and allowed to remain," he wrote to his mother. "If they ever should be freed, it should only be done when they can be removed entirely from the country." Similarly, Maria Daly reported that one of General Hunter's officers, visiting in New York, said that their black servants were "lazy, impertinent, stupid, thievish, and generally disgusting." She argued that northerners should not assist the freed blacks, "and then they will be obliged to emigrate."[11]

This was to be a white man's war. Emancipation and black enlistment could gain acceptance, if at all, only as a means of protecting the interests of white northerners. Blacks were inferior and should remain both subordinate and separate. Echoing Joseph Findley, Michigan captain William Ferry denounced all attempts "to give freedom to negroes

10. Charles B. Sartell to Thomas, November 28, 1862, in Civil War Correspondence, BHC; James W. Sligh to his wife, January 26, 1862, in Sligh Family Papers, MHC. Senator Lyman Trumbull declared in 1862 that people in the northwestern states felt a great aversion "against having free negroes come among us" (quoted in Woodward, *American Counterpoint*, 165). See also Forrest G. Wood, *Black Scare: The Racist Response to Emancipation and Reconstruction* (Berkeley, 1968), 20–21.

11. Joseph R. Findley to his mother, June 8, 1862, in Alexander T., Joseph R., and William M. Findley Papers, DU; Daly, *Diary of a Union Lady*, 121. For a discussion of Lincoln's advocacy of colonization as a reflection of racial hostility as well as humanitarian concern, see George M. Fredrickson, "A Man But Not a Brother: Abraham Lincoln and Racial Equality," *Journal of Southern History*, XLI (February, 1975), 39–58.

who would be a curse to the country & themselves instead of a source of profit & the general peace & happiness." The rights of blacks deserved no consideration according to Ferry, a Grand Rapids businessman and Democrat. "No one here in the Army cares two straws for the Negro, except only as he works," Ferry reported.[12] The war's impact on blacks seemed unimportant compared to its effects on white society and government. Just as preservation of the Union transcended emancipation as a northern objective, all issues concerning black rights were superseded by solicitude for white interests. The white North would not easily accept blacks as citizens with full and equal rights, nor even as neighbors.

This deep-seated racial prejudice led most Union soldiers to oppose enlisting blacks. They predicted that blacks could not endure the rigors of military life or the dangers of battle. Furthermore, they argued, blacks could not accept responsibility, act independently, or maintain the pride and self-respect necessary for effective military service. Hearing reports that General David Hunter was arming a regiment of blacks in South Carolina, Colonel David Strother opposed the experiment. "My belief is that any attempt to make soldiers of negroes will prove an ignominious failure and should they get into battle the officers who command them will be sacrificed," he predicted. Michigan corporal Frank Lansing wrote that his comrades were "much opposed to the raising of negro regiments & the regiment by whose side they fight will feel that instead of some one to help they have some one to look after, for their reputation for steadines while under fire is not very good." Even William Channing Gannett, a young Harvard Divinity School graduate and an abolitionist, doubted blacks' fighting abilities. "Negroes—plantation negroes, at least—will never make soldiers in one generation," he wrote from Port Royal, South Carolina. "Five white men could put a regiment to flight." Private Henry Thompson of Connecticut feared that blacks would not be inclined to fight. "I know they are all for getting out of the way when there is a battle afoot or any signs of it," he stated. "I think a drove of hogs would do better brought down here for we could eat them and the niggers we cant."[13]

12. William M. Ferry to his wife, October 31, 1862, in Ferry Family Papers, MHC.
13. David H. Strother Diary, May 17, 1862, in David Hunter Strother Collection, West Virginia University Library; Frank E. Lansing to his mother, February 8, 1863, in Frank E. Lansing Papers, BHC; Elizabeth Ware Pearson (ed.), *Letters from Port Royal, Written at the Time of the Civil War* (1906; rpr. New York, 1969), 43; Henry Thompson to his wife, March 6, 1863, in Henry J. H. Thompson Papers, DU.

Despite such vitriolic statements, many northerners who disparaged the fighting abilities of blacks still recognized that their loyalty
could prove an asset to the Union cause. The most widely advocated
means of using blacks' services was to put them to work at menial
tasks, thereby freeing white soldiers for more vital responsibilities.
"The negroes will never be of any assistance to us in any other capacity
than as labourers. We should make remorseless use of them in that
capacity," David Strother argued. Only white men were qualified for
active campaigning, which required pride, self-reliance, intelligence,
and independence. "A Nigger makes a good enough soldier for garrison and guard duty but for Field service a Hundred men is worth a
Thousand of them," concluded Captain Harrison Soule of Michigan.
Because blacks were "very scarey" they could not be depended on in
battle, Soule insisted; therefore, "they are only fit to help us in the
capacity of Laborers and watchmen." These soldiers' private opinions
echoed public statements of politicians and editors. "We do not need a
single negro in the army to fight," the governor of Iowa, Samuel J.
Kirkwood, wrote to General Henry W. Halleck, but they could relieve
white soldiers from such tasks as "making roads, chopping wood,
policing camp &c." Largely because of such sentiments, blacks were
more often put to work as menial laborers than assigned to combat
duty.[14]

Racial superiority played a large part in efforts to confine blacks to
subordinate positions. "Let the niggers be sent here to use the pick and
shovel in the broiling sun as we are now doing, and we will take a
soldier's tool—the gun and Bayonet," Pennsylvania sergeant Felix
Brannigan wrote from Virginia. "We don't want to fight side and side
by the nigger. We think we are too superior a race for that." Opponents
of black enlistment feared that such measures would open the door to
equality and enlarge black claims to full citizenship. "The negro is not
equal to a white man, and he is being put upon an equality with us in
being allowed to fight with us, and being called a united states soldier,"
Arthur Carpenter complained. Likewise, Pennsylvania sergeant Enoch
Baker predicted that "the nigger Question" would "raise a rebellion in

14. Strother Diary, March 30, 1863; Harrison Soule to his father, January 26, 1864, in
Harrison Soule Papers, MHC; Samuel J. Kirkwood to Henry W. Halleck, August 5, 1862,
in Berlin, Reidy, and Rowland (eds.), *Black Military Experience*, 85. On the use of blacks as
laborers, see Benjamin Quarles, *The Negro in the Civil War* (2nd ed.; Boston, 1969), 116, 192;
Berlin, Reidy, and Rowland (eds.), *Black Military Experience*, 487–516; and C. Peter Ripley,
Slaves and Freedmen in Civil War Louisiana (Baton Rouge, 1976), 40–43.

the army." The southern people were rebels to the government, he argued, "but they are White and God never intended a nigger to put white people Down." Allowing blacks to fight the Union's battles would force the nation to treat them with respect. Few white Yankees would tolerate this. "To claim that the indolent, servile negro is the equal in courage, enterprise and fire of the foremost race in all the world is a libel upon the name of an American citizen," the New York *World* editorialized. "It is unjust in every way to the white soldier to put him on a level with the black." Committed to maintaining white supremacy, northerners found any effort to elevate blacks repugnant. As military laborers, however, blacks could free white soldiers for more demanding and exciting military duties.[15]

Despite such opposition, the idea of enlisting black soldiers gradually shifted from abolitionist dogma to government policy. Lincoln's emancipation plans, announced in September, 1862, pointed the way. Already, under General Rufus Saxton's authority, Colonel Thomas Wentworth Higginson had begun recruiting and drilling the first officially sanctioned black regiment. Military necessity increasingly required making use of any and all available resources to suppress the rebellion. Yet Lincoln waited until he was convinced that public opinion would, however reluctantly, assent to black enlistments. Arguments against this radical step were powerful: it would show that white soldiers could not win the war alone; it would lead to slave insurrections; blacks lacked courage and fighting qualities; and it would lead to social equality. Men who opposed emancipation vehemently objected to fighting beside blacks. A New York customs official denounced "raising Negro brigades" and said that "if that was done he would wash his hands of the whole matter." Some officers resigned their commissions once black enlistment became Union policy. Arguments based on moral or political concerns could not win public acceptance of black soldiers. The only concerns that could overshadow racial prejudice were protecting white lives and preserving the Union.[16]

These were the arguments that gradually effected a reversal in north-

15. Felix Brannigan to his sister, July 16, 1862, in Felix Brannigan Papers, LC; Arthur Carpenter to his parents, May 30, 1863, in Civil War Manuscripts Collection, Yale; Enoch T. Baker, quoted in Bell Irvin Wiley, *The Life of Billy Yank: The Common Soldier of the Union* (Indianapolis, 1952), 120; New York *World* quoted in Philip S. Foner, *History of Black Americans: From the Compromise of 1850 to the End of the Civil War* (Westport, Conn., 1983), 368.

16. Daly, *Diary of a Union Lady*, 177; Quarles, *Lincoln and the Negro*, 154–55; Wood, *Black Scare*, 41–46; Voegeli, *Free But Not Equal*, 100.

ern public opinion concerning black enlistment. Among Union soldiers, the conversion process usually began with denunciations of a war in which white men died to emancipate black slaves. "It has got to be an abolition war now," complained Sergeant Charles Greenleaf of Hartford, Connecticut, "and I don't like the idea of suffering and risking my life for niggers." Private Josephus Jackson of the 12th Vermont rejoiced when he heard that a black servant had drowned. "I wish all niggers lay by the side of him," he wrote to his wife in February, 1863. "I do not think mutch of killing our Vermont boys a fighting for the black Devells," he concluded. Objecting to the government's policy regarding blacks, Jackson resigned when his nine-month enlistment expired in June, 1863, and returned to his small Vermont farm. Even antislavery proponents sometimes spoke out against the sacrifices white men made on behalf of blacks. "I believe that the onely way that A lasting Peace can be obtained is through the distruction of slavery on every foot of soil in the Union," declared Corporal Marion Munson of the 16th Michigan Regiment, "but to shoot down white men to do it is a Bace mean and A Barberous act to shoot white men and let the niger free." He argued that white men were "superior to niggers" and that soldiers did not want "to go throug the rough life of A soldier and perhaps get shot, for a d——d nigger."[17]

Eventually the argument was reduced to stark mathematical calculations of money and lives spent for emancipation. "Every niger that has been freed has cost 4 thousand dollars & one white mans life thus far," Private Henry Thompson of Connecticut declared in August, 1864, "and according to that, we shall loose 1 million of lives & every thousand nigers cost 4 million of dollars, & there is 3 million of nigers yet to free." Despite its questionable statistics and logic, this argument spread throughout the army, gaining popularity as it passed from camp to camp. The issue generated strong feelings because it deeply involved each individual soldier. Thompson stated the issue bluntly: "Shall we throw away our lives for a class of people far inferior to us in every respect people we wont associate with under any circumstances if we can avoid it. is there any man that wants to be shot down for a niger for that is what we are fighting for now and nothing else."[18]

Faced with the threat of senseless, indiscriminate death for a cause

17. Charles Greenleaf to his parents, January 31, 1863, in Civil War Letters, CHS; Josephus Jackson to his wife, February 23, 1863, in Josephus Jackson Papers, DU; Marion Munson to Joshua Van Hoosen, February 19, 1863, in Joshua Van Hoosen Papers, MHC.
18. Henry Thompson to his wife, August 17, 1864, in Thompson Papers.

they did not wholeheartedly espouse, soldiers began to think that the danger should be shared by blacks who hoped for freedom. If someone must die, they argued, let it be the black man. "I rejoice to see the negroes coming into the army," Private Edwin Wentworth of Maine acknowledged. "I am willing that they risk their lives as I mine. It is but fair." Presented as an alternative to the further sacrifice of white lives, enlistment of black troops received much greater support than it ever won on moral or ideological grounds. "You may be astonished to hear me say that the arming of the negroes is just what we want it meets with nearly universal approbation in the army," an Iowa private told his wife. "I dont care if they are one ½ mile thick in front in every Battel they will stop Bullets as well as white people." Instincts for self-preservation thus led to the realization that employment of black soldiers could help reduce white casualties. Increasingly, the war seemed an insatiable monster, indiscriminately devouring blue-clad volunteers. Bullets and artillery shells would not discriminate between white and black targets.[19]

This logic of the campfires found public expression from political leaders. According to Kansas Senator James H. Lane, who as a Union general had been an early organizer of black troops, many white soldiers would have mutinied if Lincoln had ordered blacks into service before 1863, "for not till thousands of them [whites] had been slain, and other thousands wounded and maimed, did they give a reluctant assent to receive the aid of a black auxiliary." Iowa's radical governor, Samuel J. Kirkwood, wrote to General Henry W. Halleck in August, 1862, that he would have no regrets at the end of the war "if it is found that a part of the dead are *niggers* and that *all* are not white men." He later argued more directly that he "would prefer to sacrifice the lives of niggers rather than those of the best and bravest of our white youths." Newspaper editors took up the same cause. "A white man is of as much consequence as a Negro," the Philadelphia *North American* declared in mid-1862, and "the lives of white men can and ought to be spared by the employment of Blacks as soldiers." Thus racial prejudice and disdain for black lives became incentives for accepting enlistment of black soldiers.[20]

19. Edwin O. Wentworth to his wife, May 3, 1864, in Edwin Oberlin Wentworth Papers, LC; Isaac Marsh to his wife, May 12, 1863, in Isaac Marsh Papers, DU.

20. Lane quoted in Voegeli, *Free But Not Equal*, 100; Samuel J. Kirkwood to Henry W. Halleck, August 5, 1862, in Berlin, Reidy, and Rowland (eds.), *Black Military Experience*,

Blacks' willingness to fight became increasingly significant as the North's manpower needs reached critical proportions. As the war lengthened and casualties mounted, it became increasingly difficult to obtain recruits. In August, 1863, George Templeton Strong, a prominent New York lawyer and treasurer of the Sanitary Commission, the national relief organization, wrote in his diary that the Irish "would swear at the dam Naygurs, but we need bayonets in Negro hands if Paddy is unwilling to fight for the country." Any man willing to fight should be enlisted, Union soldiers argued. "If a bob-tail dog can stick a bayonet on his tail, and back up against a rebel and kill him, I will take the dog and sleep with him," declared Captain Pythagoras Holcombe of the 2nd Vermont Battery, "and if a nigger will do the same, I'll do the same by him. I'll sleep with anything that will kill a rebel." Black lives were cheap, he insisted, compared to those of white soldiers. "What's the use to have men from Maine, Vermont and Massachusetts dying down here in these swamps," he asked a comrade in Louisiana; "you can't replace these men, but if a nigger dies, all you have to do is send out and get another one," he concluded. When a soldier seemed mere fodder for the cannon's mouth, the color of his skin did not matter. Callous disregard for black lives thus led white Unionists to view them as ideal candidates for the position.[21]

Military necessity was one of the strongest arguments for arming slaves. In the middle of 1863 Secretary of the Navy Gideon Welles confided in his diary, "All of our increased military strength now comes from Negroes." As defenders of the Union, blacks gained greater respect than white traitors. "There is not a Negro in the army that is not a better man than a rebel to this government," declared Lieutenant James G. Theaker, a former Ohio schoolteacher and farmer, who had become an instructor of black recruits. "I think that the best possible use the government can make of Negroes is to take them and make them fight against the rebels." President Lincoln had written to Horace Greeley in August, 1862, that his "paramount object in this struggle" was to save the Union. "What I do about Slavery and the colored race, I do because

85; Kirkwood quoted in Voegeli, *Free But Not Equal*, 102; Philadelphia *North American* quoted in Jack D. Foner, *Blacks and the Military in American History: A New Perspective* (New York, 1974), 34.

21. George Templeton Strong, *Diary of the Civil War, 1860–1865*, ed. Allan Nevins (New York, 1962), 347; Holcombe quoted by Henry Martyn Cross, "A Yankee Soldier Looks at the Negro," ed. William Cullen Bryant II, *Civil War History*, VII (1961), 144.

it helps to save this Union," he announced. One year later he declared that black enlistments had begun to meet this objective. "Some of the commanders of our armies in the field who have given us our most important successes, believe the emancipation policy, and the use of colored troops, constitute the heaviest blow yet dealt to the rebellion," Lincoln wrote in a public letter of August 26, 1863. "The white soldier seemed ready to welcome to his side any aid which looked to the rescue of his broken union," concluded C. W. Buckley, chaplain of a Louisiana black regiment, and the black soldier "was ready to strike for the country whose privileges and blessings he yet hopes to enjoy."[22]

If patriotic resolve did not convince all northerners that blacks should be enlisted, self-interest converted even the most bigoted potential draftee. Military reverses and a dwindling supply of new recruits led Congress to pass the Conscription Act in March, 1863, just as black recruiting commenced. John A. Wilder of Massachusetts had already begun enlisting blacks at Fortress Monroe, Virginia, in a unit that would become the 2nd Regiment, United States Colored Troops. "We wish to get the start of other states in the matter and save a draft in Mass.—do you understand?" he explained to Eben J. Loomis. Black recruits would reduce the number of white draftees. The logic was simple and direct. "Arm One Hundred Thousand Blacks, conscript them wherever they are to be found," army recruiter George L. Stearns advised the War Department's solicitor, "and you will have an army that will put down the rebellion without further draft on the northern Whites who will call on God to bless Abraham Lincoln for saving them from this dreaded conscription and effectually extirpate slavery from the land." Such a policy would also be popular, he wrote, because it would send northern free blacks far away to the South. The northern press quickly picked up the argument. "Since Congress passed the conscription bill, the opposition to the Negro enlistment has subsided," the Cleveland *Leader* reported in March, 1863. "The Negro as a . . . soldier . . . was a monster. The Negro as a substitute is very acceptable." The Conscription Act and

22. Welles quoted in Quarles, *Negro in the Civil War*, xii; Theaker quoted in Paul E. Rieger (ed.), *Through One Man's Eyes; The Civil War Experiences of a Belmont County Volunteer* (Mount Vernon, Ohio, 1974), 63; Henry Steele Commager (ed.), *The Blue and the Gray: The Story of the Civil War as Told by Participants* (2 vols.; Indianapolis, 1950), II, 1087; James M. McPherson (ed.), *The Negro's Civil War: How American Negroes Felt and Acted During the War for the Union* (New York, 1965), 192; McPherson, *Struggle for Equality*, 212; C. W. Buckley to Lorenzo Thomas, April 1, 1865, in Berlin, Reidy, and Rowland (eds.), *Black Military Experience*, 564–65.

recruiting of blacks both helped alleviate the Union's manpower short-
age. Of the two, black enlistment appeared more attractive to many
lukewarm patriots. The timing of the Conscription Act could not have
been better for those who advocated use of black troops.[23]

A single poem, more than anything else, turned such logical calculations of military necessity into a simple appeal to self-interest which
was so direct and memorable that it profoundly transformed public
opinion on the issue of black enlistment. Charles G. Halpine, a New
York journalist serving on General David Hunter's staff in South Carolina, wrote "Sambo's Right to Be Kilt" in March, 1863, as a defense of
black soldiers. Its humor was cruel and cold-blooded, but it could
persuade whites to accept black enlistment without disturbing their
deep-seated racial prejudices. Written to a familiar melody ("The Low
Backed Car"), it was easy to sing and remember.

> Some tell us 'tis a burnin' shame
>   To make the naygers fight;
> And that the thrade of bein' kilt
>   Belongs but to the white:
> But as for me, upon my sowl!
>   So liberal are we here,
> I'll let Sambo be murthered instead of myself,
>   On every day in the year.
>
>   On every day in the year boys,
>   And in every hour of the day;
>   The right to be kilt I'll divide wid him,
>   And divil a word I'll say.
>
> In battle's wild commotion
>   I shouldn't at all object
> If Sambo's body should stop a ball
>   That was comin' for me direct;
> And the prod of a Southern bagnet,
>   So ginerous are we here,
> I'll resign, and let Sambo take it
>   On every day in the year.
>
>   On every day in the year boys,
>   And wid none o' your nasty pride,

23. John A. Wilder to Eben J. Loomis, March 30, 1863, in Loomis-Wilder Family
Papers, Yale; George L. Stearns to William Whiting, April 27, 1863, in Berlin, Reidy, and
Rowland (eds.), *Black Military Experience*, 91; Cleveland *Leader* quoted in Voegeli, *Free But
Not Equal*, 105. See also Mary Frances Berry, *Military Necessity and Civil Rights Policy* (Port
Washington, N.Y., 1977), 56–57.

> All my right in a Southern bagnet prod,
>   Wid Sambo I'll divide!
> The men who object to Sambo
>   Should take his place and fight;
> And it's better to have a nayger's hue
>   Than a liver that's wake and white.
> Though Sambo's black as the ace of spades,
>   His finger a thrigger can pull,
> And his eye runs sthraight on the barrel-sights
>   From undher its thatch of wool.
> So hear me all, boys darlin',
>   Don't think I'm tippin' you chaff,
> The right to be kilt we'll divide wid him,
>   And give him the largest half.

Halpine's song quickly became popular among the soldiers at Hilton Head, and General Hunter reported to Stanton at the end of April, 1863, that their prejudices against black troops "are rapidly softening or fading out." Published under Halpine's pseudonym, "Private Miles O'Reilly," the song quickly gained nationwide popularity. It was reprinted extensively and printed in sheet music form. "Sambo's Right to Be Kilt" was particularly influential among the New York Irish, the most bitter opponents of black enlistment, and helped to reconcile them to black involvement in the war.[24]

The enlistment of blacks proceeded quickly during the first months of 1863. Early in the year, the secretary of war authorized the governors of Massachusetts, Rhode Island, and Connecticut to organize black regiments. The Bureau for Colored Troops was established in May, 1863, to regularize the method of recruiting black soldiers. The bureau organized boards to examine white candidates for commissions in these new regiments and transformed the effort to arm blacks from a haphazard and volunteer basis to a centrally controlled professional organization. By the middle of 1863, more than thirty black regiments had been organized, and both the Lincoln administration and the nation were thoroughly committed to using black troops. The two questions that remained were how black soldiers would be treated and how well they would fight.[25]

24. William Hanchett, Irish: Charles G. Halpine in Civil War America (Syracuse, 1970), 70–71, 83–84; Cornish, Sable Arm, 229–31.
25. Berlin, Reidy, and Rowland (eds.), Black Military Experience, 9–13, 37–278; Cornish, Sable Arm, 95, 130; Ripley, Slaves and Freedmen, 102–13.

When blacks were finally enlisted, racial prejudice led to discrimination and segregation. Official policy and public opinion required them to be organized into separate regiments. White soldiers strenuously objected to the prospect of serving side by side with blacks or in any way sharing the intimate contacts which camp life imposed. Despite his antislavery sympathies, Henry C. Hall of Connecticut expressed satisfaction that the first black troops he saw in Virginia remained at a distance. "I think it is well enough to make soldiers of the negroes," he confided to his sister, "but I do not think it is right to mix them with white troops for it causes a great deal of hard feeling with some. I think they should all be placed in a department by themselves."[26] Whatever white motives, the results did offer black soldiers some advantage. Keeping them in separate regiments reduced interracial contacts and "hard feeling" and increased the potential for blacks to prove their military ability. Few northerners worried, however, that the success of black troops would change their conviction that blacks were incapable of effective action. Rather, they feared that incompetent black regiments would endanger white soldiers in battle.

Such consequences could be avoided, northerners argued, only by placing inexperienced black soldiers under the command of white officers. Black men could never become officers, for they suffered from the ignorance, laziness, and indiscipline that characterized their race. William M. Findley, a civilian quartermaster clerk from Harrisburg, Pennsylvania, described for his mother the first regiments of black soldiers he saw at Hilton Head, South Carolina, in May, 1863. "They are of course under the charge of *white* officers, who doubtless keep them under the strictest discipline," he assured her; "it is the universal opinion that they make very good soldiers when kept under proper discipline." Sergeant Nathan Webb of Maine, an antislavery Republican, likewise believed that blacks needed white officers and firm control. "I believe they will, with proper discipline and good Officers, make just as good soldiers as white men," he stated. Until near the war's end, with few exceptions, blacks were not allowed to serve as commissioned officers. In Louisiana black officers were forced to resign and join the ranks as privates. Official policy stated that only white men could command black regiments.[27]

26. Henry C. Hall to his sister, October 20, 1863, in Henry C. Hall Papers, DU.
27. William M. Findley to his mother, May 15, 1863, in Findley Papers; Nathan Webb Diary, June 6, 1863, WLC.

By limiting military commissions to whites, the government greatly
expanded the promotional opportunities for white noncommissioned
officers. The prospect of becoming an officer in a regiment of "colored
troops" further increased white soldiers' self-interest in black enlistment. Writing to his brother in February, 1863, Sergeant William T.
Pippey of Massachusetts asked, "What do you think of a Captaincy in a
nigger Regt?" Pippey was soon promoted to lieutenant in his own
regiment, but many of his comrades did accept commissions in black
regiments. Commissary Sergeant William Patterson observed a "negro
Regt." in Virginia in April, 1864. "They make good looking soldiers," he
reported. Despite letters from his family, who were "much opposed to
my entering the Negro services," he took the examination and became
lieutenant of a black regiment. Similarly, Sergeant Henry G. Marshall, a
Connecticut Republican and a Yale College graduate, decided to accept
a commission in a black regiment. From Milford, Connecticut, his sister
Mary Marshall wrote that it was "especially important that negro regiments should be officered by *good* men," but she advised against his
accepting the offer. Despite her objections, Marshall became an officer
of blacks. The policy of accepting only white men as officers served
several purposes. It conformed to and reinforced racial prejudice and
provided opportunities for advancement to ambitious young white soldiers. Thus it served to increase general support for black enlistment.[28]

The same qualities that would prevent blacks from becoming competent officers enabled them to be good rank-and-file soldiers when commanded by whites. As colonel of the first black regiment organized
under federal authority, Thomas Wentworth Higginson contended
that black character traits made them naturally good soldiers. "To learn
the drill, one does not want a set of college professors; one wants a
squad of eager, active, pliant school-boys; and the more childlike these
pupils are the better," Higginson argued. Blacks were actually superior
to white troops in aptitude for drill and discipline, he concluded, "because of their imitativeness and docility, and the pride they take in the
service." Other officers commanding black troops reported similar
findings, often to their own surprise. Lieutenant James G. Theaker of
Ohio served temporarily as a drill instructor for black recruits. "I have

28. William T. Pippey to B. Y. Pippey, February 26, 1863, in William T. Pippey Papers,
DU; William Patterson Diary, April 9–July 22, 1864, SHC; Mary A. Marshall to Henry
Marshall, April 29, 1863, Henry Marshall to Hattie, May 9, 1863, both in Henry Grimes
Marshall Papers, WLC.

got relieved of my '*nigger*' command, and right glad I am, too," he informed his sister. "But I must say that they learn the drill as fast as any soldiers, for they know nothing but pay attention and obey orders. They appear to become very much attached to their officers, will follow them anywhere & do anything for them & they will *fight*." Although dependence and obedience made blacks good soldiers, such qualities hardly recommended them as candidates for full citizenship. Thus northerners could admit that blacks compiled an admirable military record without conceding that they had earned equal rights as American citizens.[29]

Sparked by racial hostility, resentment against black troops became pervasive among white soldiers. This was the first time that most northerners, especially those from rural and western areas, had come into contact with large numbers of black people, and they bitterly disliked associating with them on anything approaching an equal basis. "We have seen several Negro Regiments here," wrote an Ohio officer serving on the South Carolina coast. "They make pretty good looking soldiers but our boys dont think much of them. They still say this is a *White Mans War*." Unionists who insisted that the war's single purpose was to defend the country against rebellion denied that blacks had any role to play. Not only would their presence in northern regiments alarm southerners and compel them to resist reconciliation, but it would subject patriotic volunteers to unpleasant contact with ignorant black brutes. "What do you think of your husbands serving with 'niggers' next door to him," asked one disgruntled Pennsylvania officer. " 'Nigger officers' & 'soldiers'!! Great God!, what are we coming to, and what will become of us," he despaired. From New Orleans a Union surgeon reported that General Groves had proclaimed "that he would not disgrace his white soldiers, by permitting them to fight by the side of Niggers."[30]

The prospect of associating with blacks horrified those soldiers who feared that military rank would encourage blacks to think of themselves as equal to whites. Captain Harrison Soule of Michigan observed that the "Nigger Regiments" were "perfectly disgusting to the

---

29. Higginson, *Army Life*, 10, 30; Rieger (ed.), *Through One Man's Eyes*, 66.
30. Oscar O. Winther (ed.), *With Sherman to the Sea: The Civil War Letters, Diaries and Reminiscences of Theodore F. Upson* (Baton Rouge, 1943), 149; John D. Wilkins to his wife, February 4, 1863, in John Darragh Wilkins Letters, WLC; Robert L. Smith to General Phelps, April 14, 1863, quoted in Foner, *Blacks and the Military*, 45.

Soldiers and the men wont do any duty with the niggers." Even officers had reason for concern, he explained. "For myself to meet in the streets of New Orleans a Nigger Captain of equal rank and be obliged by Regulations to raise my Hat to him and pay the compliments of the day is more than I can do and neither will I do it or recognize a Nigger soldier or officer." Enlisted men dreaded the possibility of being ordered about by a black officer and similarly protested that they would not recognize such authority. Somehow a report reached home that a New York regiment serving in South Carolina had been punished for improper discipline by having its weapons removed and being guarded by black soldiers. Private William Pedrick was indignant. "You did not think i hope that the 115[th regiment] would be guarded by Nigers," he wrote home; "no father i think they would kill them all if they Should Die the next minute." Although blacks were seldom, if ever, given command over white troops, insults and brawls became common whenever white and black regiments were stationed close to each other. Confronted by discrimination against his regiment of black soldiers, one white officer concluded, "We have got to *win* a respect from this majority of men prejudiced against color."[31]

Such prejudice pervaded Union ranks and largely determined official policy toward black regiments. The federal government organized black soldiers into segregated units, prohibited them from becoming commissioned officers, provided them with inadequate medical and hospital care, issued them inferior arms and equipment, relegated them in most cases to fatigue duty and noncombat roles, and paid them less than white soldiers. The last point was perhaps the most troubling. "Are we *Soldiers*, or are we LABOURERS," Corporal James Henry Gooding, serving in South Carolina with a Massachusetts black regiment, asked President Lincoln in a September, 1863, letter. "We have done a Soldiers Duty. Why cant we have a Soldiers pay?" Black privates received only seven dollars per month, compared to thirteen dollars for white privates. To the objections of Frederick Douglass and others, Lincoln argued that unequal pay "seemed a necessary concession to smooth the way to their employment at all as soldiers" and urged blacks to join the service under the available conditions. Not until June,

31. Harrison Soule to his wife, April 5, 1865, in Soule Papers; William Pedrick to his parents, March 11, 1863, in Benjamin Pedrick Papers, DU; Henry G. Marshall to Hattie, March 26, 1984, in Marshall Papers.

1864, did Congress approve a pay equalization bill for black soldiers. Faced with discrimination and prejudice, blacks would have to compile an exceptional military record if they were to achieve recognition of their claims to citizenship. They did so splendidly.[32]

The battle record of black troops would be closely scrutinized to determine whether they possessed sufficient courage and determination to prove themselves men. Frederick Douglass proclaimed that military service would open the door of opportunity. "Once let the black man get upon his person the brass letters, U.S.; let him get an eagle on his button, and a musket on his shoulder and bullets in his pocket," Douglass wrote in April, 1863, "and there is no power on earth which can deny that he has earned the right to citizenship in the United States." Both friends and foes watched for signs of black weakness. "Loyal whites have generally become willing that they should fight, but the great majority have no faith that they will really do so," the New York *Tribune* declared in May, 1863. "Many hope they will prove cowards and sneaks—others greatly fear it." Nearly all could agree with General Daniel Ullman that black soldiers should be given "a fair chance." By their actions, blacks would determine their own fate. Their success or failure would shape their future position in American society.[33]

After reluctantly allowing "Sambo" the opportunity to fight and die, northerners watched carefully to see how blacks measured up as soldiers, particularly on the battlefield, where their courage, self-reliance, and manhood would be severely tested. Most observers reported favorably on their fighting abilities. "The collered Soldiers are giving a good account of them selves here," New Hampshire private Oren E. Farr wrote during the siege of Port Hudson, a Confederate stronghold on the lower Mississippi, in 1863, "and are growing in favor with evry true patriot they are brave and bare up first rate under their wounds for they have los[t] hevily." During the assault against Port Hudson, black troops equaled or surpassed the record of their white comrades, according to most reports. "A negro Regiment of 900 charged on a battery under a fire of grape and canister, took it and were unable to hold it because not supported by their support, a white Regiment," Sergeant

32. James H. Gooding to President Lincoln, September 28, 1863, in Berlin, Reidy, and Rowland (eds.), *Black Military Experience*, 385–86; Cornish, *Sable Arm*, 189.

33. Douglass quoted in Litwack, *Been in the Storm So Long*, 72; New York *Tribune* quoted in McPherson, *Struggle for Equality*, 211; Daniel Ullman to Henry Wilson, December 4, 1863, in Berlin, Reidy, and Rowland (eds.), *Black Military Experience*, 496.

Nathan Webb of Maine reported. "If I was a soldier in that Regiment, or Army even, I should ever after be ashamed to rail at a black soldier." The courage displayed by black troops convinced many who had been skeptical of their abilities. "I never believed in niggers before," a Wisconsin cavalry officer confessed, "but by Jasus, they are hell in fighting."[34]

Port Hudson was the first of three major engagements during the summer of 1863 in which black soldiers proved their ability to fight. On May 27, 1863, two regiments of New Orleans free blacks and Louisiana former slaves participated in this assault on almost impregnable Confederate fortifications. The attack failed, but black soldiers fought heroically, advancing over open ground in the face of deadly artillery fire. In his official report of the battle, General Nathaniel P. Banks concluded that "the Government will find in this class of troops effective supporters and defenders." "Let no one speak against the colored soldiers," Massachusetts private Henry M. Cross declared. "They have mingled their blood with ours on the battlefield. They have done some of the best fighting of the campaign and have lost fearfully." One white officer wrote, "You have no idea how my prejudices with regard to negro troops have been dispelled by the battle the other day." He reported that the "brigade of negroes behaved magnificently and fought splendidly" and concluded that they were "far superior in dicipline to the white troops, and just as brave."[35]

Subsequent battles provided further proof of blacks' fighting ability. In bloody hand-to-hand combat at Milliken's Bend, Louisiana, on June 7, 1863, black soldiers helped repulse a fierce Confederate assault. They won high praise for their courage and determination. "I never more wish to hear the expression, 'the niggers won't fight,'" Captain M. M. Miller of the 9th Regiment of Louisiana Volunteers of African Descent wrote to his aunt in Galena, Illinois. "I can say for them that I never saw a braver company of men in my life." Once again white soldiers acknowledged the fighting ability of blacks. "The bravery of the blacks at Milliken's Bend," observed Assistant Secretary of War Charles A. Dana, "completely revolutionized the sentiment of the army with re-

    34. Oren E. Farr to his wife, June 1, 1863, in Oren E. Farr Papers, DU; Webb Diary, June 6, 1863; Litwack, *Been in the Storm So Long*, 101.
    35. Nathaniel Banks to Henry W. Halleck, May 30, 1863, in McPherson (ed.), *Negro's Civil War*, 185; Cross, "A Yankee Soldier Looks at the Negro," 146. See also Edward Cunningham, *The Port Hudson Campaign, 1862–1863* (Baton Rouge, 1963).

gard to the employment of Negro troops." Under the leadership of Colonel Robert Gould Shaw, abolitionist and Harvard graduate, whose death at the head of his troops made him a popular hero, black soldiers fought gallantly in an unsuccessful assault against Fort Wagner, which guarded the entrance to Charleston harbor. On July 18, 1863, the 54th Massachusetts charged over the ramparts of Fort Wagner. When white regiments did not arrive in time to support the assault, the black troops had to withdraw, suffering high casualties. After Fort Wagner it was impossible to claim that blacks could not fight heroically. "It made Fort Wagner such a name to the colored race as Bunker Hill has been for ninety years to the White Yankees," the New York *Tribune* proclaimed in 1865. There would be other engagements in which black soldiers added to their record of heroism, such as their tragic charge during the Battle of the Crater near Petersburg and the Battle of Nashville, in which eight black regiments contributed to a decisive Union victory, but by July, 1863, black troops had passed the crucial test. They had proved they could fight bravely.[36]

Black soldiers felt pride in their record, and their new confidence became increasingly apparent. Edgar Dinsmore, an educated free black from Connecticut, who served in Colonel Shaw's 54th Massachusetts Regiment, boasted: "When Rebellion is crushed who will be more proud than *i* to say, 'I was one of the first of the despised race to leave the free North with rifle on my shoulder, and give the lie to the old story that the black man will not fight,' and now that he will fight no one dare deny." Wisconsin private Harvey Reid reported in September, 1863, that many blacks from Tennessee were enlisting in the army. "I have been surpised at the difference it makes in their appearance, they appear so much more independent and manly," he wrote. "They seem to consider the fact of their being *soldiers* to place them almost on an equality with whites." Even northerners who detested blacks recognized the enhanced status their military service had won for them. After watching the first black regiment from New York march through the city on its way to the front, New York Democrat Maria L. Daly commented, "Though I am very little Negrophilish and would always prefer the commonest white that lives to a Negro, still I could not but feel moved." The black soldiers' appearance surprised her. "They were

---

36. McPherson (ed.), *Negro's Civil War*, 186–87, 191, 223–39; Wiley, *Southern Negroes*, 329–33.

a fine body of men and had a look of satisfaction in their faces, as though they felt they had gained a right to be more respected," she observed.[37]

Black soldiers had finally won from northern whites a certain measure of honor for their race. It was their gallantry in battle, fighting both to defend the Union and to gain their own freedom, which brought about this change. Private Constant Hanks, a New York Republican, described the deprivations blacks had endured as slaves: "Yet in spite of all this, this same despised race are to day, by the 100,000, armed & fighting both for the defence of the Union, the maintenance of the Government against treason, & are now recognized as *men*, having rights, having proved their title to *manhood* on many a bloody field fighting freedoms battles." James T. Ayers, an Illinois recruiter of blacks, concluded in September, 1864, "Give the nigger his Liberty and A chance in the main they will do well allmost in Every Case." One of those who had to be convinced that blacks deserved to be free was Colonel David Strother, a Virginia Yankee. Early in 1862, Strother had predicted that all efforts to make soldiers of blacks would fail dismally. Their military record changed his opinion. "In this great war even the nigger has justified himself," he wrote in November, 1864. "He has exhibited himself above the barbarism of a servile insurrection and as a soldier has deported himself with a decency and discretion not inferior to the best class of whites, while in the field he has proved himself a man." Most northerners eventually came to share Strother's conclusion. Blacks had proven their manhood on southern battlefields. "Till the blacks were armed, there was no guaranty of their freedom," Colonel Thomas Wentworth Higginson reflected in 1869. "It was their demeanor under arms that shamed the nation into recognizing them as men."[38]

Overcoming prejudice and discrimination, black soldiers conducted themselves in combat "just as well and as badly as the rest," observed one white officer who had earlier warned that using blacks as soldiers would be a serious blunder. Approximately 180,000 black soldiers served in the Union army. Despite delays in accepting black recruits,

37. Edgar Dinsmore to Carrie Drayton, February 1, 1865, in Edgar Dinsmore Papers, DU; Byrne (ed.), *View from Headquarters*, 90; Daly, *Diary of a Union Lady*, 278.
38. Constant Hanks to his sister Mary Rose, December 4, 1864, in Constant C. Hanks Papers, DU; Franklin (ed.), *Diary of James T. Ayers*, 49–50; Strother Diary, November 10, 1864; Higginson, *Army Life*, 267.

they represented nearly 10 percent of all Union soldiers. Blacks suffered an astounding 68,178 casualties—more than one-third of all enlistees—including 2,751 killed in action. No one could doubt their willingness to fight and die for their freedom. Blacks provided manpower which the Union desperately needed. "This army would be like a one-handed man, without niggers," Massachusetts private Henry M. Cross wrote shortly after the assault on Port Hudson. Their conduct convinced even those imbued with racial hatred that they deserved greater respect and rewards. Far from being passive observers, blacks had played an important part in preserving the Union and liberating their people. Their role in the war increased blacks' racial pride, gave them new heroes and leaders, and earned them a right to fuller participation in American society. It also led many whites to reevaluate their racial prejudices.[39]

Charles Wills of Illinois mirrored the northern reassessment of black character. The conduct of black soldiers and the war's inexorable logic converted Wills from a virulent racist to a grudging admirer of "poor Sambo." "I don't care a damn for the darkies," Wills declared in April, 1862. As a lieutenant in the 7th Illinois Cavalry serving in Missouri and Mississippi, Wills observed the slaves who flocked to Union lines seeking freedom. Like many other officers, he appropriated a "pet negro" as a servant but soon concluded that he was "lazy and worthless" and sent him away. "You have no idea what a miserable, horrible-looking, degraded set of brutes these plantation hands are," he wrote to his sister in August, 1862. "The most savage, copper savage, cannot be below these field hands in any brute quality." Wills was concerned less with the evils of slavery or the sufferings of black plantation hands than with the potential impact of black migration on the North. "Let them keep their negroes," he concluded, "for we surely don't want our northern States degraded by them."[40]

Although Wills disliked slavery, he hated the prospect of associating with blacks. "This matter of slavery is an awful sin and I'm satisfied debases the governing race," he declared, "but if we have to keep these negroes in the country, I say keep them as slaves. Take them from secesh and turn them over to Unionists, but don't free them in Amer-

39. Litwack, *Been in the Storm So Long*, 99–103; Cornish, *Sable Arm*, 288; Cross, "A Yankee Soldier Looks at the Negro," 147; Berlin, Reidy, and Rowland (eds.), *Black Military Experience*, 27–28; Wiley, *Southern Negroes*, 315, 338–41.

40. Wills, *Army Life*, 83–123, 127.

ica." Slavery was necessary, Wills believed, to protect and discipline blacks, who "don't average the ability of eight-year-old white children in taking care of themselves." Slavery would also keep blacks in the South. "There were several gangs of negroes at work in the corn and cotton fields along the road yesterday, and I thanked God they were not in Illinois," he admitted. "Candidly, I'd rather see them and a whole crop of grindstones dumped into the Gulf, than have so many of them in our State, as there are even here."[41]

Despite such racial hatred, Charles Wills gradually altered his opinion of black soldiers. "We are all rejoicing that 'Abe' refuses to accept the negroes as soldiers," he wrote in August, 1862, after Lincoln revoked General Hunter's order for recruiting slaves. He announced that efforts to arm blacks would create "immense disaffection" in the army and would lead hundreds of officers to resign. Blacks could not be counted on as soldiers, he argued, "for a million of them aren't worth 100 whites." By 1863, Wills had begun to change his mind. During the fall of 1862, he had raised a new company of recruits in Illinois and won election as captain in the 103rd Illinois, serving in Tennessee. Although convinced that most blacks could not care for themselves as freedmen, he recognized that there were some exceptions. The Union should "arm all the latter and make them fight Rebels," he told his sister in March, 1863. "They will probably be fit for freedom after a few years as soldiers." Two months later he admitted that his views had changed considerably since the previous year. "I am by no means an enthusiast over the negro soldiers yet," he wrote. "I would rather fight the war out than arming them." Yet he declared that he would not "set up my voice against what our President says or does." He even complained about the quality of officers selected to lead black regiments. "I think poor Sambo should be allowed a fair chance and that he will certainly never get under worthless officers," he told his sister.[42]

By June, 1863, Charles Wills's conversion was complete. He had visited "the negro camps" frequently and closely observed black soldiers. "I never thought I would, but I am getting strongly in favor of arming them, and am becoming so blind that I can't see why they will not make good soldiers," he confessed. "A year ago last January I didn't like to hear anything of emancipation. Last fall accepted confiscation of Rebel's negroes quietly. In January took to emancipation readily, and now believe in arming the negroes." His only objection, he told his

41. *Ibid.*, 166–67, 106.
42. *Ibid.*, 125–27, 166–67.

sister, was a matter of personal pride. "I almost think of applying for a position in a regiment myself." Charles Wills thus typified the change in racial attitudes shared by many of his fellow Yankees. The record of black troops had earned for their race a right to expanded opportunity and to a grudging respect from their white fellow citizens in the North.[43]

FIGHTING AGAINST THEIR MASTERS

The southern response to black soldiers provides an instructive counterpoint to northern attitudes. Southerners were outraged by the presence of black troops in armies invading their sacred soil. They regarded being forced to fight against this degraded race as a humiliation deliberately inflicted by northern leaders who understood that their gentlemanly pride counted it a disgrace to enter a contest with any but one's social equals. "One of the most disgusting features in this war is the fact that negro soldiers are brought into the field against us," exclaimed Private Charles W. Hutson, a South Carolina aristocrat, who claimed that there were many blacks among prisoners captured at the first Battle of Manassas in 1861. Upon hearing that black troops had fought for the North at Milliken's Bend in 1863, Sarah Wadley, the nineteen-year-old daughter of a Louisiana railroad contractor, recoiled in disgust. "It is terrible to think of such a battle as this, white men and freemen fighting with their slaves, and to be killed by such a hand, the very soul revolts from it." Kate Stone, whose family owned 1,260 acres and 150 slaves, was similarly incensed by the black northern troops sent to raid villages and plantations near her home in Madison Parish, Louisiana. "The Yankees know they make it ten times worse for us by sending Negroes to commit these atrocities," she complained. "The Paternal Government at Washington has done all in its power to incite a general insurrection throughout the South, in the hopes of thus getting rid of the women and children in one grand holocaust." Kate Stone had reason to fear a slave revolt. Madison Parish in 1859 counted a population of 11,156, of which 9,863 were slaves.[44]

Most southerners viewed the use of black troops as a thinly veiled

43. *Ibid.*, 183–84. For other statements that black soldiers' actions reversed white prejudice see Pearson (ed.), *Letters from Port Royal*, 104; and Lorenzo Thomas to Edwin M. Stanton, November 7, 1864, in Berlin, Reidy, and Rowland (eds.), *Black Military Experience*, 171.

44. Charles W. Hutson to his mother, July 26, 1861, in Charles Woodward Hutson Papers, SHC; Sarah Wadley Diary, June 9, 1863, SHC; Anderson (ed.), *Brokenburn*, 297–98.

attempt to incite slave insurrections. Hearing a rumor that the United
States Congress had passed a bill to enlist 150,000 black soldiers, Captain Edward Guerrant, a former Kentucky schoolteacher, who after the
war became an evangelist and doctor, decried the North's intention to
send blacks "to wreak their diabolical revenge upon Southern homes."
Similarly, Ella Thomas, wife of a wealthy Georgia planter, wrote that
"this attempt to arouse the vindictive passions of an inferior race so fills
my soul with horror language fails to describe it." This dreaded prospect was depicted in even more graphic detail by Sergeant William R.
Clark of North Carolina. He wrote in March, 1864, that the South had
witnessed scenes that should inspire the wrath of all patriots against
their brutal enemies:

> To see the slaves of our Sunny South in arms against us, and see them go
> with arms in hand and threaten the lives of our fair ladies, if they spoke an
> insulting word to them, and order the wives and sisters of many of our
> brother soldiers to give them something to eat and not say a word; take
> their rings and the furniture from their houses and send it north; yes, I
> have seen our soldiers wives stripped of every thing in their houses and
> left to the mercy of those black brutal negroes; and is this not enough to
> rouse the hearts of all true southern men? Who is it would not rather have
> his lady laid in a soldier's grave as left on some bloody battle field, than to
> lay in the arms of such a brutal people.

The intense passion behind such declarations indicated that northern
employment of black soldiers had touched a raw nerve in southern
feelings. The fury of these responses portended doom for blacks captured in battle.[45]

Many Confederate soldiers proclaimed that they would offer no
quarter to black troops opposing them and that the sight of blacks in
Yankee uniforms would give them added incentive to fight to the
death. "If you ever want to see your son put up one of your old fashion
Bull Dog fights just let him come in contact with a negro Regiment,"
vowed Private William H. Phillips of Virginia. "I intend to fight them
untill I am as bloody as a Butcher." Lieutenant Edmund Patterson, an
Ohio native, who moved to Alabama in 1859 and enlisted in the Confederate army shortly after Fort Sumter, thought that no truce would be
honored in conflicts between black and white troops. "If the Yankee

45. Edward O. Guerrant Diary, February 13, 1863, in Edward Owings Guerrant Papers, SHC; Ella Gertrude (Clanton) Thomas Diary, November 10, 1861, DU; William R.
Clark to Ellen Lockhart, March 18, 1864, in Hugh Conway Browning Papers, DU.

government will persist in arming the negroes of the South and sending them against us, I believe it will amount to the 'Black Flag,'" he foresaw. "One thing I think is very certain and that is that the army in Virginia will not take negro prisoners." Other Confederates echoed Patterson's prediction. Anticipating a fight against black troops, North Carolina private Jonathan F. Coghill stated that "they will see hard times for they will howl but it will do no good for them to surrender to our boys." Returning to Kentucky during General John Hunt Morgan's raid in June, 1864, Edward Guerrant told the family slaves that "our soldiers would certainly kill them" if they were caught in the Yankee army. Guerrant concluded that southerners "would not tolerate their taking up arms against us."[46]

All too often, such threats were carried out. The most celebrated case of Confederates murdering black soldiers was the massacre at Fort Pillow on April 12, 1864. Following the Confederate capture of Fort Pillow, a Union outpost on the Mississippi River in Tennessee, approximately three hundred of its black defenders were murdered after they had surrendered. "Damn you, you are fighting against your master," one Rebel exclaimed as he shot a black soldier. Six days later, Confederates executed several black prisoners after the battle at Poison Spring, Arkansas, and then drove captured Union wagons back and forth over the bodies of wounded blacks. Such atrocities followed official Confederate proclamations, such as that of President Jefferson Davis in December, 1862, that black soldiers and their white officers would be subject to punishment under the laws of each state as instigators of servile insurrection. This could only mean the death penalty, which the Confederate Congress officially prescribed in April, 1863. Civil law offered justification for what southern soldiers in any case had determined to do. In the heat of battle, punishment of blacks came swiftly and indiscriminately.[47]

The testimony of numerous Confederate soldiers and civilians reveals that black soldiers captured in battle were often summarily executed. At the Battle of the Crater in 1864, black troops leading the

46. William H. Phillips to his parents, January 15, 1864, in William Horace Phillips Papers, DU; Barrett (ed.), *Yankee Rebel*, 128; J. F. Coghill to Pappa Ma and Mit, March 4, 1864, in James O. Coghill Papers, DU; Guerrant Diary, June 8, 1864.
47. Cornish, *Sable Arm*, 158–68, 176–77; McPherson (ed.), *Negro's Civil War*, 216–22; John Cimprich and Robert C. Mainfort (eds.), "Fort Pillow Revisited; New Evidence About an Old Controversy," *Civil War History*, XXVIII (December, 1982), 293–306.

Union assault became trapped in a pit created by the explosion of a mine under Confederate fortifications. Here they encountered a murderous crossfire from Confederate soldiers at the crater's rim. Shortly after the battle, North Carolina private Henry Biggs, son of a former United States senator, described the carnage. "It is reported that Genl. Mahone grew sick of the slaughter going on and begged his men to stop killing the negroes, and I suppose on the strength of that they captured 150 negroes," he wrote. Biggs added, "I should not have taken any of them especially after they shouted 'No quarter' which they did when they mounted the breastworks." After the battle another soldier reported that all black prisoners "would have been killed had it not been for gen Mahone who beg our men to Spare them." One of his comrades killed several blacks before General William Mahone "told him for God's sake stop." He replied, "Well gen let me kill one more," whereupon "he deliberately took out his pocket knife and cut one's throat." According to Sergeant Thomas Roulhac of North Carolina, a similar slaughter of black troops occurred during a battle at Suffolk, Virginia, in March, 1864. "We took Suffolk a few days ago & got into a fight with a negro Regiment, several of them were killed, several taken prisoner & afterwards either bayoneted or burnt," he reported; "the men were perfectly exasperated at the idea of negroes opposed to them & rushed at them like so many devils." Despite his own testimony that his comrades had fought more fiercely than usual, Roulhac concluded that "the negroes could not stand the music of bullets & their presence in an army would prove more of an incumbrance than otherwise."[48]

In addition to these instances of black soldiers massacred amid the confusion of major battles, there were reports of individual blacks wantonly killed during minor engagements. Black troops fought a skirmish with Confederates not far from the home of Samuel Agnew, a Reformed Presbyterian minister in Tippah County, Mississippi. After watching Yankee prisoners, most of them white, pass along the road under guard, Agnew reported: "The most of the negroes were shot, our men being so much incensed that they shoot them wherever they see them. It is certain that a great many negroes have been killed."

48. Henry Biggs to his sister, August 3, 1864, in Asa Biggs Papers, DU; W. C. McClellan, quoted in Bell Irvin Wiley, *The Life of Johnny Reb: The Common Soldier of the Confederacy* (Indianapolis, 1943), 314–15; Thomas R. Roulhac to his mother, March 13, 1864, in Ruffin, Roulhac and Hamilton Family Papers, SHC.

Occasionally, a former slave who had enlisted in the Union army was captured. Rebecca Davis of North Carolina reported one such instance: "Several persons say they saw Mary Newell's Alfred at Plymouth. They say he begged to be sent to his mother, but was shot, as all negroes were who were dressed in Yankee uniforms, *so I have heard.*" Alfred's having turned against his former benefactor probably sealed his fate. Such treachery on the part of formerly trusted servants enraged many southerners and deafened them to cries for mercy.[49]

Southerners reacted angrily to northern employment of black troops because they perceived the profound implications of this issue for their society. Memories of John Brown's abortive attack alarmed southerners who watched blue-uniformed blacks invade their homeland. They charged that the North sought conquest by inciting insurrection among their heretofore loyal servants. Even those who did not fear slave revolts believed that use of black troops was intended to humiliate southerners by forcing them to fight their erstwhile slaves on the field of honor. Yet these accusations cannot explain fully the violent fury of southern reactions. Southerners recognized that black soldiers who conducted themselves well in combat would disprove assertions about their race's inferiority and dependency. Once these beliefs were shattered, not only would blacks have to be granted legal rights in the North, but slavery itself would be doomed. No longer could southerners assert that slavery was necessary to protect blacks or claim to be benefactors of a helpless race. This threat to their self-image as noble guardians instinctively prompted them to retaliate against the symbols of their vulnerability. By defeating black regiments in battle, Confederates sought to prove that blacks could not stand up to white troops. By taking no prisoners they hoped to deter other blacks from fighting for their freedom. Neither purpose succeeded.

Outraged by their former slaves' disloyalty, many southerners perceived black enlistment in the Yankee army as the ultimate betrayal of the benevolences they had bestowed on their black charges. Blacks had incurred an obligation to be grateful, they believed, and evidence of disloyalty therefore justified severe punishment. Not only had black soldiers deserted their masters at a time of great danger, but they had turned against them as enemies in battle. This further dispelled the

---

49. Samuel Agnew Diary, June 13, 1864, SHC; Rebecca P. Davis to Burwell Davis, May 9, 1864, in Rebecca P. Davis Papers (typescript in possession of May Davis Hill).

southern illusion that blacks shared the paternalistic assumptions of their white masters.[50]

Once the clamor of outrage subsided, southerners were anxious to discover how well blacks performed in battle. The Battle of Milliken's Bend provided one of the first tests of black courage under fire, and southerners eagerly discussed reports of the battle. "It is said that the Yankees at the first onset left their allies and fled but the negroes fought desperately, and would not give up until our men clubbed muskets upon them," Sarah Wadley reported. Yet her fellow Louisianan Kate Stone refused to believe that blacks could fight so well. "It is said the Negro regiments fought there like mad demons, but we cannot believe that. We know from long experience they are cowards," she insisted. Her reluctance to accept information contradicting her preconceptions reveals the tenacity with which many southerners clung to long cherished beliefs about black character. The conduct of black troops in battle elicited both favorable and critical reports. Following the conflict at Milliken's Bend, Lieutenant Theophilus Perry of Texas wrote: "The negroes are said by many to have stood the bayonet charge bravely, and returned it with more daring and obstinacy than the whites. On the other hand it is said that they did not stand fire well." He concluded philosophically, "Both reports are probably true; and thus it is probable that they fought better in some places than others."[51]

Although scattered evidence of black soldiers' ineffectiveness seemed to confirm southern beliefs that they were unsuited for military service, reports of their courage under fire led some southerners to contemplate them as potential assets for the Confederate cause. Not until the end of 1864, when military reverses and dwindling resources of men and matériel began to foreshadow defeat, did Confederate authorities seriously consider enlisting black regiments. The prospect of defeat made any measure acceptable. "If I were convinced that we will be subjugated, with the long train of horrors that will follow it, unless the negroes be placed in the army, I would not hesitate to enrol our slaves and put them to fighting," Georgia Congressman Warren Akin confided to a close friend. "Subjugation will give us free negroes

50. See Eugene D. Genovese, *Roll, Jordan, Roll: The World the Slaves Made* (New York, 1974), 97–102, for an excellent analysis of southerners' sense of betrayal when blacks proved unfaithful, and pages 144–47 for an analysis of their charge of ingratitude against blacks.

51. Wadley Diary, June 9, 1863; Anderson (ed.), *Brokenburn*, 219; Theophilus Perry to Harriet Perry, June 11, 1863, in Presley Carter Person Papers, DU.

in abundance—enemies at that—while white slaves will be more numerous than free negroes. We and our children will be slaves, while our freed negroes will lord it over us." Akin's wife also feared that defeat would place southern whites at the mercy of a black majority. "I think slavery is now gone and what little there is left of it should be rendered as serviceable as possible," Mary F. Akin wrote in January, 1865, "and for that reason the negro man ought to be put to fighting and where some of them will be killed, if it is not done there will soon be more negroes than whites in the country and they will be the free race."[52]

Like their northern counterparts, some southern whites finally decided that Sambo should share the burden of fighting and dying. By November, 1864, President Davis had approved employment of slaves as soldiers, rather than risk subjugation, but opposition in Congress delayed implementing legislation until March 20, 1865. General Lee's recommendation that blacks should be armed as a matter of dire military necessity convinced Congress and many southerners to accept this drastic measure. They recognized, like Mary Akin, that this would mean the end of slavery because blacks who had served as soldiers could not be reenslaved. Yet arming blacks seemed the Confederacy's last hope. While Congress debated the proposal, Alexander Cheves Haskell, son of a South Carolina planter, declared, "I feel sure of seeing it yet done, and in this think that I recognize the principal element of our success."[53]

Few of Haskell's comrades were so sanguine about the benefits of drafting slaves. The testimony of soldiers and civilians reveals that the leading advocates were slaveowners who perceived it as a compromise necessary to sustain the remnants of slavery. To perpetuate the Confederacy, which alone could preserve their social system, many slaveowners were willing to offer freedom to bondsmen who fought for the South. Others, however, protested, arguing that any compromise of the system would lead to its demise. Nonslaveowners, on the other hand, overwhelmingly opposed all efforts to enlist black soldiers. Many enlisted men either feared that arming slaves would elevate the

52. Wiley (ed.), *Letters of Warren Akin*, 32–33, 117.
53. Louise Haskell Daly, *Alexander Cheves Haskell: The Portrait of a Man* (Norwood, Mass., 1934), 163. For a discussion of Confederate policy regarding black troops, see Robert F. Durden (ed.), *The Gray and the Black: The Confederate Debate on Emancipation* (Baton Rouge, 1972); and Bill G. Reid, "Confederate Opponents of Arming the Slaves," *Journal of Mississippi History*, XXII (October, 1960), 249–70.

blacks' social level or doubted whether blacks would actually fight for the Confederacy. As Corporal Daniel Boyd of North Carolina wrote, "i hear that they ar puting the negras in the army it wont do to put them with the white men for they wont stand it. We are nie enough on a equality with them now." Private William Phillips wrote to his father, a Virginia overseer, that the Confederacy could not survive much longer. "This bringing the Negroes in the army is certainly going to ruin us if nothing else dont," he concluded, "for they are going to fight and in six months after they are brought on the field there will be more of them in the woods all mixed up with white men than you ever see in your life."[54]

Some perceptive southerners recognized the hopeless contradiction of enlisting slaves. Ella Thomas thought that the proposal betrayed the weakness of Confederate forces and that blacks would not willingly assume the risk of combat. On November 17, 1864, she wrote in her diary: "I take a womans view of the subject, but it does seem strangely inconsistent the idea of offering to a Negro the rich boon—the priceless reward of freedom to aid us in keeping in bondage a large portion of his brethren when by joining the Yankees he will *instantly* gain the very reward which Mr. Davis offers to him after a certain amount of labor rendered and danger incurred." The Richmond *Examiner* exposed this fundamental contradiction between President Jefferson Davis' proposal to free slave soldiers and theoretical justifications of slavery. "According to his message it is a rich reward for faithful services to turn a Negro wild. Slavery, then, in the eyes of Mr. Davis, keeps the Negro out of something which he has the capacity to enjoy," the *Examiner* argued. "If the case be so, then slavery is originally, radically, incurably wrong and sinful, and the sum of barbarism." Howell Cobb pointed out a further contradiction. "You cannot make soldiers of slaves, nor slaves of soldiers," he insisted. "The day you make soldiers of them is the beginning of the end of the revolution. If slaves make good soldiers, our whole theory of slavery is wrong—but they won't make soldiers." Such inconsistencies and the dismal military situation that made it necessary to endure them brought despair to many loyal Confederates. The support some southern leaders gave to black enlistment demonstrated that their commitment to Confederate nationalism ex-

---

54. Daniel Boyd to his father, March 29, 1865, in Robert Boyd Papers, DU; William H. Phillips to his father, March 25, 1865, in Phillips Papers.

ceeded their dedication to slavery. Yet this remained a minority view. Slavery would not be sacrificed to gain independence. The effort to enlist slaves seemed a hopeless, desperate gamble. Listening to arguments for and against black enlistment and eventual emancipation, Arthur Grimball, son of a prominent South Carolina planter, feared that the end was drawing near. "We are like drowning men catching at a straw," he lamented. The desperation that finally drove the South to enlist slaves as recruits for its depleted military ranks occurred too late. The Confederate government officially began to recruit and train black soldiers only twenty days before Lee surrendered at Appomattox. None of them, apparently, ever fought for the South.[55]

THE HABIT OF INJUSTICE

Colonel Thomas Wentworth Higginson, the Boston Brahmin who commanded the first officially sanctioned black regiment, expressed confidence in the capabilities of his black troops and optimism that their military record would earn the respect of all Union-loving men. On the question of amelioration of racial prejudice, however, he soon became pessimistic. "After the experience of Hungary, one sees that revolutions may go backward," Higginson wrote in January, 1863, "and the habit of injustice seems so deeply impressed upon the whites, that it is hard to believe in the possibility of anything better."[56] Although black actions during the war altered both northern and southern judgments of black character, the habit of injustice which Higginson decried continued to shape white attitudes. Prejudice prevailed.

White views of the proper role for blacks in American society provided an inauspicious starting point for the testing of black character during the war. Southerners thought that blacks' ignorance, dependency, and subserviency consigned them forever to slavery. Lacking qualities necessary for success or even survival in a world of dangers and temptations, blacks needed guidance and control, they insisted, which only white masters could provide. Northerners found blacks

55. Thomas Diary, November 17, 1864; Richmond *Examiner* quoted in Genovese, *Roll, Jordan, Roll*, 129; Howell Cobb to James A. Seddon, January 8, 1865, in Durden (ed.), *The Gray and the Black*, 184; Arthur Grimball to his father, December 31, 1864, in Grimball Family Papers, SHC. See also Clarence L. Mohr, *On the Threshold of Freedom: Masters and Slaves in Civil War Georgia* (Athens, Ga., 1986), 275; and Richard E. Beringer, Herman Hattaway, Archer Jones, and William N. Still, Jr., *Why the South Lost the Civil War* (Athens, Ga., 1986), 368–97.

56. Higginson, *Army Life*, 47.

inferior, "brutal," and repugnant. They, too, believed that whites must retain control over all aspects of society, but instead of including blacks as a laboring class in frequent contact with their superiors, northern whites proposed to keep them at a distance. Rather than being an integral, though subordinate, component of society, as in the South, blacks would be excluded from northern society. Whereas southern whites clearly defined the boundaries of interracial contact, northerners sought to avoid the issue by precluding close interaction.

The war changed the legal and political status of blacks, but not their social position. Black contributions to the Union's war effort led directly to the permanent abolition of slavery, to citizenship and civil rights, and to the ballot box. The Thirteenth, Fourteenth, and Fifteenth Amendments ensured legal recognition for changing blacks' status. Reconstruction at first promised improved conditions for blacks, but the Republican party's commitment to its own political base proved stronger than its commitment to black rights. Social equality never received serious consideration. Nevertheless, black soldiers had gained substantial changes in the role of blacks in society. "If we hadn't become sojers, all might have gone back as it was before; our freedom might have slipped through de two houses of Congress and President Linkum's four years might have passed by and notin been done for we," Corporal Thomas Long told his fellow black soldiers in March, 1864. "But now tings can never go back, because we have showed our energy and our courage and our naturally manhood." When the black soldier fought and killed, "the whole nation with one voice proclaimed him a man and a brother," black spokesman W. E. B. Du Bois wrote long after the war. "Nothing else made emancipation possible in the United States. Nothing else made Negro citizenship conceivable, but the record of the Negro soldier as a fighter." Through their wartime actions blacks had proven their manhood and established a strong claim to equality of treatment and opportunity. Unfortunately, this did not overcome white prejudice.[57]

Black actions during the war altered both northern and southern perceptions of black character but did not eliminate deeply entrenched biases. Because some slaves remained loyal while others ran away, southerners could not detect a clear pattern of black behavior. They

57. Thomas Long quoted in McPherson (ed.), *Negro's Civil War*, 213; W. E. B. Du Bois, *Black Reconstruction in America* (New York, 1935), 104; McPherson, *Struggle for Equality*, 219–20; Cornish, *Sable Arm*, 289–91; Litwack, *Been in the Storm So Long*, 72.

were forced to weigh contradictory evidence in reevaluating black character. The faithfulness exhibited by many slaves confirmed southerners' belief in their dependency, subservience, and contentment. Yet numerous desertions weakened bonds of affection and respect for black servants, creating bitterness and indignation. Some plantation families experienced only blacks' loyalty, others only desertion. Nevertheless, most southerners had direct knowledge both of slaves who fled to the Yankees and of those who remained as faithful servants. Both conditions were widespread. Bitterness or wishful thinking, however, could make either extreme seem the prevailing norm. Evidence of black disloyalty could not easily be ignored. Interracial intimacy and friendship, which southerners claimed plantation paternalism had fostered, thus gave way to antagonism and belief that black and white had become enemies. Blacks had rejected both slavery and their masters in the most conclusive manner—by deserting to the Yankees and by fighting against their masters as enemy soldiers. Opposition to Confederate enlistment of black soldiers expressed an abiding conviction that blacks were ignorant, dependent, and unreliable and that they could function responsibly only under white domination. Belief in white superiority endured.[58]

The war tempered northern racism but did not purge it. Slaves who left their masters seeking freedom within federal lines gained recognition as supporters of the Union and as true lovers of freedom. Those who remained faithful to their masters detracted from this image, but their loyalty could be explained as the result of coercion. Since Union soldiers met relatively few of the slaves who stayed on plantations, it was logical to conclude that the great majority had sought refuge within northern lines. Many soldiers longed to be praised as conquering heroes liberating a loyal population, and even those who had no objection to slavery enjoyed the accolades given by blacks, who constituted the largest pro-Union group in the South. This distinction increased most northerners' tolerance for blacks. Yet blacks' most significant claim for recognition lay in their military record. By performing their duties as soldiers and by fighting courageously in battle, blacks won respect and proved their manhood to a skeptical nation. Nevertheless, so deeply embedded were convictions about black incompetence and dependency that even their contributions toward winning

58. Genovese, *Roll, Jordan, Roll*, 103, 130; Willie Lee Rose, *Slavery and Freedom* (New York, 1982), 83–84.

the war could not erase northern prejudice. "Shall we place 'Pompey' on the same social and political level as ourselves?" New York private Constant Hanks, an antislavery Republican, asked rhetorically. "No for the simple reason that it would be an utter impossibility[;] we have ages of civilization the start of him, whilst he has a shell of prejudice of 300 years growth that must be picked off him before he could be placed on the level of the white race." An Indiana soldier stated the northern attitude even more succinctly. "The negro never was intended to be equal with the white man," Private Arthur Carpenter insisted, "if he was the Lord would have made him so, and not permitted him to have been under the white man." Equality for blacks would not be possible, nor would most northerners even entertain the idea. The United States would remain a white man's country.[59]

Although northern and southern views of black character had altered somewhat during the war, the changes did not ameliorate American racial attitudes. The experiment with black regiments was hedged with too many restrictions and did not last long enough to produce permanent alterations in northern prejudice. In keeping with its reluctant acceptance of emancipation, the North never made a firm commitment to continued guardianship of blacks. The three constitutional amendments provided a firm foundation for later gains, ensuring that inequality would always be contrary to the nation's highest law. The Republican party, however, soon abandoned the cause of black rights. In the South, estimations of black character declined as a result of black desertion and unfaithfulness. The Sambo image of docility had merely been modified. It was too deeply rooted in southern consciousness to be eliminated. Shorn of the genial influence of paternalism, southern racial attitudes offered little hope for those seeking signs of improvement in the conditions under which blacks labored.[60]

59. Constant Hanks to his sister, ca. April, 1864, Hanks Papers; Arthur B. Carpenter to his parents and brothers, August 19, 1862, in Civil War Manuscripts Collection, Yale; Voegeli, *Free But Not Equal*, 178–82.

60. Woodward, *American Counterpoint*, 140–83; George M. Fredrickson, *The Black Image in the White Mind: The Debate on Afro-American Character and Destiny, 1817–1914* (New York, 1971), 169; Phyllis F. Field, *The Politics of Race in New York: The Struggle for Black Suffrage in the Civil War Era* (Ithaca, 1982), 226–30; and C. Vann Woodward, *The Burden of Southern History* (rev. ed.; Baton Rouge, 1968), 89–107. On postwar southern racial attitudes, see Lawrence J. Friedman, *The White Savage: Racial Fantasies in the Postbellum South* (Englewood Cliffs, N.J., 1970); Joel Williamson, *After Slavery: The Negro in South Carolina During Reconstruction, 1861–1877* (Chapel Hill, 1965), 240–99; and Fredrickson, *Black Image*, 198–227.

These changes in northern and southern perceptions of blacks were often subtle, occasionally barely perceptible. They only slightly altered the basic pattern of prejudice and disdain. Those who like Colonel Higginson hoped that the war would create a revolution in racial prejudice learned to their dismay that revolutions could indeed go backward. There would be no sudden improvement in American attitudes toward black people. The habit of injustice proved too strong.

Writing Home, illustration by David Hunter Strother, a Virginia-born Union officer
From Cecil D. Eby, Jr. (ed.), A Virginia Yankee in the Civil War *(Chapel Hill: University of North Carolina Press, 1961)*

A group of runaway slaves who sought freedom in Union lines
Library of Congress

"Though Sambo's black as the ace of spades,
    His finger a thrigger can pull,
And his eye runs sthraight on the barrel-sights
    From undher its thatch of wool."
                    Charles G. Halpine, "Sambo's Right to Be Kilt"

Colonel Robert McAllister (later Brevet
Major General), 11th New Jersey Infantry
Library of Congress

Sarah Morgan of Baton Rouge, Louisiana
*From Sarah Morgan Dawson, A Confederate Girl's Diary,
ed. James I. Robertson, Jr. (Bloomington, 1960)*

Captain Charles W. Wills, 103rd Illinois
Infantry
*From Wills, Army Life of an Illinois Soldier
(Washington, D.C., 1906)*

Sergeant Nathan B. Webb, Co. D, 1st
Maine Cavalry
*From Edward P. Tobie, History of the First Maine Cavalry
(Boston, 1887)*

A cartoonist's depiction of northerners' changing perceptions of the "rebel chivalry"

Pickets Trading Between the Lines, drawing by Edwin Forbes
Library of Congress

Private John F. Brobst, in the uniform of
the 25th Wisconsin Infantry
From John F. Brobst, Well, Mary: Civil War Letters of a
Wisconsin Volunteer, *ed. Margaret B. Roth (Madison,
1960). Reproduced courtesy of Margaret Brobst Roth*

Captain William Thompson Lusk, 79th
New York Infantry
From William C. Lusk (ed.), War Letters of William
Thompson Lusk *(New York, 1911)*

Private Harry St. John Dixon, Co. D
(Washington Cavalry), 20th Mississippi
Harry St. John Dixon Papers, Southern Historical Collection

Eliza Frances Andrews of Washington,
Georgia, in 1865
From Eliza Frances Andrews, The War-Time Journal of a
Georgia Girl, 1864–1865, *ed. Spencer B. King, Jr. (Macon,
Ga., 1960)*

Sherman's "bummers," who plundered freely during the infamous march through Georgia in 1864, confirmed southern images of Yankees.

From George W. Nichols, The Story of the Great March (New York, 1865)

A dead Confederate soldier in the trenches of Fort Mahone, near Petersburg, April 3, 1865. "I don't want to know any more about war. I have seen horible sights men with heads blowed off and legs and armes off and shot through the body."

Library of Congress

5 / PERCEPTIONS OF THE ENEMY

We are misrepresented in *every respect*, our habits, mode of life, our opinions, our feelings in the papers of the north," Henry Watson of Alabama complained in March, 1861. "That section is as badly misrepresented & vilified & as little understood here." A native of Connecticut, educated at Harvard, Watson had taken his first job as a teacher in Alabama in 1831. He remained in the state, where he practiced law at Greensboro, accumulated a plantation and slaves, and established and directed the Planters' Insurance Company. A strong Whig and Unionist, he supported John Bell and Edward Everett in the 1860 presidential campaign but gave allegiance to the Confederacy after Alabama seceded in January, 1861. Watson used the metaphor of family to describe relations between North and South and concluded that if brothers and sisters could not reconcile their differences peacefully, it would be better for one party to leave than for them to continue quarreling under one roof. Separation would be preferable to continued antagonism.[1]

The war thus began amid sectional misunderstandings and prejudices. Northerners and southerners did not really know or understand each other, and the stereotypes with which each regarded the other served as counterimages in defining their own sectional identities. Moderates in both sections deplored the false accusations that prevented fraternal ties. "A *'generation* has been educated to hate *the South'* & most earnestly is the hate returned," lamented Lieutenant William M. Ferry, a Michigan Democrat, who had been a foreman for his father's lumber business before the war. "If there is joy in this, if there is true philanthropy, if there is love of Country I cant see it." Ferry proclaimed that he was "a Democrat—not a sectionalist—proud of his whole Country—with its varied internal differences but all protected by a Common Union." By the middle of 1861, however, few Americans could remain neutral. Even those who protested against the growth of

---

1. Henry Watson, Jr., to M. L. Filley, March 17, 1861, and letter fragment, January 27, 1861, in Henry Watson, Jr., Papers, DU. Fletcher M. Green has found that most northerners who became engaged in southern agriculture, like Henry Watson, accepted slavery and southern customs (*The Role of the Yankee in the Old South* [Athens, Ga., 1972], 109–22).

sectional hatred usually concluded that they must defend their own section's rights.[2]

The Civil War thus produced conflicting emotions regarding the enemy. As citizens of the same country, northerners and southerners shared a common political, social, and cultural heritage, and for many these ties were difficult to break. Past associations between the sections often seemed more pervasive than the factors dividing them, and many individuals denounced the war as unholy and fratricidal. Numerous instances of families being divided by the war, and bizarre incidents in which men discovered that in battle they had killed members of their own families, dramatically evoked the horror of a conflict that often literally pitted brother against brother. Hatred between brothers may be unnatural or tragic, but—perhaps for that very reason—it can be extremely vicious. Rejected affection and violated trust sting the pride and unleash a fury of rage whose intensity is often proportional to previous intimacy. The Civil War thus elicited a dual response. People on both sides depicted the enemy as the embodiment of evil and fervently expressed their hatred of the foe. Occasionally, however, they reasserted the bonds of brotherhood and expressed sympathy for misguided brothers similarly victimized by a cruel war.[3]

This chapter examines sectional consciousness through individual perceptions of the enemy. In describing the character of their opponents, northerners and southerners revealed both their sense of separateness and the personal values they cherished. Images of Yankee and Rebel served as objects of invidious comparison, by which each side confirmed its own superiority.[4] The chapter first examines these sec-

2. William M. Ferry to his wife, December 9, 1862, March 15, 1863, in Ferry Family Papers, MHC. For antebellum northern views of the South, see Eric Foner, *Free Soil, Free Labor, Free Men: The Ideology of the Republican Party Before the Civil War* (New York, 1970), 40–72; and Howard R. Floan, *The South in Northern Eyes, 1831 to 1861* (Austin, Tex., 1958). Southern views of the North are examined in John Hope Franklin, *A Southern Odyssey: Travelers in the Antebellum North* (Baton Rouge, 1976).

3. For examples of families whose loyalties were divided between Union and Confederacy see Cabell Tavenner and Alexander Scott Withers Papers, DU; Bedinger-Dandridge Family Papers, DU; Gordon Family Papers, SHC; and Barrett (ed.), *Yankee Rebel*. See also Bell Irvin Wiley, *The Life of Billy Yank: The Common Soldier of the Union* (Indianapolis, 1952), 80; and B. A. Botkin, ed., *A Civil War Treasury of Tales, Legends and Folklore* (New York, 1960), 83.

4. C. Vann Woodward, *American Counterpoint: Slavery and Racism in the North-South Dialogue* (Boston, 1971), 6; David H. Donald, *Liberty and Union* (Boston, 1978), 54–56. As William R. Taylor argues, sectional stereotypes also served at times to depict good qualities that seemed lacking in one's own society (*Cavalier and Yankee: The Old South and American National Character* [New York, 1961], 335).

tional stereotypes, which the war intensified, altered somewhat, but finally confirmed. Broad generalizations, however, often mask the complexity of human experience. The war was not fought by "the South" and "the North" but by individual men and women, who shared their section's political and ideological values in varying degrees and who had significantly different personal experiences. The variety of individual perceptions is presented here through six biographical sketches which show that personal experience sometimes changed the way people viewed sectional differences. A discussion of fraternization between soldiers of the two armies reveals both the sense of kinship that still united Americans and the limited effects of such ties in reducing war's fury. Finally, these personal experiences are placed within the broader context of sectional consciousness.

IMAGES OF YANKEE AND REBEL

"One great advantage which will be gained by the war is the distinction which will be made between the northerner and southerner," Ella Thomas, wife of a Georgia planter, wrote in her diary on the first day of 1862. "The Northern and Southern people are entirely different. They are moraly and socialy as well as politicaly the antipodes of each other. This war but makes the line of demarcation broader." Freed from association with the North, southern character would be recognized for its superiority, she believed. Secession had redefined national character by drawing together all moral virtues in the Confederacy and isolating personal and social vices in the northern Union. Purified by separation, the South could attain its true greatness.[5]

Such contrasts between northern and southern character reassured southerners of their own superiority. They depicted Yankee character as a composite of moral defects, rooted in an industrial and commercial society. Images of Yankees stressed their acquisitiveness and lack of cultivation. They were a "race of clock makers and wooden nutmeg venders," capable only of "routine and mechanicle" tasks. The principal concern of all Yankees, southerners claimed repeatedly, was money—the cash nexus ruled all aspects of northern life. Only a desire

5. Ella Gertrude (Clanton) Thomas Diary, January 1, 1862, DU. The view that northern and southern people were entirely different far exceeded the facts and overlooked their common values and habits. See Taylor, *Cavalier and Yankee*, 329–35; Carl N. Degler, *Place Over Time: The Continuity of Southern Distinctiveness* (Baton Rouge, 1977), 60; and Emory M. Thomas, *The Confederacy as a Revolutionary Experience* (Englewood Cliffs, N.J., 1971), 20–22.

for profit or loot could induce northerners to fight for their country. Southerners referred to the Union army as a "mercenary horde" of "robbers and thieves" and concluded that "the soul of no northern man rises higher . . . than what he can make by any thing." Lieutenant John Hampden Chamberlayne of Virginia charged that northerners "can only work, work, work, making money. The vice is incurable too," he wrote his sister, "for they hold that this is the whole duty of man, and that he is worthiest who most unremittingly toils with his hands, or if with his brains, he must dry them up with years of mechanic toil over Day Book & Ledger." Southerners viewed the contrast between the agrarian South and the increasingly commercial and industrial North largely in moral terms. Economic differences implied cultural differences between virtuous southerners and corrupt Yankees. In comparison to the genteel Cavaliers of southern legend, Yankees seemed greedy, narrow-minded, and unrefined.[6]

According to the southern critique of Yankee character, acquisitiveness was but one aspect of a debased nature. Many Confederates viewed the war as a contest between virtue and evil. The former, they assumed, imparted strength. Georgia private H. C. Kendrick vowed that "a low a degraded set of Northern people" could never conquer "a noble and respectable squad of Southerners." With the buoyant confidence characteristic of the first months of the war, Lieutenant Henry Ewing of Tennessee, who had left the University of Virginia to volunteer, boasted, "The scum of the North *cannot* face the chivalric spirit of the South." Southerners claimed that their armies were recruited from the best families of the land and that they represented the highest ideals of manhood, valor, honor, and social responsibility. By contrast, northern politicians could raise an army only by appealing "to the lowest & vilest passions of the starving multitude in their cities to induce them to enlist." Those who joined the Yankee "horde of vandals" were described as "fierce and cruel Germans," "starving Irish, who fight for daily bread," and "Western scoundrels . . . spawned of prairie mud." These characterizations reveal an agrarian, eth-

6. Sue Sparks Keitt to Mrs. Frederick Brown, March 4, 1861, in Laurence Massillon Keitt Papers, DU; Thomas Diary, October 7, 1862; Peter Hairston to his wife, June 15, September 22, 1861, in Peter Hairston Papers, SHC: Chamberlayne (ed.), *Ham Chamberlayne*, 105. On southern rejection of materialism, see Eugene D. Genovese, *The Political Economy of Slavery: Studies in the Economy and Society of the Slave South* (New York, 1965), 28–31. For southern claims of moral superiority, see Richard D. Brown, *Modernization: The Transformation of American Life, 1600–1865* (New York, 1966), 171.

nically homogeneous South suspicious of the urban, ethnically mixed North.[7]

Such debased creatures could not be expected to possess any moral qualities. As invaders, they would be capable of extreme cruelty toward an armed foe and even toward helpless women and children. Every northerner appeared a howling fanatic, a fiendish opponent of all that was good or godly. Believing that the North sought to trample southern rights, Edward Guerrant, a Kentucky staff officer, depicted the Union army as "a fanatical mob animated by the most diabolical hate and revenge." Other southerners claimed that all traces of humanity had disappeared from Yankee souls. Lieutenant William R. Redding of Georgia described the enemy as "mean and debased Devils incarnate," and Phila Calder of North Carolina feared the war would continue until it could "satiate the blood-thirstiness of our implacable enemies."[8]

The enemy depicted by such statements was not a flesh-and-blood being but a shadowy image, conjured up by vague fears and intense emotions. Confronted by an apparently inhuman foe lacking moral principles, southerners believed that defeat would mean subjugation or extermination. They could hope for neither justice nor mercy. Northern attacks on slavery had convinced them that their fellow countrymen could no longer be trusted, and their impassioned denunciation of Yankee character derived its fury from this sense of betrayal. Their own brothers threatened their rights, liberty, and property and thwarted their quest for independence. Invasion was final proof that Yankee fanatics sought to force the South into total submission.

Hatred for the Yankee thus increased when invasion threatened southerners' homes and property. John Berkley Grimball, a wealthy South Carolina rice planter, whose plantation near Beaufort had been raided by Union troops, wrote to his son in the army: "Apart from patriotic devotion to our country's cause, we as a family have more cause to hate the Yankees than most people—for few have suffered in their property and prosperity more." A North Carolina woman watched her neighbors flee coastal areas after federal forces captured

7. H. C. Kendrick to his sisters, November 18, 1861, in H. C. Kendrick Letters, SHC; Henry Ewing to Harry St. John Dixon, May 1, 1861, in Harry St. John Dixon Papers, SHC; Peter Hairston to his wife, May 9, 1861, in Hairston Papers; David Schenck Diary, June 16, 1862, SHC; Chamberlayne (ed.), *Ham Chamberlayne*, 186.

8. Edward O. Guerrant Diary, March 8, 1862, in Edward Owings Guerrant Papers, SHC; William R. Redding to his wife, August, 1861, in W. R. Redding Papers, SHC; Phila C. Calder to Robert Calder, May 14, 1863, in William Calder Papers, SHC.

Roanoke Island. "I thought I hated the miserable Vandals before," she wrote to a friend in South Carolina, "but I never knew how intense, how bitter the feeling was until I saw the boat go by that morning loaded to the water's edge, with helpless women and children, obliged to leave so hurriedly their once happy homes perhaps forever." Less than two weeks later, she too was forced to flee inland for refuge. Convinced that their evaluation of Yankee character was correct, many southerners vowed never to forgive the cruel enemy.[9]

Confederate soldiers prayed for revenge against an enemy who had violated the rules of civilized warfare by inflicting suffering on innocent civilians. They longed to take the war into enemy territory. Georgia sergeant H. C. Kendrick insisted that Yankees must be punished for the depredations inflicted upon southern people and their property. "I feel like retaliating in the strictest sense," he wrote as Lee's army moved toward Pennsylvania in June, 1863. "I don't think we would do wrong to take horses; burn houses; and commit evry depredation possible upon the men of the North." Yet he assured his mother that he would never forget his upbringing and insult or injure any woman, however "disloyal" she might be to the Confederacy. Chivalric warfare proscribed attacks on civilians and their private property; no gentleman would insult, much less harm, a lady. "Not just retaliation alone but sound policy dictates that we should make them feel keenly [war's] wasting fury," a Virginia soldier argued. "Not a hoof should be left behind, not a grain unconsumed, not a factory, bridge, or rail road undestroyed—thus and thus only can we teach our uncivilized opponents a just appreciation of our rights and of the rules of war."[10]

Despite orders against plundering, Confederates who invaded Maryland in 1862 and Pennsylvania in 1863 fulfilled their vows of vengeance. The North must suffer, they reasoned, as the South had suffered. "They have been living as if no war existed in America," Alabama captain Elias Davis wrote from Pennsylvania in June, 1863: "It is just that they should feel the war: all persons South with few exceptions have suffered." Pennsylvania citizens were scared and submissive, a North Carolina lieutenant with the unlikely name of Iowa Michi-

9. John B. Grimball to Berkley Grimball, July 17, 1863, in John Berkley Grimball Papers, DU; Clara B. Hoyt to Fanny Hamilton, February 1, 1862, in Ruffin, Roulhac, and Hamilton Family Papers, SHC.
10. H. C. Kendrick to his mother, June, 6, 1863, in Kendrick Papers; R. H. Simpson to Annie Simpson, June 22, 1863, in Andrew Funkhouser Papers, DU.

gan Royster reported: "They know how their soldiers have desolated Virginia and they fear that ours will retaliate."[11] Lee's veterans did retaliate, though they never remained north of the Potomac long enough to inflict damage comparable to that wrought by Yankees during four years of campaigning throughout the South. These personal acts of vengeance mirrored the vandalism and destruction committed by individual northern soldiers. The only difference was that Confederate policy never officially sanctioned such action as deliberate war measures, whereas northern generals such as William Tecumseh Sherman and David Hunter became notorious for their scorched-earth policies.

Once they reached the North, Confederate soldiers obtained their first glimpses of Yankee society. The contrast between northern and southern farming surprised them. "It is the most beautiful country you ever saw, the neatest farms, large white barns, fine houses, good fences," Lieutenant Royster reported from Chambersburg, Pennsylvania, just before the battle of Gettysburg. "The whole country is covered with the finest crops of wheat, such wheat as is not seen in our country." During the invasion of Maryland in September, 1862, Colonel John B. Magruder of Virginia observed the same contrast. "This section of Md. is almost entirely settled by the Dutch who own small farms, *large barns*, which in nearly every instance are better than their dwellings, no negroes, & farm very comfortably," he reported to his father, concluding that these people had "nothing whatever in common with us." For Magruder and others, this realization of difference enhanced their pride in the southern way of life. "The country is rich in every thing necessary to man," North Carolina staff officer William Calder wrote in June, 1863, from Chambersburg, Pennsylvania. "It is literally a land flowing with milk and honey." Staying overnight in a farmer's barn, Calder observed northern life firsthand. "They live in real Yankee style," he reported, "wife & daughters & 'a help' doing all the work." Although these descriptions typified most American farms of the time, they greatly differed from the southern plantation ideal. "It makes me more than ever devoted to our own Southern institutions & customs," Calder concluded. In rejecting the northern model of prosperous small

11. Elias Davis to his wife, June 27, 1863, in Elias Davis Papers, SHC; Iowa Michigan Royster to his mother, June 29, 1863, in Iowa Michigan Royster Papers, SHC.

farms, southern planters reaffirmed their belief in the superiority of their social and economic culture, based on slavery and the plantation. Yankee acquisitiveness and respect for menial labor seemed undignified and contemptible.[12]

Northerners likewise judged southern character in derogatory terms. The Civil War uprooted northern men from isolated rural and small-town communities and transported them to a southern land they had known before only through novels, political propaganda, and popular stereotypes. From their arrival on the "sacred soil," they eagerly reported to the folks back home their impressions of the South and its people.

In many cases, direct observation rudely contradicted their preconceived images. Many northerners expected to find a society of Cavalier planters, living in elegant mansions with black servants to care for the master's every need. Such an image appealed to many young men seeking an alternative to the ceaseless struggle for advancement in New England or the Middle West. Henry G. Marshall, a young Connecticut lieutenant and graduate of Yale College, enjoyed the privilege of having a black servant during the Union occupation of Beaufort, South Carolina. "I can understand how one in this climate can easily come to be waited on & do nothing himself if he can help it," he told his mother. William Thompson Lusk, who also served as a staff officer near Beaufort, admired the former leisure and comfort of South Carolina plantation life. The mild climate, elegant mansions, and convenience of being waited on by black servants increased his tolerance for southern customs. "I have grown immensely aristocratic since in South Carolina," he confessed to his mother. "There [is] something in the air that's infectious. A few more weeks here, and I'll be able to stomach even a Bostonian." The young New Yorker, who had interrupted his medical studies to enlist, regretted the dislocations caused by war and wished "that this war had never visited us, and that the planters were once more peacefully cultivating their pleasant homes." These mansions belonged to the prominent South Carolinians whose "effervescing exuberance of gentlemanly spirit" had precipitated the war, accord-

12. Iowa Michigan Royster to his mother, June 29, 1863, in Royster Papers; John B. Magruder to his father, December 4, 1862, in John Bowie Magruder Papers, DU; William Calder to his mother, June 26, 1863, in Calder Papers.

ing to Lusk. Imbued with this attractive image of the southern Cavalier, many northerners envied the refinement and luxury which they associated with plantation life in Dixie.[13]

The Cavalier image also had negative connotations for those who objected to its aristocratic pretensions or its foundation on slavery. The Cavalier was undemocratic, backward-looking, haughty, and overbearing, characteristics that offended the North's progressive, egalitarian, democratic ideals. Neither image accurately reflected the reality of sectional character, but both symbolized aspirations that competed for dominance in shaping national character. Lieutenant Uriah Parmelee of Connecticut contrasted "the miserable huts of the *poor whites*" with the planters' mansions. "We know what the wise man said went before destruction & if there is any one trait that I have seen illustrated here in desolated Virginia it is—*Pride*," he wrote, "pride of race, pride of State, pride of wealth, pride of rule." This pride was part of southerners' inheritance, central to their way of life. "To follow its dictates is manly; to resent, to bully, to retaliate is to be—a *gentleman!*" Parmelee charged. He conceded that southern pride had some redeeming features—hospitality, refinement, and "true politeness"—but denounced its effects. Lieutenant John Wilder of Massachusetts expressed even greater ambivalence toward the Cavalier ideal. In 1863 he participated in the long siege of Charleston, which, he told his mother, "is doubtless next to Boston the most refined and cultivated place in America." Unlike William Lusk, Wilder meant this as a compliment. "All the defects of the Southern character to be found here of course but also its virtues in an eminent degree," he wrote. "Hospitality, elegance, refinement, & courage—a foe which one hates—a friend which one adores." Yet he insisted that these virtues were not sufficient "to stay her destruction." The rebellion must be crushed. "Let her go & her remembrance be a dream," Wilder concluded.[14]

The reality of southern life soon convinced most northern soldiers that the Cavalier ideal did not truly represent the South. "Notwith-

13. Henry G. Marshall to his mother, June 14, 4, 1864, in Henry Grimes Marshall Papers, WLC; William T. Lusk to his mother, November 9, December 10, 20, 1861, in Civil War Manuscripts Collection, Yale. For antebellum northern views of the Cavalier, see Taylor, *Cavalier and Yankee*, 122–35, 225–59.

14. Uriah Parmelee to his mother, September 28, 1963, in Samuel Spencer Parmelee and Uriah N. Parmelee Papers, DU; John A. Wilder to his mother, September 30, 1863, in Loomis-Wilder Family Papers, Yale.

standing their party and sectional prejudices a great many northern people, men and women, have exalted ideas of the wealth and magnificence of southern people & southern life," wrote Virginia Unionist David Strother. "To be cured of this a residence in the country will soon suffice." This had been the experience of one of his comrades, a northern Democrat, whose "romantic idea of southern life" was "sadly disenchanted" by his observations of the area near Fortress Monroe. "He pronounced the country there as the most God forsaken he had ever seen," Strother reported. Many northerners shared this conclusion. First impressions of the South and its people shocked them. Captain James W. Sligh, previously a tailor in Grand Rapids, Michigan, discovered that the people in eastern Kentucky lived in coarse log houses without windows. "They are certainly the most primitively ignorant people I ever came across—and never supposed that Ky was so far behind popular civilization," he wrote. "The land is good and capable of yielding good crops, but the inhabitens lack interprize."[15]

Union soldiers frequently concluded that the southern people suffered from lack of intelligence or incentive to improve their condition. After returning from a raid into eastern North Carolina, Connecticut private Henry Thompson reported that the inhabitants "dont know that their side have ever fired on Fort Sumpter we asked them if they didnt read it in the papers they said they never had any. they eat with their hands they have no knives & forks." Although only rudely educated himself, he was astounded by the ignorance he found in that isolated region. "I dont know what you think about such an ignorant class of people in the United States but I know what I think And I am supprised & astonished!" Indeed, he could only conclude that "the nigers are far superior in knoledge 2 the whites. I am sorry 2 say so, but all I have wrote is true as far as [I] know." After a second reconnaissance in the same area, Thompson recommended that "if they send Missionarys from home anywhere I think they had better send them here, for the natives aint more than half civilized & look like ghosts skeletons or Flyaways. . . . I supposed we were fighting a civilized class of people but I find we are not." As poverty and ignorance became for many

15. David Hunter Strother Diary, September 19, 1861, in David Hunter Strother Collection, West Virginia University Library; James W. Sligh to his wife, January 17, 1862, in Sligh Family Papers, MHC. On the question of southern laziness, see David Bertelson, *The Lazy South* (New York, 1967); and Woodward, *American Counterpoint*, 13–46.

Yankees the distinguishing characteristics of southerners, an image of the backward Rebel replaced that of the genteel Cavalier in northern perceptions.[16]

Union soldiers frequently remarked that the South was "about fifty years behind the age" and applied this judgment to areas as diverse as Tidewater Virginia, the West Virginia mountains, and Charleston, South Carolina. New York private Constant Hanks, an outspoken free-labor Republican, went even further in his contempt for southern civilization, claiming that building styles, farming methods, and even people's manners seemed to be "the relics of a bygone age." Anyone coming to Virginia from the free northern states, he told his sister, "would naturally come to the conclusion that the people of this state had gone to sleep 150 years ago & had not waked up yet." This indictment of southern backwardness carried with it an implicit assumption that the North represented a progressive culture whose national leadership was divinely ordained. Free labor had made the North a new Eden, sharply contrasted to the benighted South.[17]

Convinced of their own society's superiority, northerners believed that only Yankee common sense and enterprise could regenerate the South. Recommendations for relief included sending Yankee schoolmasters to combat southern ignorance and northern missionaries to eliminate primitive customs and morals. Private Robert J. Bates of Wisconsin listed the outmoded farming methods he observed near Murfreesboro, Tennessee: "I saw them plowing with wooden moul board plows driveing oxen with strait yokes awkward old fashioned wagons stoves are almost unknown here." Most damning of all, he charged that "there dont seem to be any enterprise in the enhabitance at all here." The solution was clear, Bates concluded, for "if we had northern farmers down here I think in a few years the country would look different." Reading poorly written letters from Confederate soldiers,

16. Henry Thompson to his wife, October 13, 1862, October 14, 1863, in Henry J. H. Thompson Papers, DU. Northern clergymen also advocated sending missionaries to the South. See Chester Forrester Dunham, *The Attitude of the Northern Clergy Toward the South, 1860–1865* (1942; rpr. Philadelphia, 1974), 204–19.

17. Nathan Webb Diary, November 18, 1863, WLC; John D. Rigg to Mary Kern, May 30, 1863, in Adam H. Pickel Papers, DU; Franklin (ed.), *Diary of James T. Ayers*, 91; Constant Hanks to Mary Rose, June 13, 1864, in Constant C. Hanks Papers, DU. See also Brown, *Modernization*, 140–48; Floan, *South in Northern Eyes*, 40; Donald, *Liberty and Union*, 54.

Lieutenant William T. Lusk, a Yale graduate, concluded that "the greatest need of the South, is an army of Northern Schoolmasters."[18]

Southerners would have to assume northern personality characteristics before they could improve their condition. Fresh infusions of Yankee virtues would be needed to repair the harmful effects of slave society. "With New England taste and enterprise to develop the resources of the country, many sections would prove an earthly paradise," Maine private Edwin O. Wentworth, a former printer, wrote from Virginia, "but with the present inhabitants, imbued as they are with the indolence and squalor superinduced by slavery, it could never be more than it has been (before the war)—the scene of ignorance, oppression, and vice." Yankees believed that southerners' ignorance and lack of enterprise prevented them from escaping the miseries of poverty, and as a result the South appeared to lag behind the North in educational, business, and material progress by about half a century.[19]

The stereotypes of Yankee and Rebel portrayed clear cultural and moral differences between North and South. Neither image accurately reflected the character of all individuals—perhaps not even of a clear majority—in either section. Yet the stereotypes reveal a great deal about sectional consciousness and about the idealized self-images of southerners and northerners, serving to a large extent as negative reference points for each side. In denouncing the Yankee as mercenary and unrefined, for example, southerners implicitly both rejected the profit motive and proclaimed their own gentlemanly virtues. Northerners likewise found the Rebels' ignorance and laziness to be exactly opposite the free-labor ideals of the progressive North. Yankee and Rebel symbolized sectional differences, which were neither as absolute nor as distinct as many people imagined. As Uriah Parmelee observed in discussing southern character, "Things appear 'mixed' in this world & motives & actions are not as clearly defined as we might wish them."[20]

18. Robert J. Bates to his parents, March 31, 1863, in Robert J. Bates Papers, WSHS; William T. Lusk to Cousin Lou, August 1, 1861, in Civil War Manuscripts, Yale.

19. Edwin O. Wentworth to his wife, March 1, 1863, in Edwin Oberlin Wentworth Papers, LC. See also George M. Fredrickson, *The Inner Civil War: Northern Intellectuals and the Crisis of the Union* (New York, 1965), 117–18; and Foner, *Free Soil, Free Labor, Free Men*, 51–58.

20. Uriah Parmelee to his mother, September 28, 1863, in Parmelee Papers.

ROBERT McALLISTER

Robert McAllister of New Jersey shared northern popular images of southerners as backward, ignorant slaveowners. Born during the War of 1812 in Juniata County, Pennsylvania, McAllister worked year-round on his father's farm, receiving only an elementary education. Even after his marriage in 1841, he continued to live on his father's property until farming became unprofitable. In 1847, he began a new career as a railroad contractor, and ten years later he moved with his wife and two daughters to New Jersey as supervisor of a construction project for the Dupuy and McAllister Company, of which he was a founding partner. Meanwhile, McAllister's brother Thompson had moved to Covington, Virginia, also as a railroad contractor. A family reunion in January, 1860, dissolved into heated arguments between Thompson, who vigorously defended southern rights, and Robert, a Republican and a devout Presbyterian, who argued strongly for the Union. The brothers parted enemies.[21]

Following the Confederate bombardment of Fort Sumter, forty-eight-year-old Robert McAllister began organizing an infantry company. A former brigadier general in the Pennsylvania militia, he soon became lieutenant colonel of the 1st New Jersey Volunteers. McAllister later explained that he was "fighting to sustain our Government and civil and religious liberty, and to tell the world that Republican Government can be sustained." Meanwhile, Thompson McAllister organized and became captain of the "Allegheny Roughs," Company A in the 27th Virginia Regiment, serving with the soon-to-be-famous Stonewall Brigade. Thompson had been "an out and out Secessionist," and he and his son both fought at Bull Run. "I am disgusted with Thompson, and *all friendship has ceased*," McAllister vowed. His brother had disgraced himself, Robert argued, so that he and his wife "could own a few miserable slaves and be ranked No. 1 in Virginia society."[22]

Lieutenant Colonel Robert McAllister soon had an opportunity to observe Virginia society firsthand. In July, 1861, he crossed the Potomac with his regiment and set up camp for the first time in northern Virginia. He described his first impressions of the South in a letter to his wife: "We are now on the sacred soil of Virginia—poor soil at that. This is a most miserable and forlorn place as any man need wish to see."

21. Robertson (ed.), *Civil War Letters of McAllister*, 3–26.
22. *Ibid.*, 459, 145, 177–78.

Southern poverty became a recurrent theme in his letters, and his indictment was harsh: "This country is sparsely settled, poorly cultivated, and the inhabitants look miserably poor. Poor miserable houses, dirty children, and pitch pine is about all they seem to raise." Poverty and "an unusual amount of ignorance" characterized even the leading families of Virginia society.[23]

McAllister attributed the poverty of Virginia farmers to their lack of enterprise. Although their farms were large, they cultivated only small and diminishing portions of them. He explained this apparent decline of southern agriculture with a military metaphor: "The lazy planter draws in his lines; the pine forest extends his pickets, followed by his line of battle, until the planter finds himself pushed back, flanked, surrounded, and ocquipying only a small portion of the farm for himself, family, and negroes. Here he stays. I would not say 'lives,' for he does not. He is deprived of all the comforts that makes home delightful in the North."[24]

Slavery had left its blighting influence on Virginia, McAllister thought, and he longed for the beauty and comforts of home. "Oh, how I would like to look once more on the beautiful green fields of the North!" he exclaimed after three years in the South. "What a Paradice to this poor, miserable, forelorn, God forsaken country! The curse of slavery has marked every acre of land, and the desolation of war has laid it all a barren wast." Returning north during the Gettysburg campaign, McAllister noticed a remarkable contrast between the land and people of Virginia and Pennsylvania. "We were coming out of a poor, miserable, forelorn country," he wrote, "to a country well cultivated, yielding a rich return for the labour bestowed, and with a prosperous and patriotic people." Even the elite of Virginia society lacked personal conveniences and accomplishments common among northern middle classes. McAllister noticed that plantation mansions were poorly furnished and that southern ladies were "not nearly so accomplished as in the North." The South had not kept pace with northern progress. "They prided themselves on family, and worshipped slavery, and fancied that they were superior to all creation," he charged. "We in the North have made rapid advances in refinement, education, and everything that is calculated to raise the scale of civilization and religion."

23. *Ibid.*, 41, 230.
24. *Ibid.*, 612.

McAllister concluded from his observation of Virginians that, "in fact, they have been standing still for the last twenty years."[25]

This lack of progress appeared to be a moral failing of southern character. McAllister depicted the war as a contest to be decided by the personal attributes of Yankees and Rebels. He believed that superior moral character would guarantee victory for the North. Marching toward Richmond in May, 1862, he predicted that the next battle "will help decide between Northern courage and Southern chivalry. That we will beat them I have no doubt."[26] Faith in the moral judgments rendered by battle, however, proved weaker than confidence in northern virtue. General George B. McClellan's defeat before Richmond did not in McAllister's eyes vindicate southern chivalry: the North was just beginning to fight.

Rumors of Rebel atrocities increased Robert McAllister's devotion to the Union and his desire for revenge against the wicked traitors. After the first battle at Bull Run, he heard reports—never proven—that Confederates had bombarded and burned Union hospitals. "The cruelty of the Rebels to our wounded has no parallel in history," McAllister charged. Southern leaders allegedly refused to allow northern ambulances to take the dead and wounded off the field. "*What a blot on Southern history*! But this will tell in our future battles," he predicted. Individual acts of cruelty stirred the flames of hatred and revenge. In 1864, McAllister came upon the bodies of several Union soldiers ambushed by Rebel bushwhackers. "From appearances they had been stripped of all their clothing and, when in the act of kneeling in a circle, they were shot in the head—murdered in cold blood by the would be 'Chivalry of the South.'" This barbarous action, he told his wife, "holds up to light the true character of those who are pushing the rebellion to the destruction of our glorious Union. Need I now tell you why our boys burnt buildings?" Desire for revenge prompted widespread destruction of Rebel property in the vicinity. Union retaliation was severe, but McAllister and others justified it as legitimate repayment for Confederate atrocities. The intensity of hatred thereby escalated with each new act of vengeance.[27]

25. *Ibid.*, 458–59, 330–31, 132. The harmful effects of slavery on the southern economy are examined in Foner, *Free Soil, Free Labor, Free Men*, 40–51; and Genovese, *Political Economy of Slavery*, 23–25.

26. Robertson (ed.), *Civil War Letters of McAllister*, 163.

27. *Ibid.*, 48–49, 558. For reports and rumors of atrocities, see Daly, *Diary of a Union Lady*, 139, 158; Felix Brannigan to his sister, June 17, 1862, in Felix Brannigan Papers, LC; and Wiley, *Billy Yank*, 346–48.

Colonel McAllister evinced little sympathy for the acute suffering among people in the South, for such was the price of rebellion. Traitors could expect no better fate. "They rebelled against this, the best of all . . . Governments, and they are reaping the bitter fruits," he proclaimed. But if the mass of southerners were as unintelligent and poorly informed as McAllister described them, they could hardly be held accountable for their treason. They very likely did not understand what they were doing. By the summer of 1862, after being appointed colonel of the newly formed 11th New Jersey Regiment, he predicted that many Rebels would gladly desert or surrender if given a chance. "A portion of them are sick and tired of the Rebellion," he wrote home. "And well they might be, for half of them don't know what they are fighting for." Unfortunately, those who did not fully understand why they were fighting were often the very ones who suffered most severely the devastation of war.[28]

Recognizing that many Rebels fought under compulsion from higher authorities, McAllister argued that the rebellion's leaders, rather than their deceived supporters, should be punished. After the arrest of Confederate commissioners James M. Mason and John Slidell in 1861, he stated: "These ringleaders are the ones that ought to suffer, not their poor deluded following." He maintained this conviction throughout the war. From the Petersburg trenches, less than two months before General Lee surrendered at Appomattox, he wrote: "If we could get the leaders of this uncalled for rebellion and hang them, what a blessing this would be to our country and the world." He did not demand that all southerners receive strict punishment because most of them had been duped by the slaveholding advocates of secession. The Rebel leaders were the only real traitors, and they must pay for their crimes.[29]

Robert McAllister compiled an impressive record of war service. He and the regiment he commanded received praise for bravery at Chancellorsville. He was twice wounded at Gettysburg and slightly wounded again in the battle of the Wilderness. Near the end of the war, he was breveted brigadier general for conspicuous conduct at Boydton Plank Road on October 27, 1864, and in July, 1865, he was appointed "Major General of Volunteers by Brevet" in recognition of "gallant and meritorious service." By then, McAllister had already returned to civilian life in Belvidere, New Jersey. Like many other enter-

28. Robertson (ed.), *Civil War Letters of McAllister*, 558, 177.
29. *Ibid.*, 94, 558.

prising Yankees, he invested in a Mississippi cotton plantation, endeavoring to prove that free labor could rejuvenate the South and enrich its sponsors. Although such business ventures sometimes succeeded, for McAllister and many others they ended in financial ruin. McAllister later served for sixteen years as general manager of the Ironton Railroad Company, which operated ore mines and a branch railway near Allentown, Pennsylvania. The family divisions resulting from the sectional conflict healed by 1870, when Robert McAllister enjoyed a "warm reunion" with his brother Thompson, the Confederate officer, who died three months later. Robert McAllister became a respected civic leader of Allentown, Pennsylvania, a successful businessman, and a regular member of the First Presbyterian Church. After suffering a stroke in 1888, he contracted Bright's disease and died on February 23, 1891. Three years later, the citizens of Belvidere, New Jersey, dedicated an impressive monument over his grave.[30]

ALEXANDER CHEVES HASKELL

Alexander Cheves Haskell clearly expressed the prevailing Confederate attitude that Yankees were ungentlemanly plunderers, fanatically determined to subjugate the South. The Yankee represented the antithesis of the southern values which Haskell and his comrades fought to defend. As the scion of an illustrious South Carolina plantation family and grandson of former Speaker of the House Langdon Cheves, Sr., Alex Haskell had more at stake than most southerners in the conflict over slavery and southern rights. In December, 1860, he graduated second in his class from South Carolina College, where he had actively followed campus political debates. A few days later his state seceded from the Union. Haskell returned home and, with his brother William, immediately enlisted in the 1st South Carolina Volunteers, an elite corps of planters' sons commanded by Colonel Maxcy Gregg. On January 8, 1861, he reported for duty at Fort Moultrie, guarding the entrance to Charleston harbor.[31]

War was a grand adventure. Haskell proudly wore his patriotic uniform of red flannel shirt and black trousers. His early letters home were filled with youthful enthusiasm and fascination with every detail of his new life. "We are living royally," he wrote on January 15. By early Febru-

30. *Ibid.*, 3–26.
31. Daly, *Alexander Cheves Haskell*, 39–51.

ary, Haskell thought war inevitable and expected it to come before Lincoln's inauguration. The northern Congress could not be trusted, he told his mother: "We cannot hope for any reason or wisdom or justice from the insane God-forsaken fanatics who are in power." Haskell proclaimed that he had enlisted to defend "our country our homes our honour and our Religion." In reciting this Confederate litany, he shared the dominant southern interpretation of the war's meaning.[32]

Subsequent efforts by the Lincoln administration to relieve Fort Sumter confirmed Haskell's belief in Yankee treachery, but the exhilarating victory over Major Robert Anderson's garrison overcame that indignation. "A glorious day it was," he wrote home, "and marked so deeply by the protecting hand of divine Providence that it calls to mind the miraculous victories of the chosen people." His only disappointment was that the Yankees offered no resistance, thereby withholding from Confederate forces the full satisfaction of victory. Nevertheless, he boasted, "It was as gallant an affair as the world ever witnessed." With a generosity born of victory, Haskell acknowledged the bravery of "our gallant foes" defending Fort Sumter, who withstood a fierce shelling before surrendering. Yet he denounced as cowardice the Yankee fleet's refusal to fight.[33]

War would not always be so glorious, however, nor the enemy so harmlessly valiant. Following the attack on Fort Sumter, Lincoln called for volunteer troops to defend the government, and Virginia seceded rather than support coercion of the South. Alex Haskell's regiment immediately volunteered to defend Virginia, and by the beginning of May it was encamped at Richmond. Haskell wrote that southern forces were preparing for "a just and righteous defence of homes & families" from a northern invasion designed for "subjugation & extermination." Resistance would be spurred on "by all the rage & hate that can be excited by the approach of an impious, piratical, bloodthirsty invader." The enemy assumed demonic proportions in Haskell's imagination, and he worried that northern soldiers were so lacking in common morality that the rules of civilized warfare would not curb their savagery. "I much fear that the Yankee horde have forgotten the laws of war & have not natural honour & chivalry enough to suggest them by the conduct they enforce," he wrote, two months before the war's first

32. Haskell to his mother, February 13, 1861, May 22, 1862, in Alexander Cheves Haskell Papers, SHC.
33. Haskell to his parents, April 17, 1861, in *ibid*.

major battle. "I think they will hang or otherwise murder any prisoners they catch at first & will keep on at it until fire & sword have driven them trembling & supplicant to ask for mercy."[34]

A few days later, Haskell reported that Union troops acting under orders from General Winfield Scott had occupied Baltimore and suppressed expressions of sympathy for the Confederacy. Based on his preconceptions of Yankee character, he believed that General Scott must already be planning "a destructive descent" upon Richmond "to glut some of his savages with plunder & strike terror into the hearts of Virginians." Northerners were not only mercenaries motivated by prospects of looting southern homes but sadistic creatures intent on terrorizing innocent civilians. Haskell went even further, portraying them as inhuman despots. "The Yankees are like ferocious monkeys, which I believe the Spanish proverb makes the most cruel wicked & capricious of tyrants," he charged. Imbued with war passions, Haskell conceded to the enemy no traits of decency or humanity.[35]

Within a month of the fall of Fort Sumter, Haskell had radically altered his perceptions of the war and of the enemy. Realizing that the gallant confrontation at Charleston would not force the North to give up the struggle, he quickly lost his former tolerance and respect for federal soldiers. Yankees now appeared to be implacable enemies, eager to invade, conquer, and destroy the South.

He no longer conceded them even military ability, complaining that the Virginians "look on the Yankees more as equals & with too much respect as a formidable invading force, to feel as we South Carolinians do the withering shame of a surrender or retreat." Exactly one month after the attack on Sumter, he wrote from Richmond: "I do hope that people in Carolina & everywhere in the South are waking up at last to the assurance that we are to have a real true & true bona fide war of terrible magnitude & intensity." Sectional antagonism had grown too bitter to permit peaceful separation or even civilized warfare. So intense was the mutual hatred, he believed, that the first prisoners both sides captured would be hanged. "Never again do I expect to see the chivalrous bowing & scraping of Fort Sumter repeated," he concluded. Haskell feared that bitter hatreds unleashed by war would overcome all restraints imposed by codes of warfare.[36]

34. Haskell to his mother, May 4, 1861, in *ibid*. See Bertram Wyatt-Brown, *Southern Honor: Ethics and Behavior in the Old South* (New York, 1982).

35. Haskell to his mother, May 8, 1861, in Haskell Papers.

36. Haskell to his father, May 6, 12, 1861, in *ibid*.

For twenty-one-year-old Alex Haskell, the war seemed to be going very well. His ardent patriotism and abilities apparently impressed Colonel Gregg, who appointed him aide-de-camp. As a staff officer, he soon rose to the rank of lieutenant and then captain. Mary Chesnut, a friend of the family from South Carolina, was now a member of the inner circle of Richmond society as the wife of one of Jefferson Davis' close friends and advisers. "We only know Alex as pious and brave and good-looking," she observed, "but they say he is ambitious most of all." According to Mary Chesnut, Haskell embodied "all human perfections" in southern character, "except that he stammers fearfully in speech." She added, however, that he "fights without let or hindrance," in true Cavalier style. The gallant young officer escaped the perils of war long enough to become engaged to Rebecca (Decca) Singleton, whom he had known for three years, and they married in September, 1861. Decca soon became pregnant. Alex Haskell seemed well on the way to becoming both a successful soldier and a happy family man.[37]

An event in New Orleans the next year again showed the ugly side of war and seemed to confirm Haskell's fears about Yankee barbarity. Since their capture of New Orleans in April, 1862, Union soldiers had been insulted, abused, and spat upon by the proud and spirited women of the city. Such challenges to federal authority soon became unbearable. Attempting to restore order through a self-enforcing regulation, General Benjamin Butler issued the notorious Order Number 28, which directed that any woman who showed contempt for a United States officer or soldier would be treated as "a woman of the town plying her avocation." Butler's "Woman's Order" quieted public displays by New Orleans ladies but outraged southern men and women, who branded him "Beast" Butler.[38]

"A few words have changed the whole complexion of the war," Alex Haskell told his mother. "All mercy all pity for their barbarous soldiery, that I have been weak enough to feel when I have seen them fleeing or in prison & suffering, has gone since the turn given to affairs in New Orleans by the barbarity of that cowardly fiend Butler." Butler's affront to women strengthened Haskell's devotion to the Confederate cause and his confidence that God's blessing would bring a southern victory. This single act fulfilled his warnings about Yankee despotism and,

---

37. Woodward (ed.), *Mary Chesnut's Civil War*, 138–39; she described Haskell's wedding in an entry for June, 1862, *ibid.*, 383–84.
38. Benjamin F. Butler, *Butler's Book* (Boston, 1892), 418.

Haskell believed, proved his assessment of northern character essentially correct. There could be no better proof of the contrast between southerners and the "barbarous" Yankees. "I feel more proud of our cause this day than I ever did before," he wrote, "now that I see from what it is that we have separated ourselves in time to save truth and honour. The Enemy confident of their triumph are beginning in the insolence of conquest to draw the veil from their true purposes and intentions. One corner has been lifted, and the picture revealed has struck a chord in every southern heart, and lighted a fire of vengeance and desperate hate, before which the ranks of our foe will melt like chaff before the flames." The first year of the war had intensified Alex Haskell's hatred of the enemy, who remained an impersonal symbol of malignant evil and savagery. Preconceptions of Yankees as immoral beings, lacking personal honor or decency, created expectations of cruelty which invasion and warfare seemed to confirm. Haskell hoped that he could satisfy his craving for revenge by participating in an invasion of the North to drive the horrors of war into the enemy's country.[39]

The tragedy of war soon caught up with the young Cavalier. Nine months after their wedding, his wife died of complications in childbirth, wrongly believing that Alex had been killed in battle. Unable to read, she refused to let anyone else touch her husband's letters and thus "died with several unopened ones on her bosom," according to Mary Chesnut. She left a baby girl, to be cared for by Haskell's family while he served in Virginia. Haskell's five brothers had all enlisted in the Confederate forces. In 1862, John Cheves Haskell lost an arm at Gaines Mill. William died at Gettysburg. Two weeks later, Charles Haskell died defending Fort Wagner during the Yankee assault, which won renown throughout the North for the fighting ability of black soldiers. Alex himself received a shoulder wound at Fredericksburg in December, 1862, and an ankle wound at Chancellorsville five months later. In October, 1864, he lost an eye during a skirmish on the Darbytown Road. By then he had been promoted to lieutenant colonel, and in that capacity Alexander Cheves Haskell—who after the war would become a successful lawyer—commanded the 7th South Carolina Cavalry during the ceremonies of surrender at Appomattox Court House.[40]

39. Haskell to his mother, May 22, 1862, in Haskell Papers.
40. Woodward (ed.), *Mary Chesnut's Civil War*, 397; Daly, *Alexander Cheves Haskell*, passim.

CHARLES WILLS

Northern hatred of southerners was similar to the loathing for Yankees that invasion spurred among southerners. Charles Wills of Illinois depicted Rebels as traitors to the Union. Yet his encounters with southerners during the war revealed that differences between Yankee and Rebel were not great and convinced him that virtue did not belong exclusively to his comrades, nor wickedness to the foe. This contradiction between assumptions and experience produced ambivalence in Wills's perceptions of the enemy.

Charles Wills, like many of his fellow midwesterners, was outspoken, confident, and open-minded. His parents had moved from Pennsylvania to Canton, Illinois, where he was born in 1840. Before the war he attended the state normal school at Bloomington. During the first wave of patriotism following the attack on Fort Sumter, Wills heeded President Lincoln's call for volunteers and enlisted in Company E, 8th Illinois Infantry. Spending his first three months training at a camp in Cairo, Illinois, he found army life a pleasant adventure. "'Tis a sure thing that as long as this war continues I will not be satisfied at home," he wrote to his sister, "and if I would there will certainly be no business." The war gave him something to do, and he enjoyed the comradeship and slow pace of camp routine. "It beats clerking ever so much!" he concluded. After his three months' service ended, he re-enlisted. "I feel as if my place is here," he explained, for young men were "needed in the army more than anywhere else."[41] Charles Wills rose rapidly in the ranks. He won promotion to sergeant in September, 1861, to lieutenant early in 1862, and to captain the following September. Serving in several southwestern states, he had numerous opportunities to meet and observe civilians in areas under Union occupation.

First impressions indicated that southerners were ignorant and backward, but Wills was more amused than shocked by differences between northern and southern customs. He was especially impressed by the women of Paducah, Kentucky. "I never saw so many pretty women in my life," he told his sister. "All fat, smooth-skinned small-boned, highbred looking women." In Mississippi, however, he was amazed by the prevalence of snuff-dipping among women and reported to his sister that "there are only two women in all Iuka that do not practice it." Dipping was common at tea parties, and girls even

41. Wills, *Army Life*, 15, 19–21.

asked their beaux to "take a dip" with them while sparking. "I asked one of them if it didn't interfere with the old fashioned habit of kissing. She assured me that it did not in the least, and I marveled." Friendly conversations with southern girls led Wills to speculate on the probable reception of Confederate soldiers in his own hometown. "About the worst feature of the case would be the southern officers sparking our girls as we do theirs now," he teased his sister, "and the worst yet is, there is no doubt the girls would take to it kindly, for they do here, and I'm satisfied there is no differences in the feminines of the two sections, except that ours do not say 'thar' and 'whar.'" Nor dip snuff, presumably.[42]

Despite such levity, Wills believed that southerners should suffer for the crime of rebellion. He disliked the outspokenness of many Rebels he met, who, "safe in the knowledge of our conciliatory principles, talk of their seceshism as boldly as they do in Richmond." Such avowed supporters of treason must be punished, Wills believed: "I'd rather see the whole country red with blood, and ruined together than have this 7,000,000 of invalids (these southerners are nothing else as a people) conquer, or successfully resist the power of the North," he vowed. "I hate them now, as they hate us." The war had made reconciliation impossible. "The feeling is too deep on both sides, for anything but extermination of one or the other of the two parties to cure," Wills proclaimed, "and of the two, think the world and civilization will lose the least by losing the South and slavery." Thus did Wills declare his belief in the superiority of northern progress and civilization. Only victory could ensure the continued progress of the Union because sectional hatred would make peaceful coexistence impossible. "I want to fight the rest of my life if necessary, and die before we recognize them as anything but Rebels and traitors who must be humbled," Wills declared.[43]

Despite his belief in the superiority of free institutions, Wills expressed no love for black slaves. He declared slavery to be an awful sin but described the plantation hands he saw as savage brutes, fit only for slavery. If they were to be freed, they should either be turned over to Yankee masters or shipped out of the country, for he did not want the northern states to be degraded by their presence. When runaway

42. *Ibid.*, 29, 99–100, 76.
43. *Ibid.*, 121, 32. Northern views of Confederates as rebels and traitors are examined in Thomas J. Pressly, *Americans Interpret Their Civil War* (2nd ed.; Princeton, 1962), 43–52.

slaves entered Union lines, however, he appropriated a "pet negro" as a personal servant and enjoyed having someone to do his chores. Although continuing to disparage blacks' character, he gradually changed his views on war policies regarding slavery. By January, 1863, he supported Lincoln's Emancipation Proclamation and six months later even favored enlisting black soldiers. Military necessity finally convinced him that such measures could aid the Union cause.[44]

Although believing that the rebellion must be suppressed and traitors punished, Wills found unauthorized acts of personal retaliation repugnant. "You don't know how thankful you ought to be that you don't live in the invaded country," he wrote from southeastern Missouri. His fellow soldiers "will go into a house and beg what they can and then steal what is left. Rough, dirty, coarse brutes, if they were all shot, our army would be better off." Wills was ashamed to be associated with such creatures. Disgusted by their thievery, he sympathized with Rebels who fell victim to Yankee plundering. In December, 1862, he wrote from Mississippi that soldiers smashed furniture and stole clothing while helpless women looked on. "Rebels though they are, 'tis shocking and enough to make one's blood boil to see the manner in which some of our folks have treated them," he told his sister. "The d——d thieves even steal from the negroes (which is lower business than I ever thought it possible for a white man to be guilty of) and many of them are learning to hate the Yankees as much as our 'Southern Brethren' do." He despaired that the army might "degenerate into a nation of thieves." Wills contrasted the destructiveness of his fellow soldiers to the peacefulness and inoffensiveness of many southerners he had met.[45]

Theft and plundering by soldiers acting without orders were deplorable, but official destruction of property could be justified as a vital war measure. "It's pretty well understood in this army now that burning Rebel property is not much of a crime," Wills wrote early in 1863. "I for one will never engage in it, until orders are issued making it duty, and then I think I can enjoy it as much as any of them." However necessary destruction might be, he found it difficult to retaliate against peaceful citizens. "Orders have been given us to put every woman and children (imprison the men) across the line that speaks or acts secesh," he re-

44. Wills, *Army Life*, 83, 123, 127, 166–67, 176–77, 183–84. For a more detailed treatment of Wills's racial views, see Chapter 4, above.

45. Wills, *Army Life*, 74, 135–36.

ported, "and to burn their property, and to destroy all their crops, cut down corn growing, and burn all the cribs." But local citizens had treated federal soldiers kindly, bringing them fruit and vegetables every day. Wills feared that orders to destroy southern property would have a demoralizing effect on his fellow soldiers: "I'd hate like the deuce to burn the houses of some secesh I know here, but at the same time don't doubt the justice of the thing."[46]

Late in the war, Wills boasted, "I do take a little private satisfaction in knowing that I have never said a word, except respectfully, to any woman in the Confederacy, that I have never touched a cent's worth of private property for my own use." He had once been part of a large foraging party that took horses and rations from some poor people, "but that was no more our fault than the war is." If the war was not his fault, neither was it the fault of most Confederate soldiers, "but of rich men and politicians who have by threats and lies induced these poor devils to leave their families to die of starvation, to fight for, they can't tell what." Most southerners were ignorant, he thought, and had been easily misled into supporting a wicked cause.[47]

By the winter of 1863, soldiers on both sides had become tired of war and earnestly desired peace—at almost any price. Wills reported that most Union soldiers "would recognize three or four confederacies to get home." Southerners likewise desired peace. "The Confederate rank and file feels the same way," he declared. "Nineteen-twentieths would vote for the United States or any other man to secure peace, but their officers and citizens control the matter." After a battle in November, 1864, the condition of enemy soldiers evoked sympathy. "Old grey-haired and weakly-looking men and little boys, not over 15 years old, lay dead or writhing in pain," Wills reported. "I did pity those boys, they almost all who could talk, said the Rebel cavalry had gathered them up and forced them in." It seemed cruel to fight such people.[48]

Whatever sympathy Charles Wills expressed for individual southerners, he could not forget that they were Rebels and must be regarded as traitors against the United States. South Carolina was the symbol of rebellion, the "mother of Harlots," as one soldier called it. When Sherman's troops reached the Palmetto State, they unleashed a fury of vengeance. "I never saw so much destruction of property before,"

46. *Ibid.*, 145–46, 124.
47. *Ibid.*, 214, 104.
48. *Ibid.*, 151, 324.

Wills reported. "Orders are as strict as ever, but our men understand they are in South Carolina and are making good their old threats." Abandoned homes were burned, and even when families remained at home, "they save their house, but lose the stock, and eatables." After one month of burning and destruction, Union forces reached the North Carolina line. As he left South Carolina, Wills looked back with satisfaction. "I think she has her 'rights' now. I don't hate her any more." Thus in the moment of victory, hatred diminished. The enemy had been conquered and punished for his misdeeds; further retribution was not necessary.[49]

Charles Wills emerged unscathed by the war. As late as January, 1864, he could claim that after thirty-three months in military service, he had not been in a single battle. At war's end, he still enjoyed military life. "I have almost a dread of being a citizen, of trying to be sharp, and trying to make money," he complained. "I am sure that civil life will go sorely against the grain for a time." Yet he rejoiced in the Union's victory. "I do from my heart thank God that I have lived to see the rebellion put down," he wrote one week after Lee's surrender at Appomattox. The Union soldiers did not destroy southern property during the joyous march from North Carolina to Washington, D.C. "They don't pretend to love our 'erring brethren' yet," Wills commented, "but no conquered foe could ask kinder treatment than all our men seem disposed to give these Rebels."[50] For Charles Wills and many of his Yankee comrades, military victory both confirmed northern superiority and reduced sectional animosity. A brave but conquered foe would easily be forgiven.

The South cast its spell over many of the former invaders. Its mild climate, its need for civilizing influences, and its apparent ripeness for economic development induced many northerners to move South after the war. Some of these "carpetbaggers" claimed high moral purpose as the vanguard of progress and enlightenment. They enforced Reconstruction's political and constitutional conquest of the South, they educated former slaves, and they brought railroads and cotton mills to the economically undeveloped region. Others, including Charles Wills, simply succumbed to the Cavalier myth, albeit somewhat modernized. After the war, Wills settled at Jeannerette, Louisiana, on the Bayou

49. Franklin (ed.), *Diary of James T. Ayers*, 74; Wills, *Army Life*, 342–43, 358.
50. Wills, *Army Life*, 210, 370, 371, 373.

Teche, as a sugar planter. Although he lived in the former Confederacy until his death in 1883, he remained at heart a Yankee and was buried in his hometown of Canton, Illinois.

SARAH MORGAN

"Until that dreary 1861, I had no idea of sorrow or grief," Sarah Morgan lamented in April, 1862. "How I like to think of myself at that time! Not as *myself*, but as some happy, careless child who danced through life." At twenty years of age, Sarah Morgan was entering adulthood amid the disruptions of a war that upset daily rhythms of life and challenged common assumptions about human nature. Before the war her life had been comfortable. Her father, Thomas Gibbes Morgan, had served as judge of the district court of the parish of Baton Rouge since 1850 and before that as collector of the port of New Orleans. Although not a member of the southern planter class, Judge Morgan enjoyed a privileged position of respect and authority. The family lived in a two-story mansion near the center of Baton Rouge and owned several black servants, whom Sarah tutored. But the Morgans remained in some sense outsiders, separate from the planter elite. Sarah resented being called one of the "Proud Morgans" or the "Aristocracy of Baton Rouge" by those, on one side, who seemed jealous of her family's wealth and influence and those, on the other, who scorned their lack of plantation respectability.[51]

The year 1861 became a dividing point both for the American people and for the Morgan family. A native of Pennsylvania, Judge Morgan never adopted the planter class's outlook, although he owned several black servants. He empathized with southern rights but denounced secession until his adopted state seceded and then grudgingly pledged support to the Confederacy. His eldest son, Philip Hickey Morgan, also was a judge in the parish of Orleans when war broke out. Like his father, he disapproved of secession. Philip Morgan, however, re-

51. Sarah Morgan Diary, May 31(?), April 7, 1862, in Francis Warrington Dawson Papers, DU. Her diary was published posthumously as Sarah Morgan Dawson, *A Confederate Girl's Diary* in 1913 and later edited by James I. Robertson, Jr. (Bloomington, 1960). Citations are to the 1960 edition. Biographical information is taken from Robertson's introduction and from the memoirs of Sarah Morgan's younger brother and her husband: James Morris Morgan, *Recollections of a Rebel Reefer* (Boston, 1917); and Francis W. Dawson, *Reminiscences of Confederate Service, 1861–1865* (1882; rpr. Baton Rouge, 1980). For a discussion of Sarah Morgan's experiences during the war, see Edmund Wilson, *Patriotic Gore: Studies in the Literature of the American Civil War* (New York, 1962), 263–77.

mained loyal to the Union throughout the war. One of Sarah's older sisters had married a United States Army officer, who in 1861 played an important role in stopping the secession movement in California. The rest of the family became ardent Confederates. Sarah's brother Gibbes, who married a cousin of President Jefferson Davis' wife, was captain in the 7th Louisiana Regiment, serving under General T. J. "Stonewall" Jackson. George Morgan served as captain in the 1st Louisiana, and the youngest brother, James M. Morgan, resigned from Annapolis, where he was a cadet, to enlist as a "rebel reefer" in the Confederate navy. The fifth brother, Harry, died in a duel—a violent "affair of honor" characteristic of the fading Cavalier ideal—in May, 1861, just as the war commenced. Six months later, the elder Judge Morgan died from a severe attack of asthma, leaving Sarah, her two remaining sisters, and their mother to maintain the family home in Baton Rouge. By the time Sarah Morgan began her journal in March, 1862, her antebellum world had been severely shaken. Like Robert McAllister, she saw her family sundered by the choice of sectional loyalties. Though not caused by the war, death had already claimed two members of her family.

In a family thus divided, Sarah Morgan could not easily believe that all enemies of the South were totally wicked. Whereas many southern ladies bitterly denounced all Yankees, Judge Morgan's daughter recognized both good and bad facets of northern character. Thus, at the war's outset, Sarah's neighbors taunted her about her Unionist relatives. "Your brother is as good a Yankee as any," they charged. "Let him be President Lincoln if he will, and I would love him the same," Sarah retorted. "If he is for the Union, it is because he believes it to be in the right, and I honor him for acting from conviction, rather than from dread of public opinion."[52] As circumstances changed, her attitudes toward the enemy alternated between hatred and respect; this ambivalence reflected her complex personal experience.

Like her father, Sarah had been a reluctant convert to secession. "I don't believe in Secession," she admitted, "but I do in Liberty. I want the South to conquer, dictate its own terms, and go back to the Union, for I believe that, apart, inevitable ruin awaits both." Nevertheless, once she became convinced that southern rights could not be secured within the Union, she supported the Confederate cause. "Though none could regret the dismemberment of our old Union more than I did at

---

52. Dawson, *A Confederate Girl's Diary*, 316–17.

the time," she wrote in 1863, "yet once in earnest, from the secession of Louisiana I date my change of sentiment." When federal soldiers entered Louisiana, Sarah Morgan regarded them as enemies.[53]

Having captured New Orleans after a stiff battle in April, 1862, virtually unopposed Union forces under General Benjamin Butler occupied Baton Rouge on May 9. "Our lawful (?) owners have at last arrived," Sarah Morgan reported bitterly. "If we girls of Baton Rouge had been at the landing, instead of the men, that Yankee would never have insulted us by flying his flag in our faces! *We* would have opposed his landing except under a flag of truce." Frustrated by restraints placed on women, she poured out her bitterness in her diary: "O! if I was only a man! Then I could don the breeches, and slay them with a will! If some few southern women were in the ranks, they could set the men an example they would not blush to follow. Pshaw! there are *no* women here! We are *all* men!" Unable to meet the enemy in battle, Confederate women developed an intense hatred of Yankees and flaunted their contempt for the invaders. Union soldiers repeatedly observed that southern women expressed more bitter feelings than the Rebel soldiers they met. "The latter seems free from personal hatred," one Union soldier commented, "while the former seem to nurse their wrath to keep it warm." Such was the case with the women of Baton Rouge.[54]

Frustrated by their enforced passivity, many Baton Rouge women displayed their defiance by jeering at Yankee soldiers, wearing Confederate emblems, and even spitting in the faces of soldiers they passed on the street. Wearing a Confederate flag pinned to her dress, Sarah Morgan joined a crowd of women taunting federal soldiers and daring them to enforce the ban on such displays. Conscience-stricken, she later confided to her diary that the Yankees proved themselves perfect gentlemen despite this "unladylike display of defiance." Her belief in northern barbarity was shaken: "With a conviction that I had allowed myself to be influenced by bigoted, narrow-minded people, in believing them to be unworthy of respect or regard, I came home wonderfully changed in all my newly acquired sentiments, resolved

---

53. *Ibid.*, 32, 317. See David M. Potter, *The South and the Sectional Conflict* (Baton Rouge, 1968), 34–83; Potter, *The Impending Crisis, 1848–1861* (New York, 1976), 448–84; and Carl N. Degler, *The Other South: Southern Dissenters in the Nineteenth Century* (New York, 1974), 166–68, 124–43.

54. Dawson, *A Confederate Girl's Diary*, 22–25; Henry Withers to his sister, December 16, 1863, in Tavenner and Withers Papers. See Bell Irvin Wiley, *Confederate Women* (Westport, Conn., 1975), 140–43, 152–53.

never more to wound their feelings, who were so careful of ours, by such unnecessary display. And I hung my flag on the parlor mantel, there to wave, if it will, in the shades of private life." Ashamed, she admitted that southern women showed less common decency than the Yankee barbarians. What had become of the vaunted southern chivalry?[55]

Sarah Morgan was too fiercely independent to conceal her new respect for federal soldiers. As a result, rumors soon circulated that Yankee officers had been seen calling at her home. Sarah believed that this story originated because she "would not agree with many of our friends in saying they were liars, thieves, murderers, scoundrels, the scum of the earth, etc." She insisted that such epithets were "unworthy of ladies" and harmed the Confederate cause rather than advancing it. When accused of not being a true southerner, Sarah Morgan retorted that her brothers were fighting for her, "so this excess of patriotism is unnecessary for me, as my position is too well known to make any demonstrations requisite." Not only did she reject the images of Yankees favored by her peers, she even refused to disparage the enemy's fighting ability. She wrote in her journal: "Shall I acknowledge that the people we so recently called our brothers are unworthy of consideration, and are liars, cowards, dogs? Not I! *If* they conquer us, I acknowledge them as a superior race; I will not say that we were conquered by cowards, for where would that place us? It will take a brave people to gain us, and that the northerners undoubtedly are. I would scorn to have an inferior foe; I fight only my equals." Despite the animosities engendered by war, an underlying sympathy remained between the fraternal enemies. Sarah Morgan would not admit that former affection for northerners had been entirely misplaced.[56]

Magnanimity toward the foe, however, disappeared amid a whirl of events. The abusive acts for which Sarah Morgan had chided her associates soon prompted General Butler to issue his notorious "Woman's Order," declaring that any woman who insulted Union soldiers would be treated as "a woman of the town plying her avocation." "These men our brothers? Not mine!" Sarah Morgan exclaimed. Butler's proclamation shattered her admiration for northern politeness and revived her hatred of Yankees. She vowed to protect her virtue from anyone who

---

55. Dawson, *A Confederate Girl's Diary*, 29–30.
56. *Ibid.*, 31–32, 79 (the published version substitutes "that excess of patriotism" for "this excess of patriotism" in the manuscript diary).

should attempt to "Butlerize" her and began carrying a carving knife in the folds of her dress. Once again she found Yankee rule oppressive. Families were prohibited from leaving Baton Rouge or sending away furniture and other possessions for safekeeping. Her patrician pride bristled at the idea of being forced to carry a pass ("just such as we give our negroes") from "some low plowman"—in this case, a Wisconsin colonel. Using an analogy close to the hearts of many southerners, Sarah complained, "Ah, truly! this is the bitterness of slavery, to be . . . governed by the despotism of one man, whose word is our law!" With all its dangers and deprivations, flight would be preferable to remaining at home under such conditions. "Oh, let us abandon our loved home to these implacable enemies, and find refuge elsewhere!" she exclaimed. "Take from us property, everything, only grant us liberty!"[57]

Although restrictions on civilian movement and activity seemed oppressive, individual soldiers sent to guard the Morgan home were polite and friendly. "It was a singular situation," she thought: "our brothers off fighting them, while these Federal officers leaned over our fence, and an officer standing on our steps offered to protect us." Certainly there were cruel and spiteful northerners, such as "Beast" Butler, but through brief encounters with Union soldiers, Sarah Morgan recognized another face of the enemy. "These people mean to kill us with kindness," she reported with astonishment. "How many good and how many mean people these troubles have shown us!" General Thomas Williams, Union commander at Baton Rouge, sent a barrel of flour to Mrs. Morgan, "accompanied by a note begging her to accept it 'in consideration of the present condition of the circulating currency,' and the intention was so kind, the way it was done so delicate, that there was no refusing it." Such acts of special kindness, in addition to friendly conversations with Yankee sentinels, again led Sarah Morgan to reevaluate her images of the enemy. Once more the conduct of her neighbors aroused her ire: "It made me ashamed to contrast the quiet, gentlemanly, liberal way these volunteers spoke of us and our cause, with the rabid, fanatical, abusive violence of our female Secession declaimers," she bristled: "Fact is, these people have disarmed me by their kindness. I expected to be in a crowd of ruffian soldiers, who would think nothing of cutting your throat or doing anything they felt like; and I find, among all these thousands, not one who offers the

57. *Ibid.*, 35–36, 53, 93–94.

slightest annoyance or disrespect." Union soldiers often found the women's defiance amusing rather than threatening. "It is a fine field for women who happen to be secesh to show their perverseness of character," a Pennsylvania lieutenant observed from New Orleans. "Many of them are so poor as to be almost wretched and yet they flaunt their senseless spite as boldly as women fit for the mad-house."[58]

Personal contact with individual federal soldiers again shook Sarah Morgan's original image of the enemy. She found these Yankees fascinating; they were, after all, the only young men in the city. Sarah had a radiant personality to match her beauty. According to observers, she was strikingly tall with clear blue eyes and golden hair tinged faintly with red. Her beautiful soprano voice lured federal soldiers to congregate in front of the Morgan mansion while she sang inside. Having noticed two soldiers looking admiringly at her one day, she exclaimed, "Dear me! 'Why wasn't I born old and ugly?' Suppose I should unconsciously attract some magnificent Yankee! What an awful thing it would be!!" The attentions of gentlemanly officers, even if they were enemies, flattered her pride and excited her curiosity. Two months later, she dreamed about marrying a Yankee officer. "That was in consequence of having answered the question, whether I would do so, with an emphatic 'Yes! if I loved him,'" she admitted, "which will probably ruin my reputation as a patriot in this parish. Bah! I am no bigot!—or fool either." Mutual curiosity of Yankee and Rebel stimulated numerous such speculations about the character of the other. Sarah Morgan's defiance of popular attitudes was unusual, but many other young ladies likewise found strangers in enemy uniform surprisingly intriguing.[59]

Yet events once again altered her image of northerners. In August, 1862, Confederate forces attempted to recapture Baton Rouge. On the eve of battle, the Morgan women fled to a plantation across the river. Not until after the war could they move back to their home, for Union soldiers ransacked it shortly after their departure. "Ours was the most shockingly treated house in the whole town," Sarah reported. "We have the misfortune to be equally feared by both sides, because we will blackguard neither." Furniture was smashed, clothes and other valu-

---

58. *Ibid.*, 67, 70, 72–73; Calvin Mehaffey to his mother, November 24, 1863, in Calvin Mehaffey Papers, WLC.

59. Dawson, *A Confederate Girl's Diary*, 61, 184. Marriages occurred between Union soldiers and women of every Confederate state. See Wiley, *Confederate Women*, 153–54; and Theodore C. Blegen, ed., *The Civil War Letters of Colonel Hans Christian Heg* (Northfield, Minn., 1936), 211.

ables stolen, mirrors and china shattered, even family portraits cut
from their frames. The destruction renewed her animosity toward the
enemy. "War to the death!" she cried. "I would give my life to be able to
take arms against the vandals who are laying waste our fair land!" The
loss of her beloved childhood home revived her Confederate loyalties,
she declared a few months later: "I have lost my home and all its dear
contents for our Southern Rights, have stood on its deserted hearth-
stone and looked at the ruin of all I loved—without a murmur, almost
glad of the sacrifice if it would contribute its mite towards the salvation
of the Confederacy."[60]

For nearly a year the Morgan women wandered from one refuge to
another, until Sarah suffered a spinal injury falling from a carriage.
With Sarah now a semi-invalid, the family found refugee life increasingly difficult. Reluctantly they returned to Union-occupied territory
and the protection of Judge Philip Morgan in New Orleans. Forced to
take a loyalty oath in order to enter the city, Sarah and her mother
refused to speak the words aloud and silently prayed for the Confederate cause and for their relatives in its army. Despite the oath Sarah
experienced "no nasty or disagreeable feeling which would have announced the process of turning Yankee." She adamantly proclaimed
her loyalty to the Confederacy: "I confess myself a rebel, body and
soul. *Confess*? I glory in it! Am proud of being one; would not forego the
title for any other earthly one."[61]

Constrained from publicly expressing her feelings so as not to
jeopardize her brother's precarious position as a Unionist judge, Sarah
chafed under Yankee rule. The war drew swiftly toward its agonizing
conclusion. In January, 1864, death claimed two of her brothers.
George died of "inflammation of the bowels" after military doctors in
Virginia treated him for the wrong disease, and Gibbes died in a federal
prison at Johnson's Island, Ohio. "I felt as though the whole world was
dead," Sarah wrote after hearing the news. "Nothing was real, nothing
existed except horrible speechless pain." Her brothers' deaths extinguished her youthful enthusiasm and joy. "When this terrible strife is
over, and so many thousands return to their homes, what will peace
bring us of all we hoped?"[62]

Having suffered the agonies of war, Sarah Morgan refused to recon-

60. Dawson, *A Confederate Girl's Diary*, 194, 175, 318.
61. *Ibid.*, 383, 317.
62. *Ibid.*, 433–34.

cile herself to the victorious enemy. Returning home in a streetcar shortly after Lee surrendered at Appomattox, she happened to meet a former childhood friend, Captain John W. Todd, a cousin of President Lincoln's wife. Before the war this Yankee officer had been her brother's friend, a daily visitor in the Morgan home, and the "sweetheart" of twelve-year-old Sarah. The war had placed an insurmountable barrier between them, Sarah wrote, and she now rebuffed this Yankee's efforts to renew their acquaintance. "Cords of candy and mountains of bouquets bestowed in childish days will not make my country's enemy my friend now that I am a woman," she vowed.[63] In the early days of the war Sarah Morgan had recognized that many of the northern soldiers she met were kind and generous. The sufferings inflicted by war, however, led her to condemn all Yankees as personal as well as national enemies. Northern and southern people could share mutual sympathy when they met each other as individuals. It was easier to hate the enemy from a distance. Having fluctuated between hatred and respect for Yankees, Sarah Morgan ended by rejecting all those, including former personal friends, who had become victorious enemies.

After the war Sarah Morgan and her mother remained in New Orleans. They did not want to return to Baton Rouge to their devasted former home. In 1866 her brother Jimmy, who had survived four years' service in the Confederate navy, moved the family to South Carolina, where he had purchased General Wade Hampton's Congaree River plantation. In 1874 Sarah married Francis Warrington Dawson, a distinguished Charleston newspaper editor and friend of her brother. Dawson, an Englishman who emigrated to America in 1861 to fight for the Confederate cause, had served during the war as a common sailor and an ordnance officer, rising to the rank of captain. He had been wounded and captured, and after Lee's surrender he remained in the South as a journalist in Richmond and then Charleston. By the time he married thirty-one-year-old Sarah Morgan, he had become a leading spokesman for the New South, promoting industrialization with the slogan "Bring the Cotton Mills to the Cotton" and condemning the Radical Republicans who dominated South Carolina's political life. In 1889 a neighbor fatally shot Dawson during a quarrel. The following year Sarah Morgan Dawson moved with her young son to Paris, where she published a popular French version of the Brer Rabbit stories.

63. *Ibid.*, 438–39.

There she died of pneumonia on May 5, 1909. Several years later her son unwrapped the slim volumes of her Civil War journal and published them under the title *A Confederate Girl's Diary*.

NATHAN B. WEBB

"This afternoon we received our arms, a Revolver & Sabre," Nathan Webb wrote in his diary on March 22, 1862. "O! that they never might have to be blackened, the one in constant use against our fellow men, the other perhaps in the blood of those heretofore our comrades and brothers." That evening Private Webb and his regiment, the 1st Maine Cavalry, crossed the Potomac and set foot for the first time on the "sacred soil" of Virginia. Six months earlier, the nineteen-year-old seminary student had left his home in Sweden, Maine. After a long period of waiting, drilling, and performing guard duty, Nathan Webb now finally prepared to meet the enemy.[64]

Webb wrote in his diary that he had enlisted to defend his country. Yet he undoubtedly acted for other reasons in addition to love of the Union. His classmates at the Maine seminary enlisted almost as a unit, and Webb did not want to be left behind. As a young man from a small community, he thrilled at the chance for adventure and travel. As a Republican, he hoped to weaken or abolish slavery. Above everything, however, Nathan Webb believed that the leaders of the rebellion must be subdued. On picket duty during his second night south of the Potomac, he tried to assess his motivations. He denounced those southerners "who through unholy ambition and love of unrighteous gain" were now attempting "by bloody war to overthrow the best, the freest government upon earth." Webb expressed more pity than vindictiveness toward the misguided Confederates, but he remained convinced that all who rebelled against the Union must be punished.[65]

Webb fought in the second battle at Bull Run in 1862, but his regiment was not engaged at Antietam or Fredericksburg later that year. After skirmishes with the Confederates at the start of the 1863 spring campaign, he commented that it was a "curious business" for "a civilized, enlightened human being" to be a hunter lying in wait to shoot another human being. "But then I would hunt and kill a man who had raised his hand in blood against my country, as soon as I would hunt and kill a

---

64. Webb Diary, March 22, 1862. Biographical information is from Webb's diary and Edward P. Tobie, *History of the First Maine Cavalry* (Boston, 1887).
65. Webb Diary, March 23, 1862.

fox which was stealing my chickens," he vowed. The Rebels must be treated as "personal enemies" seeking the life of each individual Union soldier, who "must consider the enemy of his country his own most deadly foe and show him no mercy so long as he continues in rebellion." The enemy Webb depicted remained a shadowy image. Although he insisted that sectional hatred must become personal for each soldier, he did not yet recognize the Confederates as individual humans.[66]

In explaining the sectional conflict, Nathan Webb saw slavery as the most obvious difference between northern and southern society. Contrasting the "squalid poverty" of Virginia with the "well-to-do farmers" of the North, he predicted that Maryland would "bloom and become the land flowing with milk and honey" once the "accursed institution" disappeared. He hoped that "this uprising of the slave oligarchy" would reveal the hideousness of slavery and purge the South of its "great sin." Even this opponent of slavery, however, conceded that if he had lived in the South he probably would have been "an advocate of the mild form of slavery" who hated abolitionists. Webb argued that in the South a kind and humane slaveholder could benefit the slave and society more than "a crossgrained out-and-out abolitionist." Nevertheless, he applauded Lincoln's Emancipation Proclamation. Several months after his discourse on humane slaveholders, Webb apparently reversed this opinion. He denounced the "universal idea here" that slavery was the natural condition for blacks "and that kind masters are blessings to them." He had recovered from his momentary lapse from Republican doctrine.[67]

Like most northerners, Nathan Webb expressed astonishment at the poverty and ignorance of the majority of southerners. He gawked at their "dilapidated" horses, faded dresses, "improvised" bonnets, and ramshackle buildings. "The more I see of the southern people," he concluded, "the more I am convinced that they are a poor, ignorant, arrogant set of beings." A very few were educated and well-bred, he admitted, "but the masses, even of the finest society are an ignorant, overbearing, proud, arrogant set." Most damning of all was their backwardness. "They are fifty years behind the time in all improvements and fashions and all that tends to make men good & great," Webb charged. He described Prince George Court House, in Tidewater Vir-

---

66. *Ibid.*, April 15, 1863.
67. *Ibid.*, September 9, October 28, 1862, March 1, 1863.

ginia, as a "dreary looking" and "medieval" village. "I don't see how people could live here and be contented with such little progress," he exclaimed. "If any of them ever visited the North they must have been surprised." Once again, the proud northerner boasted of his society's superiority in educational and material development. Marching through the Shenandoah Valley, Webb proclaimed that with infusions of "northern skill and enterprise" the fertile land, woefully undeveloped and blighted by southern backwardness, would "blossom as the rose." Only by the introduction of northern energy and free labor could the South become a modern, productive society.[68]

Webb's understanding of southerners improved as personal contact replaced detached observation. Conversations with several Virginia women tempered his indictment of southern character. He began to see southerners as flesh-and-blood individuals capable of feeling love, anguish, hate, and joy. Such recognition could evoke sympathy and respect. First impressions, however, did not seem promising. Two months after entering Virginia, Webb observed that the women "treat us with more scorn and derision than the males." Responding to this animosity, Union soldiers sometimes traded insults for abuse. Younger ladies, who often embodied "the most hateful form of secession," defiantly played Confederate patriotic songs on the piano and laughed derisively when Yankee officers passed by. "However, one can but notice the furtive glances made as a handsome Col. and Staff Officer rides by," Webb smugly asserted. Virginia women thus showed the same interest in the men occupying their land that Sarah Morgan had felt. Also like Sarah Morgan, they felt indignant at having to accept food and other necessities from the Union forces. "About the worst feelings I have towards them," Webb exulted, "is the satisfaction that ere long they will be begging at our feet." Only through such humiliation could their haughtiness be repaid. Webb demanded at least the satisfaction of seeing the proud southern chivalry humbled.[69]

This would not be easy. The men and women of Virginia with whom Webb discussed the causes and probable consequences of the war never wavered from their defense of slavery, secession, and the Confederate cause. While grazing his horse during a long march in May, 1862, Webb started a conversation with a woman from White

68. *Ibid.*, November 18, 1863, May 2, August 3, 1864, June 22, 1863.
69. *Ibid.*, May 27, July 21, 1862.

Plains, Virginia. When she discovered that he came from Maine, she demanded to know "'what possessed me that I should come way down there to make war upon my country-men.'" Southerners had endured northern insults for many years, she argued, but "'the abolition spirit that had seized upon the North had at last driven them to madness and they were very reluctantly obliged to resort to self defense.'" This woman had three brothers who had been in the army "since the first gun," and she vowed to disown them, "as a true Southern woman should," if they did not stay until independence was achieved. Webb tried unsuccessfully to convince her she was wrong. "I bid her good-bye, saying that I hoped she would see the error of her ways," he wrote, "and that before any of her brothers were killed, this strife would cease." Far from having humbled the pride of southern chivalry, Webb himself seemed abashed. Unable to win the argument, he could only express sympathy for the woman's suffering.[70]

Nathan Webb lacked the heart of a ruthless invader. His own hardships failed to make him bitter toward the enemy. Captured during a cavalry charge at Aldie in June, 1863, he endured privation at Belle Isle Prison in Richmond. He complained of bad food, the lack of sanitary water, and harsh guards but mentioned that some of the guards smuggled in bread, which they sold to the prisoners. After only one month in prison, Webb was paroled and returned home. In March, 1864, he won promotion to sergeant. Two months later, during a fierce hand-to-hand cavalry battle, he suffered a slight saber wound. In August, 1864, a minié ball tore open his left hip during a battle at Deep Bottom, Virginia, and he required several months of recuperation, first in a Philadelphia hospital and later at home in Maine. Solemnly, he counted the losses among his seminary classmates who had enlisted with him three years before. One comrade had died of malaria in a Louisiana bayou; a second had died in the battle of Perryville, another at Antietam, and a fourth at Aldie; one suffered a severe wound at Port Hudson, another lost a leg at Cold Harbor, and two more were in hospitals recovering from wounds; one classmate had been permanently disabled by a saber wound at Upperville, and yet another had been missing since the fight at St. Mary's Church.[71]

These numerous tragedies hardened men's hearts but did not leave

70. *Ibid.*, May 30, 1862. For further examples of Union soldiers' sympathy for southerners' suffering, see Wiley, *Billy Yank*, 351–52.
71. Webb Diary, August 15, 1864, and *passim*; Tobie, *First Maine Cavalry, passim*.

them incapable of sympathy—even for the enemy. During a raid through central Virginia in 1864, Webb expressed concern for the people whose food and property the federal troops confiscated. "We treat them civilly and excuse our foraging upon the plea that it is a necessity," he explained, "for even a three years soldier can forage with a better heart when he is obliged to than when he has salt pork and hard tack in his haversack."[72] Like Charles Wills, Webb found unauthorized theft and destruction repugnant. Military necessity justified living off the land, just as it had justified emancipation and enlistment of black troops. Northern patriots would accept any measures that would aid the war effort and preserve the Union.

Yet it was not always easy to enforce stern war measures. In August, 1864, Sergeant Webb stationed a picket to guard the house of a widow within Union lines near Petersburg. The woman said she wanted "no reminders of this unhappy struggle" and asked him to place the guard elsewhere. "Her husband and two sons had been killed in defending their home," Webb explained, "and she hated to look upon one who was a comrade of those who had killed her beloved ones." The woman walked with her little girl to the Union camp to ask the major to move the sentinel. Webb followed on foot. She gave the major a moving account of her bereavement and torment at seeing a Yankee uniform at her home. The major granted her request. "When I followed on behind her leading my horse was the first time I ever felt humbled in the presence of a Southerner," Nathan Webb confessed. "I felt heartily sorry for her and I hope she will never again be annoyed."[73]

Victorious Union soldiers might easily feel sympathy for the enemy's sufferings. The victims could only feel hatred and vengeance. On picket duty at Mount Sinai Church, Virginia, in August, 1864, Webb saw a large, rambling plantation house surrounded by slave cabins and stables. The master of the house was a Confederate infantry colonel, and the three sons served as cavalry officers. Nearly all the slaves had departed. The young ladies, accustomed all their lives to being waited upon, struggled to meet the demands of raising food and maintaining the household. "It was a sad sight to see the educated ladies with faded clothing [and] weary step brought to such straits," Webb wrote sympathetically. "It was a sad reminder of the fall of the boasted Virginia

---

72. Webb Diary, June 17, 1864.
73. *Ibid.*, August 9, 1864.

Chivalry." He thought that they must bitterly remember their former exalted status as "the beauty and pride of the country round" and keenly feel their fall to poverty. "I don't wonder that they hate us with such venom," he acknowledged. "Though they will not admit that they themselves are the cause of their sad condition they venomously curse us as the invaders and spoilers of their hearthstones." Webb still insisted that southerners deserved to suffer the consequences of rebelling against the world's best government. Yet he pitied the plight of these women. "I had much rather meet their husbands and brothers on the field than they in their bleak and dreary homes," he declared. "O Virginia how great your crime how dire your punishment."[74]

Webb's compassion had limits, however. He pitied the plight of southern women left alone to confront an invading army and recognized that many common soldiers wanted only the return of peace. Early in 1863, he wrote that the army was divided between "the two policies of kind treatment to our enemies and annihilation." Many argued that protecting private property would subdue the South more effectively than destroying everything that could aid the Confederacy. This argument corresponded to the belief that a kind master could aid the slave more than a zealous abolitionist. A soft answer would turn away wrath. "I am for kindness to the masses," Webb declared, "but death on leaders." His compassion was inversely proportional to southerners' enthusiasm for the war. "Use well those conscripted," he argued, "but rough those who volunteered." The common soldiers had been misled by wicked counselors and should be pardoned. "But to the leaders, military and civil, no mercy no leniency," Webb insisted. "Trial conviction and a rope." He hated only the leaders of the rebellion and believed that they alone should be punished. The common soldiers and civilians had expiated their sins, the former by undergoing privations and risking their lives, the latter by enduring the ravages of invasion. They could now be forgiven.[75]

Nathan Webb perceived the southern masses as victims of war. He felt no malice toward them. In April, 1863, he predicted that once Confederate leaders recognized the hopelessness of their cause they would flee the country. "Then all we will have to do," he wrote, "will be

74. *Ibid.*, August 1, 1864.
75. *Ibid.*, February 15, April 10, 1863. By early 1862, many northern ministers had assigned guilt for the war to Confederate leaders, arguing that the masses should be pitied and forgiven (Dunham, *Attitude of the Northern Clergy*, 191–94).

to send the Army home and tell them to live peaceably and again become law abiding citizens and the poor fellows will be glad of the chance." This was exactly what General Ulysses S. Grant did at Appomattox two years later. The ignorance which Webb discovered among many southerners led him to believe that they had been duped into fighting against their own interests. By January of 1864 he detected in several Richmond newspaper editorials evidence of declining morale in the South, which he attributed to antagonism between nonslaveholders and planters. "Two or three more conscriptions with wholesale exemptions of planters and wealthy men," Webb predicted, "may open the eyes of the masses just a little as to what and for whom they are fighting." Deceived by traitorous secessionists, most common soldiers deserved leniency if they would only lay down their arms.[76]

A feeling of kinship developed between some Union and Confederate soldiers. Fraternizing between picket lines, many had recognized that all soldiers shared similar experiences, dangers, fears, and hopes for peace. Even those who never met the enemy directly could sometimes perceive their common plight. This realization often assuaged their malice. Soldiers admired a gallant foe. "A true soldier cannot help having some respect for a man who openly & honorably fights him," Nathan Webb asserted, "even if his cause is wrong." Such an opponent would be considered an equal, "a foeman worthy of his steel."[77] Webb forgave Confederate soldiers because they had fought bravely and because they were willing to accept the verdict of battle. He believed that once defeated, they would live in peace. Like blacks, white southerners had earned respect on the battlefield. Webb likewise pardoned southern women, who had endured invasion and deprivations. Suffering had cleansed their sins. Only against the architects of rebellion did he demand retribution. In this respect, he typified the majority of his fellow northerners.

The war ended anticlimactically for Nathan Webb. When his three-year enlistment ended in November, 1864, he returned home. After difficult deliberations, he concluded that he did not want to be a soldier in peacetime, and, rather than commit himself to three more years of military service, he decided not to reenlist. In later years, he regretted

76. Webb Diary, April 10, 1863, January 31, 1864. On nonslaveholders and southern unity, see James L. Roark, *Masters Without Slaves: Southern Planters in the Civil War and Reconstruction* (New York, 1977), 46–48, 55–63.
77. Webb Diary, January 4, 1864.

this decision. "After getting home every letter I had from my comrades telling of their victories put again into me the old spirit and I regretted I was not with them," he wrote in 1865. "And during the last victorious days I felt as if I did wrong in leaving." The Civil War remained the most memorable period of his life. Nearly thirty years after Appomattox, even though he had moved to Boulder, Colorado, Nathan Webb still maintained contact with his former military comrades. In 1892, he contributed one dollar for a monument to be erected at Gettysburg in honor of the 1st Maine Cavalry.[78]

WILLIAM KING

Southern civilians whose lands were occupied by Yankee troops usually greeted the invaders with fear and hostility. Suffering intensified their Confederate patriotism and their hatred of the enemy. The horrors of this war, which frequently degenerated into the vicious plundering deplored by Charles Wills, led southerners to regard the Yankee as a hellish fiend incapable of moral salvation. As one wealthy Tennessee planter reported, after the invading federal army had destroyed cotton, cattle, and sheep on one of his four plantations, "The amt. of Wanton & useless distruction (to them) would better suit an army of Savages than of a Christian people."[79]

Unable to bear arms against the ruthless enemy, civilian men and women had no way to relieve their loathing for those who caused such bitter suffering. Hatred of the Yankee invader grew stonger as the war progressed. For a few southerners, however, contacts with friendly Union soldiers such as Nathan Webb altered their images of Yankee brutality. Such instances were rare, but they indicate the circumstances that could change perceptions of the enemy. Sarah Morgan's reassessment of Yankee character, for example, derived from her fiercely independent spirit, her willingness to talk openly with federal soldiers, and, at least to some extent, her background as a member of a nonplanter family with some Unionist ties. Georgia planter and Unionist William King also kept an open mind about the Yankee invaders. His brief diary, kept during the first two months of occupation by General William T. Sherman's army in 1864, records almost daily discussions of Yankee actions and character. Among southern civilians whose writings are

78. *Ibid.*, December 29, 1863, January 3, 1864, and undated footnote [1865?].
79. John Houston Bills Diary, October 13, 1862, SHC.

interpreted here, King exhibits the least hostile predisposition toward the invader.

During the summer of 1864, King had extensive personal contacts with northern soldiers, which provided ample opportunity to observe and talk with them. As Sherman's army approached Atlanta in July, 1864, the notorious "bummers" looted King's home near Marietta, in Cobb County. Learning that he was a loyal Unionist, however, federal officers apologized, punished several of the robbers, and established a guard post on his plantation to prevent further destruction. Many of King's neighbors had also been vandalized, he soon discovered: "I went to town and saw a few friends, heard added statements of depredations and believe but few in the town and county had escaped the visits and terrors of the Robbers." Taking advantage of disordered conditions, civilian bushwhackers and thieves added to the miseries of enemy occupation. As the main Union force passed on, leaving stragglers in the rear, King reported that local citizens and soldiers of both armies were "committing all depredations of plundering and murdering." Everyone in the area suffered severely, "not from the evil days of the Federal army, but from the army of Robbers which follow in its wake and from the corrupt people living among us," King wrote in his diary. "Laws are suspended and the evil passions let loose."[80]

Although he had opposed secession and supported the Union, William King shared the stereotypical southern images of Yankees. Tales of their cruelty and immorality made him apprehensive at their approach, and his first contact with Sherman's bummers seemed to confirm these fears. The behavior of the soldiers detailed to guard his plantation, however, dispelled such apprehensions. "I have suffered no more from the soldiers of the Federal Army than from those of our own Army," King wrote after living under Yankee rule for one week. "I have mingled and conversed freely with officers and privates. I have not met a single individual whose deportment and language has not been gentlemanly, nor a word nor opinion has been expressed to me in the least discourteous manner." Although he disagreed with them on many issues, King found the northern soldiers willing to discuss these topics pleasantly. Perhaps his greatest surprise was that these Yankee invaders "exhibited no exultant spirit nor expression at our army having so constantly fallen back; but more a spirit of sympathy for us, and

80. William King Diary, July 5, 7, 18, 1864, in William King Papers, SHC.

simply a desire to avoid any expression which might be painful to me."[81] These soldiers thus shared the compassion for civilian suffering exhibited by Charles Wills during Sherman's march through Georgia.

Most federal soldiers with whom King conversed shared his hatred of war and his desire for peace. As a southern Unionist, King felt alienated from both antagonists and denounced the conflict as a "cruel, stupid politicians' war." This senseless slaughter had been forced upon a happy, prosperous people by "political demagogues North and South." His friendly relations with northern soldiers convinced him that the only real enemies were the radical leaders of both sides. "This needless war is spreading mourning and distress throughout our once prosperous and almost perfectly happy country," King lamented, "if the politicians were out of the way, how soon could the afflicted people reconcile their differences, and terminate this appalling and wicked sacrifice of Life and happiness." Most of the former secessionists fled from their homes as Sherman's army approached. "How little could our disunion friends have conceived of the trials and troubles their acts were to bring upon a happy and prosperous people," King wrote. "God grant that peace may soon be restored to our afflicted country." The tragedy of war confirmed King's earlier opposition to secession and strengthened his desire to see the Union restored.[82]

The northern officers and soldiers with whom King talked expressed sympathy and friendship for the southern people; only against blacks did they exhibit hostility. It surprised and troubled King that the Yankees "all seem to hate those poor creatures." When Yankee robbers ransacked Mrs. Duncan's home, they also stole all the possessions of her servant, "old Mamie." When she asked them "to have mercy on a poor negro," Mamie told King, "they cursed her and said if she did not close her mouth they would kill her."[83] Such treatment violated the paternalistic ideal of southern planters such as William King. The words and deeds of Union soldiers were the first evidence many southerners saw of northern racial prejudice.

Despite his condemnation of cruelty and destruction, which he considered a natural result of the war, William King's image of the Yankee improved as a result of personal contact. He expressed gratitude for the

---

81. *Ibid.*, July 10, 1864.
82. *Ibid.*, July 22, 12, 25, 17, 1864. See also Pressly, *Americans Interpret Their Civil War*, 129–38.
83. King Diary, July 5, 30, 1864.

opportunity to learn firsthand about northern character and found that "everything has tended to allay any unkind feelings which I may have previously entertained and I truly wish all our ultra disunion men of the South could have enjoyed the same privilege I have." Through such personal experiences, sectional antagonism could be laid to rest. "My intercourse with them has greatly elevated my opinion of the character & feelings of the Federal Army," King concluded. Although he had supported the Union and denounced secession, William King shared his fellow southerners' dislike of Yankees. Personal encounters with the enemy altered his opinion. "All which I have seen compels me to admire the men—they do not seem to feel any hatred toward us, but speak favorably of our army and our people," he wrote in his diary, "they say we are one people, the same language, habits and religion, and ought to be one people." Sectional divisions seemed artificial and less compelling than the forces that united all Americans. King reported that federal soldiers said they had "a higher opinion of the people of the South than before the war," and he concluded that "even an ultra So. Carolinian" could no longer claim the ability to "whip 5 Yankees" by himself. "To have effected such a change of sentiment North and South toward the people of both sections," King claimed, "has been one of the favorable results of this sad war."[84] Even if his overly optimistic assessment were correct, the suffering of war was an exorbitant price to pay for a reduction of sectional animosity. Unfortunately, few southerners would share King's reassessment of Yankee character.

The South suffered too greatly at the hands of Yankee invaders for sectional stereotypes to change. Despite his new respect for individual northerners, there remained one issue on which even Unionist William King would accept no compromise. He was anxious for the war to cease; he deplored the necessity of two peoples sharing common feelings and characteristics killing each other; and he would welcome an early reestablishment of the Union. He would not, however, tolerate interference with slavery. King enjoyed talking with Union officers and soldiers, he reported in August, 1864, "but the unanimous feelings all seem to express, although opposed to War & anxious for peace, are that they cannot stop short of a restoration of the Union & the abolition of

84. *Ibid.*, July 23, 30, 10, 1864.

slavery." These northerners "generally hate the negroes, & believe they are better off as they are than to be freed," he observed, "but they say slavery is the cause of the War, and that there can be no permanent peace between the 2 sections, if slavery is allowed to remain, & to continue it would be to retain the causes for future disturbances." Such statements deeply troubled him.[85]

As a prosperous planter, William King remained a conservative Unionist. Even at the risk of sundering the Union, he would not accept the abolition of slavery, either as a moral imperative or as a military necessity. He wanted only to restore the Union as it was before the war. He told a Union officer that "if the North was contending for the Union & Constitution as they professed, an early reunion may take place, but if they intended to act in violation of the Constitution, on the subject of Slavery or in any other way, they had to subjugate the South & force it back & keep it in with many Bayonets." This would "violate all principles of a free government," he charged, and would "require years of bloody War." Northern attacks on slavery undermined King's respect and good feelings for Union soldiers and aroused stubborn resistance to reconciliation in even this most tolerant of southerners. Although he recognized the fraternal bonds uniting northern and southern people, King insisted that interference with slavery would discredit all expressions of Yankee friendship and goodwill.[86]

Despite his opposition to emancipation, William King continued to speak freely with Union officers and soldiers, even when disagreeing about war issues. In 1871, Congress established the Southern Claims Commission to recompense southern Unionists who had provided supplies to federal troops during the war. The criteria for honoring claims were strict, designed to discourage all but the staunchest Unionists from applying. Yet in 1878 William King joined twenty-two thousand other southerners who filed claims for their contributions to the Union cause. His devotion to the Union, he argued, should be recognized and rewarded. Despite King's vows of loyalty to the Union, the Southern Claims Commission rejected both of his claims, which totaled $5,895. "The claimant failed in that case to prove loyalty and there is no testimony to loyalty in the present claim," the commissioners con-

---

85. *Ibid.*, August 7, 1864.
86. *Ibid.*, September 4, 1864.

cluded. King's sympathy for the Union cause gained him no financial compensation for his wartime losses.[87]

FRATERNIZATION

Union and Confederate soldiers met each other wherever picket lines were established within shouting distance. During lulls and between battles, opposing pickets sometimes agreed to cease sniping and to enjoy a temporary peace. Robert McAllister described one of these informal truces in the Petersburg trenches: "Several times the Rebels have called upon our boys to cease firing, and we did as they desired. The boys jumped up, shook their blankets, walked around—as well as talked across to the Rebels, who done the same thing. Each time a Rebel officer would come along and order his men to fire, they would yell to our boys to keep down, as they were ordered to fire again." Shortly after the battle of Fredericksburg, a young North Carolina officer expressed surprise at the friendliness of pickets on opposite sides of the Rappahannock. "It is the strangest picket I ever saw," he wrote home. "Instead of cracking away at each other every time a head is visible each side lounges about carelessly, and talk and laugh with each other."[88]

Shouted conversations sometimes led to meetings between the picket lines, where soldiers exchanged tobacco, coffee, newspapers, and opinions about the war. Curiosity about the enemy repeatedly drew Yankees and Confederates together. "Our men & the Rebels seem determined to be together all the time," Lieutenant Charles Haydon of Michigan observed with astonishment. Lieutenant Samuel D. Sanders, a respected South Carolina physician before the war, reported that Yankee pickets at Morris Island, South Carolina, had sent across a small wooden raft containing northern newspapers, "but we sent them over some 'Christian Advocates' and 'Confederate Baptists,' hoping thereby to improve their morals some." Wisconsin private George W. Buffum obtained tobacco from Rebel pickets he met between the lines

---

87. Summary Report of Commissioners of Claims, December 16, 1879, in William King (Trustee for Sarah E. King), Southern Claims Commission Case No. 19,579, Records of the United States House of Representatives, Record Group 233, National Archives. For information about the Southern Claims Commission and the persistence of Unionism in the South, see Frank W. Klingberg, *The Southern Claims Commission* (Berkeley, 1950); and Degler, *The Other South*, 179–84.

88. Robertson (ed.), *Civil War Letters of McAllister*, 500; William Calder to his mother, January 10, 1863, in Calder Papers. See also Bell Irvin Wiley, *The Life of Johnny Reb: The Common Soldier of the Confederacy* (Indianapolis, 1943), 316–21; and Wiley, *Billy Yank*, 352–57.

near Petersburg in 1864. "We dont shute at woune a nother unles we let woune another no before we commenc fiering," he explained to his wife. "We hav orders to fier wounc in a while to ceep the pickitts in snug then we howler take care boys we are going to fier and then we lay to until we git threw." Such truces, mutually arranged by soldiers of the opposing armies, provided a brief respite from the danger of life on the picket lines. This recognition of the enemy's humanity also eventually contributed to diminishing hatred among the common soldiers. During one of these truces between the lines, Chauncey Cooke of Wisconsin talked with some of the Rebels. "It seems too bad that we have to fight men that we like. Now these Southern soldiers seem just like our own boys," he concluded. "They talk about . . . their mothers and fathers and their sweethearts just as we do." Through such meetings, soldiers of both sides realized that they shared more common values and characteristics than those that divided them.[89]

During the Atlanta campaign of 1864, large numbers of war-weary Confederates deserted to Union lines, providing Private John Brobst of the 25th Wisconsin Volunteers an opportunity to meet several enemy soldiers. These Rebel deserters assured him that they did not want to fight. "They say they are sick of war and want peace on any terms," Brobst reported. Yet he vowed that he would continue to fight "until the last foul traitor is made to bite the dust in the agonies of death" to regain "every foot of territory that the traitors claim as southern confederacy." A twenty-three-year-old farmer from the frontier of western Wisconsin, Brobst had enlisted in September, 1862. He was undecided on abolition, but he opposed secession. Personal considerations strengthened his desire for retaliation. In the battle of Atlanta on July 22, 1864, Brobst lost his knapsack, which contained a cherished picture of his fiancée, Mary Englesby. He told her that if he ever encountered the Rebel who had her picture, "I could kill him with a good heart and clear conscience."[90]

Before long, however, his encounters with Confederate prisoners altered his opinion of southerners. Two deserters had dinner with him

89. Charles B. Haydon Diary, December 23, 1862, MHC; Walter Rundell, Jr. (ed.), " 'If Fortune Should Fail'—Civil War Letters of Dr. Samuel D. Sanders," *South Carolina Historical Magazine*, LXV (October, 1964), 225; George W. Buffum to his wife, December 11, 1864, in Buffum Papers, WSHS; Chauncey Cooke, quoted in Wiley, *Billy Yank*, 356. Cf. James E. Hall, *The Diary of a Confederate Soldier*, ed. Ruth W. Dayton (N.p., 1961), 66, 128.

90. John F. Brobst, *Well, Mary: Civil War Letters of a Wisconsin Volunteer*, ed. Margaret Brobst Roth (Madison, 1960), 60, 106, 92.

one evening, and all enjoyed a pleasant conversation. After they left, Brobst acknowledged: "They were real smart fellows both of them." Union and Confederate soldiers were not fighting because they hated each other, he reasoned, for they occasionally picked blackberries together between the lines. "You must not think up there that we fight down here because we are mad," he explained to Mary Englesby, "but we fight for fun, or rather because we can't help ourselves." Surprisingly, the soldiers seemed almost free of personal hatred for the enemy. "If they would let the soldiers settle this thing it would not be long before we would be on terms of peace," Brobst concluded.[91]

Several months later, a Confederate deserter spent a few days visiting Brobst. Exactly how they met is not clear, but Brobst's account of their brief acquaintance tells an interesting story of war hatred and friendship:

December the 22nd [1864]
    . . . I have killed some time talking with a rebel deserter. He stayed with me last night. His name is James Brown. He is a very clever fellow. He is tired of war and has escaped and got safely inside of our lines. . . . We have some friendly talk about the battles we have been in. We have been hotly engaged against one another several times. The 22nd of July was one day. We have talked the scenes of that day all over several times since he has been here. He and I are going over town today so I must bid you good morning.

December the 23rd
    Well, Mary, I have something strange to tell you this morning. Yesterday, this James Brown and I got to talking about the girls as a matter of course. I told him I thought the northern girls were the handsomest and while we were talking he told me he had pictures of four northern girls. At least, he supposed they were, for he got them the 22nd of July. I wanted to see them, so he let me see them, and it was your picture, with my three sisters. I told him so, and it was some time before I could make him believe it, but I told him all that there was in the knapsack that had them in, so he gave them back to me. I tell you I was glad to get them. They have been kept very nice, just as nice as I could have kept them myself and done my best, and the result is I have been taking a long look at you this morning. I told Brown what you had written to me, that you wished you had ahold of him and you would show him what a northern girl could do. He laughed and wants me to tell you that he sends his best respects and that he has carried you in his coat pocket five months and you were docile and gentle as a lamb, never found a word of fault.

91. *Ibid.*, 80.

Having become friends with this Confederate deserter, Brobst forgot that he had once pledged to kill the enemy who had his sweetheart's picture. He even chided Mary for her bellicosity.[92]

The courage Confederate soldiers displayed in battle increased John Brobst's admiration for them. "Braver men never shouldered a musket than those rebels that came up to drive us out of our works," he wrote after a fierce battle at Dallas, Georgia. Courage in battle often earned more respect for an opponent than any other factor because soldiers recognized and applauded valor in their fellow warriors. By contrast, they scorned civilians who refused to fight. Brobst respected enemy soldiers even more after comparing their gallantry to the cowardice of many of his fellow northerners, "for every man that sympathized with the rebellion in the North are cowards, and we have more respect for those that actually took up arms against us and showed themselves men and not cowards, than we can of sneaking, low-lived, miserable cowards." Those who did not aid the Union cause were responsible for prolonging the war, he believed.[93]

John Brobst's encounters with Confederate soldiers dramatically altered his perceptions of the enemy. A recognition that northerners and southerners shared many similarities replaced vague images of sectional differences. Brobst discovered strong fraternal bonds still uniting the common people of North and South, who often did not share their leaders' sectional animosity. Like Nathan Webb, he blamed Confederate officers and politicians for fomenting the war. This distinction between wicked leaders and peaceful citizens created a false dichotomy, as revealed by the intense hatred expressed by many common people on both sides. Yet it provided a simple, satisfying explanation for the eruption of war among Americans who shared a common cultural heritage and political system.[94]

This explanation achieved increasing popularity. By 1863, war weariness permeated the ranks of both sides. Adversaries who could agree on little else concurred in their desire for peace and an end to fighting. After one battle near Vicksburg, a truce was declared while each side buried its dead. During this cessation of hostilities, Yankees and Rebels

92. *Ibid.*, 107–108.
93. *Ibid.*, 69, 144. For similar comments on the enemy's bravery by a Georgia captain, see Benjamin E. Stiles to his mother, April 29, 1862, in Mackay and Stiles Family Papers, SHC. See also Gerald F. Linderman, *Embattled Courage: The Experience of Combat in the American Civil War* (New York, 1987), 65–73.
94. Brobst, *Well, Mary*, 60. See Wiley, *Billy Yank*, 350.

met and discussed the war. "They agreed with us perfectly on one thing," a Wisconsin soldier reported. "If the settlement of this war was left to the Enlisted men of both sides we would soon go home." In April, 1863, an Alabama soldier wrote from Tennessee that his comrades were "heartily sick of the war" and that if the peace question could be submitted to Confederate and Union soldiers, "we could speedily come to an understanding." Conversations with the foe revealed that all soldiers shared common dangers, fears, and hopes for peace. Mutual problems and concerns fostered sympathy, respect, and—sometimes—even friendship among soldiers wearing blue and gray.[95]

Recognizing their common interests, Yankees and Rebels often agreed that war hatreds had been aroused and perpetuated by fanatics and politicians. Debates between Union and Confederate soldiers usually ended "by mutually wishing we had 'let those who make the quarrels be the very ones to fight,'" reported Sergeant Felix Brannigan of New York in 1863. "If the question was left to the two contending armies here," he concluded, "we would restore the Union tomorrow, and hang both cabinets at our earliest convenience afterwards." After talking with Rebel pickets, Private Edwin Wentworth of Maine concluded that he "would like to have the politicians on both sides—the leaders—shut up in a tight room and fight themselves till one side or the other were all killed, and so decide the matter, instead of us shooting at each other." Southern soldiers reported the same feelings. "If I only had the fanatics of the North and fire eaters of the South, in equal numbers in a pen together, I'd make 'dog eat dog,'" Louisiana quartermaster Robert Patrick vowed. The soldiers had thus found both a convenient scapegoat and a simple explanation of the war's causes, which enabled them to acknowledge the decency of enemy soldiers. Political leaders, not the mass of common people, had brought about the sectional conflict.[96]

Many officers feared that such sentiments would have a harmful effect on discipline and conduct in battle. It would be harder to kill personal acquaintants than unknown enemies. "The Rebs are Picket-

---

95. Stephen E. Ambrose (ed.), *A Wisconsin Boy in Dixie: The Selected Letters of James K. Newton* (Madison, 1961), 72; Henry C. Semple to his wife, April 7, 1863, in Henry C. Semple Papers, SHC.

96. Felix Brannigan to his father [late 1863], in Brannigan Papers; Edwin O. Wentworth to his wife, December 22, 1862, in Wentworth Papers; F. Jay Taylor (ed.), *Reluctant Rebel: The Secret Diary of Robert Patrick, 1861–1865* (Baton Rouge, 1959), 196.

ting on the other side and at first we were in the habit of swiming across to each other and exchanging papers and Coffee for Tobacco," reported Lieutenant Charles Greenleaf of Hartford, Connecticut, in September, 1863, "but the officers of both sides have put a stop to this." After conversing with enemy pickets across the Potomac, a Pennsylvania colonel vowed not to do so again. "It seems hard that we should be in arms against these men," he concluded. "I will talk with them no more for it will take all the soldier out of me on the day of battle." Such fears were seldom realized.[97]

However dramatic such friendly exchanges between enemy soldiers were, their importance should not be overestimated. Frequent reports of fraternization testify to the bonds of sentiment uniting soldiers exposed to common privations, but they were recognized as unusual and paradoxical events. More often than not, confrontations of Yankees and Rebels were unfriendly. In 1861, South Carolina troops exchanged insults with Michigan soldiers on picket duty in northern Virginia. "They will fire at us and yell out 'take that you d——d Michiganders,'" reported Charles Haydon. "Ours will reply 'go to h——l you d——d fools you cant hit anybody,' and all the other abusive remarks they can think of."[98]

Soldiers on picket duty spent most of their time exchanging shots with the enemy or silently guarding their stations. In the occasional conversations between the lines, most of the verbal exchanges were abusive. Yet even these shouted taunts and boastings were rare. Lieutenant Charles Wills of Illinois described a more common situation. "Our boys never have made any bargain with the Johnnies to quit picket firing, even for an hour," he wrote from the outskirts of Atlanta in July, 1864. "It would almost break the heart of one of our boys to see a Rebel without getting a shot at him." This response was more typical than the friendly meetings. "I was wishing all night that I could see a seesesh," a Pennsylvania private wrote after returning from picket duty in June, 1862, "if I should see one I dont think I could save his life for I would be apt to show him some led for I would just as leaf shoot one as look at him." These hostile confrontations lacked the emotional drama and poignancy of friendly meetings between Union and Con-

---

97. Charles Greenleaf to his parents, September 6, 1863, in Civil War Letters, CHS; Pennsylvania colonel quoted in Strother Diary, September 22, 1861.
98. Haydon Diary, September 15, 1861; Wiley, *Johnny Reb*, 321.

federate soldiers. In the exhilaration of battle, fraternal ties were forgotten, and the bloody work of death went on.[99]

The popular images of Yankee and Rebel obscured more than they revealed about the true character of northern and southern people. The personal sketches presented in this chapter indicate that sectional stereotypes do not accurately describe individuals and that they are inadequate even as generalized portraits of sectional characteristics. They tell us more about the observer than the observed. Northerners' complaints about southern backwardness, for example, reveal their own devotion to an ideal of progress.

False though they may be, sectional images have proven remarkably persistent. Even in the late twentieth century, southerners view the Yankee as mercenary, diabolical, and uncultivated. Many northerners, in turn, view the southerner as ignorant, lazy, and backward. The details and clarity of sectional stereotypes have changed over the years, to be sure, particularly with the decline of northern manufacturing and the rise of the Sun Belt in the mid-twentieth century. The sectional perceptions of Robert McAllister, Alexander Cheves Haskell, and their contemporaries originated as one-dimensional stereotypes, providing moral and social censure of the personal characteristics which each side considered objectionable in the other. Southern views of the Yankee emerged from antebellum rhetoric and literary conventions: he was acquisitive, industrious, uncultivated, and lacking in the moral sensibilities and social graces which southerners claimed as their own special virtues. Before the war, many northerners perceived southerners as Cavalier figures—haughty, aristocratic, self-indulgent, and effete. With secession and war, Rebel replaced Cavalier in northern imagery and first impressions of the South reversed many preconceptions. For northerners, the most striking features of the South were its poverty, ignorance, and lack of progress, which they considered moral shortcomings. Hatred on both sides derived from scorn of the enemy's supposed character faults and, after war erupted, from the suffering and deprivation he caused.

Sectional hatred, however, could not entirely destroy the underlying sympathy that had united northerners and southerners as Americans, sharing a common cultural heritage and political system. Although

99. Wills, *Army Life*, 278; Henry C. Snyder to his parents, June 14, 1862, in Civil War Correspondence, BHC.

hostility prevailed on both sides, many people's perceptions of the enemy transcended common stereotypes and produced sympathy, respect, and even friendship. Personal encounters with the enemy often reduced hatred. Union soldiers traversed every Confederate state, meeting southern civilians in remote rural areas and major supply centers. Soldiers of opposing armies met each other not only in battle but between picket lines during impromptu truces. Such encounters revealed that the enemy shared beliefs, fears, concerns, and hopes common to all people caught in the vortex of war. The enemy then appeared human, with a personality more complex and far less reprehensible than that portrayed in the familiar one-dimensional images.

As the horror and tragedy of war became apparent, hatred diminished. Recognizing the intense suffering invasion inflicted on the South and its people, northerners such as Charles Wills and Nathan Webb expressed sympathy for these victims of war. A few Confederates such as Sarah Morgan rejected the view that all northerners lacked any semblance of decency or honor, particularly when they met Yankees who treated them kindly. Soldiers of both sides often recognized their common hope that the war would end before more lives were sacrificed. They distinguished between ordinary people, who seemed decent and inoffensive, and political and military leaders, who had aroused sectional hatred and fomented war. Attributing evil characteristics to enemy leaders, many on both sides absolved those they thought were reluctant followers.

Northerners concluded that southerners were ignorant and backward but argued that only the rebellion's leaders should be punished. Victory had satiated their desire for revenge. As Charles Wills wrote after witnessing the devastation of South Carolina, "I don't hate her any more." Wills, Nathan Webb, and Robert McAllister all agreed that Rebel leaders deserved to suffer for their crimes but that the masses should be forgiven and welcomed back to the Union.

The Yankee, triumphant and boastful, could not be forgiven so easily. Even Sarah Morgan and William King remained unreconciled to Yankee rule and emancipation. Alex Haskell's hatred of Yankees remained more typical of southern attitudes than Morgan's and King's sympathetic views. Defeat only strengthened their conviction of Yankee wickedness. Confederate experience provided little to soften the indictment.[100]

100. Paul H. Buck, *The Road to Reunion, 1865–1900* (New York, 1959), 33.

The persistence of sectional hatred can be seen in the letters of Benedict Joseph Semmes of Tennessee. A wholesale merchant in Washington, D.C., and Memphis before the war, Semmes served as a commissary officer with the 154th Tennessee Regiment. Describing the
plundering by Yankee troops in Tennessee, Semmes wrote to his wife
in 1863 that "they shall ever be to me enemies in War—enemies in
peace." He could never forgive those "who have countenanced the
starvation & extermination of my wife & children & friends as a means
of civilized warfare." He unleashed his rage in a vitriolic diatribe
against the hated enemy:

> Teach my children to hate them & despise them, as not only our worst &
> meanest enemies but as the enemies of God & mankind. I consider it a
> solemn duty that our children and all the rising generation should be
> brought up in this spirit, for peace will come, and after it this base hypo-
> critical and detested race will endeavour to bring about the old state of
> things and our children should be taught to hate them to prevent their
> infernal designs. I could not die in peace if I thought my children would
> ever feel that the Yankee race one and all were anything but their worst
> and basest enemies socially morally & politically.

He concluded this exhortation by vowing, "No Semmes must ever be a
yankee serf." Such bitterness made reconciliation in spirit virtually
impossible for many southerners.[101]

Benedict Semmes represents an extreme example of the unrecon-
structed Rebel. Yet the depth of his hatred for the Yankee helps to
explain the persistence of sectional animosity in the twentieth century.
For many southerners, Sherman's march through Georgia and the
burning of Columbia, South Carolina, still symbolize the wickedness
of Yankee tyranny. License plates showing a Confederate battle flag or
the picture of a scowling Rebel soldier with the slogan "Hell no, I ain't
forgettin!" remind us how long the bitterness of defeat can rankle the
soul. Most southerners have long since put aside such strong sectional
hatred, but the memory of the Civil War still lives.

How accurate were these images of Yankee and Rebel? They certainly contained an element of truth. Many Yankees were mercenary
and, by Cavalier standards, uncultivated. Many southerners were impoverished, uneducated, and backward, compared to residents of the

---

101. Benedict Joseph Semmes to his wife, June 7, May 5, 1863, in Benedict Joseph
Semmes Papers, SHC. See also Wiley, *Johnny Reb*, 308–309; and Buck, *Road to Reunion*,
44–45.

antebellum North. Bell Irvin Wiley, the preeminent historian of the common soldiers of both sides, offers some interesting comparisons. Billy Yank was more literate, more interested in politics, more practical and prosaic than Johnny Reb, Wiley concludes. Johnny Reb, on the other hand, was more religious, more rural and homogeneous in background, more humorous and imaginative in his letters. Yet these differences remained largely superficial. Wiley concluded his two-volume study of Civil War soldiers by observing that "the similarities of Billy Yank and Johnny Reb outweighed their differences. They were both Americans, by birth or by adoption, and they both had the weaknesses and the virtues of the people of their nation and time."[102]

The similarities of Yankee and Rebel should not be forgotten, but neither should they obscure the deep sectional animosity that erupted in Civil War. Northerners and southerners may in fact have shared more common characteristics than the differences that divided them. Yet the pervasive perception of conflicting interests and moral viewpoints unleashed the fury of a fratricidal war. Amid the turmoil of the Civil War some individuals nevertheless recognized a glimmer of decency, courage, and humanity in the enemy. This recognition somewhat lessened war hatreds and made reconciliation possible. Sectional consciousness has persisted, however. The American people, united in most economic, social, and political matters, remain divided emotionally by the experience of the Civil War.

102. Wiley, *Billy Yank*, 346–61.

6 / THE LIMITS OF SECTIONAL CONSCIOUSNESS

Despite the bitter sectional conflict, northerners and southerners remained, in many respects, more alike than different throughout the Civil War era. Broad lines of division existed, but sectional identity never fully subsumed other personal loyalties, nor did it completely overcome internal conflicts within each section. Both Union and Confederacy faced the same wartime problems and arrived at strikingly similar solutions. Even from the outset, the Confederacy adopted a constitution with only minor revisions (for example, to protect slavery more explicitly) to the United States Constitution. Both sides likewise adopted similar responses to a wide range of issues, including enacting conscription to raise troops, issuing paper money, increasing taxes, strengthening the central government, involving civilians in a "total war" effort, and adopting such military innovations as breastworks and entrenchments. That Union and Confederacy became mirror images reflects the basic homogeneity of an American people bound by common political ideas and loyalties, reinforced by a common culture and a common tradition. Sectional conflict disrupted these ties. The sectional cleavage ran deep, but not deep enough to eliminate all traces of common American characteristics. The war thus reveals not two different civilizations, but one people divided by conflicting interpretations of common American values.[1]

Similarities in basic values should not obscure the many differences among Americans. Sectional consciousness, as discussed in previous chapters, constitutes the most pervasive and significant dividing line in popular thought during the war. This chapter examines several other issues that cut across sectional lines and even, at times, provided ties of loyalty or personal identity stronger than sectional unity. Individuals base their self-images on a broad mixture of factors, including race and ethnicity, religion, social class, gender, occupation, commu-

1. David M. Potter, *The Impending Crisis, 1848–1861* (New York, 1976), 11–14, 469–72; Potter, *The South and the Sectional Conflict* (Baton Rouge, 1968), 57; David H. Donald, *Liberty and Union* (Boston, 1978), 83–102, 121–55; Carl N. Degler, *Place Over Time: The Continuity of Southern Distinctiveness* (Baton Rouge, 1977), 93–96.

nity ties, political and ideological values, among others. Sectional loyalty constituted only one of Civil War participants' sources of personal identification. Likewise, both Union and Confederacy faced internal conflicts based on social, political, and economic interests. In demonstrating the influence of such factors, which limited sectional cohesiveness to varying degrees, this chapter focuses on five issues: state loyalty, social class, military rank, ideology and patriotism, and morale. The internal divisions caused by these factors present a valuable counterpoint to the dominant theme of sectional consciousness. Despite such limitations, sectional identity remained strong enough to sustain the conflict for four years, until the Confederacy collapsed.

A WAR BETWEEN THE STATES

Nineteenth-century Americans identified themselves as members of a particular community or as citizens of a certain state. Beyond vague feelings of national or sectional pride, their loyalties remained local. They conducted national politics as a forum dedicated to the resolution of conflicting state interests. Social customs varied from one state or region to another, even within the three sections—North, South, and West. By 1860 economic interests were not yet sources of national or sectional unification, nor had communication and transportation revolutions fully linked Americans in a nationwide chain of social interaction. Political and ideological alignments had created two opposing sectional interests by 1860, but Civil War America remained a society of local communities, with few strong forces making for national or sectional cohesion. The local perspective is best typified by the South Carolinian who thus explained his hierarchy of loyalties: "I go first for Greenville, then for Greenville District, then for the up-country, then for South Carolina, then for the South, then for the United States, and after that I don't go for anything. I've no use for Englishmen, Turks, and Chinese."[2]

Individual men and women, both North and South, continued to think of themselves as citizens of New York or Virginia or Ohio or Alabama. Early enthusiasm for the war on both sides of the Mason-Dixon line indicated regional or state pride rather than true national-

---

2. Quoted in Emory M. Thomas, *The Confederacy as a Revolutionary Experience* (Englewood Cliffs, N.J., 1971), 7–8; see Gerald F. Linderman, *The Mirror of War: American Society and the Spanish-American War* (Ann Arbor, 1974), 60–90; Robert H. Wiebe, *The Search for Order, 1877–1920* (New York, 1967), xiii, 1–43.

ism or sectional identification. Union and Confederate armies were recruited, armed, equipped, and trained by the state governments. The volunteer regiment, identified by state, became the most important unit of military organization and provided the strongest source of soldiers' identification. Governors in each state jealously guarded their control over organizing state regiments. Southerners insisted that they were fighting for states' rights, and the political difficulties created by uncompromising loyalty to individual states plagued the Confederacy and weakened efforts toward unity and cooperation. State rivalry threatened at times to dismember the Confederacy from within and even posed serious dangers to northern unity. Although such political divisions were avoided, state loyalty revealed the incomplete triumph of sectional consciousness over local identification. Many Americans, North and South, shared the attitude of Colonel Charles Wainwright, a New York Democrat, who viewed the conflict as "a war between the States of New York and others on one side, and South Carolina and others on the other side."[3]

Throughout the war, southerners described it from the perspective of their native states, praising their own state's superior virtues and contributions to the Confederate cause. As volunteers rushed to join Georgia regiments after the first thrilling victory at Fort Sumter, Ella Thomas boasted of her Georgia heritage. "I have always been proud of my native state but never more so than now," she announced. Lieutenant James A. Graham of North Carolina complained in February, 1862, that Virginia newspapers had consistently praised that state's regiments without mentioning the actions of regiments from other states. "North Carolina seems never to have a *special correspondent* to puff her up," Graham complained, "and thus other men get *all* the credit while we do our full share of the work and fighting." Lieutenant John Hampden Chamberlayne, a lawyer whose father was a medical college professor, expressed pride in both his state and his social class, merging the two identities: "How proud we are to think, and how certain we are, that there are no people quite like Virginia gentlefolks." Chamberlayne left no doubt as to his first political loyalty. Even in April, 1865, with defeat of the Confederacy inevitable, he vowed, "My duty is still

---

3. Nevins (ed.), *A Diary of Battle*, 281; Fred Albert Shannon, *The Organization and Administration of the Union Army, 1861–1865* (2 vols.; Cleveland, 1928), I, 15–50; Shannon, "State Rights and the Union Army," *Mississippi Valley Historical Review*, XII (June, 1925), 52; Frank Lawrence Owsley, *State Rights in the Confederacy* (Chicago, 1925), 76–149.

to my country, Virginia." Similar declarations also came from the opposite end of the social spectrum. "Tha ar tring every wa tha can to get ows all to voleteer for too years," Private Robert P. Boyd wrote in January, 1862, "if i have to go i am going to go and fight for south Carolina." As had Robert E. Lee, many Confederate soldiers pledged their first loyalty to their state.[4]

Northern soldiers likewise expressed pride in their home state and sought to enhance its reputation. On his way to war in 1862, Private Samuel Nichols of Brookfield, Massachusetts, worried about his state's slowness in furnishing troops and supplies. "New York and Pennsylvania and New Jersey are alive, while I am ashamed to speak of the apathy in Massachusetts," he confessed. Yet only a few weeks later, he retracted his criticism after learning that sixty regiments had been recruited in Massachusetts. "I think that perhaps I have been some severe on my home state," he admitted, "but you must ascribe it to a desire to have my state outdo all others." The state became the basic unit of identification throughout the military system. Even army hospitals were usually arranged with separate wards for each state. Harriet Eaton, a widow from Portland, Maine, volunteered as a nurse in the Washington hospitals but insisted on helping soldiers from Maine. "One of the sick boys told me he was glad to see *Maine acting*," she reported in October, 1862, "for while ladies from other States had been visiting the Hospitals he had been *ashamed* to say that no one looked after him." Soldiers and civilians identified their principal loyalty as to the state. The Union remained an abstraction. They would defend the Union, but as citizens of Maine or Pennsylvania or Michigan. Writing in the New York *Tribune* in October, 1861, historian George Bancroft warned against this parochial outlook. "Cease to be men of Massachusetts, men even of the North—be Americans," Bancroft urged the Massachusetts soldiers.[5]

Such investment of one's loyalty and pride in state rather than nation occasionally led to antagonism between representatives of different states. Because Civil War regiments were recruited and designated by

4. Ella Gertrude (Clanton) Thomas Diary, July 15, 1861, DU; James A. Graham to his mother, June 3, and February 17, 1862, in James A. Graham Papers, SHC; Chamberlayne (ed.), *Ham Chamberlayne*, 96, 325; Robert P. Boyd to his father, January 9, 1862, in Robert Boyd Papers, DU. See also Steven Hahn, *The Roots of Southern Populism: Yeoman Farmers and the Transformation of the Georgia Upcountry, 1850–1890* (New York, 1983), 119–20.

5. Underhill (ed.), *"Your Soldier Boy Samuel,"* 20, 29; Harriet Eaton Diary, October 12, 1862, SHC; George Bancroft quoted in Shannon, "State Rights and the Union Army," 59.

state, geographical biases intensified the normal military rivalries among regiments and divisions. When they passed other regiments on the march or in camp, soldiers sometimes engaged in verbal insults and bantering. "You'll see a vast deal of state pride here," Lieutenant Charles Wills of the 7th Illinois Cavalry wrote. "The 7th Cavalry don't acknowledge the Michigander troops to be more than the equals of Jeff Thompson's [Confederate] scalawags, and the Michigan boys really seem to think that the 7th regiment is not equal to one company of theirs. But I notice the generals here have all taken their bodyguards from our regiment." Similarly, Lieutenant George Ingram of Texas boasted that Arkansas soldiers lacked the dedication and fighting ability of his own state's troops. His regiment placed a Confederate flag on the dome of the Arkansas capitol building, where none had flown before. "Hurrah for the Texans. These Arkansawyers were just about to give it up before we got here," he reported.[6]

Sectional antagonism between eastern and western states surfaced repeatedly in both Union and Confederate ranks. The West's identity as a separate section did not dissolve during the conflict between North and South. "Our corps don't get along well with these Cumberland and Potomac soldiers," Charles Wills reported. "To hear our men talk to them when passing them or their camps marching, you'd think the feeling between us and the Rebels could be no more bitter." He added, "I must do the Yankees the justice to say that our men, I believe, always commence it, and are the most ungentlemanly by great odds." So intense was East-West rivalry that Lieutenant John B. Stickney of Massachusetts, whose regiment had been transferred to Mississippi, reassured his parents, "You need not fear that we are to attack Vicksburg for the Western Army are down on the 9th Corps and do not like the idea of Eastern troops coming down here to help them." Stickney predicted that the eastern regiments would be held in reserve during the attack on Vicksburg, "so that Grant's army may win all the laurels if possible." Eastern soldiers reciprocated the westerners' envy and dislike, he wrote, but "we are willing to let them do the fighting of the Southwest & win all the laurels." Shortly thereafter, a Wisconsin private stationed in Louisiana noted frequent fights between recently arrived eastern soldiers and the westerners. "I think either side would

6. Wills, *Army Life*, 66; Henry L. Ingram (ed.), *Civil War Letters of George W. and Martha F. Ingram, 1861–1865* (College Station, Tex., 1973), 21.

rather shoot at each other than the Johnnies," he reported with dismay. Harvey Reid, a Wisconsin soldier whose regiment was reassigned to Virginia in January, 1864, wrote that there was "such an incurable jealousy between the Potomac and western Armies that our position as the only western brigade in the corps can never be aught but unpleasant."[7]

Regional pride and competition stirred debates in both sections over the relative fighting abilities of the eastern and western armies. In the North, western troops enjoyed much greater success during the first years of the war than did the Army of the Potomac. "I expect the western troops will have to go to the east and take Murfreesboro and Richmond," Iowa corporal Isaac Marsh boasted in April, 1863. "There is two much Starch and Stile about the eastern troops to ever do any good." Charles Wills derided easterners' fighting ability, insisting that "the Potomac Army is only good to draw greenbacks and occupy winter quarters." Private John Brobst of Wisconsin added, "If they had done half as much as the western army, this war would have been rubbed out before this time. This army will have to go down there and take Richmond for them, poor fellows." Michigan lieutenant Charles Haydon stated in June, 1862, that he placed little confidence in the New York and Pennsylvania troops and that it was "quite probable" that they would run away during the next battle.[8]

Easterners defended their military record by claiming that western engagements were much less fierce than the hard-fought battles in Virginia. Irritated by unfavorable comparisons between western victories and the eastern stalemate, Colonel Charles Wainwright of New York complained, "They either do not or will not comprehend that the whole strength of the rebellion is concentrated in our front, and that their Western armies are made up of men and materiel of what is left over after furnishing Lee." Soldiers of the Army of the Potomac contended that they had to fight the South's best generals and troops, whereas, in the words of Michigan captain Charles Salter, "the western rebels are nothing but an armed mob, and not anything near so hard to whip as Lee's well disciplined soldiers." Easterners also disparaged the

---

7. Wills, *Army Life*, 218; John B. Stickney to his parents, July 1, 24, 1863, in Clinton H. Haskell Collection, WLC; Henry P. Whipple quoted in Bell Irvin Wiley, *The Life of Billy Yank: The Common Soldier of the Union* (Indianapolis, 1952), 323; Byrne (ed.), *View from Headquarters*, 113.

8. Isaac Marsh to his wife, April 27, 1863, in Isaac Marsh Papers, DU; Wills, *Army Life*, 144; Brobst, *Well, Mary*, 38; Charles B. Haydon Diary, June 28, 1862, MHC. On East-West rivalry, see Wiley, *Billy Yank*, 320–25.

coarseness and rowdiness of western Yankees and claimed for themselves superiority in both appearance and discipline.[9]

Confederate soldiers drew similar, though less frequent, contrasts between the fighting abilities of their eastern and western troops. South Carolina sergeant DuBose Eggleston, recently transferred from Virginia to Tennessee, claimed that "these Western troops don't know how to fight Yankees." He offered his own advice on military tactics, then continued: "These troops want us to acknowledge that these yankees fight harder than those in Va; which we won't do." The western regiments had suffered repeated defeats. "It seems that in our western campaign, everything is going wrong," Fanny Jones Erwin, daughter of a South Carolina planter, wrote in March, 1862. "The Tennesseans deserve no credit for their fighting, & are a decided disadvantage to us I think." Lieutenant George Wills, son of a North Carolina planter and Methodist minister, expressed anxiety about the ability of Confederate forces defending Mobile and Atlanta in 1864: "I can't think they fight as our troops in Va. do." Similar charges were leveled at the western troops that surrendered at New Orleans in 1862 and at Vicksburg in 1863. Mindful of Virginia's brave defense against invading armies for three years, Virginia captain Ham Chamberlayne derided the apparent irresolution of many Georgians during Sherman's devastating march to the sea. "What a pitiable, what a disgraceful contrast, does Georgia show," he jeered, "dismayed at the first invasion, cowering at first sight of a burning homestead."[10]

State and regional rivalries influenced political issues in each section. In the North, New England was singled out for special contempt, partly because of its reputation for abolitionism. As an agrarian region, the Middle West retained a suspicion of eastern business interests and an emotional dislike for New England "Yankees." Many westerners had southern origins or felt cultural and economic ties among the people of the Mississippi Valley, north and south. A few westerners even advocated reconstructing the Union with the southern states and "leaving New England out in the cold." In November, 1862, the Chicago *Times* urged western men to protect their own interests. "New

9. Nevins (ed.), *Diary of Battle*, 210; Charles H. Salter to Isabella Duffield, June 12, 1864, in Divie Bethune Duffield Papers, BHC.

10. DuBose Eggleston to Annie Roulhac, September 27, 1863, in Ruffin, Roulhac, and Hamilton Family Papers, SHC; Fanny Jones Irwin to Cadwallader Jones, March 19, 1862, in Cadwallader Jones Papers, SHC; George Wills to his sister, August 13, 1864, in William Henry Wills Papers, SHC; Chamberlayne (ed.), *Ham Chamberlayne*, 275.

England in making the negro squeal, has diverted the attention of the West from the dive she was making into Western pockets," the Chicago newspaper charged. A Pennsylvania soldier attributed part of the uproar over the dismissal of popular General George McClellan in 1862 to antagonisms toward his successor, New Englander Ambrose Burnside. "The Pennsylvania, Maryland, New Jersey and Delaware troops do not like a Yankee for their commander by any means," he explained. Civilians expressed similar resentment over New England's influence in the Union. "We are at present ruled by New England, which was never a gentle or tolerant mistress," Maria L. Daly complained in October, 1864. The wife of a respected New York City judge, Mrs. Daly was a staunch Democrat. During the dark days of early 1863, she hoped that military failure would force New Englanders out of power. "There are rumors of dissent and disunion between the Eastern and Western and Middle states," she reported. "New England will have to yield if they join against her."[11]

Similar mistrust and jealousy of those from other states repeatedly plagued the Confederacy. The prevalence of such feelings cannot easily be measured, but no state escaped the censure of zealous patriots from other states. At the beginning of the war, the border states came under greatest suspicion. Visiting army camps near Newport News in September, 1861, North Carolina lawyer David Schenck, who owned nine slaves, commented: "I am sorry to say this part of Virginia, though decidedly hostile to the North, have no warm sympathies with the South and seem to fraternise with us more to whip the Yankees than to establish a separate government." Private Harry St. John Dixon of Mississippi, who had left the University of Virginia in 1861 to enlist, criticized Virginia "for allowing herself to be Kicked out of the old Union," rather than seceding earlier with the Lower South. He predicted that "Va. in 50 yrs. would be free-soil." South Carolina private Charles Hutson, son of a wealthy Beaufort District planter, believed that the Gulf States would have to "stand alone" after the war: "These border states, with Virginia at their head, are rotten to the core in political faith." Unlike regional antagonisms in the North, where New England

---

11. William G. Carleton, "Civil War Dissidence in the North: The Perspective of a Century," *South Atlantic Quarterly*, LXV (Summer, 1966), 390–402; Chicago *Times*, November 29, 1862, quoted in George Winston Smith and Charles Judah (eds.), *Life in the North During the Civil War: A Source History* (Albuquerque, 1966), 237; William Hamilton to his mother, November 15, 1862, in William Hamilton Papers, LC; Daly, *Diary of a Union Lady*, 307.

radicals received the most severe censure, southerners most often criticized the conservative border states, whose commitment to the radical cause appeared questionable.[12]

Many patriots warned that excessive concern with state prerogatives would undermine the Confederate war effort. Colonel Laurence M. Keitt, although a leading South Carolina fire-eater and proponent of states' rights before the war, recognized the dangerous effects of such ideas on Confederate unity. Early in 1864, he worried that the southern people could not unite behind an effective leader: "They have cherished state pride and exclusiveness for eighty years, and no changes, however great, no ruin, however appalling, could make them forget it for a moment." Opposition to President Davis and the central government left the Confederacy "in mortal peril from our inability to govern ourselves," Keitt lamented. "Too many revolutions have shipwrecked upon intestine division." The states' rights doctrine for which many southerners claimed to be fighting proved a constant source of friction between individual states and the central government. Jealous to maintain the prerogatives of state sovereignty, Governors Joseph E. Brown of Georgia and Zebulon B. Vance of North Carolina withheld state troops from the Confederate army and opposed such war measures as suspension of habeas corpus, impressment of property, and conscription. Governor Brown ordered Georgia's conscription officers to refuse to cooperate with Confederate officials in enforcing conscription, which he deemed "subversive of [Georgia's] sovereignty, and at war with all the principles for the support of which Georgia entered into this revolution." Such actions by southern governors mirrored the sentiments of many soldiers and civilians. Charles W. Hutson, a gentleman private from South Carolina, denounced the proposed conscription bill of 1862 as a violation of state sovereignty and a usurpation of authority by the central government. "I should be greatly shocked to see it pass, unchallenged by my State," he told his father. State pride again interfered with Confederate authority in North Carolina, when Governor Vance and Senator George Davis protested that appointment of men from other states as tax collectors or officers of North Carolina regiments affronted the state's dignity. When a South Carolinian assumed command of Fort Caswell, North Carolina, in 1864, Adjutant

12. David Schenck Diary, September 27, 1861, SHC; Harry St. John Dixon Diary, March 21, 1862, in Harry St. John Dixon Papers, SHC; Charles W. Hutson to his mother, April 26, 1862, in Charles Woodward Hutson Papers, SHC.

William Calder reported that there was a "general outcry against any but a N. Carolinian having command in our State."[13]

In its most extreme form, this exclusiveness prompted minority factions in several states to advocate secession from the Confederacy. After July, 1863, when the tide of battle began turning against the South, a small minority of southerners advocated protecting their own states by establishing smaller and more cohesive confederations or by returning to the Union to avoid further bloodshed and destruction. Following the surrender of Vicksburg, which severed communications between East and West, representatives from the trans-Mississippi states met to discuss formation of a separate government. "In this convention they have adopted some very singular resolutions, which virtually amount to the severance of these four states from the Government at Richmond," Sarah Wadley, daughter of a prominent railroad contractor and slaveowner in Louisiana, lamented. "I feel like weeping over my country, what will we become! our enemies are those that are in the midst of us, with the Yankees we can cope." Having taken refuge in Texas when Union occupation forced her to leave her native state, Kate Stone was outraged that her new neighbors thought that Louisiana would apply for readmission to the Union. "They will believe anything against Louisiana," she exclaimed. "They seem to hate that state, and we would not give one Louisiana parish for half of Texas." Although in the end no trans-Mississippi confederation was formed, that the proposal was seriously discussed for two years indicates that some southerners faced constant temptations to place state interests above the Confederacy's survival.[14]

The strongest movement for separate state secession developed in North Carolina in 1863 and 1864. Raleigh editor William Holden, a peace advocate and strident critic of Confederate policies, combined appeals to war weariness with a desire to protect the state from northern invasion in advocating a special state convention to negotiate for readmission to the Union. Although sympathetic to Holden's desire

13. Laurence M. Keitt to his wife, January 22, 31, 1864, in Laurence Massillon Keitt Papers, DU; Joseph Brown quoted in Paul D. Escott, *After Secession: Jefferson Davis and the Failure of Confederate Nationalism* (Baton Rouge, 1978), 81; Charles W. Hutson to his father, April 13, 1862, in Hutson Papers; William Calder to his mother, September 20, 1864, in William Calder Papers, SHC. See also Albert B. Moore, *Conscription and Conflict in the Confederacy* (New York, 1924); Louise Biles Hill, *Joseph E. Brown and the Confederacy* (Chapel Hill, 1939); and Joseph H. Parks, *Joseph E. Brown of Georgia* (Baton Rouge, 1977), 265–92, 322–23.
14. Sarah L. Wadley Diary, September 2, 1863, SHC; Anderson (ed.), *Brokenburn*, 239.

for peace, a majority of North Carolinians dreaded the prospect of separate state action. "The fear I have is that we may be so silly as to subjugate ourselves," North Carolina judge Asa Biggs wrote after hearing of Holden's plan. If North Carolina seceded, "we shall soon be fighting among ourselves a civil war of the most bloody character." Sergeant William R. Clark of North Carolina declared that he wanted peace "as bad as any one in the world" but that Holden's proposal was not the answer: "I am perfectly astonished that so many of the people at home . . . listen to a man that would have North Carolina to secede from the Confederacy; have not our people seen enough of the fruits of secession? Why for us to leave the Confederacy would involve us in another war, and we would be one of the most degraded people in the world." Despite his states'-rights opposition to central government control, Governor Vance denounced Holden's proposal as treason. He finally thwarted Holden's quest for power by defeating him in the 1864 gubernatorial election. Meanwhile, at the end of 1864, Governor Joseph E. Brown, assisted by Confederate Vice-President Alexander H. Stephens and his brother Linton Stephens, called on the Georgia legislature to propose a convention of states to negotiate peace. Charges that Brown and Stephens advocated separate state secession appear groundless. They did, however, seek to reduce President Davis' military powers and to negotiate peace on the basis of state sovereignty. Brown often placed Georgia's interests above the Confederacy's. But none of the Confederate states ever came close to seceding from the southern nation.[15]

The testimony of numerous soldiers and civilians reveals that sectional consciousness never fully replaced Civil War participants' loyalty to their home states. Soldiers marched to battle under the banners of Massachusetts, Virginia, Michigan, or Alabama. They fought first for their state and second for "southern" rights or "northern" interests. For most, loyalties to state and section did not conflict. When they did, the choice was often agonizingly difficult, as it was for southerners when

15. Asa Biggs to William Biggs, January 9, 1864, in Asa Biggs Papers, DU; William R. Clark to Ellen Lockhart, March 18, 1864, in Hugh Conway Browning Papers, DU. On the Holden-Vance controversy, see Marc W. Kruman, "Dissent in the Confederacy: The North Carolina Experience," Civil War History, XXVII (December, 1981), 293–313; and E. Merton Coulter, The Confederate States of America, 1861–1865 (Baton Rouge, 1950), 534–36. For Georgia, see John Brumgardt, "Alexander H. Stephens and the State Convention Movement in Georgia: A Reappraisal," Georgia Historical Quarterly, LIX (Spring, 1975), 38–49; and Parks, Joseph E. Brown, 306–21.

their devotion to sectional interests and to the Union became mutually exclusive. States' rights was more than a political battle cry. Above all, it represented a mode of thought, common both north and south of the Mason-Dixon line, in which state pride frequently determined an individual's ideological loyalties. As a principle applied to political and military issues, states' rights impeded the Confederate quest for independence by weakening the spirit of cooperation and shared sacrifice essential for unity. Historian Frank L. Owsley may have overstated the problem when he composed an epitaph for the Lost Cause—"Died of State Rights"—but he recognized an important truth. State loyalty limited the complete realization of southern sectional consciousness. The same problem also affected the northern states, which insisted on organizing and administering the Union army as a composite of state regiments jealously guarding their separate identities. The Civil War truly was a sectional conflict waged between North and South. Loyalty to state interests, however, showed that geographical divisions could cut in several directions. In certain respects, the conflict was indeed a war between the states, at least in the minds of many participants.[16]

A POOR MAN'S FIGHT

Class consciousness likewise diminished sectional unity. The demands of war frequently override democratic principles and exacerbate social tensions. If truth is the first casualty, it is followed quickly by personal liberty and social equality. Steeped in democratic ideals and fiercely independent, nineteenth-century Americans deeply resented the intrusions of military necessity, particularly when they seemed to place disproportionate burdens on the common people. Class conflict thus threatened the unity of both Confederacy and Union. Like their counterparts in virtually every modern war, common soldiers of both armies denounced the conflict as "a rich man's war and a poor man's fight." In everything from civilian food shortages to distinctions of military rank, Civil War Americans saw the undemocratic results of class distinctions.

Class feelings erupted with particular force in the Confederacy. Southerners' strong dedication to democratic principles had always

16. Owsley, *State Rights*, 1. For a critique of Owsley, see Richard E. Beringer, Herman Hattaway, Arthur Jones, and William N. Still, Jr., *Why the South Lost the Civil War* (Athens, Ga., 1986), 203–35, 443–57. For an excellent discussion of sectionalism and nationalism in the South, see Potter, *South and the Sectional Conflict*, 34–83; and Carl N. Degler, *The Other South: Southern Dissenters in the Nineteenth Century* (New York, 1974), 116–25.

clashed with a social system in which land and slaves conspicuously revealed distinctions of wealth. The planters' revolution seemed to reinforce their privileges. Nonslaveholders claimed that the burdens of war fell most heavily on the poorer classes but that the rich would reap most of the benefits. As early as June, 1861, Mary Chesnut, wife of a prominent South Carolina planter-politician, reported that "the poor white people say why should they fight for the rich people's property." Kate Stone, whose father owned 150 slaves and 1,260 acres of prime cotton land in northeastern Louisiana, reported in March, 1862, that one of her neighbors was sharply criticized for not volunteering: "The overseers and that class of men are abusing him roundly among themselves—a rich man's son too good to fight the battles of the rich—let the rich men go who are most interested—they will stay at home." Such bitter feelings increased as the war dragged on and suffering mounted. War weariness exacerbated social class tensions. "I am out of money clothes tobacco and friends," lamented Private William Horton, an ordnance wagon driver from the hills of western North Carolina, in November, 1864. "I hope and trust to god that they is a day a Coming when poor privats will be as free as big ritch officers," Horton wrote to his sister, "this cruel war is a rich mans war and a poor mans fight but i hope that it wont always bee sow." In this complaint, Horton reiterated the slogan of common soldiers in both Union and Confederate armies.[17]

The issue that most angered nonslaveholders was the exemption from conscription of planters supervising twenty or more slaves. Faced with the pressing need for more troops, the Confederate Congress on April 16, 1862, passed the first national conscription act in American history, declaring every able-bodied white man between the ages of eighteen and thirty-five subject to military service. Later conscription acts and amendments provided exemptions for certain groups such as government officials, nurses, teachers, and factory workers, whose services supported the war effort. The most controversial exemption, passed in October, 1862, excused one overseer for every plantation having as many as twenty slaves. This "20 nigger law" symbolized for many the special privileges accorded the rich. It exacerbated class tensions by opening a breach between planters and the small

17. Woodward and Muhlenfeld (eds.), *Private Mary Chesnut*, 74; Anderson (ed.), *Brokenburn*, 95; William H. Horton to Mary H. Councill, November 30, 1864, in Mary A. (Horton) Councill Papers, DU.

farmers and nonslaveholders who were subject to the draft. The latter almost universally opposed it. One of many who denounced the exemption of planters was North Carolina private James Zimmerman. "It was done in order to get the big men out," he told his wife. Forced to enlist to avoid the opprobrium of conscription, Zimmerman warned that special privileges for the rich would weaken the Confederate cause. "There is to much speculation and to many poor fighting for the rich and the rich trying to get all the poor has after they do all the hard fighting for them," he wrote in August, 1863, "just look at the rich bigbugs whare they are and look where the poor man is that is enough to change the tide of battle." Private Wade Hubbard of North Carolina told his wife in October, 1864, that she might expect him home soon because "all of the gentel men has got out of it [the war] and i don't intend to put my Life between them and their propty." This implied threat of desertion resulted from a sense of injustice and class discrimination.[18]

The rhetoric of white democracy led the poor to oppose such privileges. If white men shared political equality, why should the poor bear the greater part of fighting and suffering? "How can we go in to battle and fight to keep the enemy back of[f] the rich man who beca[u]se he owns twenty negros is permitted to stay at home with his family and save his grain," a North Carolina soldier asked Governor Zebulon Vance in June, 1863, when requesting a furlough to harvest his small grain crop. Such concerns surfaced as early as September, 1861. "Is it right that the poor man should be taxed for the support of the war, when the war was brought about on the slave question," a citizen of northwestern Georgia asked in a letter to the Rome *Weekly Courier*, "and the slave at home accumulating for the benefit of his master, and the poor man's farm left uncultivated, and a chance for his wife to be a widow, and his children orphans?" The sense of injustice mounted as war shortages and privations increased. An anonymous writer from southeastern North Carolina warned Governor Vance in 1863, "The time has come that we the comon people has to hav bread or blood." This writer believed the reason for high prices, which "take all the

---

18. James C. Zimmerman to his wife, June 28, August 30, 1863, in James C. Zimmerman Papers, DU; Wade Hubbard quoted in Bell Irvin Wiley, *The Life of Johnny Reb: The Common Soldier of the Confederacy* (Indianapolis, 1943), 337. See also Moore, *Conscription and Conflict*, 12–26, 52–113; Escott, *After Secession*, 116–22; Stephen Ambrose, "Yeoman Discontent in the Confederacy," *Civil War History*, VIII (September, 1962), 27.

soldiers wages for a fiew bushels" of grain, was that "the Slave oner has the plantations & the hands to rais the bread stufs & the comon people is drove of[f] in the war to fight for the big mans negro." Such hardships widened the gap between the classes in southern society.[19]

Planters likewise expressed growing estrangement from the poorer classes, whom they regarded as ignorant ruffians. South Carolina planter-politician James Chesnut, a close confidant of President Davis, said in March, 1861, that he wished trains had separate coaches so he could "get away from those whiskey drinking, tobacca chewing rascals & *rabble*." Louisiana sergeant Frank L. Richardson, who left Bayside, his father's sugar plantation southwest of Baton Rouge, to enlist in the 13th Louisiana, denounced the Georgia and Alabama soldiers he met as "ignorant dirty hoosiers," nearly as deficient in speech, knowledge, reading, and writing as "cornfield negroes." Robert Patrick, a quartermaster clerk, who before the war had been a bookkeeper and deputy sheriff in southeastern Louisiana, observed that the citizens of the Alabama backwoods "appeared to be in the depths of ignorance and if 'Ignorance is Bliss,' then they are truly happy." Echoing Yankee observers, Patrick later concluded, "I was not aware that there was so much ignorance in the South until I came into the army. Here I am thrown amongst all classes." Upper-class southerners repeatedly expressed their contempt for the poor. One Louisiana plantation mistress, who was a refugee in Tyler, Texas, attended a local barbecue, as she said, "to see the animals feed." A companion insisted the food was not clean enough to eat. " 'Why,' said he, 'should we dine with plebeians?' "[20]

Because of these class divisions, planters worried endlessly about nonslaveholders' loyalty to the revolution. Without active support by the masses, the Confederacy would collapse. Secession had become necessary to protect slavery not only from Yankee attacks but from internal divisions between planters and nonslaveholders. Every southern state, possibly excepting South Carolina, suffered deep divisions over secession. The cleavages followed numerous social and political

19. Quoted in Bell Irvin Wiley, *The Plain People of the Confederacy* (Baton Rouge, 1943), 65; Rome (Ga.) *Weekly Courier*, September 27, 1861, quoted in Escott, *After Secession*, 95; anonymous letter to Vance, quoted in Charles W. Ramsdell, *Behind the Lines in the Southern Confederacy* (Baton Rouge, 1944), 47.

20. Woodward and Muhlenfeld (eds.), *Private Mary Chesnut*, 42; Frank L. Richardson to his mother, October 8, 1862, in Frank L. Richardson Papers, SHC; Taylor (ed.), *Reluctant Rebel*, 150, 190; Anderson (ed.), *Brokenburn*, 292.

fault lines within southern society, one of the least stable of which was social class. Those who owned few or no slaves expressed reluctance to support a revolt led by planters to protect their property. In Georgia and elsewhere secessionists led a double revolution to secure home rule against an external threat and then to consolidate slaveholders' hegemony against internal threats. In their private writings, planters repeatedly expressed their concerns about nonslaveholders' loyalty. The charges the latter directed against the rich slaveowners indicate that they had cause to worry. The extent of Unionism and particularly desertion among nonslaveholders indicates their conditional loyalty to the Confederate cause. All too frequently, their concern for security overshadowed their commitment to slavery. As wartime pressures sharpened class conflict, the slaveowners' government gradually lost the support of many nonslaveowners.[21]

Despite class dissension, a majority of nonslaveholders remained loyal to, if not always enthusiastic about, the Confederate cause. In some respects, slavery served their interests as well as those of the planters. It provided control over labor and visible evidence of social status to which all whites could aspire. One out of four white families owned slaves on the eve of secession, providing a broad base of economic self-interest in maintaining the institution. Above all, slavery raised poor whites above the bottom level of society and appealed to their sense of racial superiority. The argument of racial equality and unity among whites echoes through secessionists' arguments. In his famous "cornerstone" speech, Confederate Vice-President Alexander Stephens proclaimed that the new government's "foundations are laid, its cornerstone rests, upon the great truth that the negro is not equal to the white man; that slavery, subordination to the superior race, is his natural and moral condition." Stephens and other Confederate leaders hoped to secure nonslaveholders' loyalty by such appeals to racial pride.[22]

Invasion, however, soon provided an even stronger impetus for

21. James L. Roark, *Masters Without Slaves: Southern Planters in the Civil War and Reconstruction* (New York, 1977), 21–23, 55–67; Michael P. Johnson, *Toward a Patriarchal Republic: The Secession of Georgia* (Baton Rouge, 1977), xx–xxi, 85–87; and Paul D. Escott, "The Failure of Confederate Nationalism: The Old South's Class System in the Crucible of War," in Harry P. Owens and James J. Cooke (eds.), *The Old South in the Crucible of War* (Jackson, Miss., 1983), 15–28.

22. Stephens' speech, March 21, 1861, in Frank Moore (ed.), *The Rebellion Record* (11 vols.; New York, 1861–68), I, 44–49; Degler, *Place Over Time*, 76–82; Roark, *Masters Without Slaves*, 21–23.

unity. In a society beset by class tensions, slavery continued to be a potentially divisive force. It was risky to make slavery the explicit, primary justification of a revolution for which nonslaveholders were asked to fight and die. In the same manner that Abraham Lincoln subsumed agitation over slavery to the paramount need to defend the Union, Jefferson Davis tried to establish independence as the South's primary goal. At the same time that his vice-president appealed to white solidarity in defense of slavery, President Davis sought to de-emphasize slavery as the cause for secession. Davis asserted that the Confederacy stood as the true guardian of constitutional liberty, which the North sought to suppress by violating southern rights. Such arguments united white southerners in defense of "all that we hold dear"— honor, family, home, religion, and their entire social order. On such an appeal, slaveholder and nonslaveholder, rich and poor, could agree. Although they weakened southern unity, therefore, class tensions did not destroy the Confederacy.[23]

Class divisions also existed in the North, although they never posed as great a threat to internal unity as in the South. The federal government did not resort to conscription until a year after the Confederacy did. Although the Enrollment Act of 1863 contained more loopholes than its southern counterpart, its exemptions symbolized to many the problem of class discrimination. Draftees could escape military service either by furnishing a substitute or by paying three hundred dollars in commutation money. Substitution was never limited to individuals performing essential wartime services but remained available to any-one able to secure a willing substitute. Commutation, designed to keep down the prices paid for substitutes, merely put a price tag on military exemption. Wealth could enable anyone to avoid serving his country. In practice, commutation proved far more successful in raising money than troops. In the first two drafts, 85,000 out of 133,000 drafted men paid the three-hundred-dollar fee to escape service. Federal conscrip-tion eventually became a morass of inefficiency, greed, and corruption. States began offering bounties to enlistees, resulting in a complex web of recruitment brokers, substitutes, and bounty-jumpers. Through it all, one thing seemed clear: conscription placed greater burdens for military service on the poor.[24]

    23. Lewis M. Grimball to Elizabeth Grimball, November 27, 1860, Grimball Family Papers, SHC; Escott, *After Secession*, 35–41.
    24. Shannon, *Organization and Administration of the Union Army*, II, 11–46; Wiley, *Billy Yank*, 281–82; James G. Randall and David H. Donald, *The Civil War and Reconstruction*

Union soldiers denounced the entire system of conscription, particularly the commutation clause. "I believe that a *poor* man's life is as dear as a rich man's," Illinois soldier Levi Ross declared in March, 1863. The rich, having more at stake, "should sacrifice more in suppressing this infernal Rebellion and in restoring the Union and thereby save their property, homes and liberty." New Jersey private Joseph Osborn, a Democrat, who opposed emancipation but enlisted to avoid the draft, denounced commutation as a loophole that allowed rich men to escape their army obligations. "I think that allowing men to pay $300 for their exemption is a imposition on the poor people And I hope they will resist it," he wrote in March, 1863. "A rich man is no better to come out here than a poor man who can not raise $300." Although pleased that the draft would force stay-at-home patriots to fight for their country, Private William Pedrick, a Republican from Fulton County, New York, also objected to the law's discrimination against the poor. "Let them draft if they only let the $300 dollars go and take the rich With the poor," he wrote home from South Carolina, "but i say if they Let a man that has got three Hundred dollars off for that and take the poor men that has not got It to pay i hope they will not Stand it." One month later, New York City mobs responded to the first drawing of draftees' names with three days of rioting and destruction. The rioters' motives varied enormously, including everything from hatred of blacks to general social unrest and rowdiness. A major factor in provoking the so-called draft riots, however, was resentment against the class discrimination embodied in the commutation clause.[25]

Many soldiers objected to substitution and commutation because they enabled lukewarm patriots to escape service to the Union. Anyone able to pay the commutation fee could avoid shouldering his share of the burden, thus placing even greater weight on the poor and those who willingly accepted military obligations. "There are enough that can & ought to come but no they must stay & make a little more money & thus protract the war another year," Sergeant Henry G. Marshall, a Connecticut Republican, who graduated from Yale College in 1860,

---

(2nd ed.; Lexington, Mass., 1969), 313–15. As many as 42 percent of drafted men commuted to avoid service before the law was changed in July, 1864. See Eugene C. Murdock, *One Million Men: The Civil War Draft in the North* (Madison, 1971), 6–7, 197–217.

25. Levi Ross quoted in Wiley, *Billy Yank*, 282; Joseph B. Osborn to Elias Osborn, March 14, 1863, in Joseph Bloomfield Osborn Papers, LC; William Pedrick to his parents, June 1, 1863, in Benjamin Pedrick Papers, DU. Eugene Murdock contends that commutation was about equally high in "rich" and "poor" districts of New York ("Was It a 'Poor Man's Fight'?" *Civil War History*, X [September, 1964], 241–45).

complained in November, 1863. "If they don't volunteer I hope the Pres. will put in the draft & Congress will strike out the $300 clause & make *every* drafted man come." Soldiers particularly disliked the power that rich men held in determining national policies. The war benefited the wealthy at the poor's expense. "I suppose those who furnish the money, think they have a right to direct how the war shall be carried on," wrote Lieutenant Julian W. Hinkley, who had been a school-teacher in Wisconsin before enlisting when Lincoln issued the first call for troops in April, 1861, "but we whose lives are at stake, think that we have a *slight* interest in the matter, a mistaken idea of ours I suppose." The humorous tone of Hinkley's comment does not conceal a deep-seated resentment.[26]

Many soldiers felt an open antagonism against the rich stay-at-home patriots. Class resentment frequently led common soldiers on both sides to argue that the politicians and the wealthy should fight it out and let the men in the ranks go home in peace. Some soldiers acted on this premise by deserting. For a large majority, however, class divisions never overrode loyalty to the cause. Dissension in the ranks showed that factors other than sectionalism affected individual loyalties and patriotic ardor. Yet American class conflict never reached the level that it did in many European countries. It weakened the unity of Confederate and Union forces, but it never seriously disrupted either side's ability to wage war.

THE INSOLENCE OF RANK

Military rank created formal distinctions between officers and enlisted men. Army experience thus often contradicted Americans' democratic beliefs about social equality. Many soldiers resented infringements on their rights and complained bitterly that the military hierarchy forced them to surrender both freedom and dignity. Confederate and Union enlisted men alike detested their lowly status and resented officers' privileges, which mirrored class distinctions in society. The army hierarchy reinforced the influence of educated and wealthy social leaders and dramatically revealed inequalities in social status. Conversely, gentlemen who served in the ranks found the inequalities of military

---

26. Henry G. Marshall to Mary A. Marshall, November 9, 1863, in Henry Grimes Marshall Papers, WLC; Julian W. Hinkley to R. W. Wells, November 11, 1862, in Julian W. Hinkley Papers, WSHS.

life galling. Bringing class consciousness into public view, such distinctions alienated men who fought under the same flag.

The antagonism of privates toward their officers created another source of internal conflict. In the democratic armies of the Union and the Confederacy, soldiers chafed at the restrictions imposed by subordinate rank. "In the army a persons worth is measured by the position he holds," Michigan sergeant Lambert Luten, the son of Dutch immigrants, complained, "while many of our officers have not the excellence of character which entitle them to and would naturally draw respect." Shoulder straps, the insignia of officers, became the detested symbol of privileges based on rank alone. Private Jenkin Lloyd Jones, a Wisconsin Unitarian, whose parents emigrated from Wales when he was an infant, disliked being forced to stand at attention and salute officers. "'Tis hard to pay respect to unworthy beings, but we must if they have shoulder straps," he wrote. The distinctions of rank irritated junior officers as well as enlisted men. "I never was made to submit to the insolence of 'rank,'" Lieutenant William M. Ferry, a Michigan Democrat and businessman, wrote to his wife. "It takes every bit of force I have to keep cool and turn away without a word from men that because superior in rank attempt to lord it. Men that at home I would not wipe my dirty shoes on." The natural resentment of strong-willed individuals against submitting to military discipline was exacerbated when they judged those issuing the orders to be social inferiors.[27]

Confederate soldiers voiced similar complaints about inequality, especially when officers flaunted their authority or lacked the decorum of gentlemen. Enlisted men objected to the advantages enjoyed by officers, such as better rations, less marching and picket duty, and generally greater comforts. A Harvard graduate who had been headmaster of a boys' school in Minden, Louisiana, and partner in his father-in-law's cotton gin factory, Edwin Fay enlisted to avoid conscription. "I am determined not to be a private throughout this war," he vowed. "There is too much difference made between officers and privates in the army as regards conveniences," Fay grumbled. This was a recurrent theme, with numerous variations, in soldiers' letters. Resentment was particularly bitter when gentlemen became subject to the authority of their

27. Lambert Luten to Hiram Luten, June 3, 1865, in Civil War Correspondence, BHC; Jones, *Artilleryman's Diary*, 199; William M. Ferry to his wife, May 14, 1862, in Ferry Family Papers, MHC. See also Gerald F. Linderman, *Embattled Courage: The Experience of Combat in the American Civil War* (New York, 1978), 229–34.

social inferiors. "I must express my distaste to being commanded by a man having no pretensions to gentility," Harry St. John Dixon, an aristocratic Mississippi private, objected. Similarly, a Virginia private reported that an enlisted man could not sit down and eat with an officer. "What makes me feel bad about it is we have some officers who (before this war commenced) I thought myself too good to associate with," he complained. Election of officers—later abandoned because of its tendency to elevate popular rather than competent men—gave enlisted men an opportunity to reject officers who asserted too much authority and violated their conception of democratic rights. "Lowndes was not elected Captain," Private Charles Hutson, a South Carolina aristocrat, reported, "simply because . . . however excellent his qualities in other respects, [he] seemed to forget that many in the ranks were his equals at home."[28]

Although in some cases political preferment enabled incompetent men to gain commands, soldiers complained about any officer, regardless of his military qualifications, who violated their concepts of democratic rights, social equality, or personal honor. Enlisted men severely criticized officers' moral shortcomings, the most frequent charge being drunkenness. "Officers are generally drunken fellows," wrote Maine private Edwin O. Wentworth, a Republican printer and son of a clock maker. A Louisiana soldier observed that a new officer was "better able to command a bottle of whiskey than anything else." Soldiers grumbled openly about officers whom they believed to be ignorant or otherwise unfit for command. After the disastrous battle of Fredericksburg, in which Union soldiers were slaughtered attempting several charges against impregnable breastworks, New York sergeant Felix Brannigan, an Irish immigrant, voiced a feeling common among enlisted men: "It is very disheartening to see the *able* men *seniored* by *ignoramuses*." Similarly, they denounced officers who refused to share with their men the perils and hardships of battle and camp life, who displayed cowardice in battle, and who evinced personal ambition and jealousy greater than their concern for soldiers' well-being. In extreme cases, soldiers might unleash their wrath against officers. "The offersers is the miserebleist set of men you evver saw in your life," Wisconsin private George

28. Wiley (ed.), "This Infernal War," 38; Dixon Diary, November 18, 1864, in Dixon Papers; Reuben B. Hudgins to Anna Boatwright, March 31, 1863, in Thomas F. Boatwright Letters, SHC; Charles W. Hutson to his mother, September 17, 1861, in Hutson Papers.

Buffum asserted. "I hav found out the reson there is so menny kild in battle I think thair own men musters out most of them." One month later, Buffum himself died of battle wounds. Whether this charge had any basis in truth, the fact that it was believed and reported reveals the depth of soldiers' resentment. Sergeant Onley Andrus of Illinois charged that his colonel was more concerned with his own advancement than with his men's welfare. "He is looking for Stars [the insignia of a general] and is willing to sacrifice every man in his Regt to accomplish His aims," he grumbled. Yet Andrus found some comfort in thinking that in civilian life generals and privates would once again be equals. "My time will run out in course of time," he consoled himself, "& then I'll be just as good a man as he is or any other Officers either."[29]

Officers who sought the respect and cooperation of their men attempted to maintain discipline without being excessively strict because enlisted men were constantly alert to detect the slightest misstep. Volunteers resented any infringement on their liberty or rights. Lieutenant Charles Haydon of Michigan reported that new recruits objected to routine military orders. "Many of the men seem to think they should never be spoken to unless the remarks are preface[d] by some words of defferential politeness," he wrote from camp in Detroit in May, 1861. "Will the gentlemen who compose the first platoon have the kindness to march forward, or will the[y] please to halt, &c. is abt. what some of them seem to expect." A North Carolina soldier fumed at the restrictions imposed by army life. "The officers won't let him do as he likes every time, come and go when he pleases to," a neighbor back home reported in July, 1861, "and his Pa says he was the *maddest man*." Georgia lieutenant William R. Redding was sensitive to such social distinctions. "It is very contrary to my nature to punish a white man," he confided to his wife in August, 1861, "but my duty forces me to do it sometimes." Likewise, Illinois lieutenant Charles Wills consciously tried not to presume upon his rank. He boasted that the officers in his regiment pitched and struck their own headquarters tents rather than ordering enlisted men to perform that duty. "I can't bear the idea of making men who are our equals at home do our work here," he ex-

---

29. Edwin O. Wentworth to his brother and sister, January 23, 1864, in Edwin Oberlin Wentworth Papers, LC; Louisiana soldier quoted in Wiley, *Johnny Reb*, 237; Felix Brannigan to his sister, December 29, 1862, in Felix Brannigan Papers, LC; George W. Buffum to his niece, March 19, 1865, in George W. Buffum Correspondence, WSHS; Shannon (ed.), *Civil War Letters of Andrus*, 53, 71.

plained. Confederate officers sometimes did the same. "As negroes are quite scarce here now, our regiment has to do the work," Lieutenant Samuel D. Sanders, a South Carolina physician and planter before the war, reported in February, 1863. "The officers are not required to work, but the men do much better when they see us disposed to help." Such leadership by example was rare in the army, but it shows the peculiarly democratic nature of Civil War military life.[30]

Despite an undercurrent of grumbling and dissatisfaction, enlisted men usually accepted their lowly position as a temporary condition necessary for the country's salvation. They believed that their rights and freedom of action would be restored after the war. Sergeant H. C. Kendrick of Georgia hoped that his obedience to superiors would be an example for others in his company and a service to his country's struggle for independence. "I am perfectly resigned to higher authority," he told his father in June, 1863, "but while I am willing to submit to it for the good of my country, I feel my own importance no less." One month later, Kendrick was struck and killed by a minié ball at the battle of Gettysburg. This determination to preserve one's individuality and dignity, despite powerful pressures for conformity and unquestioning obedience, characterized both Union and Confederate soldiers. Enlisted men respected officers who treated them with decency and consideration. "Some men seem to feel because they are officers they are better than every body else but our officers have nothing of that," Rhode Island sergeant Henry Simmons observed with satisfaction. "I am treated by them with the utmost kindness and as an equal in *every* respect." Such confirmation of social equality became an expectation of many enlisted men, who jealously guarded their democratic rights.[31]

Gentlemen of high social standing who entered the ranks particularly objected to the inequalities of military life. Lieutenant William H. Grimball, son of a wealthy South Carolina rice planter, discovered strong resentments among the gentleman privates in his elite artillery battery. "Being gentlemen they are naturally alive to any expression of

30. Haydon Diary, May 12, 1861; Rebecca P. Davis to Burwell Davis, July 10, 1861, in Rebecca P. Davis Papers (typescript in possession of May Davis Hill); W. R. Redding to his wife, August 9, 1861, in W. R. Redding Papers, SHC; Wills, *Army Life*, 94–95; Rundell (ed.), "'If Fortune Should Fail,'" 220. See also Harold B. Simpson (ed.), *The Bugle Softly Blows: The Confederate Diary of Bejamin M. Seaton* (Waco, Tex., 1965), 2; and Linderman, *Embattled Courage*, 36–39.

31. H. C. Kendrick to his father, June 2, May 28, 1863, in H. C. Kendrick Letters, SHC; Henry B. Simmons to his wife, November 9, 1862, in Henry E. Simmons Letters, SHC.

superiority by officers to them as privates," he observed. "This is ex-
ceedingly distasteful to them and very justly so." It troubled Grimball
to think about his own brothers who served as privates, "occupying
positions not fit for gentlemen," nor could he feel pride in his own
promotion to second lieutenant. "I am ranked by men younger than
myself," he complained. Gentlemen who failed to win commissions
denounced the system that awarded military honors. Augustin L. Taveau, a wealthy South Carolina rice planter and lawyer conscripted into
the army in 1864, claimed that foreigners were receiving commissions,
"while our own *Gentlemen* of rank, birth, education and polish, are
conscripted into the *ranks* as 'common soldiers,' and then snubbed by
these popinjays; who, probably, at home are sons of tinkers." Mississippi cavalry private Harry St. John Dixon frequently objected to his
degraded status compared to that of officers who were lower on the
social scale. The son of a wealthy Mississippi planter and lawyer, Dixon
left his law studies at the University of Virginia in 1861 to join the army,
hoping to secure a "respectable" position. Confined to the ranks by
youth and inexperience, he lamented: "At home I was, at least, once a
gentleman; & I do not now altho' a private, choose to be made a dog of
by any man or set of men. It is galling to a gentleman to be absolutely &
entirely subject to the orders of men who in private life were so far his
inferiors; who when they met him felt rather like taking off their hats to
him than giving him law & gospel."[32]

College-educated planters' sons found it unpleasant to be placed in a
company composed of "a set of men that can scarcely read." Most
gentlemen who remained in the ranks, however, served in elite companies such as Hampton's Legion, the Washington Artillery, or the
Richmond Howitzers, which were composed almost exclusively of
educated and refined gentlemen. Members of such crack outfits often
preferred a private's position there to being a lieutenant in any other
regiment. There were numerous advantages in associating only with
one's social equals, as Lewis Grimball of South Carolina pointed out,
"for there is nothing to me so disgusting, as to be always in a crowd
made up of Tom, Dick & Harry." To those who complained about having disagreeable companions in the army, South Carolina private

---

32. William H. Grimball to his mother, January 12, 1863, in Grimball Family Papers,
and to his father, August 15, 1862, in John Berkley Grimball Papers, DU; Augustin L.
Taveau, letter fragment, n.d. [1863], in Augustin Louis Taveau Papers, DU; Dixon Diary,
May 18, 1863, in Dixon Papers.

Charles Hutson of Hampton's Legion answered: "There is no excuse for a young man's falling in among disreputable men, when so large a proportion of true & noble gentlemen exists in our more select companies." Being called "parlour soldiers" or "kid glove & band box soldiers" did not trouble these haughty privates, who were thankful for "having gentlemen for [their] tent-mates," and who claimed that "the pleasantness of our intercourse consoles us greatly for the discomforts we have to undergo."[33]

Because there were fewer socially elite companies in the Union army, gentleman privates were less numerous than in the South. Educated men who sought promotion could more easily transfer to other regiments or, by 1863, secure commissions in newly created black regiments. Nevertheless, some Union privates voiced complaints similar to those of southern gentlemen. "This company . . . is a sad place for a cultivated gentleman," Edward Edes of Massachusetts wrote from Virginia early in 1863, "no fit associates for a collegian & a poor company for me." Samuel Storrow, a Harvard student, who served as corporal in the 44th Massachusetts Regiment, voiced a similar complaint. "It has been one of the most unpleasant experiences as a private," he wrote home from Virginia in 1863, "to be unable to find any congenial companion and friend in my company, and to be obliged to associate with men whom nothing else could have forced me into such close intimacy with." Such arrogant consciousness of social and intellectual superiority irritated the associates of these self-styled gentlemen. Like their Confederate counterparts, Yankee soldiers denounced these snobs as "White Gloves" and "band-box" soldiers. Westerners, particularly, derided the spit and polish of many Army of the Potomac regiments. Social distinctions thus divided men of different backgrounds, creating animosity among soldiers fighting for the same cause. Soldiers especially resented such distinctions when faced with privations because of their lowly status.[34]

Enlisted men of both armies disliked the dehumanizing elements of

33. Cadwallader Jones to his sister, January 11, 1862, in Jones Papers; Lewis Grimball to Gabriella Grimball, September 25, 1863, in Grimball Family Papers; Charles W. Hutson to his mother, August 4, 1861, in Hutson Papers; Richard W. Waldrop to his father, July 23, 1861, in Richard W. Waldrop Papers, SHC; Charles W. Hutson to his mother, June 30, 1861, in Hutson Papers. See also Wiley, *Johnny Reb*, 335–39; and Roark, *Masters Without Slaves*, 59–60.

34. Edes and Storrow quoted in Wiley, *Billy Yank*, 332, 305; Leslie W. Dunlap (ed.), *"Your Affectionate Husband, J. F. Culver": Letters Written During the Civil War* (Iowa City, 1978), 168.

military discipline and objected to their loss of personal freedom. The inherent inequalities of military rank offended the individualistic and egalitarian convictions of Rebels and Yankees alike. Burdened by hard work, meager living conditions, and the onerous commands of superior officers, privates of both armies complained that they led "a dog's life." In these feelings they resembled enlisted men in all other American wars. The metaphors chosen by Civil War soldiers to describe their subordinate position, however, reveal significant differences between northern and southern conceptions of social relationships.[35]

Northern soldiers complained that the routinization and loss of autonomy required by army life reduced men to the level of machines. "One becomes as though the property of somebody else by a life in the Army," Lieutenant William Ferry, a Michigan Democrat, told his wife. "We are liable to become mere machines." Connecticut private Uriah Parmelee, who left his studies at Yale College to enlist in September, 1861, complained, "One can make no plans in the army, indulge no hopes in any particular direction, have no independence, no voice in any thing. He becomes a mere machine while he stays, & if it were not for that spark of hope which lives with nothing to feed upon, he would soon give up everything." The demands of military life seemed to require mechanical efficiency. "Private soldiers should think nothing, dread nothing, be machines, follow their leaders blindly and fearlessly," concluded Private Henry Cross, a young regimental clerk from Newburyport, Massachusetts. "Negroes are the best, foreigners the next, and thinking, *independent* Yankees the poorest." Qualities that made good soldiers thus would not make good civilians. Army nurses likewise had to adopt a cold, mechanical attitude. "No one must come here who cannot put away all feelings," declared Katherine Wormeley, a United States Sanitary Commission nurse. "Do all you can and be a machine—that's the way to act; the only way." Many soldiers, however, believed that it was possible to resist the dehumanizing influences of army life. Fritz Hollister, a young Yankee from Litchfield County, Connecticut, wrote an eloquent tribute to the human spirit's ability to withstand dehumanizing influences: "It is not necessary that

---

35. Frank Putnam Deane (ed.), "*My Dear Wife . . .*": The Civil War Letters of David Brett, *9th Massachusetts Battery, Union Cannoneer* (Little Rock, Ark., 1964), 39; Isaac Marsh to his wife and family, December 10, 1862, in Marsh Papers; Dixon Diary, January 1, April 22, 1864, in Dixon Papers; Henry E. Alvord, "A New England Boy in the Civil War," ed. Caroline B. Sherman, *New England Quarterly*, V (April, 1932), 323–24.

a man should lose his independence and manhood in order to become a soldier, and a true soldier can have the satisfaction of knowing that he is *realy* the equal of one who may be ordering him by virtue of higher rank. The superiority does not lie deeper than the 'shoulder straps,' and none but the envious or weak minded will be disturbed at being 'ordered around.' I know that the discipline & restraint of the army are unnatural. Man was never made for a machine." Union soldiers accepted a certain amount of discipline, but they resisted efforts by military leaders to instill mechanical obedience to orders.[36]

Confederate enlisted men used a different metaphor to describe their degraded status. Both planters and nonslaveholders depicted themselves as slaves to their officers, the army, or the government. For a slave society, this was a natural choice of imagery. Augustin Louis Taveau, a wealthy rice planter and scion of a prominent South Carolina Huguenot family, tried unsuccessfully to gain a military staff position to escape the draft. "I feel degraded, my spirit is broken. I feel as if I was no longer a gentleman," he wrote to his wife shortly after being conscripted in January, 1864. "I have no longer any rights, but am as mean a slave to this government, as one of my own Servants." Two weeks after enlisting in 1861, Private Frank Richardson complained to his father, a Louisiana planter, of the hardships endured by soldiers. "The life of a common soldier is a most hard and rough one," he wrote, "it is a great deal worse than that of a common field negro but those commissioned officers they are just like the owners of slaves on plantations they have nothing to do but to strut about dress fine and enjoy themselves." It is not clear how his father received such an unflattering depiction of planters. "No negro on Red River but has a happy time compared with that of a Confederate soldier," Sergeant Edwin Fay, a Louisiana slaveowner and headmaster of a boys' school, complained in 1862. "There is no telling what may happen to a soldier for he belongs to his officers much more strictly than a negro does to his master." One year later, he again complained that as a soldier he was "a bond slave worse than any

36. William M. Ferry to his wife, February 17, 1863, in Ferry Family Papers; Uriah Parmelee to his mother, March 7, 1863, in Samuel Spencer Parmelee and Uriah N. Parmelee Papers, DU; Cross, "A Yankee Soldier Looks at the Negro," 147; Wormeley quoted in George M. Fredrickson, *The Inner Civil War: Northern Intellectuals and the Crisis of the Union* (New York, 1965), 90; Fritz Hollister to Seth Hollister, n.d. [August, 1863], in Seth Hollister Papers, DU. In his study of Massachusetts political leaders' attitudes about the machine age Carl Siracusa finds a much more positive image of mechanization (*A Mechanical People: Perceptions of the Industrial Order in Massachusetts, 1815–1880* [Middletown, Conn., 1979], 76–111, 233–34).

negro." Ordered from the drill field to the guardhouse for inebriation, Private John Shanks blurted out to his captain, "I will not do it. I was a gentleman before I joined your damned company and by God you want to make a damned slave of me." Shanks thus displayed both the fierce individualism of a democratic spirit and determination not to lose his superior social status. Gentleman and slave occupied opposite ends of a social hierarchy, which to many southerners contained few middle positions.[37]

The vehemence with which southerners denounced military restrictions indicates that they were unaccustomed to limitations on their personal liberty. In their indignation over real or imagined injustices, they sometimes lacked a broader perspective. Henry C. Semple wrote to his wife in May, 1863, that he had "a very strong desire to be at home." A respected Montgomery, Alabama, lawyer and planter when war broke out, he had estimated his own worth at forty thousand dollars. Now, he explained, although he hoped to return home for a visit, "in an army one is so completely a slave that my wishes go a very small way towards their accomplishment." Enlisted men might be expected to voice such complaints, but Henry Semple was a captain of artillery, enjoying far more privileges than most soldiers. One of the Confederacy's greatest whiners was Private Harry St. John Dixon, son of a wealthy planter-lawyer from Greenville, Mississippi. A "high-toned" and vain young man, who enlisted in 1861 as a University of Virginia student, Dixon filled his war diaries with accounts of petty injustices he suffered and his demands for respect as a gentleman. "I am sick of this slavery, this drudgery," he wrote in August, 1862, after a month of marching and skirmishing. He predicted that an upcoming election of officers would elevate "men vastly my inferiors" to command. In January, 1864, he reported his anger over an unjust accusation made by his captain. "O what would I have given to have the shackles off my wrists—to feel that I was free," he wrote. "When when shall I be rid of this slavery!—this damned, hellish thraldom!" Dixon started a new diary volume on March 23, 1865, shortly after returning to camp at Columbus, Mississippi, from a one-month furlough. During this leave,

---

37. Augustin L. Taveau to his wife, January 25, 1864, in Taveau Papers; Frank L. Richardson to his father, September 4, 1861, in Richardson Papers; Wiley (ed.), *This Infernal War*, 51, 157, 285–86; John Shanks quoted in Wiley, *Johnny Reb*, 337. See also Reid Mitchell, "The Creation of Confederate Loyalties," in Robert H. Abzug and Stephen E. Maizlish (eds.), *New Perspectives on Race and Slavery in America* (Lexington, Ky., 1986), 98.

he had courted a "beautiful little blue eyed girl (as usual)" and had taken "an active part" in "weddings, parties, & tableaux & charades." When his furlough expired, he complained, "I had to resume my loathsome Slavery." Less than three weeks later, Lee surrendered at Appomattox. Harry St. John Dixon's enslavement neared its end. That a hot-blooded young patriot could pass through four years of war and spend its final weeks frolicking "with the gals" and complaining of his enslavement reveals a surprising (and unusual) lack of patriotic fervor. Only in his use of slavery as a metaphor for military restrictions did Dixon truly resemble his fellow Rebels.[38]

Nonslaveholders also compared their subordinate position in the army to that of slaves. Private Christopher Hackett, a young North Carolina farmer, objected to the lack of freedom of movement, action, and speech in the army. "I am bound down worse than the slave not only me but all private soldiers," he complained. "I think it is time for some thing to be done for we are here a fighting to keep from under northern bondage and serving under southern Masters who keep us bound more than the Master of the African." Texas private John W. Truss told his wife that military life had "shown to me the difference between a free man and a slave. It has taught me a lesson I will never forget." This bondage was all the more galling to soldiers who could not dissociate physical compulsion from mental bondage. "A soldier's life is that of a slave's, or worse," asserted Louisiana quartermaster Robert Patrick, a bookkeeper and local deputy sheriff before the war, "for he must act as the slave does while at the same time he is possessed of greater sensibility than the slave and his toils and sufferings are not confined to the physical man alone." Such a distinction enabled soldiers to compare their condition with the slave's without drawing logical conclusions about how slaves must feel toward their superiors. Denunciations of military hardship as a form of slavery belie southerners' avowed belief in the humaneness of slavery. Only by depicting blacks as subhuman could they reconcile the harsh conditions of slavery with Christian morality or belief in the dignity of man.[39]

Union and Confederate enlisted men used metaphors of machine

38. Henry C. Semple to his wife, May 29, 1863, in Henry C. Semple Papers, SHC; Dixon Diary, August 19, 1862, January 1, 1864, March 23, 1865, in Dixon Papers.
39. Christopher Hackett to his family, August 16, 1863, in John C. Hackett Papers, DU; John W. Truss, "Civil War Letters from Parsons' Texas Cavalry Brigade," ed. Johnette H. Ray, *Southwestern Historical Quarterly*, LXIX (October, 1965), 223; Taylor (ed.), *Reluctant Rebel*, 180.

and slave, respectively, to describe a similar condition of imposed restrictions. The different images they used provide a glimpse into the
social perceptions of northern and southern people. In describing the
subordinate position they occupied in the military hierarchy, Union
soldiers used the language of a burgeoning industrial society. They had
become "mere machines," anonymous cogs in a vast, impersonal structure. Southerners adopted the familiar metaphor of slave society, describing their position within a personalized social status hierarchy.
Images of machine and slave both depicted circumstances in which
freedom had ceased to exist and unthinking labor and obedience were
required. Those who denounced these conditions believed that men
had a higher calling.

These metaphors reveal a striking difference between an industrial,
"modern" North and an agrarian, "backward" South. Yet there is also
significant contrast in southerners' perception of society as a system of
hierarchical personal relationships, with a slave caste at the very bottom, and northerners' perception of an impersonal order, in which
men could be degraded to the level of inanimate machines. Southerners believed that there was no intermediate status between freedom
and slavery. An individual could be neither half-slave nor half-free.
Similarly, northerners seemed to think that there was no condition
between full manhood and dehumanization. One was either a man or
a machine. Slavery gave southerners a human model of degradation,
total lack of freedom, deprivation of rights, and subservience to the will
of superiors. Northerners believed that such a condition fell beyond
the pale of human existence. A person stripped of such rights was less
than a man: he became a "mere machine."[40]

The contrasting implications of northern and southern metaphors
should not obscure the similar feeling they convey. In vivid language,
Union and Confederate soldiers protested against their lowly status in
the army, which deprived them of liberty, power, and human rights.
Soldiers almost universally complained that rich and influential men
had created a war in which the poor had to fight the battles and bear the
heaviest burdens. These antagonisms between enlisted men and of-

40. On the conflict between the industrial North and the agricultural South see Richard D. Brown, *Modernization: The Transformation of American Life, 1600–1865* (New York,
1976), esp. 140–48, 161; George M. Fredrickson, "Blue Over Gray: Sources of Success and
Failure in the Civil War," in Fredrickson (ed.), *A Nation Divided: Problems and Issues of the
Civil War and Reconstruction* (Minneapolis, 1975), 57–80; and Thomas H. O'Connor, *Lords
of the Loom: The Cotton Whigs and the Coming of the Civil War* (New York, 1968), 154–67.

ficers transcended sectional boundaries, forming among privates on both sides a small wedge of grievance that set one social class against another. In the end, the external threat of defeat diverted class antagonisms, but their influence created internal social conflicts in both the Union and the Confederacy.

SPECULATORS AND TRAITORS

Tradition has so glorified the idealistic patriotism of both Rebels and Yankees that the extent of ideological and social divisions within each section has almost been forgotten. Despite the demands of war for sectional unity, significant numbers of Americans continued to place national or personal interests above sectional loyalty. Occasionally, this resistance to partisan appeals led to overt opposition; more often, it resulted in a simple refusal to contribute to a war based on sectional interests. The lack of patriotic unity posed an internal threat to both Union and Confederacy. Ardent patriots on each side denounced as traitors those who advocated compromise and reconciliation and condemned as speculators or slackers those whose selfish pursuit of profit or refusal to fight hampered the quest for victory. Neither side achieved complete sectional unity.

Even after Lincoln's election in 1860, most southerners did not support secession. But conservative Unionism weakened as secessionists won victories in state after state, and it virtually disappeared when, after the fall of Fort Sumter, Lincoln called for troops to suppress the southern "rebellion." Yet even when forced to choose between the South and a Union that could be maintained only by force, many southerners remained Unionists. Not all would unite, even in a war of self-defense. As postwar claims for damages filed with the Southern Claims Commission indicate, even among the South's wealthy planters, who would gain most from a war to save the slave system, hundreds maintained their Unionism to the end. Unionism remained even stronger in mountainous regions where slavery never flourished. Whether Unionism represents a truly national loyalty or merely opposition to the Confederate establishment, it reveals deep ideological cleavages within the South. Such internal enemies might cripple the struggle for independence. Most Confederate partisans were less concerned about southern Unionists as adversaries than as symbols of disunity and internal conflict.[41]

41. Degler, *Other South*, 158–87; Frank W. Klingberg, *The Southern Claims Commission* (Berkeley, 1955), 1–19. For a discussion of southern secret peace societies, see Georgia Lee

Southerners committed to the Confederate cause despised Union sympathizers, whom they accused of disloyalty or aiding the enemy. Lieutenant William R. Redding of Georgia reported in September, 1861, that the *"glorious Union men"* in western Virginia "pointed out the secessionist in their county to the Yankees and then would go with them and take their property. they took all the meal & Flour one poor old widdow had then riped her Beds & toor up her wearing apparel and left." These "infernal union men" were even threshing wheat for the federal troops, but at least five of them had been captured and were being held with the Yankee prisoners. To root out Union sympathizers in areas traversed by both armies, Confederate soldiers sometimes put on Yankee uniforms and sought information or assistance from suspected Unionists. They then arrested those who offered aid. In heavily Unionist areas of the South, particularly western Virginia, such tricks were also employed as a means of obtaining food, clothing, and supplies from a hostile populace.[42]

Unionism remained strongest in those regions of the South where slavery and the plantation system had never flourished, particularly in mountainous areas of western Virginia, Kentucky, North Carolina, Tennessee, and northern Alabama. In these remote areas, Confederate forces had difficulty establishing control. Unionist enclaves exposed Confederates to danger from internal enemies sympathetic to the northern invaders. Southern Unionists refused to renounce either their section or their loyalty to the Union. Their divided loyalties caused inner anguish for many Unionists, as well as revealing the incomplete triumph of Confederate ideology. Few Unionists actively opposed the Confederacy. They constituted, for the most part, a conservative remnant of southern nationalists. Yet the persistence of Unionism in the South provides one more example of the limits of sectional consciousness.[43]

Confederate soldiers denounced Unionists as internal enemies. Writing to his wife in June, 1861, from Martinsburg, the "H.Q. of Black Republicanism" in West Virginia, North Carolina soldier Peter Hair-

---

Tatum, *Disloyalty in the Confederacy* (Chapel Hill, 1934). The views of articulate Unionists are presented in William C. Harris, "The Southern Unionist Critique of the Civil War," *Civil War History*, XXXI (March, 1985), 39–56.

42. W. R. Redding to his wife, September 7, 1861, in Redding Papers; Samuel A. Agnew Diary, June 17, 1862, SHC; Richard W. Waldrop to his father, July 21, 1863, in Waldrop Papers.

43. Klingberg, *Southern Claims Commission*, 194; Degler, *Other South*, 158–74; William L. Barney, *Flawed Victory: A New Perspective on the Civil War* (New York, 1975), 90–91.

ston advocated arresting and disarming all suspicious persons: "We are exposing our lives for what we deem the holiest cause in the world our homes and our firesides and we must tolerate no enemies in our midst, no 'fire in the rear.' If they are not with us, let them leave the State." To Confederate patriots, regions in which Union sympathizers held sway seemed foreign territory. Returning to his native Kentucky on a cavalry raid in June, 1864, Captain Edward Guerrant observed that "although this country looked, beyond all description beautiful, it did not look or feel like my own country; did not wear the look of my native land." Invasion by the Union army had reinforced the rebel sympathies of the old men and women, Guerrant reported, but the young men had become "a shameless, spiritless, down headed, subjugated, elegantly dressed & starched set of unconscious slaves to Lincoln & his negro soldiers." Kentucky had become an enemy country. The same was true of eastern Tennessee, Guerrant soon discovered. "In no part of the South do such feelings inspire a rebel soldier, as in the East Tenn. country," he wrote in August, 1864. "Every inch of ground seems sown with treason & hatred."[44]

Confederate partisans vowed vengeance upon Unionists who either openly or tacitly proffered assistance and encouragement to the enemy. "I think that every Virginian who acts with the enemy *now* & is not true to his own State in her hour of danger, has committed the unpardonable sin at least in this world," army pay clerk Matthew Andrews of Virginia declared in August, 1861. "There is a day of Vengeance coming for all the southern Union Men, and even those who escape the dangers of the war will have a far more severe punishment to bear in the contempt in which they will be held by both parties." Mississippi private Harry St. John Dixon denounced the author of a "treasonable publication" in a local newspaper. "The culprit proposed nothing short of complete submission & slavery—reconstruction, & the old Union," he charged. "Such men want no argument but the rope, for the safety of every dear object." Occasionally such threats were carried out. Lawyer Jason Niles of Kosciusko, Mississippi, a Vermont native not entirely sympathetic to the Confederacy, recorded a neighbor's comment about southern Unionists: "Yesterday Colbert, in speaking of Nathan Sweatt, said that a man who in these times uttered disloyal sentiments ought to

---

44. Peter Hairston to his wife, June 5, 1861, in Peter Hairston Papers, SHC; Edward O. Guerrant Diary, June 10, August 17, 1864, in Edward Owings Guerrant Papers, SHC.

be shot down summarily, and if he should hear one utter such, and he had a double-barrelled gun in his hand he would shoot the offender down in a moment." One week earlier, Union sympathizer Nathan Sweatt had been lynched in a nearby swamp by men who shared Colbert's desire for retribution.[45]

Amid the fury of war, any person who failed to give active support to the Confederate cause might be labeled a traitor. There were relatively few outspoken Unionists, who would openly dispute the right of secession or advocate restoration of the Union, but the Confederacy was plagued by thousands of men who refused to volunteer for army service or contribute wholeheartedly to the war effort. "In the present sad conditions of affairs traitors are springing up in every direction," Kate Stone of Louisiana warned in February, 1862. "I would not trust any man now who stays at home instead of going out to fight for his country." Army volunteers complained about those who refused to share the war's burdens. "I do not like to grumble, yet there are those at home now, in the State of Tennessee, that ought to be in the service," declared Second Lieutenant Felix Buchanan of Tennessee. "I know several young, able boddied men, and unmaried, now at their homes laying up treasures which moth doth consume and rust destroy, relying upon the strong arms of others to establish a nation whose laws are to protect their person and property, such persons ought not to flurish." Phila Calder of Wilmington, North Carolina, bemoaned that her son, who had been actively engaged in the service for two years, had to return to his regiment after a brief furlough, "while so many hale and hearty men, & youths of this place *who have never been in service* are thronging before my eyes dressed in broadcloth & kid gloves, knowing nothing even of the hardships or privations of *the times*, much less of the jeopardies & sufferings of *a soldier's life*." She was outraged by these timid patriots, who enjoyed the comforts of peace while her son endured the hardships of war. "Even handed justice calls for redress here!" she proclaimed.[46]

Confederate soldiers reserved their most severe condemnations of stay-at-home patriots for former secessionists and political leaders who

45. Matthew P. Andrews to his wife, August 21, 1861, in Charles Wesley Andrews Papers, DU; Dixon Diary, September 1, 1863, in Dixon Papers; Jason Niles Diary, October 7, 14, 1863, SHC.

46. Anderson (ed.), *Brokenburn*, 92; Felix Buchanan to his mother, March 6, 1862, in Buchanan and McClellan Family Papers, SHC; Phila C. Calder to Robert Calder, March 26, 1863, in Calder Papers.

evaded military service. "You admonish me against indulging in bitter feelings against those people that stay at home and shun the service," Lieutenant Theophilus Perry of Marshall, Texas, wrote to his wife in July, 1863. He conceded that he could forgive those who had played no part in causing the war, "but the rabid violent secessionist who denounced all persons that differed from him, ought to have shouldered his gun at the beginning of the war; and I feel a contempt for him that I in vain would strive to repress." Many soldiers believed that those who had advocated secession and armed resistance should bear the hardships of war. "These big fighting men cant be got out to fight as easy as to make speaches," North Carolina private James Zimmerman grumbled. "How can they think we can fight when they the great leeding fighting men wont come out and help us."[47]

In April, 1862, the decline of volunteer enlistment compelled the Confederate government to enact the first of several conscription laws. Shortly before conscription was imposed, Virginia recruiting officer David Dickenson discovered that there were "some very disloyal people" in his own community. "The militia in Pittsyl[vania] are very much frightened in regard to a draft but they say that they will never go untill the draft comes and then I think it will require a force to bring some of them." Dickenson had little success in finding recruits. "I find a great many that acknowledge the importance of volenteering & dred mightly the draft but they still indulge a hope that their will be no draft & if their is that they will escape." Through both legal and illegal means, many southerners were able to escape military service. The failure of conscription to solve the army's manpower shortages indicates how serious disaffection had become. Large numbers of southerners refused to risk their lives for a cause to which they were not wholeheartedly committed.[48]

Speculators symbolized this evil spirit of selfishness and disloyalty which patriotic southerners most despised. Acting purely from self-interest, at the expense of the public good, speculators were indifferent to all appeals except that to profit. Capitalizing on their neighbors' needs, they withheld goods so as to drive up market prices, thereby undermining the Confederacy's economic foundations and creating

47. Theophilus Perry to his wife, July 17, 1863, in Presley Person Papers, DU; James C. Zimmerman to his wife, August 5, 1863, in Zimmerman Papers.

48. David V. Dickenson Diary, February 3, 23, 1862 (microfilm), UV. See Moore, *Conscription and Conflict, passim.*

scarcities of food, clothing, and military supplies. Once war broke out, the Unionist minority either chose to support the South or to remain silent rather than fight against friends and neighbors. A far greater danger was posed by self-interested citizens who exploited wartime conditions to charge exorbitant prices for food and other necessities. Individual civilians suffered heavily at the hands of these speculators, who set in motion a devastating spiral of rampant inflation and supply shortages that threatened the social stability, political authority, and military effectiveness of the young Confederacy and increased its vulnerability to northern attack.[49]

Avarice and selfishness seemed to motivate men who remained at home pursuing personal business ventures. Unchecked inflation and shortages of provisions convinced many southerners that speculators were taking advantage of the unsettled state of society to accumulate vast profits from the suffering of their fellow citizens. Captain James D. Webb, an Alabama lawyer and planter, lamented in March, 1862, "My mind has felt a gloom like the dark shadows of the night when i have seen the indifference with which some have looked on & with folded arms desired to be the recipients of the blessings without enduring the toil, whilst others have been active & energetic to speculate on the sufferings of our bleeding country regarding it only as a means to increase their ill gotten gain." Those who most boldly proclaimed their patriotism often seemed least willing to share the danger and hardship. As Theophilus Perry of Texas complained: "I have a great contempt for noisy men . . . who once valiantly talked of whipping the reluctant youths of the land off to the wars, and who themselves have ignobly speculated upon the necessities of the soldier and his family, accumulated fortunes out of the sacrifices of them that have bared their bosoms to the bayonet, and yet sculk away from danger themselves." This attitude prevailed throughout the army. Many of the most vocal civilian "patriots" were accused of placing personal financial interests above concern for the Confederacy's survival. "If you will show me a man that is trying to compell soldiers to stay in the army he is a speculator or a slave holder, or has a interest in slaves," declared James Zimmerman in October, 1863.[50]

49. Ramsdell, *Behind the Lines*, 48–51; Escott, *After Secession*, 122–25; Wiley, *Plain People*, 66–69; Hahn, *Roots of Southern Populism*, 130–32.
50. James D. Webb to his wife, March 5, 1862, in Walton Family Papers, SHC; Theophilus Perry to his wife, July 12, 1863, in Person Papers; James C. Zimmerman to his wife, October 21, 1863, in Zimmerman Papers.

As they were called on to suffer ever-increasing hardships and dangers, soldiers denounced as speculators and money hoarders those who still enjoyed the comforts of home. Following the death in battle of a close friend, Sergeant Ham Chamberlayne, a Virginia lawyer, who had been active in Richmond political and social circles before the war, deplored the spirit of selfishness exhibited by his fellow countrymen even in the presence of death. He told his mother that he would almost rather have fallen by the side of his noble comrade "than to live on among an evil & faithless generation, where all except some few like him are toiling & grasping, greedy, at spoils that may be but dead sea apples in their hands, forgetting, all, the ultimate good, the country." In May, 1862, North Carolina soldier William Calder likewise warned, "There is too much avarice, too much speculation, among our people." Civilians felt the effects of speculation in higher prices and shortages of vital commodities. Defending his decision to remain at home to care for his family, J. R. Guess of North Carolina wrote to a friend in the army: "I do sincerely believe that I would be happier in the camp, or on the march, provided my family could be well provided for, than I am at home exposed to the sharpers and speculators who are trying to crush the life out of their poor neighbors."[51]

The clamor against high prices extended from one end of the Confederacy to the other, as newspapers joined the popular denunciation of those who withheld crops and raised prices. The culmination of this protest came in the Richmond bread riot of April 2, 1863. A mob of over a thousand, mostly women, gathered in Capitol Square, then marched down Cary and Main streets, entering stores to seize provisions and clothing. The mob dispersed only after appeals by Governor John Letcher, several congressmen, and even President Davis, who threatened to have troops fire on the mob. Similar uprisings also occurred in Augusta, Milledgeville, and Columbus, Georgia. Anger and frustration among the civilian population had reached the boiling point.[52]

Patriotic southerners increasingly recognized that speculators endangered both the people's morale and the country's ability to prosecute the war. By weakening Confederate unity, they threatened to undermine efforts to repel invasion and end the war. "More and more I

51. Chamberlayne (ed.), *Ham Chamberlayne*, 68; William Calder to his mother, May 15, 1862, in Calder Papers; J. R. Guess to Levi Lockhart, January 5, 1863, in Browning Papers.
52. Emory M. Thomas, *The Confederate State of Richmond* (Austin, 1971), 118–22; Ramsdell, *Behind the Lines*, 49–50; Hahn, *Roots of Southern Populism*, 128–29.

dread the evil spirit and treason which prevails among a miserable class at home," Alex Haskell of South Carolina lamented in April, 1863: "It would shock and astonish you to hear the humblest private on his return from what should have been a joyous furlough to his home, speak in terms of unmitigated contempt and disgust of the spirit of selfishness and speculation which he has found amongst those whom he had fondly hoped to find engaged in the peaceful struggle for our salvation, as he is upon the bloody field. But so it is & almost universally." Mrs. J. R. Dixon, a Mississippi planter's wife, who had fled to Alabama as a refugee from Yankee invasion, observed in 1864 that "the majority of people in this country seem to have become hardened & have not a feeling or thought beyond money making and while this feeling pervades our country we can not expect peace." Not only did such money-making greed hinder the Confederate war effort, it also signaled the intrusion of Yankee vices.[53]

The problem of speculation became more severe as the war dragged on. As North Carolina lieutenant Jesse Person lamented in June, 1863, "The longer the war last[s], the meaner the people get, instead of getting better." Many Confederate soldiers feared that after the war these selfish speculators would usurp the social position of patriotic citizens who had sacrificed their fortunes and comforts in the war effort. "When the war ends these Vultures will have their pockets full of money & will command the respect and position that wealth always ensures," South Carolina aristocrat Lewis Grimball predicted in February, 1864, "while suffering & patriotic poverty will die uncared for and unsung." More optimistic, or determined, individuals believed that justice would eventually triumph. As Elias Davis of Jefferson County, Alabama, concluded as early as May, 1862, "These war times is their day; ours will come after the war."[54]

Frustrated by the prospect of military defeat, threatened with shortages of necessary provisions, and angered by rampant inflation, many southerners argued that speculators, rather than Union sympathizers, posed the greatest internal threat to the Confederacy's survival. These foes, they claimed, were even more dangerous than northern troops.

---

53. Alexander Cheves Haskell to his mother, April 6, 1863, in Alexander Cheves Haskell Papers, SHC; Mrs. J. R. Dixon to Harry St. John Dixon, September 19, 1864, in Dixon Papers.
54. Jesse Person to his mother, June 22, 1863, in Person Papers; Lewis M. Grimball to his father, February 8, 1864, in John Berkley Grimball Papers; Elias Davis to his parents, May 21, 1862, in Elias Davis Papers, SHC.

At the end of 1862, Martha Ingram of Hillsborough, Texas, complained that greedy neighbors were extorting the last cent from soldiers' wives and children. "My dear it seames to me that half of the people have gon wilde after money," she wrote to her husband. "I have heard men say that the Southern people were whipping themselves much faster than the Yankees could." This spirit of selfishness and indifference to the Confederate cause apparently affected large numbers of southerners. Loyal Confederates charged that by withholding their support and encouragement, speculators and submissionists virtually ensured defeat. In December, 1863, Sarah Wadley claimed that "our foes within, our inefficient and false officers, and the lukewarmness of the people are what we have [to] contend with, these are foes far more powerful than the Yankees." Rebecca Davis of Fishing Creek, North Carolina, denounced civilians who were "trying to discourage those who are doing everything and suffering everything" but who themselves contributed nothing to the cause. "It is giving aid and comfort to the enemy and virtually tying the hands of our brave soldiers in the field," she wrote to her son in the army.[55]

With the prospect of defeat looming before them during the war's final year, southerners increasingly blamed speculators and slackers for the failure of their struggle for independence. They continued to believe in southern military, as well as moral, superiority over the North. Refusing to admit that the hated Yankees could conquer them, many southerners concluded that their own lack of solidarity caused defeat. In July, 1864, Harry St. John Dixon blamed military reverses on speculation and lack of patriotism: "Had the country been true to itself—scorned speculation, placed every able bodied man in the army & been firm as it should—our lines would now be at Bowling Green & Cumberland Gap." Instead, Grant and Sherman were thundering at the gates of Richmond and Atlanta. "Intoxication, Madness, & Speculation seem to rule the hour. Speculation and the haste to get rich is ruining everything," roared Louisiana sergeant Edwin Fay in January, 1864. "The Yankees cannot conquer us but we are fast conquering ourselves." Ardent patriots argued that if all southerners remained loyal to the cause, the South could never be defeated. "When I think of the condition of our country and then of the speculators I feel indig-

55. Martha Ingram to George Ingram, December 25, 1862, in Ingram (ed.), *Civil War Letters*, 45; Wadley Diary, December 21, 1863; Rebecca P. Davis to Burwell Davis, October 15, 1864, in Davis Papers (typescript).

nant," Virginia lieutenant Thomas F. Boatwright exclaimed. "I feel and believe that if our cause fails it will be caused by them; and if this be the case what a curse will rest upon them." Speculators had become scapegoats for the Confederacy's impending defeat. Rather than concede the North's military superiority, many southerners attributed failure to internal divisions.[56]

Northern soldiers likewise denounced civilian money-makers, lukewarm patriots, and Rebel sympathizers as dangerous internal enemies. Although they believed that self-interested army contractors and cowards weakened the North's military effort, they unleashed their most stinging rebukes against Copperheads, whose sympathy for the Confederacy threatened northern morale and crippled the administration's ability to prosecute the war. Just as white southerners denounced "Yankee" characteristics such as avarice and selfishness as the greatest internal threats, northerners worried most about "Rebel" acts of opposition to the Union cause.

Union soldiers charged that army contractors and politicians sought to prolong the war so they could reap exorbitant profits; they complained that for many civilians money-making was a stronger motive than patriotism. Private Edwin Wentworth, a former newspaper printer from Maine, argued that a few politicians who were getting rich from the war hampered the army's efforts to defeat the South. "If there were not so much scheming how to make political capital out of the war, and army speculation," he insisted, "the war might have been closed, and the rebelion crushed, months ago." New Jersey corporal Joseph Osborn, son of a shopkeeper, echoed these beliefs: "I am disgusted with this war it is a bloody money making concern. Kept up by politicians for the purpose of filling their pockets. If the North was only half as united as the South we would have whipped the Rebels long ago. But as it is we can never whip the rebels." Money fever was not limited to army speculators and politicians. The entire country seemed to be infected with greed. "The mass of the people [have] turned their attention to making money, regardless of our national safety," warned New Jersey Colonel Robert McAllister.[57]

56. Dixon Diary, July 7, 1864, in Dixon Papers; Wiley (ed.), "This Infernal War," 384; Thomas F. Boatwright to his wife, May 14, 1863, in Boatwright Letters.
57. Edwin O. Wentworth to his wife, October 9, 1862, and to his father, November 10, 1862, in Wentworth Papers; Joseph B. Osborn to Louise Landau, March 16, 1863, in Osborn Papers; Robertson (ed.), Civil War Letters of McAllister, 463.

Risking their lives to defend the country in its most severe crisis, Union soldiers raged against cowards who refused to fight. These slackers remained at home, profiting from inflated prices for their goods, while honest, conscientious patriots sacrificed pleasures and risked death to defend their country. According to Edwin Wentworth, the spirit of these unpatriotic men was "exemplified by Artemus Ward, who was perfectly willing to have the rebellion crushed if it took the blood of all his relatives. He was willing to sacrifice them all, but unwilling to fight himself." Such men should be placed in the front line of every battle, Wentworth declared, where, "if they attempted to sneak away, they would meet a volley from the rear and be immolated upon their comrade's bayonets." In their letters home, soldiers exhorted neighbors to enlist and denounced the lack of patriotic fervor that had curtailed enlistments after the war's first year. Indeed, many soldiers welcomed Confederate invasions and raids, hoping that such crises would unify the North. Their expectations were disappointed. "I am almost ashamed of Penn.," Sergeant David Craft of Brownsville, Pennsylvania, confessed after hearing that Confederate forces had invaded the state in July, 1863: "Thousands of great cowardly louts who should have rushed to arms at the first prospect of invasion are found skulking while the Rebs are at their very doors." Robert McAllister wrote to his wife, "Any young able-bodied man who can possibly leave home and don't join the army now has no love for his country and does not deserve to be protected by our Government." Soldiers demanded that such slackers be forced to fight.[58]

Because of the inadequacy of enlistments, Congress in March, 1863, adopted the Union's first conscription law, which soldiers almost universally approved as a measure necessary to equalize the burdens of war. Lieutenant Charles Salter of Detroit reported that his comrades were "greatly pleased to think that the government is now bound to bring out men enough to crush the rebellion, whether they are willing to enlist, or not, there will not be much pity for these drafted men here in the old regiments." In addition to forcing slackers to share the burdens of war, veterans believed that the draft would punish southern sympathizers and stigmatize lukewarm patriots. As Isaac Marsh

58. Edwin O. Wentworth to his sister, April 3, 1864, in Wentworth Papers; David L. Craft to his sister, July 7, 1863, in David Lucius Craft Papers, DU; Robertson (ed.), *Civil War Letters of McAllister*, 325. See Linderman, *Embattled Courage*, 220–29. Artemus Ward was the pseudonymn of Charles F. Browne, a popular humorist of the wartime North.

wrote, "I want some of them infernal sympathisers that is comforting the South to have to come down and fill up our Regiment." Corporal Frank Lansing, son of a Michigan woodwright and farmer, admonished draftees that "it would have been much better to have volunteered & so got rid of the name *Conscript,* which they seem to dread more than they would the name of Convict in times of peace."[59]

Although they denounced slackers and speculators, northerners reserved their most bitter diatribes for Copperheads, who either openly sympathized with the Confederacy or opposed the Lincoln administration's military and political policies. "Copperhead" was a vaguely defined epithet applied to anyone who criticized the government or exhibited other disloyal tendencies. These political and ideological dissidents were depicted as the North's most dangerous internal enemies. Few of those denounced as Copperheads, however, actually advocated treasonable conduct. They were conservative nationalists, and their wartime slogan proclaimed, "The Constitution as it is, the Union as it was." Threatened by Republican efforts to suppress dissent, Democrats formed several small secret political societies—notably the Knights of the Golden Circle, the Order of American Knights, and the Sons of Liberty—to protect themselves and their constitutional rights. These secret societies remained small and ineffectual, yet Republicans gained political advantage by charging them with various conspiracies and treasonable acts. The Republicans formed their own secret society, the Union League, to help win elections, bolster Union morale, and support the Lincoln administration's policies. Local Union Leagues reported southern sympathizers to the War Office, demanded their removal from office, and attempted to silence critics of the war. They staged mass rallies, mobbed Copperhead newspaper offices, and contributed to Lincoln's reelection in 1864.[60]

Union soldiers believed that Copperheads posed the greatest threat to military success and condemned them as traitors. New Hampshire

---

59. Charles H. Salter to Isabella Duffield, February 21, 1863, in Duffield Papers; Isaac Marsh to his wife, March 1, 1863, in Marsh Papers, DU; Frank E. Lansing to his mother, November 13, 1863, in Frank E. Lansing Papers, BHC.

60. For a valuable historiographical analysis, see Richard O. Curry, "The Union as It Was: A Critique of Recent Interpretations of the 'Copperheads,'" *Civil War History,* XIII (March, 1967), 25–39. On the Union League and secret antiwar societies, see Frank L. Klement, *Dark Lanterns: Secret Political Societies, Conspiracies, and Treason Trials in the Civil War* (Baton Rouge, 1984); and Clement M. Silvestro, *Rally Round the Flag: The Union Leagues in the Civil War* (Ann Arbor, 1966).

private Oren Farr declared that "any one that will advocate the doctrine of our going to the South to ask terms of peace ought to be branded as a traitor and shuned by every honest man." Many soldiers thought that by withholding their support from the Union cause, Copperheads hindered efforts to subdue the rebellion. "When I see how many traitors there are, and how little union of feeling there is in the north, I some times think we shall never be able to conquer," New York private John Foote despaired in January, 1863. Disunity within the North gave southerners hope of success, soldiers believed, and thereby emboldened them to continue fighting. "We do not fear the cowardly, skulking traitor Copperhead of the North, only in the encouragement they give the enemy, & this prolongs the war," asserted Captain James G. Theaker of Ohio.[61]

Because of their political opposition to the Lincoln administration, Democrats were frequently branded as Copperheads. Such wholesale application of the epithet indicates its imprecise meaning; any person guilty of disagreeing with Republican policy or failing to contribute sufficiently to the war effort might be labeled a Copperhead. Although a majority of the party were "Peace Democrats," who opposed vigorous prosecution of the war, an important minority, called "War Democrats," supported the administration despite political differences. Their loyalty was crucial in strengthening the federal government and thereby maintaining sufficient political and military unity to restore the Union. Nevertheless, many soldiers branded all Democrats as disunionists and interpreted the party's victories in the November, 1862, elections as setbacks for the Union cause. "The results in New York and Ohio, and the successes which have resulted in the late elections to those who are openly opposed to the Administration and in fact those who not very indirectly aid the Rebellion—these are as saddening as disaster in the field," Massachusetts private Samuel Nichols claimed, "and are gloated over by the press of the enemy as much."[62]

The presidential election of 1864 aroused strong passions among Union soldiers. The Democratic party's nomination of Ohio peace ad-

61. Oren E. Farr to his wife, February 21, 1863, in Oren E. Farr Papers, DU; John B. Foote to his mother, January 4, 1863, and to his family, March 28, 1863, in John B. Foote Papers, DU; Rieger (ed.), *Through One Man's Eyes*, 128.
62. Underhill (ed.), *"Your Soldier Boy Samuel,"* 47. See also Christopher Dell, *Lincoln and the War Democrats: The Grand Erosion of Conservative Tradition* (Rutherford, N. J., 1975), 9 and *passim*; Curry, "Union as It Was," 25.

vocate George Pendleton for vice-president and its adoption of a plat-
form resolution demanding immediate efforts to reach a compromise
peace angered soldiers committed to vigorous prosection of the war.
"Every *soldier* wishes Abraham Lincoln's reelection," declared Maine
sergeant Nathan Webb, "none but 'bummers' and deserters wish otherwise." He believed that Lincoln's triumph would "do more to dis-
hearten the Rebels and crush the Rebellion than many a victory." James
K. Newton of Wisconsin rejoiced over the election results. "What I have
always thought, was, that all that was needed was to give the Copperheads of the north a whipping so that they would stay whipped, & soon
after, we would have peace," he told his mother. Despite such denunciations of Democrats as Copperheads and traitors, some soldiers continued to support Democratic candidate General George McClellan.
Captain Charles Salter of Michigan confessed that his regiment had
given McClellan three more votes than Lincoln: "I felt mortified to
think that the old Regt. after fighting the rebels for three years should
vote for the northern friends of rebellion, but it cannot be helped now."
According to those who supported Lincoln and the Union party, a
coalition of Republicans and War Democrats, this defeat of the Democratic party struck a forceful blow against northern sympathizers with
the Confederacy. The voters had rejected compromise.[63]

Frustrated by the North's inability to defeat Confederate forces,
Union soldiers blamed enemies at home for weakening their ability to
prosecute the war and vowed revenge against all such traitors. "The
traitors are not here they are at home & if they are not careful we will
give them a taste of hemp," Connecticut sergeant Henry Marshall
wrote from Virginia in 1863. He believed that the Union would triumph
"in spite of traitors at home even if we have to whip the Rebs here &
then go home & thrash those there." A civilian quartermaster clerk
from Pennsylvania declared that if he had the power he would "visit
rather severe punishment on the men who are now opposing the
Administration and thereby prolonging this horrid war and doing
more for the Rebels than if they would go into the Southern Army." The
New York draft riots in 1863 challenged federal authority to raise troops
and presented dramatic evidence of the danger posed by internal
opponents of administration policy. Soldiers railed against these al-

---

63. Nathan Webb Diary, June 7, 1864, WLC; Ambrose (ed.), *A Wisconsin Boy in Dixie*,
128; Charles Salter to Isabella Duffield, November 20, 1864, in Duffield Papers.

legedly Copperhead-inspired traitors. After hearing about "the disgraceful riot in N.Y.," Henry Marshall reported that he and his comrades "wished we could have been there to have shot down the riotous brawlers without any compunction." The riots aroused the anger of veteran soldiers, who were eager to fight against Copperheads and draft resisters. Lieutenant David Craft of Pennsylvania assured his sister that her fear of continued opposition to the draft was entirely without foundation. "Even if resistance should be attempted," Craft wrote, "nothing would please a Reg't of Veterans more than to go north and shoot a few hundred copperheads."[64]

Yankee veterans vowed that after they suppressed the rebellion, they would fight just as fiercely against northern enemies of the Union. Copperheads would be strictly punished for their disloyalty. "When this war is over I would not like to stand in Copperhead shoese," Michigan nurse Hannah Carlisle wrote from a hospital in Kentucky. "For thare is a determination on the part of Every true souldier to avenge themself & rid the country of all sush nuscunces." Soldiers eagerly anticipated the satisfaction revenge would bring. "I believe there will be a day of reckoning at the close of the war for those ten times accursed Copperheads at the North," Private Francis E. Hall of Lenawee County, Michigan, predicted. "I will fight as quick North as South." New York private William Pedrick stated that army veterans "would like to clean the copperheads out of the north" as soon as they had defeated the Rebels. "Them southern Sympathisers i would like myself to see them all drawn up in a line & hung one by one," he informed his brother, "i tell you it makes my blood boil to think about them." Similarly, Wisconsin lieutenant Julian Hinkley declared, "The English language that is its polite language does not furnish words to express my ideas of such hell pests."[65]

Hatred for Copperheads grew so intense that many soldiers came to despise them even more than southern Rebels. Though these internal dissenters professed loyalty to the Union, they weakened northern

64. Henry G. Marshall to his sister, March 1, 1863, to his family, April 2, 1863, and to the "folks at home," July 22, 1863, all in Marshall Papers; William M. Findley to his mother, March 20, 1863, in Alexander T., Joseph R., and William M. Findley Papers, DU; David L. Craft to his sister, August 28, 1864, in Craft Papers.
65. Hannah L. Carlisle to "Dear ones at home," May 18, 1863, in Carlisle Family Papers, MHC; Francis E. Hall to his sister, February 27, 1864, in Francis Everett Hall Papers, MHC; William Pedrick to Nelson Pedrick, November 4, 1863, in Pedrick Papers; Julian W. Hinkley to R. W. Wells, February 20, 1863, in Hinkley Papers.

unity and raised obstacles against the government's political and military objectives. According to a few ardent patriots, Copperheads therefore posed greater dangers than the Confederates. The latter could be defeated by military strength, whereas internal opponents could not be silenced without subverting cherished civil liberties. Rebels' treason could be explained away as the result of southern backwardness and ignorance, but for Copperheads there were no such excuses. "I think the rebels at home far meaner than the rebels of the South," an Illinois soldier exclaimed. "The latter has courage enough to meet me in open conflict while the former poor miserable sneaking hound, seeks to creep up in the dark and strike his dagger at my heart." Similarly, Connecticut sergeant Henry Hall declared, "I really hope Alex is not turning Copperhead for I despise that class of men much more than I do the rebels." Many Democrats felt the same way about Radical Republicans. They blamed the war on abolitionist fanatics, whom they despised as much as southern extremists. "I am sure, as a matter of feeling, aside from policy, I would much rather have the life of a red Republican than a Rebel," vowed New York Democrat Maria L. Daly. "I hate the thought of being of service to the arrogant, self-righteous *pharisees* of the present age who go about preaching abolitionism and who believe in no creed save their own."[66]

Angered and frustrated by delays in subduing the rebellion, northern soldiers unleashed their rage against the symbols of the North's inner conflict. Demands for retribution became strident. "You may tell evry man of Doubtful Loyalty for me up there in the north that he is meaner than any son of a bitch in hell," an Illinois soldier proclaimed. "I would rather shoot one of them a great teal [more] than one living here." He concluded that "there may be some excuse for the one but not for the other." Sergeant Charles P. Lord of Maine told his sister that he was "brim full to the overflowing with hate and contempt to the meanest of our Countrys enemies, viz. the Northern Copper Heads." This attitude prevailed in his regiment. "The[re] is nothing else on the face of this wide world that the soldiers so hate and despise as they do the northern copper heads, for whom they have much less respect than they do for the southern rebs," Lord reported. "I honestly believe that the soldiers had rather shoot a Northern Copper Head than a southern

66. David Williams to John R. Corrie, March 9, 1863, quoted in Wiley, *Billy Yank*, 286; Henry C. Hall to his sister, October 20, 1863, in Henry C. Hall Papers, DU; Daly, *Diary of a Union Lady*, 73.

rebel, they have such a perfect hatred for the[ir] principles," he concluded.[67]

Northern concern about traitors at home reflected the ideological
conflicts that plagued the Union cause. Unable to agree entirely on the
goals for which they were fighting, soldiers could at least concur in
denouncing Copperheads, who symbolized in exaggerated form the
North's failure to achieve political and ideological unity against external traitors. Copperheads provided a convenient target for the anger of
soldiers forced to endure severe hardships in a war whose objectives
were often confused and whose termination seemed distant and un-
promising of success.

Southerners, by contrast, worried much less about internal traitors.
Intimidated by secessionist zeal and threats of ostracism or revenge,
most southern Unionists either remained silent or supported their
state's cause. Yet class antagonism presented serious problems, and
southerners who endured war's hardships denounced the horde of
speculators who profited from them. These greedy villains, like the
mercenary Yankee, violated the South's concepts of honor and gra-
ciousness. Their existence revealed that southerners shared Yankee
vices. The presence of speculators thus contradicted sectional stereotypes, particularly the image of the genteel southern Cavalier. If they
prevailed, southern culture would be shattered almost as completely
as by the destruction of slavery.

TIRED OF FIGHTING EACH OTHER

As the war dragged on, soldiers and civilians on each side questioned
whether the objectives for which they fought justified increasing sacrifices. Disillusionment and desire for peace on any terms increased
dramatically as the war entered its fourth year. Desertion became a
serious problem for both armies.

Men who joined the army for nonideological reasons often became
demoralized when hardships dispelled the glamour of war. Like soldiers in all wars, many of those who enlisted in the Union and Confederate armies were motivated primarily by the promise of excitement, a desire to escape the monotony of their daily lives, or the lure of
faraway places. A holiday atmosphere pervaded the war's early

67. H. C. Bear to his wife, December 7–14, 1862, quoted in Wiley, *Billy Yank*, 286;
Charles P. Lord to his sister, June 19, September 24, and October 5, 1863, in Charles
Phineas Lord Papers, DU.

months. Many volunteers anticipated a brief, exhilarating adventure, which would end after a few minor clashes with the enemy. The lure of travel offered powerful temptations to young men who had never been far from home. They were curious to see what war was like and to participate in its grand drama. Most of the early volunteers did not foresee the hardships of military life but expected only "a glorious fight for fame and honor." Public opinion frowned on able-bodied young men who did not answer the country's call to arms, and many volunteers enlisted out of fear of public rebuke or because it was the popular thing to do.[68]

Economic pressure induced many men to enlist, especially in the North, where depression and unemployment during the war's first year made even a private's meager pay attractive. Unable to find a job in the summer of 1862, Edwin O. Wentworth, a twenty-eight-year-old printer from Maine, enlisted to provide for his family. The promise of a job made him hope that he could avoid army service, but when the offer fell through, he enlisted to claim his private's pay. Similarly, a Pennsylvania volunteer wrote to his wife in November, 1861: "It is no use for you to fret or cry about me for you know if i could have got work i wood not have left you or the children." After conscription went into effect, many volunteered for the large bounties being offered by states eager to fill their quotas. They also hoped to escape the opprobrium of being a conscript.[69]

The hardships of army life gradually weakened the morale of all but the most patriotic recruit. Soldiers complained endlessly about long marches, heavy drilling, poor rations, harsh weather, and a myriad of minor discomforts and severe rigors incident to military life. For every soldier who died in battle, three perished of disease. As one private wrote, "This killing so many men with hard work and hunger a laying

68. Anderson (ed.), *Brokenburn*, 94; Wiley, *Billy Yank*, 35–40; Shannon, "State Rights in the Union Army," 56; Wiley, *Johnny Reb*, 17. In studying a small sample of letters and diaries, Pete Maslowski concluded that Civil War soldiers were "notoriously deficient in ideological orientation" ("A Study of Morale in Civil War Soldiers," *Military Affairs*, XXXIV [1970], 122–26). Although I think he underestimates the extent of ideological commitment, his conclusions are a useful corrective to assumptions about soldiers' ideological orientation.

69. Edwin O. Wentworth to his father, July 13, 1862, to his wife, July 21, 1862, and to Catherine, October 28, 1862, all in Wentworth Papers; Enoch T. Baker to his wife, November 10, 1861, quoted in Wiley, *Billy Yank*, 38; Joseph B. Osborn to Louise Landau, October 3, 1864, in Osborn Papers; John C. Arnold to his wife, August 2, 1864, in John Carvel Arnold Papers, LC; Joseph Diltz to his wife, December 12, 1863, in Joseph Sherman Diltz Papers, DU; Joseph Findley to his mother, February 7, 1864, in Findley Papers.

on the ground and exposed to the Cold and storm is worse than shooting them." Long periods of inaction created frustration, boredom, and
listlessness. Yet defeat in battle, more than any other single cause,
crushed the ardor of soldiers. Union morale sank to its lowest depths
following the senseless slaughter at Fredericksburg in December, 1862,
and Confederates regarded the simultaneous defeats at Gettysburg
and Vicksburg in July, 1863, as their "darkest hour."[70]

The horror of war shocked each person who observed gory scenes of
battlefield or hospital. "I dont want to know any more about war,"
Connecticut private Henry Thompson declared after Fredericksburg.
"I have seen horible sights men with heads blowed off and legs and
armes and shot through the body." The ghastly experiences of battle
made a lasting impression. Edmund Patterson was an Ohio native who
taught school in Alabama and enlisted in a Confederate regiment in
1861. "To feel the warm blood of your slaughtered comrades, the one
you loved best, spurted in your face, or bespattered with his brains,
feel him clutching at you in his death agony as he falls across your feet,"
Patterson wrote after Second Manassas. "Ah! it is fearful, but it is a true
picture." A Virginia soldier, walking across a battlefield the day after a
fight, observed "a man's hand here & his body laying off to one side &
men with their heads shot off & eyes & hips & bowels shot out & the
wounded wet & freezing & in some instances drownding in the holes
of water that gathered around them in the row of corn." After the battle
of Antietam, "the rebels was laying over the field bloated up as big as a
horse and as black as a negro," reported Ohio private Joseph Diltz: "I
pased over the field too days after the fight and I tell you it Was a
horibly sight to see the dead lying over the field it Was very Warm
Wether and the smell Was offul you may form some idea of the smell
when there Was about 5 or 6,000 dead bodies decaying over the field
and perhaps 100 dead Horses . . . their lines of battel could be seen for
miles by the dead they lay along the lines like sheaves of Wheat I could
have walked on the boddes al most from one end too the other." As
soldiers grew accustomed to such scenes, they became almost indifferent to war's horrors. For many, this emotional callousness seemed
more terrible than physical suffering. "It distresses me at times when I
am cool and capable of reflection to think how indifferent we become in

70. Josephus Jackson to his wife, December 28, 1862, in Josephus Jackson Papers, DU;
Richard W. Waldrop to his father, July 18, 1863, in Waldrop Papers; Wiley, *Johnny Reb*, 244–
69.

the hour of battle when our fellow men fall around us by scores," Louisiana brigade quartermaster John Sibley wrote from the besieged city of Vicksburg in March, 1863. "My God what kind of a people will we be after our whole male population shall become inured to these scenes." Both callousness and the distress caused by this apparent indifference to suffering were common among soldiers of the two armies.[71]

These scenes of horror convinced many soldiers that victory was not worth such tremendous sacrifices. After the battle of Fredericksburg, Lieutenant Charles Salter of Michigan hoped that such battles would increase peace sentiment on both sides: "I cannot help wishing that the people of the North and South could all have seen that horrible massacre, for if they had, they would be willing to settle up the war upon any terms without ever fighting another battle." As early as the first battle at Manassas, battlefield horrors made soldiers long for peace. In August, 1861, an illiterate South Carolina private dictated the following message to his father: "Peace would be a great blessing at this time as it is at all times but to see the sufferings and privations & deaths of poor men & soldiers away from home together with the devastations spread abroad through the country shows but faintly the horrows of this unholy war." Devastation of the countryside compounded the havoc of war and led to demoralization and demands for peace among both soldiers and civilians.[72]

The terrible reality of battle destroyed romantic notions of war's glory. After the battle at Frayser's Farm, Virginia, in July, 1862, South Carolina private Robert Boyd wrote home: "i tell you thar is no fun in fighting i am in grat hops that the war wil com to an end befor long." Two months later, Boyd died in an army hospital, his great hope unfulfilled. Married soldiers were particularly anxious for the war to end so they could return to their families. "i wish this war wold com to a close an let ous all go hom," South Carolina private Fenton Hall wrote to his wife in May, 1863. "i wold like the best in the wild [world] to be hom with my loving wife an children." Private William Horton of North Carolina declared in October, 1864, that "this cruel war com-

71. Henry Thompson to his wife, December 19, 1862, in Henry J. H. Thompson Papers, DU; Barrett (ed.), *Yankee Rebel*, 48; David Dickenson to his wife, July 3, 1862, Dickenson Papers (microfilm); Joseph S. Diltz to Sidney Milledge, October 10, 1862, in Diltz Papers; John T. Sibley to E. P. Ellis, March 10, 1863, in E. John and Thomas C. W. Ellis and Family Papers, LSU. See also Linderman, *Embattled Courage*, 124–33.

72. Charles Salter to Mrs. Duffield, December 15, 1862, in Duffield Papers; Daniel Boyd to his father, August 26, 1861, in Boyd Papers.

menced with lies and it will end with lies if it ever ends and I am in hops that it will end before long for I want to go home to live with my dutch gal."[73]

Although most soldiers wanted peace only with victory, an increasing number favored peace at any price. After the fall of Vicksburg in 1863, Private Christopher Hackett heard that peace meetings were being held in his home state of North Carolina. "I pray that it may be so for I want peace on some terms or other if their meetings will be of any use in bringing about peace," he confided to his family. "The soldiers in this armey is getting verry tierd," Texas private William Stoker reported in December, 1862. "They dont think this ware will be ended by fighting." Three years of war seemed to confirm doubts about the benefits of prolonging the fighting. Private J. W. Horton of North Carolina wrote in July, 1864, that the war had resulted in a military stalemate. "So upon the hole I dont think ther is much to be made by fiting," Horton concluded. "I wish this war was over and we all could come home to stay." Suffering and hardship gradually eroded Confederate loyalty. Peace sentiment grew in proportion to wartime difficulties.[74]

Northern soldiers were even more anxious to end the war on any terms possible, partly because they suffered more defeats in the early years of the war and partly because they had less to risk than southerners in compromise or defeat. "I assure you the majority of the soldiers do not care a fig which way it goes, all they want is to end the matter," New York sergeant Felix Brannigan wrote after the battle of Antietam in 1862. Fredericksburg convinced Samuel Nichols of Massachusetts that the North could never defeat the Rebels. "Why not settle the difficulty at once without further expense and loss of life?" he asked. "We are further today from the desired result than when we commenced. Why not confess we are worsted, and come to an agreement?"[75]

War weariness created serious morale problems, weakening the unity of both Union and Confederacy. Desire for an end to fighting cut across

73. Robert P. Boyd to father, July 6, 1862, and Fenton Hall to his wife, May 29, 1863, in Boyd Papers; William A. Horton to Mrs. Mary Councill, October 18, 1864, in Councill Papers. See also Wendell H. Stephenson and Edwin A. Davis (eds.), "Civil War Diary of Willie Micajah Barrow," *Louisiana Historical Quarterly*, XVII (1934), 730.

74. Christopher Hackett to his family, August 10, 1863, in Hackett Papers; William E. Stoker, "The War Letters of a Texas Conscript in Arkansas," ed. Robert W. Glover, *Arkansas Historical Quarterly*, XX (Winter, 1961), 376–77; J. W. Horton to his uncle, July 20, 1864, in Councill Papers.

75. Felix Brannigan to his sister, September 20, 1862, in Brannigan Papers; Underhill (ed.), *"Your Soldier Boy Samuel,"* 58–59.

sectional boundaries, uniting enlisted men of the opposing armies. Their common interest led many soldiers to believe that they could end the war by laying down their arms and refusing to fight. "The soldiers on both sides are tired of fighting each other," Private Edwin Wentworth reported after Fredericksburg: "Nine-tenths of the soldiers feel the same way and are sick of the war, both northern and southern soldiers. Southern pickets have told our pickets that they were willing to throw away their guns if our pickets would do the same; and if it was once started, there is little doubt that both armies would follow suit." In April, 1863, Alabama artillery captain Henry Semple, formerly a prominent Montgomery lawyer and planter, reported that the same sentiment prevailed in Tennessee. "The men in the army generally are heartily sick of the war," Semple wrote, "& I think if the peace question could be submitted to our own troops & the troops of the enemy we could speedily come to an understanding." But although peace sentiment prevailed in each army at various times, spells of general demoralization never lasted long enough to stop the bloodshed. Whenever one army felt that its fortunes had reached the nadir of impending defeat, the other sensed improving prospects for victory and became less anxious for immediate peace.[76]

Occasionally, conditions became so intolerable that individuals sought escape from the army by deserting. Desertion in Union and Confederate armies had similar causes and produced approximately the same problems of reduced manpower and morale. Largely because of the unfavorable course of the war, desertion became a problem in the North as early as the fall of 1862, nearly a year before Confederate desertion began its dramatic increase. During the fall of 1864, a flood of desertion overtook the South. By this time, improving prospects for victory plus stricter enforcement reduced the level of northern desertion. Thus the problem worsened in the South just as it improved in the North. In the course of the war, more than 104,000 soldiers deserted from the Confederate army and more than 278,000 from the Union army. Such high levels of illegal absenteeism severely weakened the fighting strength of the two armies.[77]

Union soldiers gave many reasons for contemplating desertion, in-

76. Edwin Wentworth to his wife, December 22, 1862, January 25, 1863, in Wentworth Papers; Henry Semple to his wife, April 7, 1863, in Semple Papers.
77. Ella Lonn, *Desertion During the Civil War* (New York, 1928), 25–28, 143–45, 226, 231–35. See also Linderman, *Embattled Courage*, 173–77.

cluding the hardships of army life, inadequate food and supplies, military reverses, war weariness, and the promptings of relatives at home. The problem was greatest among conscripts, who had entered the service reluctantly and often felt little commitment to the Union cause. Fifty men from his regiment had deserted within a month, Ohio private Joseph Diltz wrote in June, 1862, but he hoped to get home without deserting. "Maby if you Would rite some big yarn about being sick and send it to me I mite get a furlow to go home," he suggested to his wife. At the end of the year he was still in the army, more discouraged than ever. On Christmas Day, Diltz wrote from a hospital in Baltimore: "I have got tiard of the War for it is no use to fight it does now good and I am going to get out of it if I can I am a going to go home this winter if I have to take a french furlow." Yet he still did not want to desert and therefore told his wife to ask the town mayor to recommend Diltz for a discharge. The desire to return home became almost universal after the defeat at Fredericksburg. "We read daily of the patriotic fortitude the heroic courage and the uncomplaining endurance of the Army of the Potomac," wrote Private Adam Pickel, a Pennsylvania Democrat, in February, 1863, "but if it were not treason to tell the truth I would say that the whole army would run home if they had the chance." Helen Whedon of Chelsea, Michigan, wrote to her brother, a lieutenant in the 20th Michigan, that the senseless slaughter at Fredericksburg was enough to kill the patriotism of everyone in the North. "I tell you Hellen, Patriotism *played out* with me some time ago, and more so after the battle over the River," Clarence Whedon responded on January 5, 1863. Three weeks later, according to official military records, Whedon deserted his regiment near Falmouth, Virginia.[78]

Some civilians openly encouraged relatives and friends to desert. After having been under enemy fire at Fredericksburg, Private Henry Thompson wrote to his wife in Fair Haven, Connecticut, that the army was completely demoralized and would not fight much longer. Dating his letter from "Camp Trials Tribulation & Desolation," he wrote: "We are all tired of the war the whole army we never shall whip them I

---

78. Joseph Diltz to his wife, June 25, December 25, 1862, in Diltz Papers; Adam H. Pickel to his father, February 8, 1863, in Adam H. Pickel Papers, DU; Clarence Whedon to Helen Whedon, January 5, 1863, in Clinton H. Haskell Collection, WLC; Michigan Adjutant General's Office, *Record of Service of Michigan Volunteers* (Kalamazoo, n.d.) XX, 100. On the problem of desertion, see Ambrose, "Yeoman Discontent," 259–68; and Lonn, *Desertion*, 127–42.

believe . . . I look at it as a great slaughter of lives." Dating her letter from "Camp Lonely," Lucretia Thompson replied:

> I have been to Williams . . . but he dont know anything about the war & cares less, & that is the way with the most of them hear they have got you all into the scrape & that is all they care for. I dont think it will be half as much disgrace to you to have you come home as it will be to stay there. when I read that perhaps you should take a long step it was all I could do to keep from laughing out loud . . . it is no worse for you than for thousands of others that is coming all the time. they all seem to think that them that does come is the wisest & smartest. dont stay for that a minute nor an hour if you see a chance improve it [do] not think of the name in these times.

Her letters were filled with complaints of loneliness and pleas that her husband return home to comfort and protect his family. In closing one letter, Lucretia added, "3000 kisses PS If you was at home the[re] would [be] something done besides sending kisses." Henry felt the same way. "I shant tell you what I dreamed last night olney I was 2 home & we was 2 bed," he wrote. By June, 1863, Lucretia Thompson suggested an audacious plan. "I have made up my mind that the only way to end the war is to have the soldiers all rise & kill off the officers & then I do think the[re] would be something done twards ending it," she told her husband. Despite such promptings and his own disillusionment, Henry Thompson served out his three-year enlistment and received an honorable discharge in the summer of 1865. Faced with similar encouragement, however, many others did take the "long step" home.[79]

Confederate deserters were motivated by the same factors, especially the lack of such necessities as food, clothing, and pay. By late 1864, military reverses created a major morale crisis and led to an epidemic of desertion and absenteeism. Cowardice was a factor for many who deserted, but more often they were prompted by homesickness and anxiety about their families' needs—a problem that grew more acute as scarcity and inflation increasingly took their toll after 1863. Lieutenant Thomas Boatwright of Virginia expressed a common worry: "Oh; it is distressing to a soldier to think that he is here bound and his family suffering for something to eat." North Carolina private James Zimmerman resented the taxes his wife had to pay to support officers in luxury,

79. Henry Thompson to Lucretia Thompson, December 21, 1862, May 30, 1863, and Lucretia Thompson to Henry Thompson, January 14, June 1, 2, 1863, in Thompson Papers.

as he claimed, while he was poorly cared for: "I feel very much like starting home sometimes when I get about half enough to eat and get to studdying how thing is going on there it makes me feel like some body was to blame and not me I am inocent of having anything to do to bring on this ware and dont feel rite suffering here as I do on account of somebodys misdoings." Private William Phillips, son of a Virginia overseer, spent two weeks in the guardhouse for overstaying his furlough in early 1863. Denied another furlough at the end of the year, he left illegally and "ran the gauntlet" home. He explained later that the reason he had taken the risk "was the pure anxiety love & Respect that I had for them [his family] and wanted to see them so very bad and also thinking that they would be glad to see me."[80]

By 1865, desertion had become a daily occurrence in the Confederate army. "I am fearful that desertion is getting to be so common that it will lessen the strength of our army," Alabama corporal Abel Crawford wrote in March, 1865. "I am *almost* tempted sometimes to take a french furlough when I think of being cut off from you and home," he confessed to his wife. Civilians frequently encouraged desertion. Late in 1864, one woman informed her soldier husband that the family had no blankets, shoes, decent clothes, or firewood and only a small amount of meal to eat. She asked him to obtain a temporary furlough to straighten things out at home. If he did not come it would soon be too late, she warned, "for we'll all . . . of us be out there in the garden in the old grave yard with your ma and mine." Her husband deserted.[81]

Rather than returning home, where conscription officers and patrols searched for deserters, some Confederate soldiers took advantage of clemency offers and fled to Union lines. Poor rations and other hardships induced Private Christopher Hackett of North Carolina to contemplate this means of escape. In March, 1864, he wrote his parents from the front lines in Virginia, asking them to read the letter in secret:

> I will have to say to you that I have resolved to try the trip . . . so you may depend upon it for I intend to get out of this war in some way. . . . And if I

80. Thomas Boatwright to his wife, March 14, 1863, in Boatwright Letters; James Zimmerman to his wife, August 16, 1863, in Zimmerman Papers; William Phillips to his parents, November 3, 1863, January 15, 1864, in William Horace Phillips Papers, DU. On the causes of Confederate desertion, see Judith Lee Hallock, "The Role of the Community in Civil War Desertion," *Civil War History*, XXIX (June, 1983), 123–34; Paul D. Escott, "'The Cry of the Sufferers': The Problem of Welfare in the Confederacy," *Civil War History*, XXIII (September, 1977), 228–40; Ramsdell, *Behind the Lines*, 23–33, 44–56; and Hahn, *Roots of Southern Populism*, 122–26.

81. Abel Crawford to his wife, March 5, 1865, in Abel H. Crawford Papers, DU.

should make the trip all right I shall expect you all that are living to come out to me. The terms offered by the Yankee authorities are if not misrepresented are of three or four kinds One is the oath of allegiance which I will never take if I can help it and another is to take the Quaker oath to not take up arms against either side and another is not an oath but is to take a parole during the war and go where you please so I have resolved to try and see what they will doo there are several of us in the club togather as you will learn from Bob we had one of the best chances when we were on picket the last time all that I fear is that we will never get another such a chance anymore.

Two months later Hackett was in a federal prison at Point Lookout, Maryland. It is not clear from surviving letters whether he was captured during the fierce fighting of the Wilderness campaign or succeeded in his plan to desert. If the latter, his hopes for kind treatment were disappointed, for he spent the remainder of the war in prison.[82]

Desertion was an extreme remedy for the common complaints of soldiers, for whom the suffering, hardships, and danger of war frequently seemed to outweigh any potential benefit. Union and Confederate leaders had to confront the problem that a majority of their citizens refused to volunteer for army service, and both sides resorted to conscription. Southern nonslaveowners abandoned the Confederate cause as often as they rallied behind the planters. When the Confederate government became unable to protect its citizens, their patriotism quickly declined. Political loyalty remained strong only in proportion to the government's ability to protect the people's interests. Many laborers and small yeoman farmers in the North evinced little enthusiasm for the Union's cause. Hundreds of thousands resisted the draft, grumbled about their political leaders and military officers, and even deserted from the army. This declining will to fight reveals that commitment to sectional interests was not deep enough to transcend personal needs, that the Civil War was not fought by solid phalanxes of idealistic warriors battling for two noble but conflicting sectional ideologies. Ultimately, such divisions weakened Confederate resistance, thereby hastening defeat.[83]

Despite these internal conflicts, enough people on each side continued to support their government's basic policies to prolong the

82. Christopher Hackett to his parents, March 26, 1864, in Hackett Papers.
83. Beringer *et al.*, *Why the South Lost*, 23–34; Potter, *South and the Sectional Conflict*, 54; Lawrence N. Powell and Michael S. Wayne, "Self-Interest and the Decline of Confederate Nationalism," in Owens and Cooke (eds.), *Old South in the Crucible of War*, 29–45.

bloody war until one side had won a complete military victory. However discouraged soldiers became with military life or the changing
fortunes of war, most of them eventually concluded that the cause for
which they fought was too important to surrender. They resolved to
finish an unpleasant though necessary task as soon as possible, so that
they could return home—proud of having done their duty. "We all got
[get] mad, sometimes, & make out like we would desert if they dident
feed us better & treat us better, but we dident hav much notion of it,"
Texas private William Stoker wrote in February, 1863. "It would be
thrown up to Priscilla for years [to come] that her par deserted the
armey [and] wouldent fight for his cuntry." Although they were tired
of war, many soldiers vowed to continue fighting until victory brought
peace. "I don't like the service & the war & shall be glad enough when
peace shall be proclaimed & I can return again to my books & peaceful
pursuits," Connecticut soldier Henry Marshall wrote in December,
1863. "For all that I am in for it to the end." Confederate soldiers voiced
the same determination. "I am as tired of this cruel war as any body,"
North Carolina sergeant William R. Clark declared in February, 1864,
"but I am willing to fight to the last, and will stand it as long as any
body." Despite class tensions, backwoods farmers formed the back-
bone of the Confederate war effort. Among some Georgia up-country
units, the death toll reached 40 percent. This loyalty did not signify
complete agreement with political leaders, however. As one upcountry farmer, who "volentarily Entered the Service," pointedly insisted,
"Mr. Davis and me does not put the same construction" on things.
Southern yeomen often fought for a "liberty and independence" distinct from the slave system. They often remained indifferent to slaveowners' appeals. Yet they continued to shoulder the burden of fighting
and dying to resist Yankee tyranny.[84]

Soldiers on both sides believed that they must continue the struggle for victory so that those who had lost lives, property, or security
would not have made such sacrifices in vain. As a Virginia soldier
proclaimed, "We have suffered too much to give up now."[85] Sustained
by this resolve, most Union and Confederate soldiers remained loyal to

84. Stoker, "War Letters of a Texas Conscript," 387; Henry G. Marshall to his sister,
December 13, 1863, in Marshall Papers; William R. Clark to Ellen Lockhart, February 15,
1864, in Browning Papers; Hahn, *Roots of Southern Populism*, 132–33.
85. Thomas F. Boatwright to his wife, August 6, 1863, in Boatwright Letters.

their cause. War weariness and declining patriotism could not end the fighting.

Sectionalism was not the only issue dividing Civil War Americans, as this chapter clearly shows. Individuals shaped their own sense of personal identity according to a wide range of attributes, including many, such as occupation, religion, and gender, that lie beyond the range of this study. In other areas of group identity, Civil War participants expressed opinions, fears, and hopes unrelated to sectional consciousness. Rivalries among individuals from different states—particularly between eastern and western states—demonstrate an alternative geographical identity in striking counterpoint to North-South sectionalism. Tensions between rich and poor and between officers and enlisted men indicate social cleavages that crossed sectional boundaries. Likewise, internal ideological conflict produced animosities such as those revealed by Union soldiers' startling statements that they hated Copperheads more than southern Rebels. Finally, the decline of morale and the relatively high incidence of desertion reveal that sectional loyalties could not sustain large numbers of individuals throughout four long years of war.

These limits of sectional consciousness, however, did not prevent a final military settlement. Peace advocates never reached a wide audience, and even war weariness did not begin to weaken the Confederacy seriously until the winter of 1864–1865. State rivalry, class conflict, and the inequality of military rank created small fissures in sectional unity. Nevertheless, the exigencies of war prevented these internal divisions from seriously threatening either the Union or the Confederacy. As long as the fighting lasted, most southerners supported the Confederate cause and most northerners supported the Union. Whether such a clear sense of sectional identity would outlast the war would depend on individuals' responses to the experience of victory or defeat.

EPILOGUE / VICTORY AND DEFEAT

When the fighting finally stopped in the spring of 1865, Civil War participants began the difficult transition to a new social order. The Confederacy had crumbled, slavery had been abolished, and the Union remained intact. Both victors and vanquished had to adjust to changing circumstances. The war had focused attention on sectional differences, but it had also challenged many sectional stereotypes. The response of southerners to defeat and of northerners to victory would determine the contours of sectional consciousness for a new generation. The writings of Robert McAllister of New Jersey and Eliza Frances Andrews of Georgia clearly show the differing experiences of victory and defeat. Their reactions to events of 1865 reflect the common elements of popular thought in the two sections.

The surrender of General Robert E. Lee at Appomattox on April 9, 1865, and of General Joseph E. Johnston in North Carolina on April 26 marked a complete military victory for Union forces. From Burkeville Junction, near Appomattox, Robert McAllister of the 11th New Jersey rejoiced. In his narrative report of the final campaign, sent to his wife, he described the army's celebrations:

> At 3:30 p.m. it was announced officially that Lee had surrendered. What a scene followed! . . . Greeting, congratulations and cheering beggars description. Shoes and hats flew high in the air. Speeches were made, called for loudly, but could not be heard for the cheering at every sentence. The Star Spangled Banner waved high in triumph—high and low, back and forth, over a sea of upturned faces. . . . All knew that by the surrender of Lee and his army the greate contest was over. The war was ended, and we could return to our homes with the proud satisfaction that it has been our privilege to live and take part in the struggle that has decided for all time to come that Republics are not a failure.

McAllister had completed an admirable record of service. A New Jersey railroad contractor before the war, he became lieutenant colonel of the 1st New Jersey Volunteers in 1861, at the age of forty-eight. One year later he assumed command of the 11th New Jersey as its colonel, a rank he held through most of the war. Wounded twice at Gettysburg and

once at the Wilderness, he was breveted brigadier general for conspicuous conduct in the October 27, 1864, engagement at Boydton
Plank Road near Petersburg. McAllister welcomed peace as the closing
chapter of a successful military career.[1]

President Lincoln's assassination, coming only five days after Appomattox, mingled grief with the victory celebrations. As a dedicated
Republican, Robert McAllister shared the North's intense mourning
for the fallen commander. "Oh, what a loss to the country and the
world! What a crime before God and Heaven!" McAllister lamented.
"We all feel miserable. The Army was and is united for Lincoln and the
administration. The soldiers loved him." This tragedy could alter the
course of reunion, McAllister believed. "The South will face worse than
if the President had lived," he predicted. "But God's ways are not our
ways. Oh, may He lead us as a nation in safety. May peace and tran-
quility once more reign over our unhappy land." McAllister rejoiced
that peace had arrived. "The war is over and will soon be closed up.
Then we can all return to our homes," he wrote on April 21, 1865. "I feel
like going home to enjoy the ballance of my life with my dear family,"
he added. McAllister thus prepared for a speedy return to civilian life.
He had done his duty; the Union was preserved.[2]

The progress of sectional reconciliation following the war would
depend on the responses of black freedmen and southern whites. In a
lengthy letter to his wife, dated April 26, 1865, McAllister recorded his
observations about these two groups. From conversations with blacks
and Rebels he had gained direct knowledge of their views. His report
reveals as much about his own attitudes as about those of the people he
met. Because of its careful recording of conversations and its unfiltered
commentary, it is worth quoting at length:

> The other day Dr. Welling and I walked slowly along the road towards
> Farmville. We had gon but a short distance when we met three men,
> careworn and tired, walking down the road. We soon entered into conver-
> sation with them and learned that they had been conductors on this
> railroad. . . . These men lived in Richmond and Petersburg. They were
> hurrying home to their families and hoped to get into business again.
> They are heartily sick and tired of the war and expressed a wish to turn
> back to the Union.

1. Robertson (ed.), *Civil War Letters of McAllister*, 607–608. Biographical information in
this section is from Robertson's "Introduction," *ibid.*, 3–26.
2. *Ibid.*, 609, 611.

The next party we met was two darkeys. We came up with them while they were resting. We asked them where they were going.

"Home, massa, home," they replied. "We hab been down to de Junction to buy horses."

"What?" said the Doctor. "Buy horses?"

"Yes," one answered. "We went to see if you'uns would gib us a horse so dat we could make some corn. If we'uns could only get de horse, we could turn up de ground, plant de corn, and hab some bread for to keep our families."

"That is a capital idea," I said. "Show yourselves to be men. Plant corn, hoe potatoes, and make an honest living for your families. You are free, but show to us, and to the world, that you are worthy of that freedom. But tell us, where are you going to get the land to work?"

A cunning smile played over their broad faces. "Why, you'uns own de land," they said. "We'uns will work it for you. Your army got it."

"But where is your master?" we asked.

"Massa tell us to get horses and go to work. Massa will work too, and all will share alike."

We told them that they could not make a better bargain than that one and to go to work at once and lose no time, as the season was advancing rapidly. They seemed to fully understand this. All they wanted was the horses to "make corn." They had left one of their number down at the junction to do what he could to get a horse while they were walking home—twenty-five miles above here—to attend to the work.

I liked the spirit of these men. They seemed anxous and determined to do something to make a living. They were laboring under many difficulties to accomplish their object. They were fully aware that they were free. They seemed to realize their new position and the responsibility resting upon them relative to supporting their families. The next party we met were colored men also on the hunt for horses. They seemed to evince the same spirit as the first.

A short distance further on we came upon a Rebel soldier laying and resting himself under the shade of a small tree. He was a youth 19 years old, of rather delicate make, dressed in a Rebel uniform careworn and very despondent. On approaching him I said, "Well, sir, where are you going?"

He answered, "Home, sir, home—way down on the York River below Gloucester Point."

We then asked him if he was paroled, to which he replied in the affirmative. He belonged to Lee's army and was captured with the rest. He was an artillery man and belonged to a battery. Though a Private, he had been well raised. His manners were good, showing education and culture. He had been raised in easy circumstances and knew nothing of hardships until he entered the Rebel army. He was reserved at first, but kind words caused him to open his heart. He talked freely of their army and their difficulties. He said that we had outnumbered them and out generaled them, that their army had become completely demoralized, deserted and threw away their guns.

Then, with tears in his eyes, he said, "What could General Lee do with such an army?"

He admitted that they were completely whipped and that there was nothing left for them but to submit.

The Rebel soldier went on to enumerate the hardships and lack of provisions that destroyed the Confederate army's ability to continue fighting. When he finally parted from the two Yankees, McAllister reported, he did so "with many thanks for our kindness to him." McAllister added a final commentary: "What a subject for reflection! What a mountain of responsibility is resting on the shoulders of the leaders of this Rebellion, North and South. The cry is against them for their deception."[3]

Robert McAllister's observations indicated good prospects for peaceful reunion. Black freedmen apparently understood the obligations emancipation entailed and seemed willing to meet their new responsibilities. Confederate soldiers and citizens told McAllister that they accepted defeat and welcomed peace. They expressed little of the bitterness that must have weighed heavily on them. "There are no guerillas here," McAllister reported from Burkeville Junction on May 1. "The people are all well disposed and glad to cease this war on our Government." Two days later, as his regiment began the long march north to Washington, McAllister repeated this conclusion. "It is amusing to hear the Rebels talk about their once would-be Confederacy," he observed smugly. "They all say that 'the Confederacy has gone up the spout.' They all talk for the Union now, except a few rabid ones." This response offered hope for a speedy reconciliation. Many southerners, particularly weary veterans, did quickly accept defeat, but many others did not. Reconstruction of the Union would be a long, tortuous process.[4]

Robert McAllister and his comrades in the 3rd Brigade returned to Washington for the grand review of the federal armies on May 25–26, 1865. McAllister's wife and daughter journeyed to the capital for this event. They stayed with him in camp outside the city for a week or two.

3. *Ibid.*, 612–15.
4. *Ibid.*, 615–16. Paul H. Buck concluded in 1937 that "when the war ended it was the soldiers who first forgave" (*The Road to Reunion, 1865–1900* [New York, 1937], 245). On southerners' initial acceptance of defeat and the difficulties of Reconstruction, see Eric L. McKitrick, *Andrew Johnson and Reconstruction* (Chicago, 1960).

One final duty remained for General McAllister. On June 2, he issued a general order to the officers and soldiers of the 3rd Brigade, congratulating them on their "brilliant career," which would now become "a matter of history": "The war is over, the contest is ended. The glorious old flag of our country—consecrated by the blood of our fallen heroes—under the folds of which you have so often, so long, and so gallantly fought and bled—and to defend which your comrades have died—now floats in triumph over our land. The war brought us to the field. Peace returns us to our homes. Our work is done, and we go to enjoy the fruits of our victories with our friends in the several States represented in this command." Robert McAllister then returned home to Belvidere, New Jersey. He later worked for sixteen years as general manager of the Ironton Railroad Company in Allentown, Pennsylvania, where he became a respected civic leader, businessman, and member of the First Presbyterian Church. Following his death in 1891, the citizens of Belvidere prevailed upon his widow to have the beloved general buried in his former hometown. Three years later, they dedicated an impressive monument, purchased by Belvidere residents, over his grave.[5]

In his response to the Union's triumph in 1865, Robert McAllister had articulated the opinions shared by a majority of northerners. Rebel leaders should be punished, they argued, but the majority of southerners should be forgiven and welcomed back to the Union. Blacks should be given an opportunity to enjoy the rewards of freedom, northerners believed, although few shared McAllister's optimism that they would succeed. Magnanimous in the moment of victory, most Union veterans argued for a rapid reconciliation. "They are willing to admit that we have whipped them, and that is all that we want of them," Wisconsin private John Brobst reported after talking with Joe Johnston's war-weary veterans in April, 1865. Political and civilian leaders did not share such lenient views, however, and the hostile confrontations of Reconstruction ensued.[6]

The collapse of the Confederacy profoundly affected southern men and women. The memory of defeat would last for generations and remains vivid for many of their descendants. The end of the war

5. Robertson (ed.), *Civil War Letters of McAllister*, 619.
6. Brobst, *Well, Mary*, 135–36. See Buck, *Road to Reunion*, 3–74.

brought three cataclysmic changes to the South: the bitterness of defeat, the disruption of slavery and patterns of race relations, and the triumph of Yankee values and customs. These changes occurred simultaneously during the spring and summer of 1865. For a time, the world seemed turned upside down.

The personal impact of defeat is clearly seen in the journal of a young Georgia woman, Eliza Frances Andrews. Born in 1840 in the county seat of Washington, Georgia, Fanny Andrews was the second daughter and sixth child of Judge Garnett and Annulet Ball Andrews. A successful lawyer and circuit-rider for the superior court, Judge Andrews also owned nearly two hundred slaves, who worked on his Georgia property northwest of Augusta and a Mississippi Delta plantation managed by one of his sons. The family lived at Haywood, a stately eighteenth-century mansion, to which seven Doric columns had been added during the Greek Revival period. Despite his prominent position in the circles of plantation society, Judge Andrews remained a firm Unionist throughout the war. Elected to the Georgia legislature in 1860, he could not stop the tide of secession that soon swept over his state. Fanny, however, embraced the Rebel cause, secretly sewing Confederate flags which she hid from her parents. Her three older brothers enlisted, without objection from their father. Throughout the war years, the generational split between Unionist parents and Confederate children created tensions within the family.

When General Lee surrendered at Appomattox, Fanny Andrews was twenty-four years old. Defeat tasted bitter. "It is all over with us now, and there is nothing to do but bow our heads in the dust and let the hateful conquerors trample us under their feet," she lamented. "I am crushed and bowed down to the earth, in sorrow, but not in shame. No! I am more of a rebel to-day than ever I was when things looked brightest for the Confederacy." Within a few days, ragged veterans of Lee's army began to arrive in Georgia. "Everybody is cast down and humiliated, and we are all waiting in suspense to know what our cruel masters will do with us," Andrews reported on April 25, 1865. "Think of a vulgar plebeian like Andy Johnson, and that odious Yankee crew at Washington, lording it over southern gentlemen!" She occupied her time cooking for the returning soldiers, many of whom "break down and cry like children" when talking about the surrender. Yet humiliation turned to hatred, remorse to resistance. "The more misfortunes overwhelm my poor country, the more I love it," Andrews proclaimed;

"the more the Yankees triumph, the worse I hate them, wretches!" This pledge of continued loyalty to the Confederacy echoed throughout the South. Torn by dissension during the war, southerners found their greatest unity at the moment of defeat.[7]

The conquering Yankee represented everything that southerners had struggled against for decades. They feared that Yankee vices would supplant their Cavalier virtues, that Yankee tyranny would suppress their cherished liberty, that Yankee abolitionism would sunder their control of race relations. Even if blacks were freed voluntarily, it would be difficult to incorporate them into southern society, Fanny Andrews wrote. "And to have a gang of meddlesome Yankees come down here and take them away from us by force—I could never submit to that, not even if slavery were as bad as they pretend." Not only did the Yankees destroy slavery, they also disrupted long-established patterns of race relations. Union troops entered Washington on May 5, beginning a period of military rule. Apart from complaints of confiscation and oppression, what troubled Fanny Andrews most was the way these Yankees mingled with blacks. She decried their "negro balls," at which white soldiers danced with black women, and charged that the Yankees had set up brothels in the center of town, where they conducted orgies that "kept everybody on the square awake with their disgraceful noise." Yankee soldiers "strutted about the streets on Sundays with negro wenches on their arms," Andrews charged, "and yet their officers complain because they are not invited to sit at the tables of southern gentlemen!" By violating such racial taboos, the Yankee conquerors outraged southern sensibilities. Such conduct could not be forgiven.[8]

Southerners' responses to racial intermingling echoed their reaction to northern use of black troops. Both actions seemed deliberately designed to insult southern honor. As Fanny Andrews complained on June 22, 1865: "I hope the Yankees will get their fill of the blessed nigger before they are done with him. They have placed our people in the most humiliating position it is possible to devise, where we are obliged either to submit to the insolence of our own servants or appeal to our

7. Eliza Frances Andrews, *The War-Time Journal of a Georgia Girl, 1864–1865*, ed. Spencer Bidwell King, Jr. (1908; rpr. Macon, Ga., 1960), 171–72, 185, 188. See James L. Roark, *Masters Without Slaves: Southern Planters in the Civil War and Reconstruction* (New York, 1977), 103–106; Buck, *Road to Reunion*, 44–45.

8. Andrews, *War-Time Journal*, 127, 267, 306–308.

Northern masters for protection, as if we were slaves ourselves—and that is just what they are trying to make of us. Oh, it is abominable!" The social order had been inverted. Southern whites felt like slaves to the victorious Yankees, while their erstwhile servants flaunted their new independence. Like her fellow slaveholders, Fanny Andrews clearly understood both the symbolism and the reality of slavery. Yet she expressed sympathy for misguided blacks. "Poor darkeys, they are the real victims of the war, after all," she wrote. "The Yankees have turned their poor ignorant heads and driven them wild with false notions of freedom." Such efforts to "elevate the negro" would have disastrous consequences, she predicted. "The higher above his natural capacity they force the negro in their rash experiments to justify themselves for his emancipation, the greater must be his fall in the end, and the more bitter our sufferings in the meantime," Andrews declared. "A race war is sure to come, sooner or later, and we shall have only the Yankees to thank for it." She thus anticipated the dark days of Reconstruction and the white backlash of the Ku Klux Klan. By destroying racial control, the North would unleash violent confrontation as southern whites and blacks struggled to reestablish patterns of social interaction.[9]

A more immediate test of the war's impact on race relations lay in personal dealings between masters and their former servants. White southerners closely watched blacks for signs of rebelliousness or disloyalty. "The negroes, thus far, have behaved fairly well, except where they have been tampered with," Fanny Andrews reported on May 9, four days after Union troops arrived. "Not one of father's has left us, and they are just as humble and obedient as ever." One month later, she reported that the family's slaves had behaved so well "that I feel more attached to them than ever." She had a long talk with "mammy," who said that "none of our house servants ever had a thought of quitting us." Despite such reassurance of black loyalty, Andrews also wrote that her mother hoped to get rid of Emily, who "has a savage temper" and had been impudent. "She says she would enjoy emancipation from the negroes more than they will from their masters," Fanny stated. Unable to control their slaves, many whites shared this

9. *Ibid.*, 308, 277, 316. Many planters compared their condition under Union occupation to that of slaves. See Roark, *Masters Without Slaves*, 155.

feeling that emancipation would free them from responsibility for blacks' welfare. Judge Andrews, however, retained his sense of paternalistic obligation, declaring that "he would never let any of his negroes suffer as long as he had anything to share with them." For southern slaveholders, this internal conflict between responsibility and rejection proved deeply troubling. Their responses to black freedmen remained ambivalent or contradictory.[10]

Fanny Andrews regretted the disruption of personal loyalty and affection between masters and servants. "I feel sorry for the poor negroes," she wrote on June 18. "They are not to blame for taking freedom when it is brought to their very doors and almost forced upon them." Yet when they left, she stated, "I can't help feeling as if they are deserting us for the enemy, and it seems humiliating to be compelled to bargain and haggle with our own servants about wages." The loss of blacks' loyalty became even more troubling when southerners saw it transferred to the hated Yankees. Black character traits made them incapable of independent judgment and action, Andrews charged. This portended tragedy, both for blacks and for the South: "They are like grown up children turned adrift in the world. The negro is something like the Irishman in his blundering good nature, his impulsiveness and improvidence, and he is like a child in having always had someone to think and act for him. Poor creatures, I shudder to think of what they must suffer in the future, and of what they are going to make this whole country suffer before we are done with them." Such consequences, however, remained in the future. The immediate problem was the loss of affection and loyalty between the races. Andrews lamented the new names blacks assumed as a symbol of their independence and newly recognized maturity. Dignified names, often taken from former masters of long ago, replaced servile nicknames. "Instead of 'maum Judy' and 'uncle Jacob,' we shall have our 'Mrs. Ampey Tatoms,' and our 'Mr. Lewis Williamses,'" Andrews reported derisively. "The sweet ties that bound our old family servants to us will be broken and replaced with envy and ill-will." Newly freed blacks wanted nothing more than to break the shackles and reminders of the

10. Andrews, *War-Time Journal*, 236, 292–93. For blacks' response to emancipation, see Leon F. Litwack, *Been in the Storm So Long: The Aftermath of Slavery* (New York, 1979), 167–267; and Joel Williamson, *After Slavery: The Negro in South Carolina During Reconstruction, 1861–1877* (Chapel Hill, 1965), 32–79.

past. If ties of genuine affection occasionally had to be sundered, that was a small price to pay for freedom and dignity. Yet their former masters often found this difficult to accept.[11]

Defeat and emancipation forced a reassessment of sectional identity. For southerners, this would be a long process, as they fought to retain as much as possible of the past while bowing to inevitable changes. Fanny Andrews, like her fellow southerners, feared the loss of sectional distinctiveness. In April, 1865, Andrews wrote that "Mr. Adams, our little Yankee preacher," had adopted southern views but still talked and dressed like a Yankee. "What is it, I wonder, that makes them so different from us, even when they mean to be good Southerners!" she mused. "You can't even make one of them look like us, not if you were to dress him up in a full set of Georgia jeans." Beyond this difference of manners and appearance, the war had interposed a seemingly unbridgeable chasm of hatred and bitter memories. "I used to have some Christian feeling towards Yankees," Andrews continued, "but now that they have invaded our country and killed so many of our men and desecrated so many homes, I can't believe that when Christ said 'Love your enemies,' he meant Yankees."[12]

By July, 1865, Fanny Andrews worried that the South would become indistinguishable from the North. "It is sad to think how things are changing," she lamented, after reporting that blacks had become insolent to southern whites. "In another generation or two, this beautiful country of ours will have lost its distinctive civilization and become no better than a nation of Yankee shopkeepers." This warning has been repeated—either in sorrow or in hopefulness—ever since Appomattox. Like many southerners who have feared the loss of sectional identity, Fanny Andrews continued to proclaim the superiority of southern customs and character. "Notwithstanding all our trouble and wretchedness, I thank heaven that I was born a southerner,—that I belong to the noblest race on earth—for this is a heritage that nothing can ever take from me," she boasted in August, 1865. "The greatness of the southern character is showing itself beyond the mere accidents of time and fortune; though reduced to the lowest state of poverty and subjec-

11. Andrews, *War-Time Journal*, 319–40, 347. On blacks' adoption of new names, see Eugene D. Genovese, *Roll, Jordan, Roll: The World the Slaves Made* (New York, 1974), 444–50; Williamson, *After Slavery*, 309–11; Litwack, *Been in the Storm So Long*, 247–51.
12. Andrews, *War-Time Journal*, 148–49.

tion, we can still feel that we are superior to those whom brute force has placed above us in a worldly state." Andrews concluded that she was proud of her poverty when she remembered "in what a noble cause all was lost."[13]

The period just after Appomattox marked the beginning of the myth of the Lost Cause that enabled southerners to feel vindicated for their heroic sacrifices on behalf of a noble cause that was doomed from the outset. They could thus accept defeat by a more powerful nation while still claiming moral superiority. The plantation legend of moonlight, magnolias, and mint juleps also appealed to northerners. It offered both sides an idealized vision of an alternative civilization more attractive than the increasingly industrialized North. For most southern whites, the war's principal legacies would be hatred of Yankees and the romantic myth of the Lost Cause.[14]

Fanny Andrews fully shared these beliefs. After the war, she turned to teaching and writing for a livelihood. She taught for several years in the public schools of Yazoo City, Mississippi, where her brother had established a law practice. From 1885 to 1897, she taught at Wesleyan Female College in Macon, Georgia. Throughout this period, she wrote numerous stories, essays, novels, poems, and works of criticism. By the time of her death in January, 1931, Eliza Frances Andrews had earned recognition as a popular author and had been invited to address the International Academy of Science in Italy. Henry W. Grady, the apostle of the New South, called her novel *Prince Hal, Or the Romance of a Rich Young Man* (Philadelphia, 1882) "the most powerful work" he had seen from "the pen of a Southern writer in many years." In 1908, Fanny Andrews published her diary of the turbulent period from December, 1864, to August, 1865, under the title *The War-Time Journal of a Georgia Girl*. In the prologue she paid tribute to the Confederate veteran: "His cause was doomed from the first by a law as inexorable as the one pronounced by the fates against Troy, but he fought with a valor and

13. *Ibid.*, 351, 380–81. On southern efforts to retain a separate sectional identity, see Carl N. Degler, *Place Over Time: The Continuity of Southern Distinctiveness* (Baton Rouge, 1977), 1–25.
14. Rollin G. Osterweis, *The Myth of the Lost Cause, 1865–1900* (Hamden, Conn., 1973); Paul M. Gaston, *The New South Creed: A Study in Southern Mythmaking* (New York, 1973), 167–86; Frank E. Vandiver, "The Confederate Myth," *Southwest Review*, XLVI (Summer, 1961), 199–204.

heroism that have made a lost cause forever glorious." Forty years after Appomattox, Fanny Andrews glorified the Old South:

> It was a mediaeval civilization, out of accord with the modern tenor of our time, and it had to go; but if it stood for some outworn customs that should rightly be sent to the dust heap, it stood for some things, also, that the world can ill afford to lose. It stood for gentle courtesy, for knightly honor, for generous hospitality; it stood for fair and honest dealing of man with man in the common business of life, for lofty scorn of cunning greed and ill-gotten gain through fraud and deception of our fellowmen—lessons which the founders of our New South would do well to lay to heart.

Fanny Andrews thus summarized the southern defense of plantation civilization and the Lost Cause. Even brute force could not diminish the South's moral superiority to Yankee culture.[15]

This study of sectional consciousness indicates the powerful emotional legacy of the Civil War. "It was an experience that was probably felt more deeply than anything else that ever happened to us," explains Bruce Catton. "We cannot hope to understand it unless we share in that feeling, simply because the depth and intensity of the feeling are among the war's principal legacies." Likewise, Henry Steele Commager writes that of all America's wars, "it is the Civil War that has left the strongest impression on our minds, our imagination, and our hearts."[16] This emotional legacy can be seen more clearly through examination of personal letters and diaries than in battle accounts and official pronouncements.

Emerging victorious from a long and costly war, the North recognized its military power and economic strength. The verdict of combat seemed to justify the moral superiority of the Union cause. The federal army's destructiveness, however, led many northerners to feel shame for their soldiers' actions and to doubt the morality of their conquest. The South, by contrast, was forced to admit its lack of military and economic might. Nevertheless, continued faith in the virtue of the Confederate cause and renewed certainty of northern immorality strengthened convictions of southern honor and righteousness. This

15. Henry Grady quoted in Andrews, *War-Time Journal*, xv; *ibid.*, "Prologue," 14–15.
16. Bruce Catton, *Prefaces to History* (Garden City, N.Y., 1970), 8; Henry Steele Commager (ed.), *The Blue and the Gray: The Story of the Civil War as Told by Participants* (2 vols.; Indianapolis, 1950), I, xiii.

became a central tenet of the Lost Cause legend that sustained southern pride after Appomattox.

Defeat united the South. Even the comparatively minor divisions revealed by war were largely healed by a sense of common suffering and a feeling of resentment against the hated conquerors. As Thomas Pressly concluded, "The common experience of defeat and the omnipresent desire to vindicate the South . . . provided the most important foundation for the emotional and intellectual unity characterizing the postwar South—a unity greater than that of either the South of the 1850s or the South during wartime." As an oppressed minority, southerners joined together to resist Yankee domination.[17]

Whereas defeat strengthened southern unity, victory perpetuated northern internal conflicts. Lacking the common bond of suffering and subjugation, northerners had no unifying force as strong as the South's. Even Reconstruction and "bloody-shirt" politics were directed toward securing Republican political control in a divided North more than toward chastising the South. The North was uncertain of the meaning of its victory because it had never fully agreed on its reasons for fighting. Some believed that the Union had made a commitment to black equality, others that the South must be punished and controlled. Yet a majority apparently desired only a return to peace and national unity. Reconstruction foundered on the shoals of this divided purpose.[18]

Sectional distinctions became less significant for northerners as they sought to reunite the nation and minimize internal conflicts. Victory also assuaged bitterness, dissolving hatred for the vanquished foe. Proclamations of sectional brotherhood and reconciliation similarly indicated efforts to heal—or at least disguise—sectional divisions. Such feelings contributed to northern willingness to forgive southerners. Only a few Rebel leaders, who had deluded the majority of Confederate supporters, should be punished.

For the South the war's primary legacy was increased hatred of the Yankee invader. Southerners viewed the war as an unjustified assault on their rights and liberty, committed by fanatical, immoral Yankees, who had disrupted harmonious relations between the races, destroyed slavery, confiscated their property, violated their rights, stifled their

17. Thomas J. Pressly, *Americans Interpret Their Civil War* (2nd ed.; Princeton, 1962), 106.

18. See C. Vann Woodward, *The Burden of Southern History* (rev ed.; Baton Rouge, 1968), 89–107; and Stanley Hirshson, *Farewell to the Bloody Shirt: Northern Republicans and the Southern Negro* (Bloomington, 1962).

liberty, desolated their land, and destroyed their homes. Reconstruction perpetuated Yankee domination and humiliated southern pride and independence. Southerners vowed everlasting hatred of Yankees and taught their children to hate the evil conquerors. Sherman's devastating march to the sea and the infuriating spectacle of former slaves sitting in state legislatures seared the southern mind. Such experiences could neither be forgotten nor forgiven.

Overt signs of sectional hostility declined during the latter part of the nineteenth century, as southerners accepted northern gestures of reconciliation and sought to share the benefits of economic growth and social stability. The myth of the Lost Cause permitted southerners to believe in their moral superiority despite defeat. Many northerners shared a romanticized image of the plantation South, which reduced sectional antagonism. A small but influential group of southerners adopted a New South "creed" that called for industrialization and economic growth based on the northern model. Beneath the surface of this public reconciliation, however, an underlying sectional animosity remained. Although there were few public utterances of sectional hatred by the 1890s, southerners privately continued to despise Yankees and to remember Sherman's march through Georgia and the years of Reconstruction as unforgivable outrages. In an essay titled "The Scourge of the Invader," Richard M. Weaver wrote in 1943: "This is an unhappy chapter to record in the history of any nation and the deep psychological wounds it left postponed reconciliation indefinitely." Such feelings surfaced again during the civil rights movement, when many white southerners denounced interference by "outside agitators" from the North.[19]

The Civil War had a tremendous impact on the American people. The nation's crisis became a personal crisis for individuals who participated in its momentous events. The war was the most significant experience of many people's lives. For years after, it would be remembered, debated, and examined as people sought to determine the relationship of their own experience to national events. Amid the bloody strife, participants had recorded their daily actions and thoughts. Through these individual accounts of the war, we can begin to understand the personal legacy of the sectional conflict.

19. Buck, *Road to Reunion*; Osterweis, *Myth of the Lost Cause*; Gaston, *New South Creed*; Richard M. Weaver, *The Southern Tradition at Bay: A History of Postbellum Thought* (New Rochelle, N.Y., 1968), 259.

BIBLIOGRAPHY

PRIMARY SOURCES

Manuscript Sources

Burton Historical Collection, Detroit Public Library
  Civil War Correspondence
  Divie Bethune Duffield Papers
  Frank E. Lansing Papers
Connecticut Historical Society, Hartford
  Civil War Letters
Duke University Library, Manuscript Department, Durham, North
  Carolina
  Charles Wesley Andrews Papers
  William B. G. Andrews Papers
  Bedinger-Dandridge Family Papers
  Asa Biggs Papers
  James Locke Boardman Papers
  Robert Boyd Papers
  Hugh Conway Browning Papers
  James O. Coghill Papers
  Alonzo B. Cohen Papers
  Mary A. (Horton) Councill Papers
  David Lucius Craft Papers
  Abel H. Crawford Papers
  Henry M. Crydenwise Papers
  John Cumming Papers
  Francis Warrington Dawson Papers
  Hider D. Dickens Papers
  Joseph Sherman Diltz Papers
  Edgar Dinsmore Papers
  Henry Kyd Douglas Papers
  Oren E. Farr Papers
  Alexander T., Joseph R., and William M. Findley Papers
  John B. Foote Papers
  Andrew Funkhouser Papers

John Berkley Grimball Papers
John C. Hackett Papers
Robert G. Haile Papers
Henry C. Hall Papers
Constant C. Hanks Papers
John Herr Papers
Robert Bruce Hoadley Papers
Seth Hollister Papers
Robert W. Honnoll Papers
Josephus Jackson Papers
Laurence Massillon Keitt Papers
Charles Phineas Lord Papers
John Bowie Magruder Papers
Isaac Marsh Papers
James R. Martin and Robert Wilson Papers
Robert Anderson McClellan Papers
Marshall McDonald Papers
Charles Jewett Morris Papers
Samuel Spencer Parmelee and Uriah N. Parmelee Papers
Benjamin Pedrick Papers
Presley Carter Person Papers
William Horace Phillips Papers
Adam H. Pickel Papers
William T. Pippey Papers
Alonzo Reed Papers
Sarah A. Rootes Papers
Irby H. Scott Papers
Helen L. and Mary Virginia Shell Papers
Evin Smith Papers
Charles H. Sowle Papers
Joseph D. Stapp Papers
Augustin Louis Taveau Papers
Cabell Tavenner and Alexander Scott Withers Papers
Ella Gertrude (Clanton) Thomas Diary
Henry J. H. Thompson Papers
Henry Watson, Jr., Papers
Worth Family Papers
James C. Zimmerman Papers

Library of Congress, Manuscript Division, Washington, D.C.
  John Carvel Arnold Papers
  Felix Brannigan Papers
  William Hamilton Papers
  Joseph Bloomfield Osborn Papers
  Edwin Oberlin Wentworth Papers
Louisiana State University Libraries, Louisiana and Lower Mississippi
  Valley Collections, Baton Rouge
  Priscilla "Mittie" (Munnikhuysen) Bond Papers
  Audley Clark Britton and Family Papers
  E. John and Thomas C. W. Ellis and Family Papers
  Samuel J. Lance Papers
  Joseph D. Shields Papers
Michigan Historical Collections, Bentley Historical Library, University
  of Michigan, Ann Arbor
  Carlisle Family Papers
  DeLand Family Papers
  Ferry Family Papers
  Francis Everett Hall Papers
  Charles B. Haydon Diaries
  Sligh Family Papers
  Harrison Soule Papers
  George E. Woodbury Letters
  Joshua Van Hoosen Papers
National Archives and Record Administration
  Southern Claims Commission Records, Record Group 233, Records
    of the United States House of Representatives
Southern Historical Collection, Library of the University of North Car-
  olina at Chapel Hill
  Samuel A. Agnew Diary
  Mrs. John Berry Papers
  John Houston Bills Papers
  Thomas F. Boatwright Letters
  Bond and Fentriss Family Papers
  Buchanan and McClellan Family Papers
  William Calder Papers
  Tod R. Caldwell Papers
  Alexander Donelson Coffee Papers

John Hamilton Cornish Papers
Susan Cornwall Diary
Elias Davis Papers
Harry St. John Dixon Papers
Harriet Eaton Diaries
Belle Edmondson Diary
Silas Everett Fales Papers
William O. Fleming Papers
David Gavin Diary
Gordon Family Papers
James A. Graham Papers
Grimball Family Papers
John Berkley Grimball Diary
Meta (Morris) Grimball Diary
Edward Owings Guerrant Papers
Peter Hairston Papers
Eben Thomas Hale Papers
Alexander Cheves Haskell Papers
Charles Woodward Hutson Papers
Cadwallader Jones Papers
H. C. Kendrick Letters
William King Papers
Mackay and Stiles Family Papers
Jason Niles Diary
William Patterson Diary
Nimrod Porter Books
W. R. Redding Papers
Frank L. Richardson Papers
Roach and Eggleston Family Papers
Iowa Michigan Royster Papers
Ruffin, Roulhac, and Hamilton Family Papers
David Schenck Diary
Benedict Joseph Semmes Papers
Henry C. Semple Papers
Henry E. Simmons Letters
Frank F. Steel Letters
Isaac Barton Ulmer Papers
Sarah L. Wadley Diary
Richard W. Waldrop Papers

Walton Family Papers
Henry Clay Warmouth Papers, Magnolia Plantation Record Books
William Henry Wills Papers
State Historical Society of Wisconsin, Archives Division, Madison
Robert J. Bates Papers
George W. Buffum Papers
Julian W. Hinkley Papers
University of Virginia Library, Manuscripts Department, Charlottes-
ville
Eugene M. Cox, "Border Guard" Roll Book (microfilm)
David V. Dickenson Papers (microfilm)
West Virginia and Regional History Collection, West Virginia Univer-
sity Library, Morgantown
David Hunter Strother Collection
William L. Clements Library, University of Michigan, Ann Arbor
Andrew Brockway Papers
Lucius W. Chapman Diary
Clinton H. Haskell Collection
Henry Grimes Marshall Papers
Calvin Mehaffey Papers
Isaac G. Seymour Papers
Nathan Webb Diaries
John Darragh Wilkins Papers
Yale University Library, Manuscripts and Archives Department, New
Haven, Connecticut
Civil War Manuscripts Collection
Diaries (Miscellaneous) Collection
Loomis-Wilder Family Papers
Tarleton Family Collection
Terry Family Papers
Manuscripts in private possession
E. R. Berry Letters, in possession of John Sickler
Rebecca P. Davis Papers (typescript), in possession of May Davis Hill

Published Letters and Diaries

Alvord, Henry E. "A New England Boy in the Civil War." Edited by
Caroline B. Sherman. *New England Quarterly*, V (April, 1932), 310–44.
Ambrose, Stephen E., ed. *A Wisconsin Boy in Dixie: The Selected Letters of
James K. Newton*. Madison, 1961.

Anderson, John Q., ed. *Brokenburn: The Journal of Kate Stone, 1861–1868.* Baton Rouge, 1955.

Andrews, Eliza Frances. *The War-Time Journal of a Georgia Girl, 1864–1865.* Edited by Spencer Bidwell King, Jr. 1908; rpr. Macon, Ga., 1960.

Barrett, John G., ed. *Yankee Rebel: The Civil War Journal of Edmund DeWitt Patterson.* Chapel Hill, 1966.

Baxter, Nancy Niblack, ed. *Hoosier Farm Boy in Lincoln's Army: The Civil War Letters of Pvt. John R. McClure.* N.p., 1971.

Blegen, Theodore C., ed. *The Civil War Letters of Colonel Hans Christian Heg.* Northfield, Minn., 1936.

Brobst, John F. *Well, Mary: Civil War Letters of a Wisconsin Volunteer.* Edited by Margaret Brobst Roth. Madison, 1960.

Byrne, Frank L., ed. *The View from Headquarters: Civil War Letters of Harvey Reid.* Madison, 1965.

Cash, William M., and Lucy Somerville Howarth, eds. *My Dear Nellie: The Civil War Letters of William L. Nugent to Eleanor Smith Nugent.* Jackson, Miss., 1977.

Chamberlayne, C. G., ed. *Ham Chamberlayne—Virginian: Letters and Papers of an Artillery Officer, in the War for Southern Independence, 1861–1865.* Richmond, 1932.

Cross, Henry Martyn. "A Yankee Soldier Looks at the Negro." Edited by William Cullen Bryant II. *Civil War History,* VII (1961), 133–48.

Daly, Louise Haskell. *Alexander Cheves Haskell: The Portrait of a Man.* Norwood, Mass., 1934.

Daly, Maria L. *Diary of a Union Lady, 1861–1865.* Edited by Harold Earl Hammond. New York, 1962.

Dawson, Sarah Morgan. *A Confederate Girl's Diary.* Edited by James I. Robertson, Jr. Bloomington, 1960.

Deane, Frank Putnam, ed. *"My Dear Wife . . .": The Civil War Letters of David Brett, 9th Massachusetts Battery, Union Cannoneer.* Little Rock, Ark., 1964.

Dunlap, Leslie W., ed. *"Your Affectionate Husband, J. F. Culver": Letters Written During the Civil War.* Iowa City, 1978.

Eby, Cecil D., Jr., ed. *A Virginia Yankee in the Civil War: The Diaries of David Hunter Strother.* Chapel Hill, 1961.

Franklin, John Hope, ed. *The Diary of James T. Ayers, Civil War Recruiter.* Springfield, Ill., 1947.

Gerow, R. O., ed. *Civil War Diary (1862–1865) of Bishop William Henry Elder.* Natchez, n.d.

Hall, James E. *The Diary of a Confederate Soldier*. Edited by Ruth Woods Dayton. N.p., 1961.

Higginson, Thomas Wentworth. *Army Life in a Black Regiment*. 1869; rpr. Boston, 1962.

Ingram, Henry L., ed. *Civil War Letters of George W. and Martha F. Ingram, 1861–1865*. College Station, Tex., 1973.

Jaquette, Henrietta Stratton, ed. *South After Gettysburg: Letters of Cornelia Hancock, 1863–1868*. New York, 1956.

Jones, Jenkin Lloyd. *An Artilleryman's Diary*. [Madison], 1914.

Jones, Margaret Mackay, ed. *The Journal of Catherine Devereux Edmondston, 1860–1866*. N.p., n.d.

Key, Hobart, Jr., and Max Lale, eds. *The Civil War Letters of David R. Garrett*. Marshall, Tex., n.d.

Lusk, William C., ed. *War Letters of William Thompson Lusk*. New York, 1911.

McConnell, Charles, ed. *Army of the Cumberland: Diary of William McConnell, Private Co. I, 15th O.V.V.I.* Tiro, Ohio, 1899.

McLarty, Vivian Kirkpatrick, ed. "The Civil War Letters of Colonel Bazel F. Lazear." *Missouri Historical Review*, XLIV (1949–50), 254–73; XLV (1950–51), 47–63.

Miers, Earl Schenck, ed. *When the World Ended: The Diary of Emma LeConte*. New York, 1957.

Myers, Robert M., ed. *The Children of Pride: A True Story of Georgia and the Civil War*. New Haven, 1972.

Nevins, Allan, ed. *A Diary of Battle: The Personal Journals of Colonel Charles S. Wainwright, 1861–1865*. New York, 1962.

Pearson, Elizabeth Ware, ed. *Letters from Port Royal, Written at the Time of the Civil War*. 1906, rpr. New York, 1969.

Rieger, Paul E., ed. *Through One Man's Eyes: The Civil War Experiences of a Belmont County Volunteer, Letters of James G. Theaker*. Mount Vernon, Ohio, 1974.

Robertson, James I., Jr., ed. *The Civil War Letters of General Robert McAllister*. New Brunswick, N.J., 1965.

Rundell, Walter, Jr., ed. " 'Despotism of Traitors': The Rebellious South Through New York Eyes." *New York History*, XLV (October, 1964), 331–67.

———. " 'If Fortune Should Fail'—Civil War Letters of Dr. Samuel D. Sanders." *South Carolina Historical Magazine*, LXV (July, October, 1964), 129–44, 218–32.

Shannon, Fred A., ed. *The Civil War Letters of Sergeant Onley Andrus.* Urbana, Ill., 1947.

Simpson, Harold B., ed. *The Bugle Softly Blows: The Confederate Diary of Benjamin M. Seaton.* Waco, Tex., 1965.

Stephenson, Wendell H., and Edwin A. Davis, eds. "The Civil War Diary of Willie Micajah Barrow." *Louisiana Historical Quarterly*, XVII (1934), 436–51, 712–31.

Still, William N., Jr., ed. "The Civil War Letters of Robert Tarleton." *Alabama Historical Quarterly*, XXXII (Spring–Summer, 1970), 51–80.

Stoker, William E. "The War Letters of a Texas Conscript in Arkansas." Edited by Robert W. Glover. *Arkansas Historical Quarterly*, XX (Winter, 1961), 355–87.

Strong, George Templeton, *Diary of the Civil War, 1860–1865.* Edited by Allan Nevins. New York, 1962.

Swint, Henry I., ed. *Dear Ones at Home: Letters from Contraband Camps.* Nashville, 1966.

Taylor, F. Jay, ed. *Reluctant Rebel: The Secret Diary of Robert Patrick, 1861–1865.* Baton Rouge, 1959.

Truss, John W. "Civil War Letters from Parsons' Texas Cavalry Brigade." Edited by Johnette H. Ray. *Southwestern Historical Quarterly*, LXIX (October, 1965), 210–23.

Underhill, Charles Sterling, ed. *"Your Soldier Boy Samuel": Civil War Letters of Lieut. Samuel Edmund Nichols.* Buffalo, 1929.

Wiley, Bell Irvin, ed. *Confederate Letters of John W. Hagan.* Athens, Ga., 1954.

———. *Letters of Warren Akin, Confederate Congressman.* Athens, 1959.

———. *"This Infernal War": The Confederate Letters of Sgt. Edwin H. Fay.* Austin, Tex., 1958.

Williams, Robert W., Jr., and Ralph A. Wooster, eds. "Camp Life in Civil War Louisiana: The Letters of Private Isaac Dunbar Affleck." *Louisiana History*, V (Spring, 1964), 187–201.

Wills, Charles W. *Army Life of an Illinois Soldier: Letters and Diary of the Late Charles W. Wills.* Washington, D.C., 1906.

Winther, Oscar O., ed. *With Sherman to the Sea: The Civil War Letters, Diaries and Reminiscences of Theodore F. Upson.* Baton Rouge, 1943.

Woodward, C. Vann, ed. *Mary Chesnut's Civil War.* New Haven, 1981.

Woodward, C. Vann, and Elisabeth Muhlenfeld, eds. *The Private Mary Chesnut: The Unpublished Civil War Diaries.* New York, 1984.

ESSAY ON SECONDARY SOURCES

For citations of historical works on specific topics, consult notes for each chapter. Several interpretive books that have proven particularly valuable for this study of personal attitudes deserve special mention. Bell I. Wiley is the preeminent authority on Civil War soldiers. His companion volumes, *The Life of Johnny Reb: The Common Soldier of the Confederacy* (Indianapolis, 1943), and *The Life of Billy Yank: The Common Soldier of the Union* (Indianapolis, 1952), provide a detailed description of soldiers' daily lives. Bruce Catton's many volumes on the Civil War, particularly *This Hallowed Ground* (Garden City, N.Y., 1956), and *A Stillness at Appomattox* (Garden City, N.Y., 1953), are masterpieces of military history written in sparkling literary style. For the general political and social background in the North, Allan Nevins, *The War for the Union* (4 vols.; New York, 1959–71), provides a valuable narrative survey; David M. Potter, *The Impending Crisis, 1848–1861* (New York, 1976), offers a superb analysis of sectionalism and the coming of war; and James G. Randall and David Donald, *The Civil War and Reconstruction* (2nd ed.; Lexington, Mass., 1969), is a standard text. Confederate political and social developments are fully treated in E. Merton Coulter, *The Confederate States of America, 1861–1865* (Baton Rouge, 1950); and Clement Eaton, *A History of the Southern Confederacy* (New York, 1954). William L. Barney, *Flawed Victory: A New Perspective on the Civil War* (New York, 1975), presents a stimulating reinterpretation of war issues. Among many excellent new studies of secession, those I found most valuable are Stephen A. Channing, *Crisis of Fear: Secession in South Carolina* (New York, 1970); Michael P. Johnson, *Toward a Patriarchal Republic: The Secession of Georgia* (Baton Rouge, 1977); and William L. Barney, *The Secessionist Impulse: Alabama and Mississippi in 1860* (Princeton, 1974).

Ideological issues of the Civil War period are discussed in Thomas J. Pressly, *Americans Interpret Their Civil War* (2nd ed.; Princeton, 1962); Eric Foner, *Free Soil, Free Labor, Free Men: The Ideology of the Republican Party Before the Civil War* (New York, 1970); Eugene D. Genovese, *The Political Economy of Slavery: Studies in the Economy and Society of the Slave South* (New York, 1965); and George M. Fredrickson, *The Inner Civil War: Northern Intellectuals and the Crisis of the Union* (New York, 1965). Paul C. Nagel, *One Nation Indivisible: The Union in American Thought, 1776–1861* (New York, 1964), presents a stimulating analysis of the meaning of the

Union for antebellum Americans. David H. Donald, *Liberty and Union* (Boston, 1978), evaluates sectional differences within the context of American nationality and homogeneity.

White racial attitudes are admirably explored in Winthrop D. Jordan, *White over Black: American Attitudes Toward the Negro, 1550–1812* (Chapel Hill, 1968); and Joel Williamson, *The Crucible of Race: Black-White Relations in the American South Since Emancipation* (New York, 1984). For the Civil War era, see V. Jacque Voegeli, *Free But Not Equal: The Midwest and the Negro During the Civil War* (Chicago, 1967); George M. Fredrickson, *The Black Image in the White Mind: The Debate on Afro-American Character and Destiny, 1817–1914* (New York, 1971); and Willie Lee Rose's brilliant *Rehearsal for Reconstruction: The Port Royal Experiment* (New York, 1964), which provides compelling insights into northern efforts to convert slaves into free laborers. The war's impact on slavery has been examined from the perspectives of both master and slave. Two excellent treatments of slaveholders are James L. Roark, *Masters Without Slaves: Southern Planters in the Civil War and Reconstruction* (New York, 1977), which is a model of historical scholarship; and James Oakes, *The Ruling Race: A History of American Slaveholders* (New York, 1982). For the war's impact on blacks, see Leon F. Litwack's brilliant study, *Been in the Storm So Long: The Aftermath of Slavery* (New York, 1979); and Eugene D. Genovese, *Roll, Jordan, Roll: The World the Slaves Made* (New York, 1974). Also valuable are Benjamin Quarles, *The Negro in the Civil War* (2nd ed.; Boston, 1969); Bell Irvin Wiley, *Southern Negroes, 1861–1865* (Rev. ed.; New Haven, 1965); Clarence L. Mohr, *On the Threshold of Freedom: Masters and Slaves in Civil War Georgia* (Athens, Ga., 1986); and Dudley Taylor Cornish, *The Sable Arm: Negro Troops in the Union Army, 1861–1865* (New York, 1956).

Stimulating discussions of sectional differences are presented in William R. Taylor, *Cavalier and Yankee: The Old South and American National Character* (New York, 1961); Carl N. Degler, *Place over Time: The Continuity of Southern Distinctiveness* (Baton Rouge, 1977); David M. Potter, *The South and the Sectional Conflict* (Baton Rouge, 1968); W. J. Cash, *The Mind of the South* (New York, 1941); and Paul H. Buck, *The Road to Reunion, 1865–1900* (New York, 1937). C. Vann Woodward's masterful essays in *The Burden of Southern History* (Rev. ed.; Baton Rouge, 1968), and *American Counterpoint: Slavery and Racism in the North-South Dialogue* (Boston, 1971), contain provocative explorations of sectional issues. A valuable discussion of southern Unionists is presented in Carl N. Degler, *The Other South: Southern Dissenters in the Nineteenth Century* (New York, 1974). Paul D. Escott, *After Secession: Jefferson Davis and the Failure of Confederate Nationalism* (Baton Rouge, 1978), analyzes the Confederacy's internal divisions.

Finally, several valuable collections of primary sources deserve special mention. The voluminous *The War of the Rebellion: A Compilation of the Official Records of the Union and Confederate Armies* (130 vols.; Washington, D.C., 1880–1901) constitutes an inexhaustible mine of official documents and reports, but, largely because of its official nature, it was not heavily used for this study of popular thought. In comparing personal opinions with more public statements, however, I found the following documentary collections valuable: Ira Berlin, Joseph P. Reidy, and Leslie S. Rowland, eds., *The Black Military Experience* (Cambridge, England, 1982), which is Series II of Freedom: A Documentary History of Emancipation, 1861–1867; Henry Steele Commager, ed., *The Blue and the Gray: The Story of the Civil War as Told by Participants* (2 vols.; Indianapolis, 1950); Dwight L. Dumond, ed., *Southern Editorials on Secession* (New York, 1931); Robert F. Durden, ed., *The Gray and the Black: The Confederate Debate on Emancipation* (Baton Rouge, 1972); James M. McPherson, ed., *The Negro's Civil War: How American Negroes Felt and Acted During the War for the Union* (New York, 1965); Howard C. Perkins, ed., *Northern Editorials on Secession* (2 vols.; New York, 1942); and George Winston Smith and Charles Judah, eds., *Life in the North During the Civil War: A Source History* (Albuquerque, 1966).

Index